EXAM CRAM™

ASVAB

Karl W. Riebs

Kalinda Reeves

D1386003

International Standard Book Number: 0-7897-3258-0

Library of Congress Catalog Card Number: 2004108922

Printed in the United States of America

Eighth Printing March 2009

10 09   8

Trademarks

Warning and Disclaimer

Bulk Sales

Que Publishing offers excellent discounts on this book when ordered in quantity for bulk purchases or special sales. For more information, please contact

U.S. Corporate and Government Sales

1-800-382-3419

corpsales@pearsontechgroup.com

For sales outside the U.S., please contact

International Sales

international@pearsoned.com

Publisher
Paul Boger

Executive Editor
Jeff Riley

Acquisitions Editor
Carol Ackerman

Development Editor
Steve Rowe

Managing Editor
Charlotte Clapp

Project Editor
Tonya Simpson

Copy Editor
Linda Seifert

Indexer
Heather McNeill

Proofreader
Leslie Joseph

Technical Editors
Terry Hanson
Will Schmied

Publishing Coordinator
Pamalee Nelson

Multimedia Developer
Dan Scherf

Page Layout
Bronkella Publishing

To the outstanding men and women of the U.S. Armed Forces.
—Karl Riebs

*To my friends and family who have supported and encouraged me during
the writing process.*
—Kalinda Reeves

About the Authors

Karl W. Riebs graduated with Merit from the United States Naval Academy in 1992. He served in the Pacific Fleet as a Surface Warfare Officer aboard the guided missile destroyer *USS Chandler* (DDG-996) and on the staff of Commander, Destroyer Squadron 23. His assignments included deployments to the Persian Gulf, Somalia, and Central America. He was awarded the Navy Commendation Medal and the Southwest Asia Service Medal. Karl currently resides in Delafield, Wisconsin.

Kalinda Reeves got her start writing as an ELINT analyst in the Air Force, writing research papers. Since then, she has accumulated more than 17 years experience writing research, business, technical, and engineering documentation for government, military, and civilian customers. Her focus is computer/network hardware and software writing, and certification writing. During her writing career she has written more than 50 nonpublic documents for various customers, addressing system- and circuit-level hardware; uniquely developed, hardware-specific programs; and programs that were implemented across government and military communications systems. In addition, she has been a freelance writer for 10 years, during which time she co-authored five networking-genre books for public distribution.

Kalinda makes her home in Heron, Montana, and when she is not writing she home schools her children and indulges her many hobbies, including amateur (Ham) radio, cooking, gardening, all manner of crafts, drama writing and directing, mentoring aspiring writers, and hiking the beautiful trails of Big Sky Country.

About the Technical Editors

Will Schmied, who has served in the U.S. Navy for more than 12 years in the nuclear power field, is a systems engineer for a Fortune 500 shipping and logistics company. As a freelance writer, Will has worked with many publishers, including Microsoft and Que. Will has also worked directly with Microsoft in the MCSE exam-development process and is the founder of the popular MCSE certification portal, www.mcseworld.com. Will holds a Bachelor's degree in mechanical engineering technology from Old Dominion University along with his various IT industry certifications.

Will has previously authored several other publications for Que Publishing, including *MCSE Implementing and Managing Exchange Server 2003 Exam Cram 2 (Exam 70-284)* (2004), *MCSE 70-293 Training Guide: Planning and Maintaining a Windows Server 2003 Network Infrastructure* (2003), and *MCSA/MCSE 70-291 Training Guide: Implementing, Managing, and Maintaining a Windows Server 2003 Network Infrastructure* (2003).

Will currently resides in Desoto County, Mississippi, with his wife, Chris; their children, Christopher, Austin, Andrea, and Hannah; their dogs Hershey, Joe, and Charlie; and their cats, Smokey and Evin. When he's not busy working, you can find Will enjoying time with his family or dishing out a serious frag-fest on his Xbox.

Terry Hanson is a 24-year veteran of the U.S. Air Force. He holds an AAS Instructor of Technology and Military Studies and was an instructor while in the Air Force. Terry was part of a team involved in updating training material at the initial technical training schools and was responsible for developing and executing training programs ranging in length from two weeks to six months. He currently works as a contractor for the U.S. Air Force as a technical advisor and trainer.

Acknowledgments

Thank you to Carol Ackerman for her support and dedication. I also want to express my appreciation for the professional and courteous armed forces recruiting personnel I encountered in the course of my research. And most of all, I am grateful to my wife Amy and son Samuel for their encouragement, patience, and understanding throughout this project.

—Karl Riebs

I would like to extend my sincere thanks to the team at Que Publishing for the hard work and guidance provided during this project. It takes a team effort to put a book into production, and I would like to recognize a few members of the team with whom I had close interaction. Thanks to Carol Ackerman for keeping us on track, coordinating the on-going submissions, and for providing us with motivation and encouragement when we needed it. Thanks also to Linda Seifert and Tonya Simpson for smoothing out my grammar practices and to Terry Hanson and Will Schmied for providing me with valuable technical guidance. In addition, I need to thank all the folks who worked in the background, and whose names I will never know who helped to get this book to publication.

In addition, I couldn't have completed this book without the love, patience, understanding, and support of my family and friends.

—Kalinda Reeves

We Want to Hear from You!

As the reader of this book, *you* are our most important critic and commentator. We value your opinion and want to know what we're doing right, what we could do better, what areas you'd like to see us publish in, and any other words of wisdom you're willing to pass our way.

As an executive editor for Que Publishing, I welcome your comments. You can email or write me directly to let me know what you did or didn't like about this book—as well as what we can do to make our books better.

Please note that I cannot help you with technical problems related to the topic of this book. We do have a User Services group, however, where I will forward specific technical questions related to the book.

When you write, please be sure to include this book's title and author as well as your name, email address, and phone number. I will carefully review your comments and share them with the author and editors who worked on the book.

Email: feedback@quepublishing.com

Mail: Jeff Riley
        Executive Editor
        Que Publishing
        800 East 96th Street
        Indianapolis, IN 46240 USA

For more information about this book or another Que Certification title, visit our website at www.examcram2.com. Type the ISBN (excluding hyphens) or the title of a book in the Search field to find the page you're looking for.

Contents at a Glance

Table of Contents

Introduction

Welcome to the *ASVAB Exam Cram*. In the pages of this book you will find tips and essential information you will need to score your absolute best on the Armed Services Vocational Aptitude Battery (ASVAB).

You might be taking the ASVAB to explore your aptitude for a variety of civilian careers, or to begin the process of enlistment in the armed forces. Either way, you want your performance on the ASVAB to showcase what you already know and demonstrate your readiness to achieve proficiency in the vital skill sets called for by the modern military and civilian workplaces. Simply put, the better you perform on the ASVAB, the greater your career opportunities will be.

The goal of the ASVAB is straightforward. It is not designed to trip you up or screen you out. It is basically a tool you can use to introduce yourself to your prospective employer and take control of your own future.

Much like military service itself, success on the ASVAB requires disciplined, targeted preparation. A soldier heading into battle carries only the essential equipment for survival in the field and victory in combat. Your *ASVAB Exam Cram* preparation is your "combat gear" for an assault on the ASVAB. Our goal is not to try to teach you all the material you need to know about every topic. Instead, we will provide you with focused review materials and key tactical insights for overcoming potential problem areas. We leave out all the fluff to keep your pack light and all your energies focused on the objective.

Let's get started!

Taking the ASVAB

The ASVAB is administered by the Department of Defense (DoD) and is free of charge. It comes in several forms; however, the tests themselves (and the preparation techniques required) are not all that different. The ASVAB tests are as follows:

➤ **ASVAB 18/19**—Administered in over half of all U.S. high schools as part of the "Career Exploration Program," this version is used as a tool for students and guidance counselors to assess career aptitude (both civilian and military). This test comes in a paper version and consists of eight sections. See your guidance counselor for more information, or visit www.asvabprogram.com.

➤ **Paper Version ASVAB**—Administered by recruiters for use in direct enlistment into the armed forces it contains eight subject area sections (see Table 0.1 below) and may also contain a ninth section called "Assembling Objects." Contact a recruiter from the service branch of your choice to schedule the test.

➤ **CAT ASVAB**—The Computer Adaptive Test (CAT) is also administered by recruiters for use in direct enlistment into the armed forces. This version is becoming more common, is given only at Military Entrance Processing Stations (MEPS), and, in some areas, may be the only version available. The main difference between the CAT and paper version is that the CAT adapts (or adjusts on the fly) to determine your level of ability. The better you do on the early questions, the higher the level of difficulty you can reach, and the higher you can score. The downside is that you don't have the option to skip over and return later to a tough question that has you bogged down. The CAT ASVAB contains nine or ten sections ("Shop" and "Auto Information" sections may be separated), including the "Assembling Objects" section. Contact a recruiter from the service branch of your choice to schedule the test.

If you are taking the ASVAB through a recruiter, he or she may accompany you to the test site and wait for you to complete the test. You may even be offered a ride to and from the test location. Do not allow yourself to feel pressured to hurry through the test so that you don't inconvenience the recruiter. They are just doing their job. Yours is to focus on the test and do your best.

When you add up the time required for each section of the test (see Table 1) and throw in extra time for administration, the ASVAB takes about three hours to complete. In between sections of the CAT-ASVAB, you may take a short break before moving on. If you take longer than two minutes before advancing to the next screen, your computer terminal will lock up on you. This will require the proctor to come to your terminal and key in the password to resume testing. There is no penalty for locking up your terminal in this way, but it can be distracting to the other test takers.

Table 1	ASVAB Test Sections		
Order	Section	Number of Questions	Time Allowed
1	General Science	25	11 minutes
2	Arithmetic Reasoning	30	36 minutes
3	Word Knowledge	35	11 minutes
4	Paragraph Comprehension	15	13 minutes
5	Mathematics Knowledge	25	24 minutes
6	Electronics Information	20	9 minutes
7	Mechanical Comprehension	25	19 minutes
8	Shop and Automotive Information	25	11 minutes
9	Assembling Objects	16	9 minutes

Taking the ASVAB in no way obligates you to join the military, but it is an excellent way to begin a conversation with a recruiter to help you gather information about possible career fields and job opportunities that might be open for you. You also can use the Internet to research military occupations. Each branch of the armed forces has its own website, as listed here:

➤ **Army**—www.army.mil

➤ **Air Force**—www.af.mil

➤ **Navy**—www.navy.mil

➤ **Marine Corps**—www.usmc.mil

➤ **Coast Guard**—www.uscg.mil

As an alternative, you can visit www.careersinthemilitary.com or www.military.com to get an overview of each branch.

Arriving at the Exam Site

After you have studied the material, taken the practice tests, and reviewed your weak areas, you are academically ready to take the ASVAB. But your preparation doesn't end there. To ensure your readiness you need to be well rested, on time (which, as for any professional appointment, means that you should arrive 10–15 minutes early) and comfortably, but appropriately dressed. Essentially this means that you should wear casual, but professional, clothes and shoes. Don't waste the recruiter's time by missing or being late to your appointment and don't waste your time by pulling an all-nighter before the test that prevents you from being at your sharpest. Along with being well rested, make sure you have eaten a good meal before test time; you'll need your energy. Once the test starts, the proctor may excuse you momentarily to use the restroom, however, it is best to take care of that need before the test begins. Here's what you'll need to take with you to the test site:

➤ A picture ID (such as driver's license)

➤ A completed Form 680 (the equivalent of an admissions ticket, your recruiter will have this form and help you fill it out)

Scratch paper and pencils will be provided at the test site

In the Exam Room

Chances are good that you will not be the only test-taker in the exam room on the day of your ASVAB. Whether there are only a few or as many as 20 others, remember that everyone works at his or her own pace. Just because someone else may zoom through the test and finish ahead of you, doesn't mean that you are falling behind or need to pick up the pace. Work at your own pace, being mindful of the time limits for each test section, in the same way that you practiced when working through the sample tests in this book.

The test environment will be professional and quiet. There will be a proctor to help you with any questions, provide you with extra pencils and scratch paper if you need, and to unlock your computer terminal if you take too long to answer a question or read the sample question instructions; both situations will cause your screen to "lock up," thus preventing you from proceeding without assistance.

Answer sheets for the paper version of the ASVAB resemble any other standardized testing form. You must completely and neatly fill in the bubble corresponding to your answer choice. The CAT ASVAB instructions and questions appear in white lettering on a blue screen background. You may also have a specially labeled keyboard on which you can only select from the keys A, B, C, D, E, Enter, Spacebar, or HELP. Don't skip over the instructions. Read them carefully and follow them throughout the test.

When you complete each section of the test you will be notified on screen and then can move on to the instructions and examples for the next section. At the end of all sections, you will be expected to check out with the proctor and to turn in your pencils and all scratch paper (used and blank). Nothing leaves the testing room. For the CAT ASVAB your recruiter will likely be able to give you your score the next day.

Study and Exam Preparation

Regardless of the testing format you are taking, the old saying that "practice makes perfect" applies. The more effort you put into reviewing and practicing (under test-like conditions) the type of questions you'll be facing, the better you will do.

About This Book

Each Exam Cram chapter follows a regular structure and contains graphical cues about important or useful information. Here is the structure of a typical chapter, including special features that may be used to highlight key points:

➤ **Opening Hotlists**—Found on the first page of each chapter, these lists highlight terms, concepts, and information you will need to become familiar with throughout the chapter.

➤ **Topical Coverage**—The heart of the chapter, this is a summary of the subject matter vital to success on that subject area of the exam.

➤ **Notes and Tips**—These are useful pieces of information, shortcuts, or more efficient ways to tackle a type of exam question.

➤ **Exam Alerts**—Here is your "heads up" for items you can be certain will show up on the exam.

➤ **Exam Prep Practice Questions**—Each chapter contains a set of 10–15 practice questions to help you solidify your understanding of the material covered. The correct answer is given along with an explanation of why it is correct and why the other choices are not. Use these questions to pick out weak areas you should review before taking the Sample Exams at the back of the book.

➤ **Need to Know More?**—Found only on the CD-ROM, this is a listing of other sources of information to hone your skills in a particular way.

Using This Book

You may use this book according to your own needs. Everyone should begin with the Self Assessment to gauge his or her particular strengths and weaknesses and to get a feel for the ASVAB. Treat all practice exams as though they were the real thing. Find a quiet place, use a timer, and don't allow yourself to be interrupted until the time is up.

After you've completed the Self Assessment, review your personal objectives in taking the ASVAB. Everyone should focus effort on preparing for the four sections that comprise the Armed Forces Qualification Test (AFQT). You must achieve a minimum score on the AFQT for the different branches of the service. The sections that make up the AFQT are: Word Knowledge, Paragraph Comprehension, Arithmetic Reasoning, and Mathematics Knowledge.

If you find yourself short of time before your ASVAB test date, study the areas of weakness identified in your Self Assessment and be sure to at least skim every chapter to absorb the Tips, Exam Alerts, and Cautions.

Ideally, you will take the time to move steadily through each chapter, taking note of areas in which you need to do additional study. This will prepare you to take the Practice Exams found at the end of the book. Treat this book like a study outline and don't hesitate to mark it up, highlight key information, and fold down the corners of important pages for future reference. Also note that at the very end of this book are answer sheets you can use for your practice exams.

We hope you enjoy using this Exam Cram book and that as a result of your focused preparation you will be well on your way toward a rewarding career.

Self Assessment

This self assessment is included in this *ASVAB Exam Cram* to help you evaluate your current readiness to tackle the ASVAB exam. It will also help you understand what material and skills you need to master as regards the topic of this book—namely, those on the ASVAB exam. In this self assessment, we also provide you with resources and recommendations to increase your skill and ability levels before you take the ASVAB. However, before you tackle this self assessment, let's talk about concerns you might have when pursuing the ASVAB exam, and what an ideal ASVAB candidate might look like.

The ASVAB in the Real World

In this section, we describe an ideal ASVAB candidate, knowing full well not all candidates will meet this ideal. In fact, our description of that ideal candidate might seem a little scary, but it is an attainable goal. Annually, the Department of Defense (DoD) administers the ASVAB to more than 900,000 candidates at more than 14,000 high schools and post-secondary schools, in addition to 65 Military Entrance Processing Stations, nationwide. Your ASVAB scores are good for two years after you take the exam. If you didn't do as well as you like on the first attempt, you can retake the ASVAB after 30 days, but after that, you have to wait for 6 months to test again.

Because the Introduction provided you with the test subjects, we will pick up from there to show you how school counselors and the military use your scores to help you determine your direction in life. The ASVAB measures your aptitude on multiple levels and because of its flexibility, is one of the most widely used aptitude exams in the world. The ASVAB indicates your overall academic ability and predicts how well you will do in a variety of military and civilian occupations. Different combinations of the ASVAB test scores form other composite scores, as follows:

➤ The Career Exploration Score is a composite that helps students as they explore their future career options. The CES gives students a sense of their verbal, math, and science and technical skills so they can create effective goals toward future careers.

➤ The Military Careers Score is a composite that enables students to compare their skills and abilities with other job incumbents in various military careers. Go to the military careers website at www.careersinthemilitary. com to find job descriptions for about 1,409 enlisted and officer military careers.

➤ The Military Entrance Score, also called the Armed Forces Qualification Test (AFQT) score, determines whether you have scored high enough to meet the entrance requirements for military service. The minimum percentile you will need varies between military service branches and between career fields within a given branch.

Although the ASVAB gives any test-taker an overall understanding of his or her academic skills, you must remember it is the primary tool the military services use to determine eligibility into the armed services. Four critical scores comprise your AFQT score, which are as follows:

➤ Arithmetic Reasoning

➤ Word Knowledge

➤ Paragraph Comprehension

➤ Mathematics Knowledge

However, don't concentrate only on those skill areas; your scores in the other areas determine how you will qualify for specific military careers. If you are planning on going into the military, and you want to target a career field, then you can visit these websites to find out what the necessary scores are for that career field:

➤ Air Force: www.military.com/ASVAB/0,,ASVAB_MOS_USAF.html

➤ Army: www.military.com/ASVAB/0,,ASVAB_MOS_Army.html

➤ Marine Corps: www.military.com/ASVAB/0,,ASVAB_MOS_USMC.html

➤ Navy: www.military.com/ASVAB/0,,ASVAB_MOS_Navy.html

➤ Coast Guard: http://usmilitary.about.com/library/milinfo/cgjobs/ blcgjobmenu.htm

You can get all the real-world motivation you need from knowing that many others have gone before you and all you have to do is follow in their footsteps. If you're willing to tackle the process seriously and do what it takes to acquire the necessary experience and knowledge, then you can take the ASVAB exam successfully. If fact, we've designed this Exam Cram and the

Practice Exams on the companion CD to make it as easy on you as possible to prepare for the exam.

The Ideal ASVAB Candidate

Just to give you an idea of what an ideal ASVAB candidate is like, we provide some relevant statistics about the background and experience such an individual might have. Don't worry if you don't meet these qualifications; areas where you fall short simply indicate where you'll have to do more work. In some cases, it may mean you have to learn entirely new skill sets.

The Department of Defense (DoD) says you can take the ASVAB if you are in the 10th, 11th, or 12th grade of high school, or if you are a post-secondary school student. Although most of the material on the test is knowledge you should have learned in a normal high school regimen, some of the material is a little outside the norm.

Most students have taken the most common high school courses, but some of the skills and abilities the ASVAB tests are not in an average curriculum. For instance, most students have taken these high school courses:

> ➤ **English**—You need to know how to interpret a written passage according to word usage and context. In addition, you need to understand what words mean, although some of the words on the test may not be familiar to you.

> ➤ **Mathematics**—You need to understand basic math principles, such as adding fractions and determining percentages. You also need to understand basic Geometry and Algebra I.

> ➤ **General Science**—This covers basic life and earth science and a little actual biology. Remembering your high school biology lessons should get you through this module easily.

> ➤ **Assembling Objects**—This module tests your competence in spatial relations. There is no real way to prepare for this module, as most of it is common sense and determining which patterns go together.

However, a good portion of students have not taken the following courses and have no practical experience in them:

> ➤ **Electronics**—You need to understand basic electronic and electrical principles.

> ➤ **Automotive**—This module tests your knowledge on primary car and engine functions.

➤ **Shop**—This information is not too hard, but you have to have some understanding of basic carpentry and tools.

➤ **Mechanical**—You should have an understanding of work load and other basic physics and mechanics principles.

To do well on all areas of the exam, you should be proficient with the basic principles of each of the skill areas listed. However, you don't really need any experience in any of these areas, as long as you understand the fundamentals of each skill. On the test, you may do well on some of these areas, whereas others may give you some problems. If you are weak in some areas, then put forth the time and effort to focus on them.

Put Yourself to the Test

We have put together the following series of questions and observations to help you determine how much work you must do before you take the ASVAB exam, and what resources you can consult on your quest. *Be absolutely honest in your answers*, or you'll end up wasting time on an exam you're not ready to take. There are not right or wrong answers, only steps along the path to exam success. Only you can decide where you really belong in the broad spectrum of aspiring candidates. However, two things should be clear from the outset:

➤ Your high school education should get you through the most crucial parts of this test.

➤ Although hands-on experience is a plus, it is not absolutely necessary.

Educational Background

Before you take the ASVAB, you need to have an assessment of your current education levels and whether you are ready to proceed with the exam. If you are a high school junior or senior, you are most likely ready to take the ASVAB. However, if you have been out of school for a while, your best bet is to spend a good bit of study time on the fundamentals.

1. Have you recently taken a CAT, ACT, SAT, or other standardized aptitude test? [Yes or No]

   If Yes, you can use your scores from those tests to determine how you will do on four of the most important ASVAB test modules: Arithmetic Reasoning, Mathematics Knowledge, Word Knowledge, and Paragraph Comprehension.

If No, then you haven't really lost anything. However, you will need to pay close attention to how well you do on the ASVAB practice exams and then study accordingly.

2. Are you a high school graduate? [Yes or No]

If Yes, then most of the material on the ASVAB won't give you too much of a headache, except for perhaps the vocational skills. In all, it just depends on what you studied in high school.

If No, then you must first finish high school or take your General Education Development (GED) exam. You can take GED classes through your local high school, community college, or even online. The military won't even look at you until you get your GED or a high school equivalency diploma.

3. Have you ever taken any vocational classes, through your high school curriculum or through a local voc-ed, trade, or technical school? [Yes or No]

If Yes, then you are ahead of the game! All you have to do is thumb through your textbooks and refresh yourself on the material.

If No, then you should go to the library and check out books on the skills for which you have no knowledge. As an alternative, you can take self-study courses online. Here are some books that we recommend:

➤ **English**—*Word Smart: Building an Educated Vocabulary* by Adam Robinson (Princeton Review, 2001, ISBN 0375762183; Also, see www.gmatquiz.com/gmat-prep/ for a free download of math and verbal training.

➤ **Math**—*Everyday Math for Dummies* by Charles Seiter (For Dummies, 1995, ISBN 1568842481).

➤ **Science**—*Earth Science the Easy Way* by Allan D. Sills (Barron's Educational Series, 2003, ISBN 0764121464); *Schaum's Outline of Biology* by George H. Fried (McGraw-Hill, 1998, ISBN 0070224056).

➤ **Mechanics**—*Basic Physics: A Self-Teaching Guide* by Karl F. Kuhn (John Wiley & Sons, 1996, ISBN 0471134473).

➤ **Automotive**—*Auto Repair for Dummies* by Deanna Sclar (For Dummies, 1999, ISBN 0764550896).

➤ **Electronics/Electricity**—*Understanding Basic Electronics* by Larry D. Wolfgang (American Radio Relay League, 1996, ISBN 0872593983); *Basic Electricity* by the Bureau of Naval Personnel (Dover Publications, 1970, ISBN 0486209733).

➤ **Wood Shop**—*Getting Started in Woodworking: Skill Building Projects that Teach the Basics* by Aime Ontario Fraser (Taunton Press, 2003, ISBN 1561586102).

➤ **Assembling Objects**

4. Do you have any practical experience in any of the skill areas we have discussed? [Yes or No]

If Yes, then you don't need to spend much time at all dedicated to studying those areas for which you have experience. You can spend extra time on other areas of academic or skill weakness.

If the answer is No, then that's okay. Although you do still need to study, experience just gives you a leg up and is not essential to understanding the principles on the exam.

Hands-On Experience

Although we have stated that experience is not necessary for successful completion of the ASVAB exam, there truly is no substitute for experience to develop proficiency. But you don't have to have been employed in that particular skill to be proficient. Using a particular skill set regularly will give you all the experience you need. For example, if you write articles for your school or local newspaper, then you have experience with the English components of the exam. You gain wood shop experience if you have helped your dad build a shed, or if your hobbies include working on your car's engine, then that qualifies as automotive experience.

Testing Your Exam Readiness

Whether you attend training classes on specific topics to get ready for the exam or use written materials to study on your own, some preparation for the ASVAB exam is essential. Although the test is free, you want to do everything you can to pass on your first try, and that's where studying comes in.

For any given test subject, consider taking a class if you've tackled self-study materials, taken the test, and failed anyway. The opportunity to interact with an instructor and fellow students can make all the difference in the world.

If you can't afford to spend money taking classes, you should still invest in some low-cost practice exams from commercial vendors. These exams can help you assess your readiness to pass a test better than any other tool. Besides the one included with this Exam Cram, several other publishers, such as Peterson's, have ASVAB practice exams, some available for download online. In addition, you can find a free practice test at www.military.com.

We have included practice questions at the end of each chapter, plus practice exams in Chapters 11 and 13 of this book and more practice exams on the companion CD, so if you don't score well on the chapter tests, you can study more and then tackle the test in Chapter 11. If you want to take more practice tests, consider purchasing additional study and test material from the following websites:

➤ www.learnatest.com/military/home.cfm

➤ www.asvabpractice.com

➤ www.petersons.com

If you have taken a practice exam and scored 75% or better on each module, then you're probably ready to tackle the real thing. If your score isn't above that crucial threshold, keep at it until you break that barrier. If you haven't taken a practice exam, then you should arrange to do so fairly soon. Obtain all the free and low-budget practice tests you can find and get to work. Keep at it until you can break the passing threshold comfortably.

When it comes to assessing your test readiness, there's no better way than to take a good-quality practice exam and pass with a score of 75% or better. Ideally, you should shoot for 80+%, just to leave room for the "weirdness factor" that sometimes shows up on exams; and the ASVAB has a couple of questions that fall into that category.

Recruiters currently have access to a computer-based program that gives a mini-ASVAB right in their offices. This computerized test asks questions in only the four main test areas the military uses to determine the overall ASVAB score. For most people, this mini-test gives a pretty good indication of how well they will score on the actual ASVAB exam.

You should also cruise the Web looking for discussions or chats that provide recollections of test topics and experiences recorded by others. These will help you anticipate topics you're likely to encounter. You can find two such discussion groups at these sites:

➤ http://forums.military.com/1/OpenTopic?a=frm&s=78919038&f= 078192862

➤ http://p068.ezboard.com/fpxzoneopenmilitaryforumfrm4

When you visit a discussion group, it's okay to pay attention to information about questions. However, you can't always be sure the answers are correct. So, use the questions to guide your studies, but don't rely on the answers to lead you to the truth.

Assessing Your Readiness for the ASVAB Exam

Once you have assessed your readiness, undertaken the right background studies, obtained any hands-on experience that will help you understand the necessary skills, and reviewed the many resources of information to help you prepare for the ASVAB exam, you'll be ready to take a round of practice tests. When your scores come back positive enough to get you through the exam, you're ready to go after the real thing. If you follow our assessment regime, you'll not only know what you need to study, but you'll know when you're ready to make a test date at your local high school or Military Entrance Station.

Good luck!

General Science

Terms you'll need to know:

- ✓ Atom
- ✓ Matter
- ✓ Elements
- ✓ Metals and nonmetals
- ✓ Chemical bonds and reactions
- ✓ Acids, bases, and pH
- ✓ Work, energy, and power
- ✓ Velocity and acceleration
- ✓ Mass and fluids
- ✓ Convection, conduction, and radiation
- ✓ Frequency, amplitude, and wavelength
- ✓ Magnetism
- ✓ Organism

- ✓ Cell
- ✓ Photosynthesis
- ✓ DNA and chromosomes
- ✓ Community and population
- ✓ Ecosystem and biome
- ✓ Food chain
- ✓ Producers and consumers
- ✓ Crust, mantle, and core
- ✓ Igneous, sedimentary, and metamorphic rock
- ✓ Atmosphere and front
- ✓ Solar system, orbit, and eclipse

Concepts and techniques you'll need to master:

- ✓ States of matter
- ✓ Newton's laws of motion
- ✓ Pascal's, Archimedes', and Bernouli's principles
- ✓ Thermal energy transfer
- ✓ Doppler effect
- ✓ Classifying organisms
- ✓ Identifying the purpose of human body systems

- ✓ Identifying the function of parts of a cell
- ✓ Understand plant and animal cells
- ✓ Identifying biomes
- ✓ Cloud formation
- ✓ Identifying Earth's layers
- ✓ Identifying the planets in the solar system

The first hurdle you need to clear, the General Science test, covers the entire range of scientific knowledge in 25 questions over 11 minutes. Your key to success here is focusing your review on the most heavily weighted subjects:

➤ **Physical Science**—Chemistry and Physics

➤ **Life Science**—Biology, Human Anatomy and Physiology, and Ecology

Together, these areas make up more than 80% of the questions on the exam. In the remaining five or so questions, you will test your knowledge of Earth and Space Science, including Geology, Oceanography, Meteorology, and Astronomy.

Taking the General Science test first is a good way to get into the exam mind set. This section is important to you if you want to be a medical corpsman, meteorologist, or other scientific field specialist. If your goals lie elsewhere, do the best you can here and get in a rhythm of thinking and answering questions before the Verbal and Mathematics sections. These four sections make up your AFQT (Armed Forces Qualification Test) score, which determines your eligibility to enlist.

Physical Sciences

The physical sciences, physics and chemistry, attempt to measure and explain the physical world in which we live. In this section, you will look at the universal method of scientific inquiry and review the standard units of measurement. The ASVAB is loaded with questions about the physical sciences. Beginning with the field of chemistry, you will brush up on matter and atomic structure, chemical elements, and the periodic table. Using this information, you will consider how chemical elements bond to form molecules and react with each other. Turning to physics, you will define key concepts of mechanics: work, energy, power. Mechanics is the study of how physical objects move. You will cover Newton's laws of motion and then proceed to the special case of fluids in motion. Finally, you examine several other kinds of energy, including: thermal energy, light energy, and magnetic energy.

Scientific Method: Observation and Measurement

All modern scientific fields share certain characteristics. *Scientific method* is the way in which scientists seek to explain the phenomena they observe. Scientific method follows this path:

➤ Making observations of natural phenomena.

➤ Taking measurements.

➤ Formulating hypotheses (educated guesses that may be tested).

➤ Conducting experiments to determine the validity of the hypothesis.

Hypotheses that stand up to experimentation are regarded as scientific law.

Units of Measurement

In addition to having a standard observation methodology with the scientific method, scientists have developed standard (called SI, or *Système International*) units of measurement to simplify communication and allow comparisons. Table 1.1 illustrates some of the more common SI base units.

Tables 1.1 and 1.2 contain basic information about the SI base units of measurement and the metric system's prefixes. If you are already familiar with these, you can skip right on by. If you are less familiar, you should take a minute to refamiliarize yourself with this material. You will not likely see test questions strictly on this material; however, questions will contain the terms and the more comfortable you are with them the better.

Table 1.1 SI Base Units		
Quantity	**Unit**	**Symbol**
Length	Meter	M
Mass	Kilogram	Kg
Time	Second	S
Electric current	Ampere	A
Temperature	Kelvin	K
Amount of a substance	Mole	Mol

You're no doubt already familiar with some of the base units listed in Table 1.1 and their multiples, such as centimeters or kilograms. Table 1.2 outlines some of the more common unit prefixes used in the SI system.

Table 1.2 SI Unit Prefixes		
Multiple	**Prefix**	**Symbol**
10^6	Mega	M
10^3	Kilo	k
10^{-1}	deci	d
10^{-2}	centi	c
10^{-6}	micro	m
10^{-9}	Nano	n

Most of the questions on the General Science test are standard "read and choose an answer" multiple choice questions. Don't be thrown off track, however, when you see problems—especially in the Physical Sciences—that require you to solve problems using simple equations, such as the formula for work, or the equation: Distance = Rate * Time. The emphasis here is on understanding the key relationships expressed by the formula, not on testing your math skills—that will come later!

Chemistry

Chemistry is the science of matter. Chemists study matter in all its forms and pay particular attention to the changes it undergoes. The ASVAB contains a number of chemistry questions on topics such as the different states of matter, the structure of the atom, chemical elements, bonding, reactions, and solutions. You will review each of those topics next.

Matter and Atomic Structure

Matter is anything having mass and occupying space. It exists in the universe primarily in three states, listed in order of increasing density:

➤ **Gas**—Gases have definite mass, but variable volume and shape.

➤ **Liquid**—Liquids have definite mass and volume, but variable shape.

➤ **Solid**—Solids have definite mass, volume, and shape.

All matter is made up of *atoms*. Atoms, in turn, are composed of subatomic particles (protons, neutrons, and electrons) as illustrated in Figure 1.1.

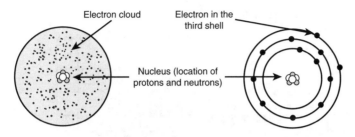

Figure 1.1   The atom and its subatomic particles.

➤ **Protons**—These particles are located in the nucleus and have a +1 relative charge.

➤ **Neutrons**—These particles are located in the nucleus and have no charge.

➤ **Electrons**—These particles are located in orbital "shells" around the nucleus and have a –1 relative charge.

Periodic Table of Elements

Substances made up of only one kind of atom are called *elements*. Some elements include Helium (He), which is used to fill blimps; Nitrogen (N), which is found in fertilizer and plant food; and Oxygen (0_2), which hospitals may supply to patients. Chemists have organized all the stable elements that occur in nature or have been created in the laboratory into the *Periodic Table of Elements*. The Periodic Table lists elements in order by their atomic number. The atomic number (the number of protons in each element's nucleus) is like a fingerprint in that it positively identifies an atom as being of a certain element.

As you can see in Figure 1.2, each element is represented by a square containing the following items of information:

➤ The alphabetic abbreviation of the element's name

➤ The element's atomic number

➤ The element's atomic mass (the average mass of all the naturally occurring isotopes of the element)

Periodic Table of Elements

IA	IIA												IIIA	IVA	VA	VIA	VIIA	VIIIA

(Periodic table figure)

1. The atomic number equals the number of protons in the atom.
2. The number of protons equals the number of electrons in the atom.
3. The number of neutrons in the most common isotope equals the atomic mass (rounded to the nearest whole number) minus the atomic number.

Atomic Number — 1

Atomic Symbol — **H**

Atomic Mass — Hydrogen 1.0

Types of Elements Key
- Alkali metals
- Alkaline earth metals
- Transition metals
- Lanthanides
- Actinides
- Poor metals
- Semi-metals
- Non-metals
- Noble gases

| La | Ce | Pr | Nd | Pm | Sm | Eu | Gd | Tb | Dy | Ho | Er | Tm | Yb | Lu |
| Ac | Th | Pa | U | Np | Pu | Am | Cm | Bk | Cf | Es | Fm | Md | No | Lr |

Figure 1.2   The Periodic Table of Elements.

> Isotopes are atoms of the same element (that is, possessing the same number of protons) that have different numbers of neutrons. The mass number of an element is simply the number of protons plus neutrons contained in an atom's nucleus.

As you look at the Periodic Table you might notice a dark, bold line stair-stepping its way across the table. This line represents (with a few exceptions) the division of elements into two major groups: *metals* and *nonmetals*. The following list details these further.

➤ **Metals**—Metals are located to the left of the line and comprise the majority of elements in the table. Some familiar examples include: Fe (iron), Ti (titanium), Au (gold), and Na (sodium). Metals do not combine with each other, but do combine with nonmetals. Metals share certain physical properties, including electrical and thermal (heat) conductivity, hardness, a high melting point, and a shiny appearance.

➤ **Nonmetals**—Nonmetals are located to the right of the line. Nonmetals combine with metal and sometimes with each other. Their physical and chemical properties are roughly the opposite of metals. Nonmetals are poor conductors, are soft, and have lower melting and boiling points. As a result, some nonmetals, such as H (hydrogen), O (oxygen), N (nitrogen), and Cl (chlorine) can exist as gases at normal temperatures.

Chemical Bonding

In the natural world, elements may be found alone or in combination with other elements. When two or more different kinds of elements combine (chemically bond) to form a different material, the result is called a *compound*. There are two basic methods by which elements chemically bond:

➤ **Ionic bonds**—These chemical bonds are formed when electron(s) are transferred from one atom to another. Atom(s) that gain or lose an electron, and thus acquire a charge, are called *ions*. The compounds formed by ionic bonding have a strong, crystalline structure with high boiling and melting points.

➤ **Covalent bonds**—These chemical bonds are formed when a pair of electrons is shared between the atoms.

Chemical Equations and Reactions

As chemical elements come in contact with each other, they may react. Chemical reactions take place in several forms, and chemists describe these reactions by writing equations that represent the elements and proportions involved.

Chemical equations are similar to mathematical equations, with the substances on the left side of the equation called *reactants*, and the substance(s) on the right side called *products*. Numbers are assigned to show the proper ratio of atoms of each element participating in the reaction. The following are the three main types of reactions, along with an example equation for each:

➤ **Synthesis reaction**—The formation of a new compound from a synthesis, or combination, from two or more different substances.

Example: $H + O_2 \rightarrow H_2O$

➤ **Decomposition reaction**—The breakdown of one compound into two or more different substances.

Example: $CaCO_3 \rightarrow CaO + CO_2$

➤ **Replacement reaction**—The exchange or elements or compounds as a result of the reaction.

Example: $2Na + 2H_2O \rightarrow H_2 + 2\ NaOH$

In each type of reaction, the *Law of Conservation of Mass (or Matter)* states that the quantity of mass (or matter) of the product must be equal to that of the reactants. In other words, matter can neither be created nor destroyed in a chemical reaction.

Remember that the *Law of Conservation of Mass (or Matter)* states that the quantity of mass (or matter) of the product must be equal to that of the reactants. For example, when mixing one hydrogen element with one oxygen element you get H_2O (water), as evidence in this equation:

$H + O_2 \rightarrow H_2O$

Solutions, Solvents, and Concentration

A *solution* is a homogeneous (uniform throughout) mixture comprised of a *solute* (a substance that is dissolved) dissolved into a *solvent* (the dissolving substance). A commonly found example is salt water, which can be formed by adding the solute NaCl (sodium chloride) to the solvent water (H_2O). The solution formed has the same properties throughout.

A *solute* is a substance that is dissolved and a *solvent* is the substance that does the dissolving.

Another characteristic of a solution is that its components can be varied. When more of either solvent or solute is added to the solution, a change occurs in the concentration of the solution. For example, let's say you are mixing up some instant lemonade. You pour water into a pitcher and then add the lemonade powder. What happens? The powder is the solute in this example and it is dissolved into the water, which is the solvent. The concentration of your lemonade is determined by the specific quantity of water and powder used. To change the concentration you must either add more powder (to increase the concentration) or water (to decrease the concentration.)

One way of expressing the concentration of a solution is in terms of *molar concentration*, using the following formula:

Molar concentration (M) = moles of solute/liter of solution

A *mole* is the amount of a substance that contains Avogadro's number (which is equal to 6.02×10^{23}) of units. For example, one mole of HCl (hydrochloric acid) contains 6.02×10^{23} molecules. Because atoms and molecules are so small and combine in such vast numbers, the mole makes calculations simpler (just as the ton is helpful when working with extremely heavy objects).

NOTE | Amedeo Avogadro, an Italian chemist and physicist, theorized that equal volumes of gases existing at identical temperature and pressure contain an equal number of molecules. This number, which would be called Avogadro's number, was determined through experimentation.

There is a limit to the amount of solute that can be dissolved by a solvent into a stable solution at any given temperature. When that limit is reached, the solution is saturated. Unsaturated solutions contain less than the maximum amount of solute. Supersaturated solutions, on the other hand, contain more than the normal maximum quantity of solute. These solutions are unstable and, when disturbed, undergo a process called *precipitation* in which all the excess solute settles out of the solution.

Acids, Bases, and pH

Acids are substances that give up a proton (producing an H+ ion) when in an aqueous (water) solution. They turn blue litmus paper red and have low pH numbers. Acids are also sour tasting; lemon juice and vinegar are acids. Finally, acids neutralize bases.

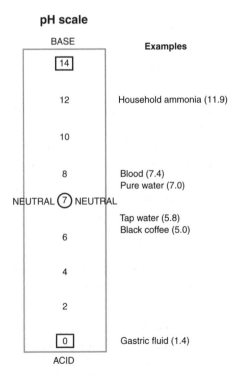

Figure 1.3 The pH scale.

Bases are substances that accept a proton (producing an OH- ion) when in aqueous solution. They turn red litmus paper blue and have high pH numbers. Bases are bitter tasting (think ammonia) and have a soapy, slick feel. Bases neutralize acids.

pH is measurement of the relative acidity or alkalinity of a solution, which is determined by its concentration of hydrogen ions. Chemists have created a pH scale that ranges from 0 to 14. On this scale, pure distilled water has a pH of 7, which is neutral. Solutions with pH less than 7 are acids and those with pH greater than 7 are alkalines (also called bases).

Figure 1.3 illustrates the pH scale, along with several common solutions and their pH levels.

Carbon and Organic Chemistry

Organic chemistry is a specialized field of study focusing on carbon-based molecules. The significance of carbon is its presence in all living things on the earth, as well as in the fossil fuels we burn to power the machinery of modern life.

Physics

Physics is the science concerned with the relationship between matter and energy in all its forms. It is another broad field that we need to break down into digestible sections.

Beginning with the field of physics called mechanics, you will review the concepts of work, energy, and power. Mechanical energy can take several forms, including kinetic energy and potential energy. You will define these types of energy and review Newton's Laws of Motion, before moving on to the special case of fluids in motion. The review concludes with a tune-up on thermal (heat) energy, light energy, and magnetism. There is a lot to cover here and physics questions make up a significant block of ASVAB questions.

Work, Energy, and Power

The terms *work*, *energy*, and *power* are commonly used in our language and mean different things in various contexts. To a physicist, however, they each have a specific, precise meaning.

➤ **Work**—In a flat plane, *work* is the product of an object's displacement (distance moved in the direction of a given force) and the force used to move the object. The SI unit of force is the *Newton (N)* and the SI unit of work is the *Joule (J)*. The equation for work is

Work (W) = force * displacement.

➤ **Energy**—*Energy* is the ability to do work. The SI unit of work is the *Joule (J)*. Although energy comes in many different forms, (such as chemical energy, electrical energy, nuclear energy, and so on), when we are concerned with the energy of objects in motion, there are two main types of energy to consider:

> ➤ **Kinetic energy**—This is the *energy of motion*. When you swing a hammer and strike a nail, the resulting work is done by kinetic energy.

> ➤ **Potential energy**—This is *stored energy*. Energy is stored in an object as a result of its position or configuration. Imagine a skier riding to the top of a slope. On reaching the top, the skier has stored up a supply of potential energy in her body as a result of the work done to transport her mass to a position where gravity can act on it.

➤ **Power**—This is the rate at which work is done. The SI unit of power is the *Watt (W)*. Or, in equation form:

Power (P) = work / time = (force * displacement) / time

The Energy of Motion

Sir Isaac Newton formulated three Laws of Motion that laid the foundation for the entire field of mechanics, which is the study of the energy of motion. To understand these basic laws, let's first define a few terms:

➤ **Speed**—The scalar (that is, quantity only, with no information as to direction) expression of distance traveled per unit of time.

➤ **Velocity**—The vector (that is, containing quantity and direction information) expression of distance traveled (called *displacement*) per unit of time.

➤ **Acceleration**—The change in the velocity of an object over the amount of time required to make that change. (The acceleration of gravity on an object is independent of the object's mass and is a universal constant, $g = 9.8$ meters/second^2.)

➤ **Force**—The push or pull that imparts motion on an object.

➤ **Mass**—A measure of the quantity of matter in an object. An object's mass is constant, regardless of the gravitational force acting on it. Weight, by contrast, is simply a measure of the gravitational force acting on an object's mass. For example, due to the weaker gravitational pull of the moon, a person would weigh less on the moon than he or she does on earth. Mass—the amount of matter out of which you are made—would remain constant.

Newton's three Laws of Motion are as follows:

1. An object at rest will remain at rest and an object in motion will remain in motion in a straight line, unless it is acted upon by some net force.

2. If a net force acts on an object, it will cause the object to accelerate in direct proportion to the magnitude of the net force and in inverse proportion to the mass of the object.

3. For every action or force that one object places on a second object, the second object places an equal and opposite (in direction) reaction on the first.

 Newton's Second Law leads us to define *momentum (p)* as the product of the mass (m) of an object and its velocity (v). In equation form:

$p = m * v$.

Fluids

Fluids are substances that can *flow*. Both liquids and gases are fluids. Fluids exert pressure on their containers due to the constant, random motion of their molecules. The SI unit of pressure is the *Pascal*. The formula for pressure is

Pressure = Force / Area (in meters squared)

Three basic principles govern the behavior of fluids:

➤ **Pascal's Principle**—Any change in pressure applied to a confined, incompressible fluid is transmitted uniformly to every part of the fluid. This principle underlies the incredibly useful mechanical advantage provided by hydraulics.

➤ **Archimedes' Principle**—An object that is submerged (either completely or in part) in a fluid is buoyed up by a force that is equal to the weight of the fluid it displaces. The ability to predict the force of buoyancy, which operates in opposition to gravity and keeps ships and swimmers afloat, also allows for advances in lighter than air travel.

➤ **Bernoulli's Principle**—As the velocity of a moving fluid increases, its ability to exert pressure decreases. This principle, when applied to the fluid called air, is at the root of hydrodynamics and aerodynamics and explains how an airplane's wings produce the lift required for flight.

Thermal Energy

Thermal energy, or *heat*, is the energy created by the internal movement of a substance's molecules. Heat flows from a substance that is hot to a cooler substance with which it comes into contact. The SI unit of measurement for heat is the *calorie*. There are three ways that thermal energy is transferred:

➤ **Convection**—Heat transfer occurs through actual displacement of a lower temperature part of a medium by a higher temperature part. Because physical mass movement is required, convection can only take place in a fluid.

➤ **Conduction**—Heat transfer occurs within a medium (such as a steel rod or a copper wire) through the flow of "free" electrons. For this reason, electrical conductivity and thermal conductivity go hand in hand.

➤ **Radiation**—Heat transfer occurs through electromagnetic waves and so does not require direct contact between the two mediums. In fact, energy transfer through radiation does not even require a connecting medium. This is best seen when considering how the sun heats the earth, via radiation, across the vacuum of space.

Waves

Heat is not the only form of energy that can be transmitted through waves. Sound travels in waves and light also exhibits wave-like properties. In physics, waves are disturbances that move progressively through a medium in a given direction with repeating peaks and valleys of motion. Figure 1.4 demonstrates a wave.

A Waveform

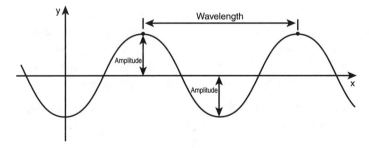

Figure 1.4   A sinusoidal wave.

When discussing a wave, you must consider the following items:

➤ **Frequency (Pitch)**—The number of complete waves passing a point in one second.

➤ **Amplitude**—The value of the maximum height of the wavelength above the mean value of the wave.

➤ **Wavelength**—The distance between two consecutive peaks in the wave.

The *Doppler Effect* is a phenomenon of waves generated by a moving source or detected by a moving observer. In the case of sound waves, when a listener hears a noise source approaching, its *pitch* (frequency) appears to increase the closer it gets. The moment the noise source passes its nearest point to the listener and begins moving away, its pitch appears to decrease. (Think of how an emergency vehicle's siren sounds as it goes past.) This phenomenon is useful in many applications, including radar, sonar, and sonograms.

Light can behave as a wave in a number of ways. Each color in the rainbow is made up of light of a different wavelength and frequency. This is demonstrated when light passes through a prism, which *refracts* (bends) the light causing the different frequencies to separate. Here are some terms you should be familiar with:

➤ **Refraction**—The bending of light when it passes from one medium (such as air) into another (such as the glass of a prism). Different wavelengths of light bend at different angles. The reason for this bending is that light—like all waves—slows down when traveling through a denser medium.

➤ **Reflection**—The "bouncing" back of light rays toward their source when they hit a surface. The angle at which light strikes a surface (called the angle of incidence) is equal to the angle at which it is reflected.

➤ **Lenses**—A lens is an optical device used to refract light. Concave lenses are recessed in the middle and curved out at their edges in the direction of the light source; they cause light to diverge, or spread out. Convex lenses are curved out at the middle and are recessed at their edges away from the light source; they cause light to converge, or focus.

➤ **Mirrors**—Mirrors are optical devices used to reflect light. Concave mirrors focus light and convex mirrors spread it out.

Magnetism

Magnetism is the study of magnets, their properties, and their effects on other materials. Magnets attract iron, steel, and other materials with high iron content. Metals alloys with iron content are called *ferrous metals*. The earth is a magnet because of its dense iron core. Magnets have a north and a south pole. If you place the north pole of one magnet next to the north pole of another, the magnets will move away from (or repel) each other. If, however, you place the north pole of one magnet next to the south pole of another magnet, they will move together (or attract).

Together the north and south poles of a magnet form a magnetic field in which the magnetic forces of attraction and repulsion are exerted. A useful characteristic of a magnetic field is that when a conductive wire is moved through it (or vice versa), an electrical current is generated in the wire. The discovery of this concept led to the invention of electrical generators and motors.

Life Sciences

Up to this point in our General Science review we have looked at scientific fields dealing with nonliving things. The Life Sciences, including: Biology, Anatomy and Physiology, and Ecology, are devoted to the study of living organisms and their interactions. Beginning with Biology, you will review the basic system of classifying organisms according to type. Next you will brush up on cells—the basic building block of living things. Turning to Human Anatomy and Physiology, you will review the function and interrelationships of the human body's major systems. Finally, our Ecology review begins with the definition of major terminology and culminates in a discussion of Earth's biomes and the food chain which links together all Earth's organisms.

Biology

Biology is the study of life and living things, called *organisms*. All organisms go through a process of birth, development, reproduction, death, and decomposition. Organisms consume energy throughout their lifespan and ultimately recycle energy back into nature. Life is a process in which individual organisms have beginnings and endings, but attempt to preserve a continuing cycle of existence of their species. Let's now look at how organisms are classified into groups and then review some key facts about cells.

Taxonomy (the Classification of Living Things)

The enormous job of classifying (or organizing into groups) all living things took its currently accepted form in the eighteenth century, and is known as the *Linnaean System*. Organisms are classified according to shared characteristics, physical structures, or traits. From broadest to narrowest, these groupings are seen in Table 1.3.

Table 1.3 How Organisms Are Classified	
Classification	**Example (Human Beings)**
Kingdom	Animalia
Phylum	Chordata
Class	Mammalia
Order	Primates
Family	Hominidae
Genus	Homo
Species	sapiens

In everyday conversation we refer to ourselves simply as "people" or "human beings," yet biologists must be more precise in order to differentiate between the many varieties of similar organisms that exist and evolve over time. The example given in Table 1.3 contains the complete and exact scientific name for present day human beings. The top level of the classification (the Kingdom) represents the broadest group with which humans share similar characteristics. We have more in common with animals than with plants or fungi, for example. By the time you have worked your way down the classification hierarchy to the narrowest grouping (species) you find that you are now describing only one organism.

Most often you will see organisms referred to using a binomial (two name) abbreviation of their classification, which uses only their Genus and Species (for example, Homo sapiens for humans, or Ornicus orcas for killer whales).

Biologists recognize five distinct kingdoms of organisms, as defined in Table 1.4. Every living organism belongs to one and only one of these kingdoms. Although this may seem like common sense now, it represented a significant step forward in our knowledge and has allowed biologists to organize their discoveries and better understand the organisms they study. Although you will not be required to memorize the correct kingdom for every organism, the ASVAB does contain questions relating to the animal kingdoms, so be sure to give Table 1.4 a look.

Table 1.4	Kingdoms	
Kingdom	**General Characteristics**	**Examples**
Monera	Single cell; no true nucleus	Blue-green algae
Protista	Single cell; true nucleus, membrane	Amoebas
Fungi	Multicell; eat by external digestion followed by absorption	Slime molds, fungi
Plantae	Multicell. Almost all plants make their own food through photosynthesis.	Ferns, flowering plants, trees
Animalia	Multicell; may be carnivores, herbivores, or omnivores	Birds, reptiles, mammals, jellyfish

Cells

Cells are the smallest unit of life. They contain distinct parts, as seen in the plant cell diagram in Figure 1.5, and perform the basic functions of life. *Cytoplasm* is the name for all parts of a cell, except for the cell membrane (sometimes called plasma membrane). The cytoplasm includes the *organelles*, or compartmented sections, which perform the cell's various life functions and chemical reactions. The organelles are described in Table 1.5.

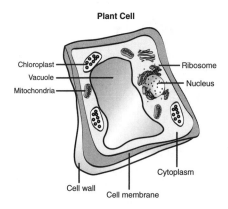

Figure 1.5   A plant cell.

The ASVAB might ask you to identify the various parts of a cell or, given the name of a particular part, identify its function. You do not need to spend too much time memorizing the entire table, but you should be somewhat familiar with the terms presented in Table 1.5.

Table 1.5 The Parts of a Cell	
Organelle	**Function(s) Performed**
Nucleus	Controls cell functions, contains all genetic instructions in chromosomes.
Endoplasmic reticulum	Manufactures proteins and lipids.
Golgi bodies	Transports proteins.
Lysosomes	Recycles materials.
Ribosomes	Synthesizes proteins.
Mitochondria	Extracts energy from carbohydrates.
Vacuole(s)	Stores waste and other materials.
Chloroplasts (plant cells only)	Performs photosynthesis (converting solar energy to chemical energy for making the cell's food.)
Cell walls (plant cells only)	Supports and protects cell.

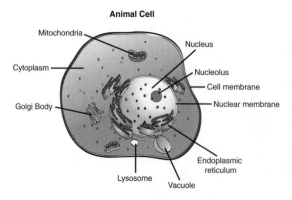

Figure 1.6 An animal cell.

Photosynthesis

As you can see from the previous two figures, there are several key differences between plant and animal cells. Before moving on, let's take a closer look at the phenomenon, unique to the Plant Kingdom, of *photosynthesis*.

Photosynthesis is the process by which plants create their own food. Plants contain chloroplasts within their cells. Chloroplasts in land plants appear green because of chlorophyll, a green, light-absorbing pigment. Absorbed light (solar energy) is then used to convert carbon dioxide (CO_2) and water (H_2O) into carbohydrates, which the plant uses for food. A beneficial byproduct of this reaction is the release of oxygen (O_2) and water (H_2O) to the atmosphere.

Cell Division and Genetics

Cells reproduce through a process called *cell division*. They can replicate themselves because of the hereditary (or genetic) information contained within the nucleus of the parent cell. Each nucleus contains chromosomes, which in turn contain *deoxyribonucleic acid* (DNA) molecules. DNA provides a set of instructions that governs the entire cell's function, growth, development, susceptibility to disease, and more.

Most human cells contain 46 chromosomes. Sex cells (sperm and ova), however, each have only 23 chromosomes. This allows for even sharing of the male and female partners' genetic information at fertilization. When the 23 chromosomes from the male cell join with the 23 chromosomes from the female cell, the resulting cell has 46 chromosomes.

Cell division can happen in one of two ways:

➤ **Mitosis**—A process in which a cell makes two exact copies of itself by first duplicating its chromosomes and then splitting in two. Each new cell receives a set of chromosomes that perfectly matches that of the parent cell. Mitosis occurs in most of the human body's cells.

➤ **Meiosis**—A specialized, two-step process leading to the production of sex cells. One parent cell produces four daughter (or son) cells, each with half the number of chromosomes of the parent cell.

Human Anatomy and Physiology

Anatomy deals with the study of the structure of an organism or body and Physiology focuses on the functions and processes of a body's vital systems. These two related subjects are of great importance to the military, and so receive significant attention on the ASVAB, because of the great need for medical knowledge in every branch of the service. You will certainly see several questions coming from the material presented here.

Bodily Systems

The body is a complex set of interrelated systems, all working to allow the human organism to fulfill its life functions. Here is a look at those systems:

> **Musculoskeletal system**—The skeleton is made up of bones, which provide strength, protect the internal organs, and produce blood cells. Muscles attach to the skeleton, allowing the body to move and perform vital functions.

> **Nervous system**—Nerve cells (called *neurons*) are located all over the human body; they receive stimuli from the surrounding environment and transmit those stimuli to the brain in the form of electrical impulses. The brain processes this input and controls the body's response. The central nervous system deals with input from the neurons in the spinal cord and brain, whereas the peripheral nervous system involves neurons from all other areas of the body (skin, internal organs, and so on).

> **Endocrine system**—The endocrine system controls the body through a release of *hormones* (produced in the endocrine glands) into the blood stream. Specific hormones target specific organs and only affect them. Examples of these hormones include: thyroid hormone, affecting the thyroid's ability to regulate metabolism; and insulin, affecting the pancreas by decreasing the concentration of blood sugar.

> **Respiratory system**—The respiratory system includes the mouth, nose, throat, and lungs (and other organs). It enables the body to inhale air, filter out the oxygen needed for life, and exhale the unnecessary (waste) gases (primarily carbon dioxide). The lungs transfer oxygen to the blood stream where it is transported throughout the body via the circulatory system.

> **Circulatory system**—Like an interstate highway system, the circulatory system's job is to transport oxygen and nutrients throughout the body and remove waste. The heart pumps the blood out into a network of arteries, arterioles, and capillaries, which direct blood to all parts of the body. Blood makes its return trip to the heart by way of the capillaries, venules, and veins.

> **Lymphatic system**—The lymphatic system supports the circulatory system by returning fluids to the blood and helping to fight infections.

> **Digestive system**—Comprised of the mouth, esophagus, stomach, small intestine, large intestine, rectum, and anus, the digestive system ingests and breaks down food. The usable nutrient particles are absorbed into the body and the unusable particles are removed and evacuated from the body.

➤ **Excretory system**—The body's waste disposal system is controlled by the kidneys, which filter waste products from the blood. This waste travels from the kidneys to the bladder via the ureter. The waste, called *urine*, is stored in the bladder until it is removed from the body via the urethra.

➤ **Reproductive system**—Human reproduction requires the union of the male and female reproductive systems. The *male* organs produce and transport *sperm*, which seek to fertilize the *female ovum*. If fertilization takes place, a *zygote* is formed. The zygote attaches itself to the wall of the female's uterus to develop into a fetus. If no fertilization occurs, the blood rich lining of the uterus is removed from the body through the process of *menstruation*.

Ecology

Organisms constantly interact with each other and with their environment. On a planet with limited resources and limited space being shared by all living things, the study of these interactions—a field of science called *ecology*—takes on great importance. Here are a few important ecological terms:

➤ **Biome**—Regions that share similar climate and soil type, resulting in similar populations of plant and animal life.

➤ **Community**—The sum of the various populations that live within a particular habitat (common geographic location).

➤ **Population**—A grouping of a certain species within a habitat.

➤ **Ecosystem**—A community and its environment.

➤ **Predator**—An organism that utilizes other living organisms as its food source, but does not live in or on its prey.

➤ **Prey**—A living organism that becomes a food source for another living organism.

➤ **Parasite**—An organism that lives in or on another living organism (host) and obtains the nutrients it needs from the host's tissues.

➤ **Symbiosis**—A mutually beneficial relationship between two or more species, which causes them to maintain close and continuous contact.

Biomes and Ecosystems

Ecologists have divided the life sustaining areas of the planet (which together make up the biosphere) into *seven biomes*.

1. **Tundra**—With permanently frozen soil, plant life on the tundra consists of short-rooted plants and shrubs. Located in the northern portion of the northern hemisphere, tundra is a region of vast plains, short
   summers, and long, brutal winters. Animal life includes bears, reindeer,
   wolves, and other rugged species.

2. **Taiga (Coniferous forest)**—Located to the south of the tundra, taiga
   contains coniferous (or evergreen) trees. Although the winters are not
   as extreme as in the tundra, they are long and severe. Animal species
   include bears, elk, rabbits, and many others.

3. **Deciduous forest**—Located south of the taiga, these forests contain
   leafy trees. The milder climate allows for four distinct seasons. Animals
   such as deer, raccoons, squirrels, rabbits, and fox live here.

4. **Savannah**—These grasslands exist in a wide belt that includes the mid-
   western United States, Africa, parts of South America, and the massive
   central plains of Eurasia. There are few trees and rainfall is unreliable.
   Animal species include a variety of grazing and burrowing animals such
   as gophers, moles, snakes, hawks, antelope, giraffe, lions, and ele-
   phants.

5. **Tropical rain forest**—This is a region of extremely high humidity,
   rainfall, and temperature. Dense vegetation extends from the forest
   floor to the tall canopy of trees and vines. Tropical rain forests are
   found in the mid-latitudes surrounding the equator in Central and
   South America, Africa, and also in Southeast Asia. Animal species
   include birds, snakes, monkeys, panthers, and countless insect species.

6. **Desert**—A region of extremely low humidity and precipitation. Plant
   life is scarce, but may include low scrub or cacti. Deserts may be hot or
   cold and have large temperature swings between day and night. Animal
   species (including small rodents, snakes, lizards, and kangaroo) possess
   specialized survival skills to manage the temperature swings and scarce
   water supply.

7. **Marine**—Water covers almost three-fourths of the planet's surface.
   The marine biome contains countless plant and animal species and can
   be further subdivided into several distinct zones. The scientific field of
   oceanography is devoted to the study of the marine biomes.

Food Chain

All organisms must consume energy to live. To describe the interrelationships of the various organisms within a community, ecologists construct food chain diagrams. Food chain pyramid diagrams are useful tools to help ecologists express the delicate balance of various communities within an ecosystem. Just as with a literal chain, when one link is greatly weakened or removed, the entire chain fails. Figure 1.7 illustrates one example of a food chain pyramid. The larger area at the bottom of the pyramid contains producers and the shrinking size of each successive layer of consumers reflects the relative proportion of each type of organism in a community.

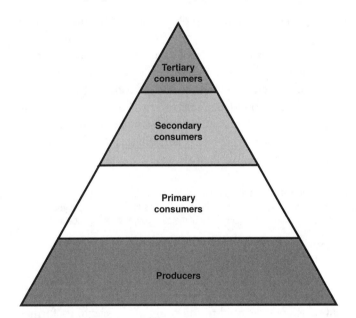

Figure 1.7 A food chain pyramid.

Table 1. 6 Food Chain Example	
Group	**Example**
Tertiary consumers	Eagles
Secondary consumers	Snakes
Primary consumers	Small rodents
Producers	Blackberry bushes

Producers make their own food. Consumers are unable to produce their own food so they feed on other organisms. Primary consumers feed on producers; secondary consumers feed on primary consumers, and so on. Another group—the decomposers—is also present in every food chain. decomposers, such as bacteria and fungi, eventually break down all members of the food chain into simple organic compounds. Decomposers are nature's great recyclers.

Earth and Space Sciences

The Earth and Space Sciences are made up of: Geology, Meteorology, and Astronomy. Geology is the study of the earth and this review covers the earth's composition and types of rocks, as well as an overview of the earth's geological eras dating back to its formation. Meteorology, or the study of the earth's atmosphere and its climate and weather, and Astronomy (the study of space in the objects in space) round out our review. You can move fairly quickly through this section. If you are pinched for time before the test, you can skim this section and go back to the Life and Physical Science sections to brush up on any areas where you feel a little shaky.

Bearing in mind that these final scientific fields are weighted much less heavily on the ASVAB than those we have just covered, here are some key concepts you should know. Although you won't face every one of them on your test, you can count on seeing at least a few.

Geology

Geology is the field of science devoted to the study of the earth, its formation and composition, and its ongoing processes of change. Although not heavily tested on the ASVAB, there are some basic geology items you should be familiar with as discussed in the following paragraphs.

The earth is composed of three main layers:

➤ **Crust**—The outermost layer of the earth, the crust varies in thickness from as little as 5 miles under the ocean to 40 miles beneath mountain ranges. It is made up of rock, mainly granite and basalt.

➤ **Mantle**—Located directly beneath the crust, the mantle makes up approximately 85% of the earth's volume. The upper mantle is rigid like the crust. The thicker, lower mantle behaves more like a slowly moving fluid and contains pockets of molten rock. The mantle reaches approximately 1,800 miles below the earth's surface.

➤ **Core**—The center of the earth is made up of nickel-iron; it has a fluid outer layer and a solid inner core. The core is responsible for generating the earth's magnetic field and is approximately 1,400 miles across, representing about one-third of the earth's mass.

Geologists have classified three major types of rocks, whose differences are primarily the result of how they are formed:

➤ **Igneous**—Formed by cooling lava (the name for magma that reaches the earth's surface.

➤ **Sedimentary**—Formed by the compacting and cementing together of sediment (small rock, mineral, and even organic particles).

➤ **Metamorphic**—Formed by the transformative effects of extreme heat, pressure, or chemical action on existing rock.

Analyzing rock deposits and fossils, geologists have been able to establish a timeline to trace the earth's development from its formation up to the present day. The following list highlights this timeline:

1. **Precambrian Era (4.6 billion to 570 million years ago)**—Beginning with the earth's formation, this era was marked by violent volcanic activity and mountain formation. Primitive life forms date back to this period, but few fossil records of this life survive.

2. **Paleozoic Era (570 million to 245 million years ago)**—Continents were formed. Fish, amphibians, reptiles, and land plants emerged.

3. **Mesozoic Era (245 million to 66 million years ago)** —Dinosaurs lived and became extinct, along with a number of other species.

4. **Cenozoic Era (66 million to present)**—Many species of mammals have developed and flourished during this period, during which the last Ice Age ended.

Meteorology

Military forces have always been impacted by the effects of the weather. Predicting weather begins with understanding climate. Climate, the prevailing weather patterns in an area over a long period of time, depends on many factors. The key factors to review for the ASVAB are the atmosphere and clouds, which are a part of the water cycle by which the earth recycles water from the oceans into the atmosphere and back to the earth again. You begin with the atmosphere.

The Atmosphere

The *atmosphere* makes life on earth possible and protects all living things from the sun's harmful ultra-violet rays. The atmosphere is like a blanket of gases surrounding the planet. Its four layers are

1. **Troposphere**—Extends from the surface to an altitude of approximately 10 miles. Its composition is 78% nitrogen, 21% oxygen, and 1% of a variety of other gases. The troposphere contains most of the earth's clouds and its weather. As altitude increases, temperature and barometric pressure decrease.

2. **Stratosphere**—Extends from 10 miles to 30 miles above the earth's surface. This important layer contains the ozone layer. Although there is very little water vapor in the stratosphere, some clouds (e.g., cumulonimbus and cirrus) exist there. Although pressure continues to decrease with altitude, temperature increases.

3. **Mesosphere**—Extends from 30 to 50 miles above the earth's surface. Temperature and pressure decrease with altitude. This is the atmosphere's coldest layer.

4. **Thermosphere**—Extends from 50 to 300 miles above the earth's surface. Temperature increases dramatically and pressure decreases with altitude.

Clouds

Clouds are formed when water vapor is carried into the air by rising warm air currents that begin to cool as they continue to rise. When the temperature of the droplets reaches the dew point, they condense into water droplets (or tiny ice crystals). When the droplets are big and heavy enough they precipitate out of the cloud as rain, sleet, hail, or snow.

There are three basic types of clouds:

➤ **Stratus**—Flat, layered clouds.

➤ **Cumulus**—Clumplike clouds with strong upward currents of air, leading to elongated, tall shapes. Cumulonimbus clouds are thunderstorm clouds.

➤ **Cirrus**—Striped, wispy, high-altitude clouds.

Fronts

When two air masses of differing temperature and humidity come in contact with each other, the line that separates them is called a *front*. Meteorologists speak of warm fronts and cold fronts when describing the movement of the leading edge of these air masses through a region.

Astronomy

People have always been fascinated by what they have seen in the night sky. Astronomers have expanded our knowledge about space and the universe greatly over the centuries, and our knowledge continues to grow ever more rapidly as we peer out and send probes deep into "outer space." For the purposes of the ASVAB, what you need to know mostly involves the solar system.

The Solar System

The solar system consists of the sun and everything that orbits it. Table 1.7 presents the nine planets of our solar system.

Table 1.7	The Planets in Our Solar System			
Planet (Listed Closest to Farthest from Sun)	Type	Rank by Size (Large to Small)	Has Ring(s)?	Has Moon(s)?
Mercury	Rock	8	No	No
Venus	Rock	6	No	No
Earth	Rock	5	No	Yes
Mars	Rock	7	No	Yes
Jupiter	Gas	1	Yes	Yes
Saturn	Gas	2	Yes	Yes
Uranus	Gas	3	Yes	Yes
Neptune	Gas	4	Yes	Yes
Pluto	Rock	9	No	Yes

Here are some astronomy terms worth knowing:

➤ **Orbit**—The path an object follows through space as it travels around another object. The shape of an orbit is determined by the force of gravity acting on the objects and by the laws of motion.

➤ **Light year**—The distance light travels (through a vacuum, such as space) in one year. The light year is the standard unit astronomers use to measure or describe distances between objects in the universe. One light year equals approximately 5.9 trillion miles.

➤ **Eclipse**—The obscuring of the moon (lunar eclipse) when the earth's shadow passes over it, or the obscuring of the sun (solar eclipse) when the moon passes directly between the earth and sun.

Exam Prep Questions

1. Which of the following is the third planet from the sun?
   - ❑ A. Mars
   - ❑ B. Earth
   - ❑ C. Venus
   - ❑ D. Neptune

2. Which instrument do meteorologists use to measure wind speed?
   - ❑ A. Hydrometer
   - ❑ B. Altimeter
   - ❑ C. Wind sock
   - ❑ D. Anemometer

3. What are the product(s) of a neutralization reaction?
   - ❑ A. An acid and a base
   - ❑ B. Water
   - ❑ C. A salt and water
   - ❑ D. A base

4. How many atoms are present in five molecules of water (H_2O)?
   - ❑ A. 3
   - ❑ B. 5
   - ❑ C. 10
   - ❑ D. 15

5. When a ray of light passes from air into water it...
   - ❑ A. slows down.
   - ❑ B. speeds up.
   - ❑ C. is absorbed.
   - ❑ D. is unchanged.

6. Which biome is characterized by its permanently frozen soil?
   - ❑ A. Taiga
   - ❑ B. Savannah
   - ❑ C. Deciduous forest
   - ❑ D. Tundra

7. Which of the following organelles is found in plant cells but not in animal cells?
   - ❑ A. Cell walls
   - ❑ B. Lysosomes
   - ❑ C. Cell membranes
   - ❑ D. Smaller vacuole

8. The SI unit for work is the…
   - ❏ A. Newton
   - ❏ B. Calorie
   - ❏ C. Joule
   - ❏ D. Watt

9. Convection currents transfer heat through
   - ❏ A. Electromagnetic waves
   - ❏ B. Mass movement of a fluid
   - ❏ C. Flow of free electrons
   - ❏ D. Refraction

10. Which system of the human body is responsible for releasing hormones into the blood stream?
   - ❏ A. Reproductive system
   - ❏ B. Lymphatic system
   - ❏ C. Circulatory system
   - ❏ D. Endocrine system

Exam Prep Answers

1. **The correct answer is B.** Earth is the third planet from the sun. Answer A is incorrect because Mars is the fourth planet from the sun. Answer C is incorrect because Venus is the second planet from the sun. Answer D is incorrect because Neptune is the eighth planet from the sun.

2. **The correct answer is D.** The anenometer measures wind speed, and sometimes direction. Answer A is incorrect because the hydrometer is used to measure the specific gravity of liquids. Answer B is incorrect because altimeters measure altitude, or the height above a reference point such as sea level. Answer C is incorrect because the wind sock only indicates wind direction.

3. **The correct answer is C.** A neutralization reaction is a chemical reaction where the reactants are an acid and a base, and the products are a salt and water.

4. **The correct answer is D.** The number of atoms in a molecule is found by looking at its formula. For one molecule of H2O, there are 2 atoms of hydrogen and 1 atom of oxygen, for a total of 3 atoms. But this question asks for the number of atoms present in 5 molecules of H2O. So, since 5×3 = 15, the answer is 15 atoms.

5. **The correct answer is A.** When light passes from one medium (like air) into a denser medium (like water) it slows down and bends in a process called refraction.

6. **The correct answer is D.** Tundra, located in the northern portions of the northern hemisphere, is known for its permanently frozen soil. Answer A is incorrect because the taiga is a biome characterized by its coniferous forests, which could not survive in permanently frozen soil. Answer B is incorrect, because the savannah is a grassland region located in the more central latitudes and containing all manner of burrowing animals. Answer C is incorrect because deciduous forests require an even milder climate, which allows for four distinct seasons.

7. **The correct answer is A.** Cell walls are not found in animal cells, only in plant cells. Answers B, C, and D are incorrect because both plant and animal cells contain lysosomes, cell membranes, and a smaller vacuole.

8. **The correct answer is C.** The Joule is the SI unit for work. Answer A is incorrect because the Newton is the unit for force. Answer B is incorrect, because a calorie is a measurement of heat energy (specifically, one calorie is equal to the amount of heat required to raise the temperature of one gram of water by one degree centigrade). Answer D is incorrect because the Watt is the unit of power (one Watt is equal to one Joule per second).

9. **The correct answer is B.** Convection is the form of heat transfer that occurs through an actual displacement (i.e., mass movement) of a lower temperature part of a medium by a higher temperature part. Answer A is incorrect because heat transfer through electromagnetic waves is called radiation. Answer C is incorrect because the flow of free electrons is how heat is transferred by conduction. Answer D is incorrect because heat energy is not transferred through refraction, which is a phenomenon occurring when a wave (such as light) bends as it changes speed passing from one medium into another medium of different density.

10. **The correct answer is D.** The endocrine system controls bodily functions by releasing hormones into the blood stream. Answer A is incorrect because the reproductive system includes only the organs relating to reproduction. Answer B is incorrect because the function of the lymphatic system is to fight infections and support the circulatory system by returning fluids to the blood. Answer C is incorrect because the circulatory system's function is to transport oxygen and nutrients throughout the body's cells while removing waste.

Arithmetic Reasoning

Terms you need to understand:

✓ Sum
✓ Product
✓ Difference
✓ Quotient
✓ Percent
✓ Ratio
✓ Fraction
✓ Decimal
✓ Interest rate
✓ Series
✓ Proportion
✓ Probability

Concepts you need to master:

✓ Solving word problems
✓ Performing simple arithmetic operations on whole numbers, decimals, and fractions
✓ Recognizing patterns in a series of numbers
✓ Calculating the average of a group of numbers
✓ Drawing pictures or simple data charts to help organize data provided in word problems
✓ Writing simple algebraic formulas and solving for a single variable

Arithmetic Reasoning tests your problem solving skills as much as your knowledge of basic mathematics. In fact, you may find that the arithmetic is the easy part of these problems. As we will see later, understanding what each problem is asking for and organizing the data you need are the keys to solving word problems. And that is most of what you will be seeing on this test. This chapter is broken down into three sections: a review of basic arithmetic, a review of reasoning and problem solving skills, and a practice exam question set with answers and explanations provided to help you identify any weak areas in your preparation and help you focus your review efforts further.

The Arithmetic Reasoning section of the ASVAB asks you to solve 30 questions in 36 minutes. Your exam proctor will provide you with ample scratch paper and pencils. Don't be shy, take all you need before the test starts so you don't have to interrupt the exam and waste time asking for more in the middle of the test. Calculators, watch calculators, and cell phones are not allowed in the test area.

The Arithmetic Reasoning (AR) section is important for several reasons. First, it is a part of the all important AFQT, which determines your eligibility to enlist. Second, demonstrated math skills are important in opening the doors for you into the increasingly large number of high-tech military occupational specialties. Finally, the AR section is a great opportunity to tune up for both the Mathematical Knowledge and the Paragraph Comprehension sections that come later.

Arithmetic: A Review

Arithmetic is the area of mathematics that involves making computations with real numbers. These computations are done using four basic operations: *addition*, *subtraction*, *multiplication*, and *division*. Let's begin our review with the alphabet of arithmetic: numbers. Table 2.1 provides a refresher on the various types of number sets you will encounter. Take a moment now to review the differences between each set of numbers so that on the test you won't have to stop to think what is meant by a "real number" or an "integer" before solving a problem.

Arithmetic Operations

Here is where the action is. Arithmetic operations are the verbs (action words) in the sentences making up word problems. They are what you do to the numbers to turn them into the right answer to the question being asked. Look at Table 2.2 to review the terminology found in ASVAB word problems and what it translates to in terms of arithmetic operations.

Table 2.1	Types of Number Sets	
Name of Set	**Definition**	**Examples**
Natural numbers	The counting numbers (that is, positive integers)	1,2,3,4...
Whole numbers	The natural numbers and zero	0,1,2,3,4...
Integers	The natural numbers, their opposites, and zero	...–4,–3, –2,–1,0, 1,2,3,4 ...
Rational numbers	Any number that can be represented as a fraction	–2/3,–1/2, 0,1,5/4,8.25
Irrational numbers	Numbers that can't be expressed exactly as a fraction. (When expressed as a decimal, they have infinite, nonrepeating decimal places.)	Pi=3.1415926... $\sqrt{2}$=1.4142135... $-\sqrt{5}$=–2.236068...
Real numbers	The set of all rational and irrational numbers	...–$\sqrt{5}$, –2/3, 0, 1, 5/4, Pi, 8.25...

Table 2.2	The Language of Arithmetic
What the Word Problem Says...	**What the Word Problem Means...**
Find the *sum*	Add
Find the *difference*	Subtract
Find the *product*	Multiply
Find the *quotient*	Divide

Although you are no doubt very familiar with performing the four basic arithmetic operations on integers (see Table 2.1 if you're still unsure of what an integer is), the ASVAB also requires you to perform these operations in more "real-life" scenarios. These scenarios often involve fractions, decimals, ratios, and percents. Let's review each of these now.

Fractions

Fractions represent partial quantities. For example, if you have three quarters in your pocket, you have less than a dollar. This could be expressed as a fraction: 3/4 dollar, to indicate that a dollar is made up of four parts and you have three of them.

Each fraction is made up of two numbers. The number above the line is called the *numerator* and the number below the line is called the *denominator*. A fraction with a denominator larger than its numerator (such as, 1/2, 3/4, or 5/8) is called a *proper fraction*. If the fraction's numerator is equal to or greater than its denominator (as in 4/4, 8/4, or 10/8), the fraction is *improper*. To convert an improper fraction into a proper fraction, simplify (if possible; see example that follows) and then divide the denominator into the numerator to create a mixed number. Here's an example given an improper fraction of 12/9:

1. Simplify (by removing the common factor 3 from both numerator and denominator)

   12/9 = 3*4/3*3 = 4/3

2. Convert to mixed number:

   4/3 = 1 1/3

3. Goes into 4 one time with a remainder of 1, so the new numerator is 1.

   Another way of looking at this is

   4/3 = 3/3 + 1/3 = 1 + 1/3 = 1 1/3

To convert a mixed number into an improper fraction, as you might need to do to perform an operation on it, you simply reverse this process.

Addition and Subtraction with Fractions

To add or subtract two fractions you must first find their *common denominator*. This can be done by multiplying the two denominators. Don't forget that what you do to one half of a fraction you must do to the other. Here's how it looks:

> **Addition**

$$5/8 + 1/3 = (5/8)(3/3) + (1/3)(8/8) = 15/24 + 8/24 = 23/24$$

> **Subtraction**

$$3/4 - 2/3 = (3/4)(3/3) - (2/3)(4/4) = 9/12 - 8/12 = 1/12$$

 Depending on the resulting fraction, you may have to simplify or convert it to a mixed number to get the correct answer.

Multiplication and Division with Fractions

To multiply and divide with fractions, no common denominator is needed. To multiply fractions all you have to do is multiply the two numerators to obtain the numerator of the product fraction, and multiply the two denominators to find its denominator. Here is an example:

$$5/7 * 1/2 = 5*1 / 7* 2 = 5/14$$

Division of fractions is accomplished by inverting the divisor (the quantity being divided into another quantity) and then multiplying to produce the correct answer. The following is an example:

$$3/8 / 2/3 = 3/8 * 3/2 = 9/16$$

Decimals

A decimal expresses a fraction with a base of 10. Table 2.3 gives you some examples of decimal fractions.

Table 2.3 Decimal Fractions		
Decimal	**Fraction**	**Spoken Equivalent**
0.3	3/10	three-tenths
2.6	26/10 or 2 6/10 or 2 3/5	two and six-tenths
0.04	4/100 or 1/25	four-hundredths

Any fraction can be converted into a decimal by dividing its denominator into its numerator, like this:

$$3/4 = 0.75$$

```
    0.75
4)3.00
  2 80
    20
    20
     0
```

Addition and Subtraction with Decimals

All you have to do is line up the decimal points in the numbers you are adding or subtracting. Then, proceed as if you were working with whole numbers.

For example:

1. Find the sum of 53.746 and 6.15.

```
 53.746
+6.15
 59.896
```

Note that the decimal points are lined up and carry straight down to the answer.

2. Subtract 476.36 from 1003.1.

```
 1003.10
−476.36
  526.74
```

Once again, note that the decimal points are lined up and carry straight down to the answer.

Multiplication and Division with Decimals

To multiply two decimals, write them as they are and multiply. Then you insert a decimal point in the product so that the product has the same number of decimal places as the sum of the decimal places in the two original numbers. The following is an example:

What is the product of 44.672 and 39.1?

44.672	(3 decimal places)
× 39.1	(1 decimal place)
44672	
402048	
134016	
1746.6752	(3+1=4 decimal places)

To divide a decimal into any number, you move the decimal point in the divisor to the right until it appears as a whole number. Then move the decimal point in the dividend the same number of places to the right. The quotient will have its decimal point at the same place as the dividend now does. The following is an example:

Divide 350.175 by 3.45. What is the quotient?

Steps 1 and 2 3.45)350.175 becomes 345)35017.5

Step 3:

```
        101.5
345)35017.5
    345
     517
     345
     1725
     1725
        0
```

Note how the decimal point in quotient lines up with adjusted decimal point in dividend.

Putting Fractions and Decimals to Use on the ASVAB

Some typical questions in the Arithmetic Reasoning section include specialized applications of decimals and fractions within word problems. These problems will deal with *percent*, *interest rate*, *ratio*, *scale*, and *proportion*.

If you are taking the CAT ASVAB be aware that the better you do on the early questions, the deeper the computer will drive you into the more complex applications of these concepts. This is good news because that means you are doing well. Take heart. Also, be sure to focus on this section so you'll be ready to ace Arithmetic Reasoning.

Percent and Interest (Rate)

Percent literally means, "per hundred." In other words, a percent is a way to express the frequency of some occurrence (like winning at checkers or getting people to vote for you in an election) by stating how many times it happens out of each 100 chances of it happening. For example:

Karl shoots 50 free throws (FT) after basketball practice, making 39 of them. What percent of his free throws did he make?

Solution:

FT made / chances = 39/50 = 78/100 = 0.78 = 78% (percent)

Or, you might be asked to work backward from a percent to obtain a solution, as in this example:

Alex scored a 98% on her math test. If each question was worth one point and the test had a total of 200 possible points, how many questions did she get right?

Solution:

98% = 98/100 = x/200

(where x = number of points Alex got for right answers)

100x = 19600

x = 19600/100

x = 196

And, because each question was worth one point, the number of points Alex earned (x) also equals the number of questions she answered correctly.

You can also use percentage to calculate the interest rate. In these problems, a percent expresses the amount of change of some quantity (say, money in a savings account or the amount of interest charged on a loan). Let's take a look at an example of this type of problem:

Kevin earned a $1,000 bonus for meeting his performance goals. If he invests it in an account, which offers a 5% annual interest rate, how much money will he have in the account at the end of one year (assuming he makes no withdrawals during that time)?

Solution:

Interest = principal * interest rate =

$1,000 * 5% = $1,000 * 0.05 = $50

Total in account = principal + interest earned =

$1,000 + $50 = $1,050

There are many varieties of this problem. Be sure to read carefully to understand exactly what the problem is asking for. If you provide the correct answer to the wrong question, you get zero points for your effort.

Another twist you may face is the compound interest problem. *Compounding* is the accelerating accumulation of savings over time due to reinvestment of the interest earned on the principal invested. Let's return to the example of Kevin and his $1,000 bonus to see how compound interest problems work.

Suppose Kevin keeps his $1,000 in the account with its 5% annual interest rate (just another way of saying that interest is compounded annually) for three years without making any withdrawals and reinvests the interest he earns each year into his account. How much money will there be in his account at the end of the three years?

Because this is a more complex problem, you might want to start by drawing a quick table (like Table 2.4) to help you keep track of the results of your calculations. Begin by filling in what you already know (that is, Kevin has $1,050 in his account at the end of year 1) and then fill in the remaining squares as you make the calculations shown in Table 2.4.

Table 2.4 Compound Interest Sample Problem Solution	
At the End of Year...	**Total Money in Account**
1	$1,050 (calculated in original example)
2	$1,102.50 (calculated as follows)
3	$1,157.63 (final answer, calculated as follows)

So, in year 2:

Interest = principal * interest rate =
$1,050 * 5% = $1,050 * 0.05 = $52.50

Total in account = principal + interest earned = $1,050 + $52.50 =
$1,102.50

And in year 3:

Interest = $1,102.50 * 5% = $1,102.50 * 0.05 = $55.125 ~ round to
$55.13

Total in account = $1,102.50 + $55.13 = $1,157.63

The term "rate" is also used on the ASVAB to describe other quantities, such as speed. Problems involving rate of travel (for example, "If a car is driving at a rate of 70 miles per hour, how far will it go in 3 1/4 hours?") or rate of change ("If a tree is growing at a rate of 3 inches each year, how much taller will it be in 50 years?") are also common.

Ratio, Scale, and Proportion

Ratios are useful in describing the relationships that can exist between objects or quantities. Fractions can be written as ratios by simply changing the notation (for example, 3/4 is equivalent to the ratio 3:4). When you possess information about ratios, you can often use that information to determine other unknown quantities by establishing a proportion. Here's how that's done:

If the ratio of basketball cards to baseball cards in George's collection is 3:4 and George has 225 basketball cards, how many baseball cards are in his collection?

1. Establish a proportion.

3/4 = 225/x, where x = number of baseball cards

2. Solve for x.

3x = 900

3x/3=900/3

x = 300 baseball cards

You can check your answer, and verify the proportionality of the two ratios, by simplifying the fraction 225/300. When you divide both numerator and denominator by 75, the result is 3/4. Expressed as a ratio you have 3:4, the original ratio.

Scale is an expression of relative dimensions (such as the relationship between a map and a city, or between a model airplane and the real airplane). Scale can be represented as a fraction, but you'll most likely see it on the ASVAB expressed as a ratio. The following example will help you understand scale.

Visiting a new city, Adriana consults a map to determine how far she must walk to get from her hotel to the lakefront. On her map, the distance is 3 inches. If her map's scale is 1 inch for every 2 miles, how far must she walk?

Scale = 1 (inch) : 2 (miles), so you can establish a proportion, 1/2 = 3/x, where x = number of miles Adriana must walk.

1/2 = 3/x

x = 6 miles

Reasoning: Using Arithmetic to Solve Your Problems

Now that you've reviewed arithmetic you can turn to what the AR section is really testing: your reasoning and problem solving abilities. The men and women of today's armed forces are constantly facing challenging situations and confronting problems that require them to call on their prior knowledge and experiences, to make good observations, and then to roll all that data together to reason their way to a solution. In real life, just as in word problems, you can find yourself flooded with data and dazzled by the details. In the military, people are trained to get through tough scrapes by following set procedures on which they have drilled over and over. That is your best approach to success on the mathematics sections of the ASVAB, too. So, next let's take a brief look at two types of reasoning problems that appear on the ASVAB (word problems and series) and how to approach each.

Word Problems

In the section ("Putting Fractions and Decimals to Use on the ASVAB"), you worked through several examples of the types of word problems you will encounter. Although different word problems might require different arithmetic operations and might appear differently when you read through them the first time, there are some fundamental approaches that you can take to see through the camouflage and attack the simpler math problem that lies underneath.

How to reason your way through word problems:

1. **Read the problem carefully to find the "hidden" equation**—This may mean that you skim read first to get the general idea and type of question. Then, you should go back over the question "with pencil in hand" to translate the central question being asked into the language of math: An equation using the arithmetic operations reviewed here.

2. **Draw a picture or chart to organize the data**—If the problem you are working on has a truckload of data, unload the truck and put the data into a form you can use or at least keep track of as you work toward the answer.

3. **Write out all your calculations on the scratch paper provided**—Don't skimp on paper, grab a handful before the test begins and if you run out, ask for more. Also, be sure you number the problem you are working on and write out your calculations legibly so you don't make

goofy mistakes. It is faster to work through a problem methodically than to rush to the end, fail to come up with an answer, have no idea how you got there, and have to start over from scratch.

4. **Check your answer**—Apply common sense. If the question asks what 50% of 200 is and you come up with an answer of 400, you should be able to tell just by looking at it that you did something wrong. On the CAT ASVAB you only get one look at each question, so at least be sure your answer could be correct before moving on. Of course, you can also go back over your calculations from start to finish to be sure.

5. **Work as far as you can get into the problem before guessing**—If you are up against a two-part word problem (one that asks you to perform two, separate operations to reach the answer) and you can solve the first step but not the second, you should do so. Working deep into the problem may help you eliminate one or two of the answer choices and increase your odds of guessing right should it come to that. (Remember, if you are flat out guessing you have a 1/4 or 25% chance of getting it right; eliminate one answer and your odds increase to 1/3 or 33%; better yet, eliminate two choices and your odds of success are even.)

Series

Far and away most of the problems you will see on the AR section are word problems. You may, however, catch a glimpse of another kind of reasoning problem: the series. Series problems ask you to identify a pattern in a series of numbers and then to predict which numbers would come next if the series were to continue. You may see a simple series question, such as:

Find the next number in the series that begins: 1, 2, 4, 7...

The key here is figuring out the pattern. Look at the relationship between adjacent numbers to determine what operation is being performed. Again, making a table (like Table 2.5) on your scratch paper will help you visualize the series so that you can discern its pattern.

Table 2.5 Series Sample Problem #1		
Number	**Next Number**	**Operation Performed to Get There**
1	2	+ 1
2	4	+ 2
4	7	+ 3
7	?	?

By writing it like this you can no doubt see the pattern right away. To get each next number in the series, you add a number to the last number that is one more than the number that was added to get it. So, for the next number after 7, you add 4. This gives you your answer: the next number in the series is 11.

Actual test problems, however, can get much trickier than this last example. Be prepared for series containing fractions, decimals, or involving multiple operations. Here is an example of the last type:

Find the next three numbers in the series that begins: 3, 9, 7, 21, 19...

Again, seek out the pattern. There are a couple of operations at work here. We begin by making Table 2.6 to record what we know from the question.

Table 2.6	Series Sample Problem #2, First Step	
Number	**Next Number**	**Operation Performed to Get There**
3	9	*3, or square the number
9	7	–2
7	21	*3 (we can rule out squaring)
21	19	–2
19	?	?

Okay, so first you square the number to get the next number and then you subtract two from that for the next, and so on. Now that you've picked up on that pattern, filling in the rest of the blanks is easy. Table 2.7 continues where Table 2.6 left off.

Table 2.7	Series Sample Problem #2, Final Step	
Number	**Next Number**	**Operation Performed to Get There**
19	57	*3
57	55	–2
55	165	*3
165	163	–2
163	?	?

Exam Prep Questions

1. Jordan was her basketball team's leading scorer. In two preseason games she scored 18 and 22 points. In the regular season she had 14-, 20-, 20-, 16-, and 25-point games. What was her regular season scoring average?

   ❑ A. 18.5 points per game

   ❑ B. 19.0 points per game

   ❑ C. 19.3 points per game

   ❑ D. 20.0 points per game

2. Sam needs one more block to finish building his toy castle. He reaches into his block bin without looking. If the bin contains 5 yellow, 3 blue, and 2 red blocks, what is the probability that Sam will pick out a blue block?

   ❑ A. 20%

   ❑ B. 23%

   ❑ C. 30%

   ❑ D. 50%

3. Amy's recipe calls for combining 1 cup of whole wheat flour, 1/2 cup of oat flour, and 1/4 cup of spelt flour. What is the total amount of flour in the recipe?

   ❑ A. 1 3/4 cups

   ❑ B. 2 1/4 cups

   ❑ C. 2 1/3 cups

   ❑ D. 2 1/2 cups

4. Rafael scored an 85% on his science final exam. If each question was worth 5 points and there were a total of 300 possible points on the test, how many questions did Rafael answer wrong?

   ❑ A. 4

   ❑ B. 5

   ❑ C. 9

   ❑ D. 12

5. Find the next two numbers in the series beginning with 1, 4, 1 1/3, 5 1/3, 1 7/9...

   ❑ A. 16/9, 4/9

   ❑ B. 7 1/9, 2 10/27

   ❑ C. 4 1/9, 2 10/27

   ❑ D. 5 1/3, 4/3

6. The department of public works has determined the city's total residential water usage to be 100,000 gallons each day. Of that amount, 35% is for personal use and 20% is used for landscaping purposes. How much more water is used for personal use than for landscaping purposes?

❑ A. 15,000 gallons/day
❑ B. 20,000 gallons/day
❑ C. 35,000 gallons/day
❑ D. 55,000 gallons/day7. A car passes a sign that reads, "Chicago 161 miles." Assuming that the driver can keep his cruise control set at 67 miles per hour (mph) the entire way, approximately how long will it take him to reach Chicago?

7. A car passes a sign that reads, "Chicago 161 miles." Assuming that the driver can keep his cruise control set at 67 miles per hour (mph) the entire way, approximately how long will it take him to reach Chicago?

❑ A. 2.2 hours
❑ B. 2.4 hours
❑ C. 2.7 hours
❑ D. 3.0 hours

8. What is the quotient of .639 / .2 ?

❑ A. 0.03195
❑ B. 0.3915
❑ C. 3.195
❑ D. 39.15

9. The Acme Manufacturing Company produces 5,600 widgets each week. If its production on Monday and Friday is only 1/2 that of its daily production rate for Tuesday through Thursday, then how many widgets are produced on Wednesday?

❑ A. 1,600
❑ B. 1,875
❑ C. 2,250
❑ D. 2,800

10. Donna bought a pair of shoes for $38.50. On her way to the cashier, she saw a sign advertising a "buy one pair, get a second pair for 40% off" sale. She grabbed a pair of sandals that were originally marked $18.99. Assuming that sales tax is included in the marked prices, how much money did Donna spend in total?

❑ A. $46.09
❑ B. $46.10
❑ C. $48.50
❑ D. $49.89

Exam Prep Answers

1. **The correct answer is B.** There is extra information here. Don't be distracted by preseason games, the question is asking for regular season scoring average.

   (14+20+20+16+25)/5 = 19.0.

2. **The correct answer is C.** This is a probability question. Probability can be expressed as a fraction, ratio, or percent. In this case, the answer is a percent. To determine the probability of picking a blue block, you only need to know how many blue blocks there are and how many total blocks are in the bin (which equals the number of chances you have to pick a blue block).

   3 blue blocks / 10 total blocks (i.e., 5 yellow + 3 blue + 2 red)
   3/10 = .30 = 30%

3. **The correct answer is A.** Here you are asked to add fractions. Remember that the first step is to find a common denominator, and then the rest is easy.

   1 + 1/2 + 1/4 = 8/8 + 4/8 + 2/8 = 14/8

   Now you have to convert the improper fraction to a mixed number and simplify the proper fraction part to match the format of the answer choices.

   14/8 = 1 6/8 = 1 3/4

4. **The correct answer is C.** This question is similar to an example problem earlier in the chapter—with a few twists. Reading the problem carefully, you'll notice that each problem is worth 5 points now, and the question is asking for the number of wrong answers.

   85% = 85/100 = r/300, where r = points Rafael got for right answers
   100r = 85 * 300
      r = 25500/100
      r = 255 points

   Next, subtract Rafael's points from the total possible points to find the number of points he missed.

   300 − 255 = 45

To find w (which is equal to the number of wrong answers) use the formula

w = points missed / points per question
    = 45 / 5
    = 9 wrong answers

5. **The correct answer is B.** This is a series question in which the pattern involves two alternating operations being performed. It also contains a twist in that you must convert back and forth between improper fractions and mixed numbers, simplify, multiply, and divide fractions. Begin by making a table like Table 2.8.

Table 2.8	Practice Exam Question #5 Solution	
Number	**Next Number**	**Operation Performed to Get There**
1	4	*4 (or + 3, can't tell yet)
4	1 1/3	/3 (convert 1 1/3 to 4/3 to see more clearly the operation performed)
1 1/3	5 1/3	*4 (rule out +3 because, 1 1/3 = 4/3 and 4/3 * 4 = 16/3 = 5 1/3)
5 1/3	1 7/9	/3 (16/3 / 3 = 16/9 = 1 7/9)
1 7/9	**7 1/9**	***4 (16/9 * 4 = 64/9 = 7 1/9)**
7 1/9	**2 10/27**	**/3 (64/9 / 9 = 64/27 = 2 10/27)**
2 10/27		

You will find it easier in this case to convert to improper fractions and keep working in improper fractions until you have completed the next two numbers in the series. Then you can convert back to mixed numbers to match the answer choice format.

6. **The correct answer is A.** This question asks you to use percents to calculate the proportion of various elements of a whole (that is, total residential water usage) and then compare those elements to arrive at the answer.

Personal use = 100,000 gallons/day * 35%
    = 100,000 * .35
    = 35,000 gallons/day

Landscaping = 100,000 gallons/day * 20%
    = 100,000 * .2
    = 20,000 gallons/day

Therefore, personal use minus landscaping = 35,000 – 20,000 = 15,000 gallons/day.

7. **The correct answer is B.** This rate(speed) problem also includes the use of rounding to give an approximate answer.

161 miles / 67 miles/hr = 2.403 hours ~ 2.4 hours

8. **The correct answer is C.** Straight division problem with decimals for divisor and dividend. No frills here, but beware of transposing digits and of decimal point placement. Look back to the decimal division section of the chapter for a review if you are still confused here.

9. **The correct answer is A.** To sort out the clues in this problem, you should begin by sketching a quick production chart for each day of the week. This gives you a good visual that will help you create the simple algebraic formula needed to solve the problem.

From a careful reading of the question, you learn that the daily production rate is constant for Tuesday through Thursday. You can organize what you know in the form of a table like Table 2.9. Monday's and Friday's rates are described as a fraction of that rate. So let's call the Tue through Thu rate "r". And because Wednesday's rate is equal to r, when you solve for r, you solve the problem. You also learned that the total week's production is equal to 5,600 widgets.

Table 2.9   Practice Exam Question #9 Solution

Mon	+Tue	+Wed	+Thu	+Fri	=	Week total
r/4	+r	+r	+r	+r/4	=	5600

So,

$$3 * r + 2 * (r/4) = 5600$$
$$3r + r/2 = 5600$$
$$2 * (3r + r/2) = 5600 * 2$$
$$6r + r = 11,200$$
$$7r = 11,200$$
$$r = 11,200/7$$
$$r = 1,600 \text{ widgets}$$

10. **The correct answer is D.** To solve this percent problem you need to keep track of the facts and calculate the correct sales price for the second pair of shoes. If you don't pay attention, you might calculate the discount instead and (depending on whether you round correctly to the nearest penny) choose answer A or B.

Total $ = cost of 1st pair + cost of 2nd pair

= $38.50 + (original price of 2nd pair – discount)

= $38.50 + ($18.99 – ($18.99 * .4))

= $38.50 + ($18.99 – $7.60)   {round $7.596 to nearest penny}

= $38.50 + $11.39

= $49.89

Word Knowledge

Terms you'll need to understand:

✓ Connotation
✓ Context
✓ Denotation
✓ Synonyms
✓ Prefix
✓ Suffix
✓ Root word

Techniques you'll need to master:

✓ Building your vocabulary
✓ Understanding words according to their usage
✓ Understanding words according to their construction
✓ Knowing the differences between denotation and connotation

In essence, we live in a communications-centric society. To cope in that society, you must be able to read and understand what you are reading. The beginning of overall reading comprehension lies within adept vocabulary skills—understanding individual words as they appear in context. The Word Knowledge and Paragraph Comprehension sections of the ASVAB assess your ability in vocabulary skills and reading comprehension.

The Word Knowledge module contains 25 questions (the CAT-ASVAB has 16 questions), which you will need to answer in 11 minutes, or 8 minutes on the CAT-ASVAB. To achieve your 70%, you need to answer 18 questions correctly; to achieve 80%, you need to answer 20 questions correctly.

The Word Knowledge portion of the ASVAB tests your knowledge of both common and not-so-common words. This section measures your ability to choose the correct meaning of a word, in context, and choose an appropriate synonym or meaning.

Much of the Word Knowledge module is simply word recognition and knowing the meaning of words. Because vocabulary is an essential part of reading comprehension, you need to get a good handle on this section to prepare you for the Paragraph Comprehension module. In each question on the test, you will see a sentence that contains one underlined word. Your job is to select a word or phrase that has the closest meaning to the underlined word. For example, a Word Knowledge question might look like the following, wherein you must choose a word that means approximately the same as the underlined word:

His behavior was <u>atypical</u>.
- ○ A. usual
- ○ B. abnormal
- ○ C. bizarre
- ○ D. calm

If you are an avid reader, or if you are simply adept at learning and using new words, this section will not be too difficult. However, because we can't all be familiar with all the words of the English language, we have to employ a few tools and methods of discerning what unfamiliar words mean. The following sections teach you about word usage and give you tips for maneuvering through the murky waters of word usage.

Building Your Vocabulary

There is nothing difficult about expanding and improving your word knowledge—it is simply a matter of practice and deliberation. The most important habit you can cultivate, if you haven't already, is to start reading more, especially material that is a little difficult for you. That doesn't mean you have to pick up a college-level physics book or a database programming manual. If you currently read popular fiction, perhaps you can start reading other fiction books in the same genre as those you enjoy, but that have a more advanced writing style. For example, if enjoy adventure novels, you can try some books by Tom Clancy or John Grisham, which contain more difficult, and sometimes technical, words. By doing this, you will encounter words that are new to you, but you can still keep up with the context as presented in an enjoyable story line.

When you come across an unfamiliar word, look it up in the dictionary as soon as possible. That way, you can derive the full meaning of the word. After you look up the word, try to use it a couple of times so you understand not only the meaning and spelling of the word, but how to use it correctly in conversation, too.

If you want to score high on the Word Knowledge portion of the ASVAB, you should develop habits of reading avidly, consulting a dictionary when you need to, playing word games—such as Scrabble—and being aware of other opportunities to improve your language and vocabulary skills through usage.

Throughout this book, you will encounter words with which you may not be familiar. This is an excellent opportunity to use your vocabulary building skills.

Understanding Context

When you are reading and come across an unfamiliar word, you can often look at the context to help you figure out at least an approximate definition for that word. The other words in the rest of the sentence or paragraph influence and clarify the unfamiliar word and provide its context. The context provides a setting for the word. Further, context clues help provide meaning and usage for the word. The most common context clues are discussed in more detail later in the chapter, but they are listed as follows:

➤ Experience clues

➤ Definition clues

➤ Example clues

➤ Comparison clues

Even if you don't know a certain term, you can put together clues from the context, a clue's tip-off phrase, or a suggested idea, to formulate a guess as to the meaning of a particular word. In addition, a sample context is a sentence or a part of a sentence that clarifies a definition, distinguishes similar meanings, and illustrates the level and mode of usage. For example, the test might present the following type of question:

> The nice young man <u>courteously</u> opened the door.
> ○ A. Hastily
> ○ B. Rudely
> ○ C. Slowly
> ○ D. Politely

In this type of question, you need to find a synonym for the underscored word. By understanding the rest of the words in the sentence, you can assume that the young man was kind and polite in opening the door.

Although you might not always be able to look up a new word promptly, seeing the new word in its proper context is very important. You are more likely to remember a new word presented in context than if you were to simply study words from a list. The first couple of times you come across a new word, you might ignore it and skim to the next familiar word. However, after several encounters, you will begin to recall other times you have seen that same word. You are also likely to start noticing incidences of the new word when you hear it in conversation or on the radio or television. When you do learn its definition, you are more likely to remember it because of your experience with that word.

Experience Clues

Sometimes, you can guess at the meaning of an unfamiliar word simply because you have had a similar experience to the one the sentence or paragraph discusses. We can all relate to a number of common experiences, such as feelings you have upon receiving an award for commendable work, the death of a loved one, or falling in love. For example, consider this sentence: "Not even the caterer's late arrival could take away from the bride's euphoria." You might not understand the term *euphoria*, but you understand the extreme happiness that a bride feels on her wedding day, and you can therefore vaguely understand that *euphoria* means an exaggerated buoyancy and sense of bodily health.

Definition or Paraphrase Clues

Sometimes you can determine the meaning of a word by the way the writer describes the word by defining or paraphrasing it. We call this description a *definition*, or *paraphrase*, *clue*. A definition clue is one that actually defines a term, and a paraphrase clue is a phrase that restates the term in question.

You will often find definition clues in science and technical books, where the writers must constantly define new terms. Sometimes, commas set off the definition or paraphrase, which immediately follows the target word. In other instances, the definition or paraphrase comes later in the sentence or paragraph. The phrase *is called* or the word *is* often indicates a definition clue. For example, "The set of rules that govern how Microsoft programs run is called the Windows Operating System," shows how the phrase Windows Operating System is defined in usage.

Example Clues

In some instances, writers provide you with examples of the unfamiliar word that help you figure out its meaning. Often, parentheses, commas, or dashes offset an example clue. For example, in this sentence, "You can use almost any legume— such as black, navy, and kidney beans—to make a rich and hearty soup," the offset words tell you what a legume is, even if you have never farmed or cooked and have no idea what a legume is.

Noticing examples can help you infer the meaning of a word, and expressions like the following often precede an example clue:

➤ *such as*

➤ *for example*

➤ *for instance*

➤ *to illustrate*

➤ *including*

Comparison and Contrast Clues

You can also discern the meaning of a word through *comparison clues*, wherein a writer compares or contrasts one word or point with another. A *comparison* clue tells you how things are the same, whereas a *contrast* clue tells you how things are different.

For example, examine this sentence, "Mike is rather withdrawn and subdued today and is rather lacking in his usual display of bonhomie and zeal". You might not understand the word *bonhomie*, but you most likely understand the word *withdrawn*. From this contrast, you can determine that Mike does not want to socialize today and that bonhomie means that Mike is normally of a genial, social nature and is very enthusiastic about life in general.

If you pay attention, you will see introduction words that tip you off that you have a comparison clue, like these:

➤ *but*

➤ *however*

➤ *instead*

➤ *although*

➤ *though*

➤ *on the other hand*

➤ *still*

Words like these, on the other hand, often introduce comparison clues:

➤ *and*

➤ *another*

➤ *like*

➤ *as*

Synonyms and Homonyms

When you look up a specific word in the dictionary, you often see three other categories of words listed in addition to the word itself. *Antonyms* are words that have an opposite meaning to the original word; however, because the ASVAB test does not cover antonyms, neither will we. You will also see two other categories of words in the dictionary, *synonyms* and *homonyms*, which the test does address. The following sections discuss each of these categories and what to watch out for on the test.

Words and Their Synonyms

Synonyms are words that have similar, but not exactly the same, meanings. The Word Knowledge section of the ASVAB will test your knowledge of word meanings and synonyms. The test will present you with an underlined word, and ask you to choose a synonym for that word from a list. As you learn new words, ensure that you also learn the meanings and synonyms for that word. For example, the test may give you this type of question:

The best synonym for <u>irrigate</u> is

- ○ A. moisten
- ○ B. aggravate
- ○ C. manuever
- ○ D. wade

You must choose the word with the nearest meaning to "irrigate" from the list, which will be answer A, moisten.

Remember, a synonym matches the part of speech of the original word. This means that a verb has another verb as a synonym, and a noun has a noun as its synonym. For example, in the list above, irrigate is a verb, therefore, the synonym for irrigate will also be a verb, which is moisten.

Although you can normally substitute a given word for its synonym, you won't necessarily achieve a direct translation in meaning by doing so. In these situations, the difference in meaning between synonyms is a matter of specificity. Take, for instance, this sentence, "The boy ate his supper," as compared to "The boy devoured his supper." Although the essence of both sentences is the same—that the boy has, in some manner, ingested his meal—the specificity and connotation of the two phrases are distinctly different because "ate" indicates a placid attitude toward consuming his meal, whereas "devoured" indicates an urgency and speed to the same basic activity. Because of the variations in meaning between words, you cannot always directly substitute synonyms.

On the Word Knowledge module, you are presented with lists of words or meanings from which to answer synonym questions. More than one of the choices might be a viable answer; choose the one that has the closest meaning and context. In addition, some of the choices might be very closely related in meaning. Make sure that you understand the context, if one is provided, of the word and choose carefully.

Using a Thesaurus

You will often see two types of synonym-listing books: a *dictionary of synonyms* and a *thesaurus*. The dictionary of synonyms is fairly straightforward; you simply look up your target word from an extensive list of alphabetically organized words to find synonyms of your target word. The word listing does not necessarily keep contextual synonyms together.

Using a thesaurus is a bit different. Because *Roget's International Thesaurus* is the most popular and most extensive thesaurus, we will use it as our example. First, look up your target word in the index in the back of the book. The index lists words alphabetically. Second, in the listing under your target word, find the desired context. Last, follow the numerical reference to the contextual listing. The book arranges the categories in numerical order, and the numbers of the categories on each page are at the top outer corner of the page. In this listing, you will find not only your target word, but also all the synonyms within a specific context.

Confusing Homonyms

In addition to misunderstanding a word's denotation, a writer can also make mistakes in diction because he confuses the word he intends with a homonym of that word. *Homonyms* are words that sound alike but have different spellings and meanings.

 Be sure that you can recognize homonyms and how they are spelled. A homonym can change the entire context of a sentence.

For example, "The hare on the back of his neck stood up," doesn't make a lot of sense until you understand that *hare* should be its homonym, *hair*. To keep from making the same, confusing mistake, you should consult your dictionary whenever you are unsure of a word's exact meaning. Remember that both meaning and spelling count in the Word Knowledge section of the test. Table 3.1 lists some common homonyms.

Table 3.1 Common Homonyms	
Word	**Homonym**
accept (receive)	except (other than)
affect (have an influence on)	effect (result)
allude (refer to indirectly)	elude (to avoid)
allusion (indirect reference)	illusion (false perception)
bare (unclothed)	bear (to carry; an animal)
board (plank of wood)	bored (uninterested)
brake (stop)	break (smash)
buy (purchase)	by (next to)
cite (quote an authority)	sight (to see); site (a place)
desert (abandon)	dessert (after-dinner course)
elicit (bring out)	illicit (illegal)
fair (average, lovely, or gala)	fare (a fee)
fourth (after third)	forth (forward)
gorilla (large primate)	guerilla (type of warfare)
hear (perceive by ear)	here (in this place)
heard (past tense of hear)	herd (a group of animals)
hole (opening)	whole (complete)
lead (heavy metal)	led (to have guided)
lessen (make less)	lesson (something learned)
meat (flesh)	meet (encounter)
no (opposite of yes)	know (be certain)
passed (past tense of pass)	past (after, or time gone by)
patience (forbearance)	patients (people under medical supervision)
peace (absence of war)	piece (a portion)
plain (unadorned or clear)	plane (carpenter's tool, aircraft, or geometric space)
presence (to be on hand)	presents (gifts)
principal (most important; head of a school)	principle (basic truth or law)
rain (precipitation)	reign (to rule); rein (a strap to control an animal)
raise (build or lift up)	raze (tear down)
right (correct; opposite of left)	rite (religious ceremony); write (enscribe)

Understanding Denotation and Connotation

Language is symbolic in that we use it to represent ideas, objects, and feelings. Because language is only representative, you can interpret any given statement in more than one way. Sometimes the difference is simply literal versus figurative interpretation. *Denotation* and *connotation* are two more tools you can employ to discern the meaning of an unfamiliar term. For a writer to express herself precisely, she must understand both the denotations and connotations of words, and use that understanding to convey to the reader her exact intent.

Denotation

A word's *denotation* is the strict dictionary definition of that word and refers to the actual thing or idea it represents. In other words, a denotation is the actual meaning of the word without reference to the emotional associations it can arouse in a reader.

If a writer wants her readers to fully grasp her meaning, she must use words according to their established denotations to avoid meaning something she didn't intend and end up confusing the reader. An example of a misused word is represented in this sentence, "Her dissent was gradual and hesitating." This is homonym confusion—and subsequently denotation confusion—at its best. Although a dissent (disagreement) may be gradual and hesitating, the most likely denotation is that of descent (travel downward), which makes a lot more sense.

However, even with the apparent objectivity of a dictionary definition, you will still encounter certain language challenges on the denotative level, because a word can have multiple denotations. For example, the dictionary lists more than 20 distinct meanings for the word *low*. As a result, you can say, "A low wall bordered the field," and you can also say, "John was feeling low today." The same word, used in two different contexts, has two distinctly different meanings. This ambiguity of word meanings can give you a bit of an obstacle in understanding new words. Considering that, ensure that when you read you understand both denotation and context to get the precise meaning of the word as it is used.

In technical or scientific books you are less likely to find a great number of words with multiple denotations than you are, for instance, in a fictional work. In these kinds of books, you have a one-to-one correspondence between word and meaning. For example, if you see the term *transistor* or *operating system*, you will perceive each of those terms in only one context each, that being electronic circuitry (for transistor) or a set of governing operating rules for your computer (for operating system).

Be aware that words can have more than one denotation and connotation. Be sure to read the question in the correct context and then choose an answer based on the most correct contextual meaning.

Connotation

Although writers can make mistakes in denotation, a writer is more apt to miss the right word by misjudging its *connotation*. *Connotation* refers to the emotional or psychological associations a word carries with it. The connotation of a word goes beyond its strict meaning to express the feelings, thoughts, and images the word suggests or evokes.

You can see an example of the difference between connotation and denotation by examining the phrase *United States of America*. The denotation is as follows: "A federal republic of North America, including 50 states, and the District of Columbia, the Canal Zone, Puerto Rico, the Virgin Islands of the United States, American Samoa, Guam Wake, and several other scattered islands of the Pacific." Pretty dry and neutral, huh? Now, compare the connotation of the same phrase, which includes government, patriotism, national pride, and a feeling of republic and oneness with other Americans. As you can see, the connotation is quite different from the denotation.

Because of the subjective nature of language, it has the power to create unpredictable psychological responses. Some connotations are personal, deriving from one's particular experiences, whereas others carry emotional overtones by virtue of the way the writer presents the word.

For example, the word *home* evokes a different response from someone who came from a happy childhood and home than that evoked in someone who had an unhappy home life. Several types of connotation can influence the way you think about a word, which are as follows:

➤ **Positive (favorable) connotation**—Words that make people feel good

➤ **Negative (unfavorable) connotation**—Words that provoke a negative emotional response

➤ **Neutral connotation**—Words that cause no emotional reaction at all

Depending on the intent of the writer, he will choose either favorable or unfavorable connotations to communicate his point. Most journalistic writing uses favorable connotations for the sake of political correctness and to avoid alienating readers. Scientific or technical documents typically use a neutral connotation. Politically motivated writing normally uses highly charged connotations, both favorable and unfavorable, to achieve the desired impact.

Words also have formal and informal connotations. When you speak with or write to older people, people who are in a position of authority, or others you do not know well, you are most likely to use words with formal connotations. An example would be using the term *grandmother* instead of a denotative, yet less formal, equal like *gramma*. Formal connotations tend to be either neutral or favorable. When you speak with or write to your friends, you are most likely to use words with informal connotations.

Finding Word Meaning Through Structure

You can often determine the general meaning of a word by its structure. Compound words have a root word, which might not be a whole word, either preceded by a prefix or followed by a suffix.

Although the English language, especially in the United States, has considerable influence from many different languages, most English root words and prefixes come from Latin or Greek and still carry the same meaning they did in the original language. Your job is to learn the most common prefixes and roots so you can determine a word's meaning from its structure. By learning the most common standard prefixes, roots, and suffixes, you can improve your vocabulary and spelling skills immensely.

Root Words

Root words generally keep the same meaning as they had in the original language, whether it be Latin, Greek, or another mother language. Most of our root words are derived from Latin and Greek; Table 3.2 provides a list of some of the most common Latin and Greek roots, what they mean, and examples of English words containing them.

Table 3.2	Common Root Words	
Root	**Meaning**	**Example**
anthrop	man; human	anthropomorphic
aster, astr	star	astronomy, astrology
audi	to hear	audible, audience
bene	good, well	benefit, benevolent
biblio	book	bibliography
bio	life	biology, autobiography
dic, dict	to speak	dictator, dictionary
equ; aequ	equal, same	equivalent
fer	to carry	transfer, referral
fix	to fasten	fix, suffix, prefix
geo	earth	geography, geology
gram	written or drawn	telegram
graph	to write	geography, photography
jur, jus	law	jury, justice
lingue	language, tongue	linguistics
log, logue	word, thought, speech	astrology, biology, neologism
manu	hand	manual, manuscript
meter, met	measure	metric, thermometer
op, oper	work	operation, operator
par	equal	parity
path	feeling	pathetic, sympathy
ped	child	pediatrics
phil	love	philosophy, anglophile
phon	sound	phonics
phys	body, nature	physical, physics
psych	soul	psychic, psychology
sci	know	science
scrib, script	to write	scribble, manuscript
tele	far off	telephone, television
ter, terr	earth	territory, extraterrestrial
vac	empty	vacant, vacuum, evacuate
verb	word	verbal, verbose
vid, vis	to see	video, vision, television
voc	call, voice	vocation

Prefixes

Prefixes are standard syllables that attach to the front of root words to modify the root word and provide specificity and meaning. For example, the prefix *pro* added to the beginning of the root *logue*, results in the word prologue, which means "before the word, thought, or speech." When you think of multisyllabic words as simply puzzle pieces, it becomes much easier to determine their meanings. Table 3.3 provides a list of the most common prefixes you will see in everyday language.

Table 3.3 Common Prefixes		
Prefix	**Meaning**	**Example**
a-	on, in	aboard, asleep
a-, an-	not, without	achromatic
ab-, a-, abs-	away, apart from	abdicate, amoral
ad-, a-, ac-, af-, ag-, al-, an-, ap-, ar-, as-, at-	near to, toward, without perceptible force	adhere, ascribe, allude, annex, append, attract
ambi-	both	ambidextrous
amphi-	both or all sides, around, both kinds	amphichroic, amphibious
ante-	before	anteroom, antenatal
anti-	against	antibiotic
bi-	two	biannually, biped
bio-	life	biophysical
circum-	around	circumvent
co-, com-, col-, con-, cor-	with, together	combine, collide, concur, correspond
contra-	against	contradict
counter-	opposite to	counterclockwise
de-	away, off, remove, completely, undo, opposite of, down	depart, debark, derail, debrief, detract, decline
di-	twice, double	dichotomy, dipole
dia-, di-	across, through	diameter
dis- (di-, dif-)	apart, away from	disperse, digress
en-, em	to cover, into	encircle, empathy

(continued)

Table 3.3 Common Prefixes *(continued)*

Prefix	Meaning	Example
epi-, ep-, eph-	among, besides, upon	epigram
ex-	out, former	exhale, ex-president
exo-	outside	exoskeletal
extra-	outside of, beyond	extrasensory, extralegal
fore-	prior to	forewarn
hyper-	excessive, over	hyperactive
hypo-, hyp-	less than, under	hypodermic
icon-, icono	image	iconographer
in-, il-, im-, ir-	into, on, within	include, immigrate
in-, il-, im-, ir-	not, without	inapt, impossible
infra-	below, beneath	infrastructure
inter-	together, between	intercultural
intra-	within, inside of	intracellular
juxta-	near, next to	juxtaposition
macro-	large, long	macroclimate
mega-	large, powerful	megalith
meta-	changed, with, beyond	metabolic, metaphysics
micro-	enlarges, one-millionth part of, abnormally small	microphone, microjoule, microcosm
mini-	small	minibus, miniskirt
mid-	middle point	midsentence
mis-	wrong, bad, amiss	misbrand, miscreant
multi-	much, many	multitask, multitude
non-	not	nontoxic, nonduty
ob-, o, oc-, of-, op-	against, toward, to	obstruct, omit
ortho-	correct, straight	orthopedics
out-	external, surpass	outcast, outrun
over-	above, superior, excessive, move down	overbuild, overlord, overdose, overthrow
peri-	around, near	perimeter

(continued)

Table 3.3 Common Prefixes *(continued)*		
Prefix	**Meaning**	**Example**
post-	after, behind, later	postwar
pre-	before	prepaid, preempt
pro-	before, on behalf of, favoring	prologue, propitiate, pro-life
pseudo-	false, resembling	pseudonym, pseudopod
re-	back, again	reexamine, reunify
retro-	backward	retrogression
semi-	half, partly	semiconductor
sub-, suc-, suf-, sug-, sum-, sup-, sur-, sus-	below, under, nearly, lower, division of	subfloor, subdermal, sublateral, subagent, subcouncil
subter-	beneath, secretly	subtend, subtitle
super-	above, surpassing	supersonic
supra-	above, beyond	supraorbital
syn-, syl-, sym-, sys-	together, with	symbiosis
tele-	distant, far away	telephone, telepath
trans-	across, surpassing	transarctic, transphysical
un-	not, reversal	unadorned, unchain
under-	beneath, inferior, insufficient	undertow, under-god, underpowered
ultra-	surpasses, excessive	ultrasonic

Suffixes

Suffixes, yet another piece of the word structure puzzle, are standard syllables attached to the end of a word to modify and further specify its meaning. Although some suffixes add meaning to the root, most often the addition of a suffix also changes the part of speech (that is, verb, adjective, adverb, or noun) of the original word. In many cases, the suffix gives us clues to indicate which part of speech a particular word is.

For example, if you add an *-ist* suffix to the word *art*, you have *artist*, or one who displays the characteristics of art. In this case, both the root and the modified word are nouns. However, if you add an *-istic* suffix to the word *art*, you have *artistic*, which demonstrates a change of the root from a noun to an adjective. Table 3.4 demonstrates some common suffixes you should know.

 Inflectional endings, such as the plural *-s*, possessive *-'s*, past tense *-ed*, and comparative *-er* or *-est*, appear at the end of a word, but they do not change that word's grammatical function.

Table 3.3   Common Suffixes

Suffix	Meaning	Example
-able, -ble, -ible	able to, fit to	salable, edible
-al	pertaining to	betrayal
-cide	killer or destroyer	insecticide
-clasm, -clysm	break, destroy	cataclysm
-cracy	government, rule by	aristocracy
-er, -or, -ess, ist	one who	painter, artist
-escense, -escent	becoming	effervescent
-fer	to bear, produce	aquifer
-ful	full of	peaceful
-fy	to make	satisfy
-ish	like, similar to	piggish
-ism, istic	characteristic of	barbarism
-ize, ise	to cause to be; to become; to engage in	sterilize, crystalize, theorize
-latry	worship of	idolatry
-less	without	dauntless
-mancy	divination, prophecy	necromancy
-mania	excessive like of, psychosis	pyromania
-oid	resembling	humanoid
-ous	full of, having	zealous
-phobia	dread of, fear of	hydrophobia
-scope	instrument for viewing	telescope
-sect	cut, divided	bisect

Exam Prep Questions

In the following questions, look at the underlined word and pick out the most appropriate synonym or definition from the list. Pay attention to context as you choose your answer.

1. When adults speak to children, they will often <u>metaphorize</u>.
   - ❑ A. Change form or structure
   - ❑ B. Use an allegory
   - ❑ C. Use colorful language
   - ❑ D. Condescend

2. Before the Geneva Convention, <u>genocide</u> was a frequent tool of war.
   - ❑ A. Massacre
   - ❑ B. DNA studies
   - ❑ C. Ancestry
   - ❑ D. Overthrow

3. The new recruits understood their <u>subordinate</u> status.
   - ❑ A. Conquered
   - ❑ B. Less
   - ❑ C. Underwater
   - ❑ D. Lower

4. The lieutenant declared that the soldier's behavior during the mission was <u>supererogatory</u>.
   - ❑ A. Superfluous
   - ❑ B. Questioning
   - ❑ C. Bad
   - ❑ D. Good

5. The judge was compelled to <u>proscribe</u> the youth's activities.
   - ❑ A. Assign
   - ❑ B. Support
   - ❑ C. Engrave
   - ❑ D. Prohibit

6. The pilot corrected the plane's <u>attitude</u> in mid-flight.
   - ❑ A. Temperament
   - ❑ B. Bearing
   - ❑ C. Height
   - ❑ D. Loudness

7. Tom saw the <u>inanimate</u> object through his binoculars.
   - ❏ A. Lively
   - ❏ B. Non-mammalian
   - ❏ C. Large
   - ❏ D. Lifeless

8. Marge studied the <u>chronological</u> listing meticulously.
   - ❏ A. Time-oriented
   - ❏ B. Chemical
   - ❏ C. Extensive
   - ❏ D. Alphabetical

9. The congressman proposed a bill to revamp <u>immigration</u> laws.
   - ❏ A. To leave a country
   - ❏ B. To enter a country
   - ❏ C. Pilgrimage
   - ❏ D. Submerge

10. The aurora borealis is <u>phenomenonal</u>.
    - ❏ A. Celestial
    - ❏ B. Mystical
    - ❏ C. Sense-oriented
    - ❏ D. Breathtaking

Exam Prep Answers

1. **The correct answer is B.** *Metaphorize* means to liken one object to another by speaking of it as if it were that other; an allegory. Answer A refers to metamorphosis; C refers to animated conversation; D means to talk down to. Therefore, answers A, C, and D are incorrect.

2. **The correct answer is A.** *Genocide* is the deliberate and systematic massacre of a racial, political, or cultural group. Answer B refers to genetics; C refers to genealogy; D refers to revolution. Therefore, answers B, C, and D are incorrect.

3. **The correct answer is D.** *Subordinate* means lower in rank, order, or class; secondary; inferior to; or controlled by an authority. Answer A refers to being subjugated; B refers to being less in quantity or quality; C refers to submerged. Therefore, answers A, B, and C are incorrect.

4. **The correct answer is A.** *Supererogatory* means an observation or action that goes beyond what is necessary for the task (superfluous). Answer B refers to interrogatory; C refers to derogatory; D refers to exemplary. Therefore, answers B, C, and D are incorrect.

5. **The correct answer is D.** To *proscribe* something is to prohibit or forbid it as harmful. Answer A refers to prescribe; B refers to endorse; C refers to inscribe. Therefore, answers A, B, and C are incorrect.

6. **The correct answer is B.** *Attitude*, in addition to meaning a person's state of mind, can also mean physical position. Although A also means attitude, you must look at the context to determine the correct denotation. C refers to altitude, and D refers to audibility. Therefore, answers A, C, and D are incorrect.

7. **The correct answer is D.** *Inanimate* means not endowed with life or spirit. Answer A refers to animated, the antonym of inanimate; B refers to other than fur-bearing animals; C refers to immense. Therefore, answers A, B, and C are incorrect.

8. **The correct answer is A.** *Chronological* means an arrangement in order of occurrence or time. Answer B deals with properties and composition of substances; C refers to a large listing; D refers to sorting according to the first letter of a word. Therefore, answers B, C, and D are incorrect.

9. **The correct answer is B.** *Immigration* is when a person enters a new country to establish residency. A refers to emigration, which is when a person leaves her birth country; C refers to a long journey; D refers to immerse. Therefore, answers A, C, and D are incorrect.

10. **The correct answer is C.** *Phenomenonal* means something visible or directly observable through the senses, such as an appearance, action, change, or occurrence of any kind. A pertains to those things which are heavenly or divine; B pertains to those things that have a spiritual character or reality beyond the comprehension of human reason; D means astounding or overawing. Therefore, answers A, B, and D are incorrect.

Paragraph Comprehension

Terms you'll need to understand:

✓ Context
✓ Inference
✓ Summary
✓ Literal interpretation
✓ Figurative interpretation
✓ Applied interpretation
✓ Topic
✓ Denotation
✓ Connotation
✓ Comprehension
✓ Subject matter
✓ Plot
✓ Theme
✓ Tone

Concepts you'll need to master:

✓ Reading for content
✓ Looking for the stated details
✓ Using deduction to answer questions
✓ Using inference to draw conclusions
✓ Developing a summary

The Paragraph Comprehension (PC) module of the ASVAB tests your ability to obtain information from written material. The questions will measure your ability to understand several literary comprehension concepts, which include the following:

➤ Identify stated and reworded or paraphrased facts

➤ Develop a sequence of events

➤ Draw inferred conclusions based on referred statements

➤ Specify main ideas and topics

➤ Understand the purpose and tone

If you are taking the paper ASVAB, the PC module contains 15 questions, which you will need to answer in 13 minutes. The CAT-ASVAB contains 11 questions that you will need to answer in 22 minutes, so the CAT-ASVAB actually gives you more time per question than the conventional ASVAB. To achieve your 70%, you need to answer 11 questions correctly on the conventional ASVAB and 8 questions correctly on the CAT-ASVAB. To achieve 80%, you need to answer 12 questions and 9 questions for the conventional and CAT-ASVAB, respectively.

In this test section, you will read a battery of literary passages and then answer questions based on information you should have gleaned from your reading. You should read each paragraph carefully, and then choose the answer option that best completes the statement or answers the question. These questions fall into four general types, as follows:

➤ Detail Questions

➤ Context and Word Meaning

➤ Inference Questions

➤ Summary Questions

Most of us have a good handle on the English language and just as many spend our leisure time reading books on a variety of subjects for work, school, or pleasure. However, statistics state we retain only 10–20% of what we read. Sometimes the percentages are lower and we come away from a written article with absolutely no understanding or recollection of what we have just read, either because we have no interest or no experience in the discussion topic. In addition, studies show retention, comprehension, and reading speed are all interrelated.

To help you do your best, we are providing a crash course in literature comprehension. Many test-takers are daunted by the paragraph comprehension segment because they do not read fast, they don't get a lot out of visual learning, their information retention skills are deficient, or they don't understand different writing styles and elements of literary interpretation.

This chapter shows you how to analyze a paragraph to understand its meaning—both referred and inferred—and to answer questions about what you have just read.

Reading for Details

Reading for details is just that. Before you start reading, fix these questions in your mind so you can be alert to their answers as you read: *When? Where? Who? What?* and *Why?* The answers to the detail questions are straightforward and require no supposition on your part, and if you have a general framework of main ideas and structure, you can better comprehend and retain the details that you will read later. Take this paragraph for example:

"A small organization of farmers in Canada and the northern Great Plains, fearing that introduction of bioengineered wheat would cost them vital markets among skeptical consumers in Europe and Asia, fought for five years to kill the crop. In the process, they formed a tactical alliance with environmental groups that oppose genetic engineering in principle. Their efforts set off broad debate among farm groups and in state legislatures."

A detail question might ask you about a specific detail or fact from the segment you just read. The test might ask you, "Who was the adversary against bioengineered wheat?" or "What initiated the farming and legislative debates?"

 The ASVAB contains a lot of detail questions. Make sure that you can distinctly answer each of these questions: Who? What? When? Where? and How?

Reading for Comprehension

Reading for comprehension requires a bit more effort to accomplish than reading for stated details. To make your reading and comprehension more productive, ask yourself these fundamental questions before you read each test question:

➤ Who or what is the passage about? What is the subject matter or topic?

➤ Who is the main character?

➤ Where does this story take place? What is the setting?

➤ What is the time frame? When does this story occur?

➤ Why was this story written? What is its purpose and theme?

➤ How is the story organized? What is the plot?

➤ What is the point of view?

➤ What is the atmosphere and tone? Is the author being argumentative, persuasive, or informative?

➤ What is the language usage (figurative/literal)?

We discuss each element of the preceding questions in the sections that follow. Understanding how these elements work together will help you answer the comprehension questions of the ASVAB.

Subject Matter

The subject matter is the whole picture of the passage—like a tapestry—that consists of the characters, actions, settings, and properties concerned with the passage. Normally, finding the subject matter will be a fairly easy task, especially if the piece directly identifies the subject matter, such as "Elias" by Leo Tolstoy. The subject matter of this story is Elias, his actions, his life, and the reactions of those with whom he came in contact.

Main Character

The *main character* is a critical component of many passages you read. Discerning the main character answers the question, "Around whom, or what, is the story centered?" The characters are the actors in a literary work, and the main character is like the lead actor. Although we normally think of main characters as people, they can also be animals, such as the rabbit Hazel in Richard Adams's *Watership Down*. Characters may even be creatures from another planet, such as the Martians in Robert Heinlein's *Stranger in a Strange Land* or even robots, like C3PO and R2D2 in the film *Star Wars*.

You can discern information about the characters through statements the narrator makes directly, the character's dialogue and manner of speech, the character's actions, and the reactions of other characters to them.

Setting

Setting refers to the place and time in which the story happens. Sometimes the author will directly specify the setting, whereas other times the reader must interpret stated details to determine the setting and time. If the author does not directly state the setting, then you can use other detail clues, such as the ones below, to help you determine the setting.

➤ **Names of people and places**—It is safe to assume that if there are several characters in the story with names like Pierre, Marie, and Jacque, the story is most likely taking place somewhere in France or in another primarily French settlement, such as Montreal, Canada.

➤ **Styles of clothing**—If you read a piece that discusses women wearing corsets, hoop skirts, and sun bonnets, then you can guess that you are reading a piece on the antebellum South.

➤ **Dialects, language usage, and mannerisms that suggest region or time**—In Sir Walter Scott's *Rob Roy*, the author uses a heavy Scottish/English dialect that clearly indicates region, but not necessarily time, whereas Joel Chandler Harris's *Uncle Remus Stories* uses an Old-South dialect that easily places both region and time. Although Jane Austen's *Sense and Sensibility* does not use specific dialectal, the genteel language usage and mannerisms indicate both region and time.

In addition, if you read "Let me infold thee, and hold thee to my heart," or "What is man, that thou art mindful of him?" then you would have a pretty good idea that you are reading a piece that occurs, or was written in, the Elizabethan era. However, keep in mind modern-day Amish communities still use some of those same terms, so context is important.

➤ **Unusual terms**—While every age of humankind has its own unusual sayings and terms, some give you an idea as to the period of the story. For example, the term "groovy" is specific to pop culture of the early 1970s. If your character is riding in a "hansom," then they are riding in a horse-drawn carriage, probably in the 1800s, and if you are reading about a Pentium Processor, you can deduce you are talking about recent computer technology.

➤ **Tools or equipment**—If you read that a man is using a plow horse, drawing water from a well with a bucket, or is rounding up cattle on horseback, you can assume the story took place in the 1800s, possibly in the Old West. Conversely, if you read about using spaceships for interplanetary travel, you can guess the story occurs in the future.

> ➤ **Dates**—Dates let you correlate ideas within a time frame so you can develop a fuller sense of the setting. Specific dates, such as May 15, 2004, at 2:00 p.m. let you know the precise day and time. However, "John plowed his field in spring 2004," gives you only a rough idea of the time John plowed his field, which you can narrow down to a time frame of three or four months. Further, if you read, "Computers became available to the public in the latter half of the 20th century," then you have a still-less specific time frame to deal with.

Point of View

Point of view is the position from which the events of the story are told or observed. Sometimes, the author uses an *omniscient*—all knowing—point of view, meaning the narrator tells everything about characters and events, including thoughts and emotions. At other times, a narrator uses a point of view restricted to how one character sees, does, and thinks about events and other characters. Most often, this will be first-person narration, wherein the narrator is part of the story and can relate his own feelings, thoughts, and actions. However, it may also be objective, wherein the narrator can relate only the actions of the characters but not the thoughts or feelings of any of the characters.

Action and Plot

Action and *plot* refer to the sequence of events in a story. Plots may be very simple or very complicated. In some instances, such as in Leo Tolstoy's *War and Peace*, there may even be more than one plot in a story. You must be able to identify events, their order, and their importance. In some instances, you may be required not only to identify events and actions that are directly stated, but also to interpret an event that the passage only suggests.

Time Clues

Time words, such as meanwhile, after, before, until, next, during, finally, and as, are clues that can help you follow the order of events of a story. For example, read the following two sentence sets, noting the key time words "before" and "after."

> ➤ The singer smiled before her performance; The singer smiled after her performance.

> ➤ The singer frowned before her performance; The singer frowned after her performance.

After reading these passages, you should be able to order the following events correctly for each passage:

1. singer performs

2. singer smiles

3. singer frowns

In which set of sentences was the singer's performance successful? You will see questions that ask you to conclude, by virtue of the stated facts, an unstated assumption about the passage.

Verb Tenses

Verb tenses also give you clues to constructing a plot sequence. For instance, "Charlotte sailed gracefully down the staircase, looking anxiously for Jackson. She had taken much care with her hair and dress in preparation for the party later that evening." The verb phrase "had taken much care" tells you that even though the sentence about dressing comes after the sentence about coming down the stairs, Charlotte dressed first, and then came down the stairs for a party yet to happen.

Grouping Sequences

Not every event or action in a story is as equal in importance as every other event or action. You need to understand how to group events together into important scenes and note any unusual details that do not fit or seem to stand out. Analyze the following passage to extricate the important information and eliminate the unimportant details.

In 2002, Tombstone Hearse Co. began building handcrafted Old West-style casket carriers that are pulled by a modified Harley-Davidson Road King. To create this "Hawg Heaven" vehicle, they took a regular bike and turned it into a motortrike equipped with gears that allow it to pull heavier loads. The hearse allows for most casket sizes. David Follmar is a retired cabinetmaker who came up with the idea 12 years ago, and with the help of a construction expert, he has franchised the idea and has a network of in-service hearses in areas ranging from Texas to Michigan and New Jersey. Tombstone's hearse has traditional amenities but features a glass-enclosed carriage with curtains and tassels. Four gold lanterns adorn each corner, and it's fitted with a black vinyl top. Tombstone's drivers dress in white tuxedo shirts, string ties, black pants and Calvary style knee-high boots with a single spur. For any guy or gal who has sat in a Harley seat all their lives, it is the only fitting way to take that farewell ride.

This article has a good mixture of important and unimportant details. After reading this passage, what are the important details that the writer includes to get the message across? Here are some of them:

➤ Tombstone Hearse Company has created an Old-West style, Harley-Davidson hearse.

➤ The hearse company has franchises in several states.

➤ The target sector for this type of hearse are men and women who ride Harley-Davidsons.

Now, what are the unimportant details? Any thing that doesn't contribute to the crux of the message is secondary in importance, or not important at all, such as the following:

➤ That the creator came up with the idea 12 years ago

➤ The descriptive details of the hearse

➤ The dress of the hearse drivers

These things do not point to the main message of the article. Of course, you read each passage with a particular goal in mind. If you are writing about hearse design, then the details of the hearse will be important to you. Likewise, if you are researching Old West attire in contemporary settings, then the clothing of the hearse drivers will be important to you.

Reading for Content, Comprehension, and Context

A writer must choose words carefully because they are the only tool he has at his disposal for expressing an idea, a mood, or a feeling. A writer will choose words for either their denotations (literal meanings) or their connotations (figurative or suggested meanings or associations). Reading requires the ability to read and comprehend at two distinct levels, *literal* and *figurative*, and interpretation at a third level, the *applied* level.

Reading for Content—The Literal Level

When you read at the literal level, you read to focus on information the author has directly stated. It's a "what you see is what you get" approach to understanding. This level is also denotational in its interpretation and relies solely on referenced detail. For example, read the following paragraph to find the directly related information.

"The woman was tiredly weeding her garden, but then she slowly stood to see the approaching car. She was old and partially blind, but she didn't see a need of accepting help from others or admit that she needed help running her farm."

This passage directly tells you the following:

➤ The character was a woman.

➤ The woman was tiredly weeding her garden.

➤ The woman stood slowly.

➤ The woman was old.

➤ The woman was partially blind

➤ The woman didn't feel she needed help from outsiders.

➤ The woman lived on a farm.

Although you might visualize the details that the paragraph states, you don't need to think too much to understand the full context of what the paragraph is stating and you understand everything that is stated is literal in its context.

Although understanding the written word at the literal level is the first step toward understanding any form of writing, common words will sometimes have special or double definitions. Further, even in the same language, many people use different words to mean the same thing because they have different ways of speaking. For example, if you ask for a soda on the East Coast, then your waiter will normally ask you, "what kind?" However, if you live in the Midwest and ask for a soda, you will most likely receive just a plain soda water. These multiple word meanings may cause some of us obvious reading problems. So, if you read a question and a word doesn't make sense in the context with which you normally associate it, try using the context clues within the sentence and paragraph to help you look at the word in a different context, and thereby gather its intended meaning.

Reading for Context—The Interpretive Level

When you read at the interpretive comprehension level, you read the information as the author presents it at the literal level, and then apply your intuition, personal experience, and knowledge to draw conclusions about the story or fill in unstated information. This interpretation relies heavily on figurative language, which departs from the literal meaning and requires an interpretive, or inferred, understanding. To *infer* is to take the information as the author presents it and conclude what it means, even though the author does not tell you directly. For example, read the following elaboration of the paragraph in the previous section:

"The bent figure was lost amid the beans, peas, and tomatoes, wearily pulling the unwanted intruders from the fertile soil of her tiny patch of heaven, while a gentle breeze stirred her sun-paled dress. A faint noise in the distance caused her to raise her silvery head and shade her eyes with her hand. The wind stirred up the dust that was rolling down the road, and the green speck continued to get larger as it led the dust storm. However, the faded, blue eyes still didn't see...didn't see the approaching joy and laughter...didn't see the bright little voices destined to fill her day. In the summer heat, a cow softly lowed and the hens busily clucked and pecked in the yard. The weeds grew in the garden, and the grass in the yard grew tall. The neighbors had urged her to let them fix the barn, which needed so much work, but the urging went unheeded, for to her, visitors were cause for spending afternoons in the shade of the porch. The whole place looked unkempt and run-down, but her clouded eyes didn't see it that way. They saw only peace and a little bit of heaven on earth. It was her home, as it always had been."

You get the same information from this paragraph as you did from the previous one, but not in such explicit terms. This passage gives you enough information to visualize and infer the fact that the character is a woman, she is old, she can't see well, she is tired, she is weeding her garden, she lives on a farm, and refuses help. While the passage states none of these points directly, you interpret the material from a figurative, or inferred, standpoint.

 The ASVAB test contains several passages in which you must infer information. Read the question carefully and broaden your scope of what you think the question is asking. If you get snagged up, answer according to your instinct and move on.

If you don't understand when to apply figurative interpretation of a passage, you may experience some reading difficulties. You must recognize whether you are supposed to understand a given word or phrase at the literal level, the interpretive level, or both. Sometimes, common sense can help you to recognize figurative language by interpreting the context of that word or phrase. You must know when to apply both literal meanings and figurative meanings to any given word or phrase. If you fail to read figurative language on an interpretive level, the context will probably make little or no sense, and you will miss the intended context. However, you should keep in mind that an expression an author intended as figurative can make perfect sense literally, although the meanings might be very different, and on the other hand, sometimes the author wants you to read on both levels at the same time—symbolism or analogy.

Word Meanings and Context

Remember the discussion in the previous chapter on synonyms and context? As you go through the Paragraph Comprehension battery, you need to keep those same principles in mind. Words can have different meanings, both literally and figuratively, depending on how and where they're used.

Comparisons

In any written work, you will find many types of figurative comparisons you must recognize and then interpret to understand the work fully. Authors usually draw comparisons between known and unknown people, animals, places, objects, or events, to help you understand the unfamiliar by paralleling it with something familiar. Although figurative language employs several kinds of comparisons, we will address only those types you will likely see on the ASVAB, which are *similes*, *metaphors*, and *personification*, and another type of figurative writing that employs language on more than one level by using *symbolism* and *irony*. We describe each of the comparison types here.

➤ **Similes**—These compare two things that are unlike each other, but that share some characteristic, by using the words *like* or *as*. The author usually does not provide an explanation and it is your responsibility to determine the shared characteristics to gain information about the unknown object.

Example—"To hold America in one's thoughts is like holding a love letter in one's hand—it has so special a meaning." — E.B. White

➤ **Metaphors**—Like similes, metaphors compare things of two different classes. However, instead of using like or as, a metaphor is an implied comparison in which the author describes one thing in terms of another.

Example—"Thy word is a lamp unto my feet and a light unto my path" — Psalm 119:105

➤ **Personification**—This also makes use of comparisons at the interpretive level to clarify a point or create a vivid image. Personification assigns human qualities or characteristics to inanimate objects or animals.

Example—"The seasons prayed around his knees, Like children round a sire: Grandfather of the days is he. Of dawn the ancestor." — Emily Dickenson

➤ **Symbolism**—This uses words to convey both a literal meaning in and of itself, but also representing something beyond itself. Compared to a metaphor, which does not have meaning on a literal level, a symbol says one thing on a literal level and means it literally, figuratively, and symbolically and sometimes on multiple levels.

Example—"…Two roads diverged in a wood, and I—I took the one less traveled by, And that has made all the difference." … Robert Frost

➤ **Irony**—This uses words to convey the opposite of their literal meaning.

Example—A trip to the dentist is always the highlight of my day.

Idioms

Idioms are expressions wherein you cannot determine their overall meaning by the meaning of the individual words in the expression. In addition, idioms do not normally follow the conventional rules of grammar. Unfortunately, looking at the context of the idiom won't help much, either. A given society or generation usually assigns a nonliteral definition to an idiom and understands that definition by repeated use. You must learn definitions of idiomatic expressions just like you learn new words. For example, "The man's retirement came upon him like a thief in the night." Although you could conjecture several different meanings, the one we all relate to it is that his retirement came upon him unexpectedly.

Reading at the Applied Level

The third level of comprehension—the *applied level*—requires you to determine the appropriateness of the author's use of figurative language. Unfortunately, applying what you have read becomes difficult if the figurative language doesn't present a clear picture. It may compare things with no shared characteristics, or it may compare too many things at once.

At the applied level, you go beyond understanding the passage on a literal and interpretive level to make judgments, evaluations, and generalizations. Applied-level questions include the following:

➤ Does the story express a universal truth?

➤ Is the author convincing in his descriptions?

➤ Are the language and comparisons appropriate to the characters?

➤ Are the characters justified in their actions? Are the actions commendable?

➤ Can you relate to the character's experiences? Have you ever had similar feelings?

After you read some of the questions on the test, you might have to take the material as it is presented and answer the preceding questions to judge the characters and their actions, evaluate the work as a whole, or identify your emotional response to the work. When you do these types of tasks, you are working at the applied level.

Developing a Summary

The final type of item we need to address is that of developing the ability to summarize the context of the passage.

 You will see summary questions on the test. Be sure you can effectively create a summary of a passage. You can practice creating summaries as you watch the news or read the daily paper.

To develop a summary, you need to read the passage on all three levels (figuratively, literally, and applied), then remember the questions you asked in the very beginning of this chapter, which are: *Who, What, When, Where,* and *Why?* You should be able to reach a conclusion that draws together the elements of each of these questions, and that will summarize the passage you read. For example, analyze the following statement:

"Minerva, a great horned owl, is the only animal in the world, in the wild, with surgically implanted artificial lenses. Veterinary ophthalmologists confirmed that the owl had cataracts in both eyes, which prevented her from seeing and catching prey. Because the bird was only about a year old and otherwise healthy, doctors and volunteers decided to rehabilitate the bird in a four-hour procedure to remove both cataracts and implant artificial lenses. Even though an owl weighs only about 4.4 pounds, their eyes are much bigger than a human's and are much different because they are adapted for nocturnal hunting. Experience with this owl will help doctors in designing lenses for other birds in the future, possibly endangered species, such as condors and eagles. After her eyes healed and Minerva could catch live prey, the team fitted her with a radio transmitter and released her in the same place in Wisconsin from where she had been rescued."

Now that you have read this passage, you need to come up with a summary statement. Think of it as developing a newspaper headline—short and to the point. Ask yourself these questions:

➤ Who or what is the passage about?

➤ What is the point of the passage?

➤ When did the passage take place?

➤ Where did the passage take place?

➤ Why is this passage important?

Your job is to take all the answers to these questions and condense them. You might come up with something like this: "Wisconsin Owl First Wild Animal to Get Eye Surgery." Then, you will look at the answers the test provides and pick the one that most closely resembles your summary statement. If you look at the test options first, you may become misled because of the similarity. The best option is to come up with your own answer first and then select the answer that best matches your summary statement.

Improving Your Reading Abilities

Because this is a timed test, as all the components of the ASVAB are, you need to be able to process information quickly. Everyone doesn't interpret and extract information from a literary piece at the same speed. Some people can read quickly and retain enough information to answer the questions. However, others take a bit more time to understand what the author is trying to say, especially if the piece is technical, mathematical, or scientific in nature or is otherwise outside the boundaries of normal reading exposure.

To that end, in the remainder of the chapter we are including a section on tips you can employ to increase both your reading speed and information retention.

Improving Your Comprehension

Reading is a fundamental skill for succeeding in life and takes years to fully develop. Most people use reading as their primary tool for learning, and as a means to understanding the world around them. However, some of us struggle with reading effectively. Often the point of failure may be speed, comprehension, or basic word skills.

First, we need to understand that reading is a sequential process, wherein each new skill builds on previously learned skills. Each step in this process relates to one of the three components of reading: *decoding*, *comprehension*, and *retention*.

Decoding

First, we recognize letters represent the sounds of spoken words, which, as we map letters to the sounds they represent, enables us to begin to put together whole words. By breaking words into syllables and component sounds, we can sound out words—decode them. Normally, and with practice, decoding becomes an automatic process that allows us to read words, even if we don't know their meanings.

Comprehension

Next, we learn to understand—*comprehend*—the written word. *Comprehension* depends on the ability to decode and master sight words. When word recognition becomes automatic, we can concentrate on the meaning of whole sentences and paragraphs as we read instead of focusing on individual words. During this process, we also learn to simultaneously connect information within the context of a selection, relate what we are reading to what we already know, and stay focused.

Retention

Finally, we learn to *retain* what we have read. To do this, we must organize and summarize the content and connect it to what we already know. Research shows we forget 40–50% of the material we read within about 15 minutes after we read it. Therefore, immediate recall is essential for continued reading retention. To improve your retention skills, after you read each section of material, recall the highlights of what you have read, and then ask yourself the same questions (Who, What, When, Where, and Why?) you used before you read the section and answer them in your own words.

Improving Your Reading Speed

We all have some idea whether we are fast, intermediate, or slow readers. A fast reader can achieve about 500–600 words per minute, and the normal college-level reader reads at about 250–350 words per minute on fiction and nontechnical material. If you need to improve your reading speed, you can train yourself to read faster with greater comprehension and retention, all it takes are these three things:

➤ The desire to improve

➤ The willingness to try new techniques

➤ The motivation to practice

The first thing you need to realize is that skimming isn't reading. When you skim, especially on sections as small as those presented on the ASVAB, you will miss a lot of important information. You should push yourself to read written material, as the author presents it, only faster than your normal speed. To do this, you will need a newspaper, a stopwatch, and lots of practice.

Training yourself to read faster does not mean you will loose your comprehension level, quite the opposite: Because pushing yourself to read faster requires greater concentration, you diminish time for focusing on one word or a group of words. This also helps with the problem of subvocalization, or reading aloud to yourself.

You need to understand that your reading speed relates directly to your interest or experience in the material, so the more you know about a subject, the faster you can read about it. However, you shouldn't try to keep one reading speed for all topics; some things deserve a slower reading speed and greater comprehension level, such as contracts.

Habits That Reduce Your Reading Rate

Because of the close relation between speed and understanding, increasing your reading rate often parallels an greater comprehension, and vice versa. For this reason, learning to read rapidly and well presumes that you have the vocabulary and comprehension skills to go beyond your current level.

The factors that cause slow reading also cause lowered comprehension. As you increase your reading rate, you might actually see better comprehension. However, if you simply try to read faster without improving your reading habits, you will probably notice decreased comprehension. Some habits that reduce your reading rate are as follows:

➤ **Reading word by word**—You might be suppressing your reading rate by believing that you can improve your comprehension if you spend more time on individual words. However, word reading actually restricts your contextual understanding of the written piece. Learn to sight read common words and phrases. Sight reading is when you automatically recognize common words without actually "reading" them, words such as these: and, but, the, however.

➤ **Subvocalization**—Reading aloud or internally vocalizing—where you hear the words in your head—for the sake of comprehension inhibits your reading speed.

➤ **Eye movement**—You should get into the habit of accurately placing your eyes on the page and developing a rhythm of movement as you read.

➤ **Rereading**—Rereading indicates an inability to concentrate. If your reading speed is about 250 words per minute, you will normally reread about 20 times per page. This slows your reading speed and inhibits your contextual understanding. A very slow reader regresses more frequently, giving his mind time to wander, impairing his ability to concentrate.

➤ **Lack of concentration**—Many things contribute to not being able to concentrate, such as not enough sleep, high sugar intake, stress, and physical distractions. You can counter these problems by eating a solid breakfast, meditating, getting enough rest, and going to the bathroom before you begin.

➤ **Lack of practice**—Increase your daily reading activity and spread it over a wide range of subjects. The more you read, the greater your comprehension, retention, and speed.

➤ **Inability to determine which details are important and which are not**—Learn to ask yourself the elemental questions of who, what, when, where, and why? This will help you sort out the important facts. Conversely, you should not try to remember every detail of the story, but should concentrate on remembering selectively.

Tips for Increasing Your Reading Rate

Ideally, you will achieve a maximum increase in rate by establishing the necessary conditions, which are as follows:

➤ Be sure you don't need corrective lenses, as very slow reading is often due to vision problems.

➤ Don't read individual words. Try to concentrate on sight-reading (knowing common words by sight instead of pronouncing them), key words, and meaningful ideas.

➤ Avoid regressing and rereading.

➤ Develop a wider eye-span to help you read more than one word at a glance. This will help you to read by phrases or thought units instead of word by word.

Adjusting Your Reading Rate

If you try to use the same reading rate on all material, regardless of content, then you will not read as effectively as you might otherwise. You should adjust your rate to complement both the reading purpose and the difficulty of the material. You will achieve your maximum rate on material you find easy, familiar, or interesting. Conversely, you will achieve your minimum rate on material that is unfamiliar in content and language structure or material you must digest thoroughly.

For example, if you see a comprehension question that addresses advancements in computer technology, and you happen to be interested in such, then you will read at your maximum rate. However, if you have a technical question on electronics and you have no interest or experience in that field, then your rates will bottom out.

Adjust your rate according to the subject and difficulty of the material and with your ability to understand that type of material. To understand information, scan at a rapid rate. To determine the value of material or to read for enjoyment, read according to your feeling. To read analytically, read at a moderate pace to permit interrelating ideas. As a rule, you should decrease your speed under these circumstances:

➤ The piece has unfamiliar terminology that is not clear in context.

➤ The passage has difficult sentence and paragraph structure. Slow down enough to untangle them to understand the context.

➤ You have unfamiliar or abstract concepts. Look for applications of your own, as well as understanding those of the author.

➤ You are reading detailed, technical material. This includes complicated directions, statements of difficult principles, or subjects with which you have little or no experience.

➤ You want to achieve detailed retention on the material.

You should increase your speed when you have the following conditions:

➤ Simple material with few new ideas

➤ Unnecessary examples and illustrations

➤ Detailed explanations and idea elaborations on material that you already understand

➤ Generalized ideas or restatements of previous material

By keeping your reading attack flexible, you can adjust your rate sensitivity from article to article and even within a given article. Practice this technique until a flexible reading rate becomes natural to you.

Tips for Success on the Reading Comprehension Battery

Now that we have covered all the aspects of getting through the Paragraph Comprehension module, let's summarize how you can answer the questions both quickly and accurately:

➤ Quickly read each paragraph to glean the important details.

➤ Reread the paragraph to ensure that you understand the information, how it relates to the main point, and any figurative language or inferred details.

➤ Be sure you look at each question and that you understand the question that you're being asked. Keep an eye out for superlatives such as these: least, greatest, except, not all, always, every, and never. You should also read all the possible answers, even if you think you already know the correct answer.

➤ Be objective. Although you might not agree with the author's viewpoint, answer the question based only on the information in the passage.

➤ Because this is a timed test, you must keep moving. If you cannot decide on the best answer when you first read the question, close your eyes, take a deep breath to clear your mind, and start again. If you are still stuck, guess and move on to the next question. This is especially important on the CAT-ASVAB, because its adaptive nature does not give you opportunity to revisit any missed questions.

Exam Prep Questions

1. American tolerance for the homeless dilemma is waning, though no one desires to be homeless, and no one begs because it amuses them; being homeless is degrading and robs a person's self-respect. Although the government has implemented programs that increase opportunities for people to get housing, those programs usually profit only a small sector of the population. Furthermore, because the poor are often discriminated against within these programs, they usually have no choice but to live in shoddy housing that quickly becomes derelict and uninhabitable, thus creating a yet larger homeless population when these people must move out onto the streets. However, the government's housing policies seem unfair and inequitable, and without a place to call home, these disenfranchised Americans do not have access to the most basic rights, such as the right to vote, the right to privacy, the right to family integrity, and the right to liberty itself.

The main idea of this paragraph is

- ❑ A. Government makes people homeless.
- ❑ B. Current housing policies are inequitable and ineffective.
- ❑ C. Americans should be more tolerant of the homeless.
- ❑ D. The homeless should have more liberties.

2. Contrary to popular belief, modern-day homesteaders tend to be well-educated people from city and suburban areas who have decided to revolt against their urban existence. Usually, these homesteaders are middle-aged and have spent a significant portion of their adult lives in the country, whether at summer houses, getaway cabins, or otherwise vacationing or escaping from the stresses of everyday life. Because they are well educated, most of these new pioneers have well-reasoned rationalizations for choosing their alternative lifestyle. However, they aren't ideological, nor are they purists, and they fully realize that their survival in the country depends on a substantial practicality. The modern homesteader's role in this new separation movement seems to oppose the ideals of urban America and its corporate and industrial mind set and can best be defined as almost revolutionary or radical in concept.

According to the paragraph, modern-day homesteaders are

- ❑ A. Young and idealistic
- ❑ B. Raised in the country
- ❑ C. Not well educated
- ❑ D. Middle-aged and pragmatic

3. In the light of the induction of the North American Free Trade Agreement (NAFTA), the question that lingers in most American's minds today is why American industry can't compete with foreign markets and why American jobs are crossing the borders, to our neighbors' financial benefit. Americans as a whole have seen a marked increase not only in manufacturing jobs, but also in the quantity of American products available on the market, and our overall manufacturing quality has improved—even our foreign competitors recognize these points. But the fact remains that Americans can't compete on the global market, and by all indications, we will continue to diminish in that capacity. The bottom line is that American workers cannot produce a product of like quality as cost-effectively as most of our foreign competitors. American workers have a higher standard of living, including better living conditions, cars, and necessary amenities such as health insurance, that requires them to be paid more than off-shore workers who, in most cases, make less than a dollar an hour. There is no technological advantage to either side, because both sides of the market have the same quality of machinery and use the same technology. There's no quantity or production rate advantage to either side, because a steel worker in Pittsburgh can work as effectively as a steel worker in China, and a seamstress in Mississippi can sew at the same speed as a seamstress in the Philippines. The cost of labor is the only advantage that our foreign competitors have. For an American manufacturer to see the same bottom line as a foreign competitor, his workers must produce at a rate of five times that of their overseas equal.

According to this paragraph, which aspect of manufacturing does not occur equitably on both sides of foreign trade?

❏   A. Labor costs
❏   B. Machinery and technology
❏   C. Manufacturing quality
❏   D. Ability of workers

4. When James Madison drafted the First Amendment, his intent and purpose was not only to allow the press to question the actions and motives of our elected officials, but also to limit the powers of Congress in restraining that free speech. Those limitations applied only to Congress, and did not extend to the individual states. The drafter's intention was to bring the powers of Congress to bear, so that they could not make any laws that infringed upon freedoms of speech and press. The focus was not that freedom of speech should be prized inordinately, but that the powers of Congress should be limited, lest they deem it necessary to squelch all forms of political criticism. The salient point of the First Amendment was that it protected the independence of the legislature at the state level while curtailing Congressional jurisdiction and imposition on a national level.

According to this paragraph, what was the original purpose of the First Amendment?

- ❑ A. To guarantee Americans free expression, regardless of the consequences.
- ❑ B. To control Congress's authority over the states.
- ❑ C. To endorse a free press.
- ❑ D. To make Congress more powerful.

5. The girl tossed restlessly in her bed. How she wished that she could once again run in the bright sunlight—feel the wind upon her face—hear the birds sing their gay, lilting notes. Outside, she heard the voices of the other children, laughing gleefully at some game. If she closed her eyes, she could see them—Jan, Lilly, Pete, Michael—and she was forgotten by them all. She looked spitefully at the flowers on the bureau, hating the drawings and cards strewn about her room. She kicked at her blankets with all the force she could muster from her weak legs and thought to herself, "Maybe someday...."

According to this passage, what can we infer about the condition of the girl?

- ❑ A. That she was grounded to her room.
- ❑ B. That she had a slight cold.
- ❑ C. That she had been ill for a long time.
- ❑ D. That she didn't want to play with the other children.

6. "Mrs. Jennings was so far from being weary of her guests, that she pressed them very earnestly to return with her again from Cleveland. Elinor was grateful for the attention, but it could not alter their design; and their mother's concurrence being readily gained, everything relative to their return was arranged as far as it could be." — Jane Austen

In the paragraph, what is the meaning of the term "design"?

- ❑ A. Desires
- ❑ B. Way of living
- ❑ C. Particular purpose
- ❑ D. An artistic pattern

7. "I went to the woods because I wished to live deliberately, to front only the essential facts of life, and see if I could not learn what it had to teach, and not, when I came to die, discover that I had not lived. I did not wish to live what was not life, living is so dear; nor did I wish to practice resignation, unless it was quite necessary. I wanted to live deep and suck out all the marrow of life, to live so sturdily and Spartan-like as to put to rout all that was not life, to cut a broad swath and shave close, to drive life into a corner, and reduce it to its lowest terms, and, if it proved to be mean, why then to get the whole and genuine

meanness of it, and publish its meanness to the world; or if it were sublime, to know it by experience, and be able to give a true account of it in my next excursion." — H.D. Thoreau

In the passage, what does Thoreau not desire from his life in the country?

- ❏ A. To live deliberately
- ❏ B. To live deep
- ❏ C. To have wealth
- ❏ D. To reduce life to its lowest terms

8. Cisco Systems, Inc. and the FBI are investigating the theft of portions of the core source code that runs Cisco's networking gear. Source code is the raw software that interacts with computer hardware, of particular interest to hackers who can use it to find security weaknesses to exploit networks. The source code is part of the company's Internetwork Operating System (IOS) that runs the Cisco-built hardware that composes much of the Internet backbone. It consists of millions of lines of source code, and there are hundreds of versions of it in existence. However, Cisco is not sure which version of the software was stolen. A Russian website, SecurityLab.ru, posted some of the code online but the culprit of the theft is still unknown. The code theft might be serious, resulting in new security problems, or the missing code may not contain any significant vulnerabilities.

What is the main idea of the paragraph?

- ❏ A. Cisco source code runs the backbone of the Internet.
- ❏ B. Cisco source code was stolen.
- ❏ C. Source code will open vulnerabilities to hackers.
- ❏ D. Source code contains millions of lines of code.

9. During his years at Stanford, Richard Rodriguez gained special insight, which he records in his autobiography, *Hunger of Memory.* He relates one remarkable impression that he gained during his time lecturing in ghetto high schools. In this passage, he talks about the attitude displayed by the students in these schools. In particular, he notes the remarkable style and physical grace that these students exude, pointing out that he has seen more dandies in ghetto schools than he had ever found inside middle-class high schools. He also observed that these students do not carry the attitude of casual assurance that is prevalent at Stanford. In his estimation, the ghetto girls seem to mimic high-fashion models, wearing dresses of bold, forceful color, accentuating figures that are elegant and long, that pose with an almost theatrical stance. Too, he notes that the boys wear shirts that fit tightly against their muscular bodies, and by their own show of physical strength, they display images of strength in contrast to their own, powerless

future. Because of their youth, the effects of years of bad nutrition do not show; neither does the bitterness and jaded outlook of great disappointment tell in them, for to realize such is fatal to their youthful exuberance. For now, they are absorbed in their own youth, their movements are confident, smooth, and dance-like, and their attitudes are of strength and hope.

What can you infer about the students in the ghetto high school?

❑ A. That ghetto students have good physiques.

❑ B. That ghetto students want to disguise their poverty by their dress.

❑ C. That ghetto girls like bold colors.

❑ D. That poverty cannot quench personal pride and zest for life.

10. "Psychological observations of a man's capacity for retrospectively supplying a whole series of supposedly free reason for something that has been done confirm the assumption that man's consciousness of freedom in the commission of a certain kind of action is erroneous." — Leo Tolstoy

In the passage, what does the term "retrospectively" mean?

❑ A. Defensively

❑ B. To do over

❑ C. In hindsight

❑ D. To go backward

Exam Prep Answers

1. **The correct answer is B.** Current housing policies are not sufficiently fair and effective enough to alleviate homelessness. Although government policies are not doing anything significant to help the homeless, the government does not make people homeless; therefore, A is incorrect. Although it is true that society needs to be more tolerant of the plight of the homeless, that is not the focus of the article, therefore C is incorrect. The homeless have all the same liberties that you and I do; however, their plight keeps them from fully exercising their basic rights; therefore, D is incorrect.

2. **The correct answer is D.** As stated in the passage, the new homesteaders are not young and idealistic; therefore, A is incorrect. While the homesteaders have spent much time as adults in the country, the article does not say that they were raised in the country; therefore, B is incorrect. The article clearly states that the homesteaders are well educated; therefore, C is incorrect.

3. **The correct answer is A.** The passage states that labor in second-world countries is cheaper than in the United States. The same machinery and technology for manufacturing is available to both sides, therefore B is incorrect. Both sides can achieve the same product quality, so C is incorrect. The ability of workers from both sides is the same, so D is also incorrect.

4. **The correct answer is B.** The framers of the Constitution included the First Amendment to control Congress's authority over the individual states. According to the passage, the intent of the First Amendment was not to guarantee unlimited, uncontrolled freedom of expression for the American people; therefore, A is incorrect. The First Amendment was not written to endorse a free press, so C is incorrect. The First Amendment was to limit Congress's power; therefore, D is incorrect.

5. **The correct answer is C.** Details in the story pull together to give the impression that the girl had been sick in her room for a long time. The passage says nothing about punishment; therefore, A is incorrect. The flowers, cards, and weakness in her legs does not indicate a slight cold, therefore B is incorrect. From the passage, it is clear that she wanted to play with the other children; therefore, D is incorrect.

6. **The correct answer is C.** A design is a particular purpose or intent. It does not mean a desire, so A is incorrect. Neither does it mean a way of living; therefore, B is incorrect. Although a design can mean an artistic pattern, the context does not support this interpretation; therefore, D is incorrect.

7. **The correct answer is C.** He states, "to live so sturdily and Spartan-like", or sparsely. Because he did desire to live deliberately, to live deep and to reduce life to its lowest terms, choices A, B, and D are incorrect.

8. **The correct answer is B.** That Cisco source code was stolen is the point of the story. That Cisco equipment and source code run the Internet is additional information that adds on to the main point, therefore A is incorrect. Choices C and D are valid information, but simply contribute to information about the source code, and are therefore incorrect choices.

9. **The correct answer is D.** The point is that not even poverty can suppress the personal pride and youthful zeal of the young. The passage describe the physiques of the boys as being muscular and the girls as being slender, but not all ghetto students are so built. The description applies more toward the pride and grace with which the students carry themselves rather than their physiques; therefore, A is incorrect. That students dress well does not mean that they are pretending that they are not poverty-stricken, but that they dress with pride and care, therefore B is incorrect. Although the passage does state that the girls wear bold colors, it is not a main point that you should infer; therefore, C is incorrect.

10. **The correct answer is C.** To look at a situation retrospectively, is to look at it in hindsight, or after it has already happened. It doesn't mean defensively, so A is incorrect. Redo or re-accomplish means to do over; therefore, B is incorrect. Retrace is to go backward; therefore, D is incorrect.

Mathematics Knowledge

Terms you need to understand:

- ✓ Algebraic expression
- ✓ Area, volume
- ✓ Perimeter, circumference
- ✓ Constants, variables
- ✓ Prime numbers
- ✓ Angle
- ✓ Types of triangles
- ✓ Quadrilaterals
- ✓ Least common multiple
- ✓ Greatest common factor
- ✓ Exponent

Concepts you need to master:

- ✓ Factoring and expanding algebraic expressions
- ✓ Using data from a word problem to write an equation
- ✓ Solving equations
- ✓ Solving inequalities
- ✓ Using basic geometric formulas and calculations

With the word problems of the Arithmetic Reasoning section in your rear-view mirror, you are ready for the second—and final—mathematics section of the ASVAB. The stakes are still high in terms of your enlistment eligibility, but if you are one of the many people who dread elaborate word problems, this section should be more within your comfort zone.

In the Mathematics Knowledge section the aim is to assess your comprehension of algebra, geometry, and some more advanced arithmetic computation. Regardless of your fondness for math, the material you'll be working with in this section should at least be somewhat familiar. The ASVAB covers topics addressed in basic middle- and high school-math classes.

 The Mathematics Knowledge test will contain some short word problems. You will be asked, for example, to read a sentence or two that describes a mathematical relationship. Your task, then, will be to rewrite this relationship in the form of a simple equation and to solve for the variable in question. These problems are aimed at testing your ability to use basic algebra and geometry to solve "real life" problems.

Taking the Mathematics Knowledge Test

Time is usually not a factor on this test. You have 24 minutes to answer 25 questions. There are two ways to ensure that you don't run out of time before you run out of questions.

First, don't skimp on your studying and review before taking the ASVAB. You will know you are ready when you begin to feel comfortable with each type of problem. Do as many practice questions as you can and pay close attention to the explanations of the solutions. If you are still unsure, go back to the review chapter or even your school math book for more detailed explanations.

Second, don't "freeze up" on the test and spend too long on any one problem. You all have felt that sudden chill during a test when you were faced with a question you didn't know how to attack. What to do? The answer to this question depends on whether you are taking the CAT-ASVAB or the paper version. On the paper version, if you see "one of those problems" you just skip right over it. Mark the question in your test booklet and return to it later, after you have worked through all the "easier" questions in the section. If you find that you have to guess in the end, you'd much rather guess on a question you are unsure how to solve than on a question that you could have readily solved if you'd had the time.

Unfortunately, the CAT-ASVAB doesn't give you the option to skip and return. Here you have to make a judgment call as to how long *is* too long to spend on any one question. Let's do the math to come up with a simple rule of thumb. Because you have 24 minutes to answer 25 questions, you have a little over 57 seconds for each question. We don't advocate that you become an incessant clock-watcher (it can become a hypnotic time-waster to stare at the computer's time remaining clock). Instead, you can keep track of your pace by checking every few questions to see that the time remaining (in minutes) is greater than the number of questions remaining. If so, then you are pacing yourself well. If you find you're spending more than a minute on a problem and are still not sure whether you are on the right track, cut your losses with a best guess based on the work you have already done.

More Fun with Numbers

In Chapter 2, "Arithmetic Reasoning," you reviewed different sets of numbers and the four basic operations you can perform on them. Now you will look at some other special types of numbers and operations that you will see on the Mathematics Knowledge test.

Factors and Multiples

Working with the set of counting numbers (1, 2, 3, 4...) called *natural numbers*, every number in the set (with the exception of the number 1) can be broken down into two other subsets: *prime numbers* and *composite numbers*.

A composite number is a number that can be expressed as a product of two or more natural numbers other than itself and 1. For example, the composite number 9 = 3*3. These other numbers are called *factors*. Continuing with this example, a complete list of the factors of the number 9 includes {1, 3, 9}.

A prime number is a number whose only factors are itself and 1. For example, 3 = 3*1. You might be given two numbers and asked to find their greatest common factor. Here's how it's done:

Find the greatest common factor of 24 and 64.

Factors of 24: 1, 2, 3, 4, 6, 8, 12, 24

Factors of 64: 1, 2, 4, 8, 16, 32, 64

So, 24 and 64 have the factors 1, 2, 4, and 8 in common. Among those, 8 is the greatest common factor.

You also need to be familiar with the term *multiple*. The multiples of a number are the set of numbers formed by multiplying a number by other numbers. For example, the first six multiples of the number 7 are

7*1=7

7*2=14

7*3=21

7*4=28

7*5=35

7*6=42

You might be given two numbers and asked to identify their least common multiple, as seen in the following example:

Find the least common multiple of 6 and 9.

Multiples of 6: 6, 12, 18, 24, 36, 42, 54...

Multiples of 9: 9, 18, 27, 36, 45, 54...

So, if you used the simplest way of finding a common factor (that is, by multiplying the two numbers together to get 54) you would not have found the least common multiple. By writing out each number's multiples in order, you found that the least common multiple actually is 18.

The Factorial (!)

Another concept that you should be familiar with is the factorial. *Factorial* means the product of all the natural numbers from 1 through the number preceding it and is represented by the exclamation mark (!) in mathematical formulas. Thus,

➤ One factorial = 1! = 1 * 1 = 1

➤ Two factorial = 2! = 2 * 1 = 2

➤ Three factorial = 3! = 3 * 2 * 1 = 6

➤ Four factorial = 4! = 4 * 3 * 2 * 1 = 24

Exponents and Roots

Exponents are a handy form of notation used in higher-level arithmetic and algebra to indicate when a number is multiplied by itself a specified number of times. Exponents come with their own special notation. Here are some examples:

$31 = 3$

$32 = 3*3 = 9$

$23 = 2*2*2 = 8$

$104 = 10*10*10*10 = 10,000$

As you can see, the number written in superscript indicates the number of times the base number is multiplied by itself. Other ways of expressing 3^2 include "3 squared" or "3 raised to the power of 2."

The *square root* of a number is the factor of that number that, when multiplied with itself, yields the original number. For example, the square root of $9 = 3$, because $3*3 = 3^2 = 9$. In this example, 3 is called a perfect square because it is a whole number. The square root of 5 is not a perfect square because it equals $2.236068...$.

The *cube root*, the third root, of a number is a factor of that number that, when multiplied with itself twice, yields the original number. For example, the cube root of $8 = 2$, because $2*2*2^2 = 8$.

Operations with Negative Numbers

Everything you've done so far in this chapter has been with positive numbers. On the test you will also need to know how to work with negative numbers.

Working with Addition and Negative Numbers

Remember that adding a negative number is the same as subtracting the same positive number. Keep the number line in mind while you at these examples:

$8 + (-5) = 8 - 5 = 3$

$-7 + (-4) = -7 - 4 = -11$

Working with Subtraction and Negative Numbers

Similarly, subtracting a negative number is equivalent to adding the same number, as seen in the following examples:

$9 - (-1) = 9 + 1 = 10$

$-3 - (-12) = -3 + 12 = 9$

Working with Multiplication and Negative Numbers

When two negative numbers are multiplied, their product is always a positive number. When a positive number is multiplied with a negative number, the product is a negative number, as seen in this example:

$$-10 * (-6) = 60$$
$$13 * (-4) = -52$$

Working with Division and Negative Numbers

When two negative numbers are divided, their quotient is a positive number. When the dividend and the divisor are of opposite sign, the quotient is a negative number. The following examples demonstrate this:

$$-10 / (-2) = 5$$
$$32 / (-8) = -4$$

Working with Exponents and Negative Numbers

Basically, exponents follow the same rules as regular multiplication. A negative number raised to an even power, such as $(-3)^4$, will always have a positive answer. A negative number raised to an odd power, such as $(-3)^5$, will have a negative answer. The only other catch is in interpreting the notation. For example:

$$(-6)2 = 36,$$

but

$$-62 = -(62) = -36$$

Why is this? Complex mathematical equations (those containing more than one operation) are performed according to a strict set of rules governing which operations are performed in what order. In the second example, the order of operations tells you to first complete any operations within parentheses $(6^2) = 36$, and then to perform the multiplication $-1 * 36 = -36$.

Order of Operations

Following these surefire rules for solving expressions or equations containing multiple operations will make the difference between a right and a wrong answer on many different questions in the Mathematics Knowledge test.

In military terms, knowing your Order of Operations cold is a "force multiplier," having a disproportionately large impact on your score. No matter how good you are at performing the various mathematical operations, you can't get to the correct answer if you perform the operations out of order.

So, here are four basic rules to live by:

1. Perform operations inside parentheses (or other groupings) first.

2. Perform exponent and root operations.

3. Perform multiplication and division, moving from left to right.

4. Perform addition and subtraction, also moving from left to right.

To see how these rules work in practice, let's try this example:

$3(8*2-6)^2 + \sqrt{9}(4+1) - 25/5$

$= 3(16-6)^2 + \sqrt{9}(5) - 25/5$ RULE 1

$= 3(10)^2 + \sqrt{9}(5) - 25/5$ RULE 1

$= 3(100) + (3)(5) - 25/5$ RULE 2

$= 300 + 15 - 5$ RULE 3

$= 315 - 5$ RULE 4

$= 310$ RULE 4

Algebra

Algebra is the area of mathematics where you are asked to solve for unknown quantities that are represented by letter symbols. Algebra generalizes on the basic arithmetic concepts reviewed previously, and so is especially useful in solving many real-world problems. For example, $5^2 = 25$ is a specific expression. In algebra, you can generalize that relationship to state that $x^2 = x * x$ for any number x (including the specific number 5 from the first example).

Algebraic expressions contain *constants* (definite numbers), *variables* (letter representations of number values), *mathematical operations*, and *grouping symbols* (such as parentheses). Let's look at an example to identify the different components of an algebraic expression:

$3x + 4(x - 3)^2$

Constants: 3, 4, 3 and ^{2}

Variable: x

Operations: Multiplication: 3x = 3 * x; multiplication: 4(x – 3)2 = 4 * (x – 3)2; addition: +; subtraction: –; and exponent.

Notice that in algebra, the multiplication sign is implied and doesn't need to be written when a constant appears next to a variable or when two variables appear next to each other (as in xy = x * y).

Grouping(s): () In this example, the terms x and 3 are grouped together within parentheses. In addition to parentheses, grouping symbols can include brackets [] and braces {}. Grouping symbols call for operations on the terms within the grouping to be performed first.

 The algebra questions on the ASVAB are not designed to trip you up. Still, I was told by one recruiter that if a candidate gets tripped up on the mathematics sections of the test, more times than not, algebra is the culprit. What is the moral of the story? Pay close attention to your algebra review!

Algebraic Equations

Equations are mathematical expressions in which the quantity to the left of the equal sign is equivalent to the quantity to the right of the equal sign. Algebraic equations can be solved by isolating the variable in question on one side of the equation. Let's look at an example of this principle:

$9x - 7 = 74$. Solve for x.

Remember, to keep the quantities on each side of the equal sign equal, whatever you do to one side of the equation you must do to the other.

So,

$9x - 7 = 74$

$9x - 7 (+7) = 74 (+7)$ (add 7 to each side)

$9x = 81$

$9x/9 = 81/9$ (divide each side by 9)

$x = 9$

Because this example required you to perform more than one operation to solve for x, it is called a *multistep equation*. Most algebraic equations you see on the ASVAB will be multistep rather than the simpler one-step equation ($x + 1 = 3$) variety.

Performing Operations with Algebraic Expressions

Each of the four arithmetic operations may be performed on algebraic expressions. Here's how it is done.

Algebraic Expressions with Addition

Only like terms can be combined. Like terms are expressions containing the same variable, raised to the same power. For example, $2x + 7x = 9x$. The expressions $2x^3 + 4x$ cannot be combined because in the two instances where x appears, it is raised to a different power. Similarly, $3x + 4y$ cannot be combined because the two variables x and y indicate different quantities.

Algebraic Expressions with Subtraction

Again, only like terms can be combined. For example, $16y^2 - 9y^2 = 7y^2$.

Here is a more complicated example:

Subtract $(x^2 - 2x + 9)$ from $(4x^2 + 8x - 5)$.

Solution:

$(4x^2 + 8x - 5) - (x^2 - 2x + 9)$

$= 4x^2 + 8x - 5 - x^2 + 2x - 9$

$= (4x^2 - x^2) + (8x + 2x) - (5 + 9)$

$= 3x^2 + 10x - 14$

Algebraic Expressions with Multiplication

Using the distributive property, algebraic expressions can be multiplied by multiplying each term of the first expression by each term of the second expression and then adding together the like terms. Here are three examples of how to multiply algebraic expressions:

Example 1:

$(11x^5)(2x^3)$

$= 22x^8$

First you multiply the constants, then you multiply the variable terms by adding their exponents.

Example 2:

$5z^9(z^4 - 2z + 1)$

$= 5z^{13} - 10z^{10} + 5z^9$

You simply multiply each term of the first expression $(5z^9)$ by each term of the second expression and add.

Example 3:

$(y^3 - 1)(y^2 + 5)$

$= y^3y^2 + 5y^3 - y^2 - 5$

$= y^5 + 5y^3 - y^2 - 5$

Again, use the distributive property of multiplication and combine like terms, if you can, to get the answer.

Algebraic Expressions with Division

To divide algebraic expressions, divide the constant terms and then divide the variable terms.

Example 1:

$6x^5/2x^3 = ?$

$6/2=3$ and $x^5/x^3=x^5{-}3=x^2$

So, $6x^5/2x^3 = 3x^2$

Example 2:

$(12y^2 + 8y) / 2y$

$= 6y + 4$

Factoring Algebraic Expressions

Algebraic expressions also can be factored, and you might be asked to do so on the test. Remember that *factoring* is the process of dividing a quantity or expression into its basic components. To reach the basic component level, you must first find the highest common factor of each term in the expression.

Example 1: Find the factors of $9x^3 + 12x^2$.

Solution: First, find the largest number (constant) that divides into each term. In this case that number is 3.

$(9x^3 + 12x^2) / 3 = 3(3 \ x^3 + 4x^2)$

Then, find the largest variable factor that divides into each term. In this case that variable is x^2.

$(9x^3 + 12x^2) / x^2 = x^2(9x + 12)$

Putting it all together you have your answer,

$(9x^3 + 12x^2) / 3x^2 = 3x^2(3x + 4)$

Example 2: Find the factors of $y^2{-}81$.

Solution: Factoring involves thinking backward and forward. In this problem, you have to try to picture what two expressions, when multiplied together, produce $y^2{-}81$.

Start by drawing the groupings for the two factors, and then work to fill them in with what you already know.

$y^2{-}81 = (y \quad)(y \quad)$

You know that $y*y = y^2$ and you also know that $81 = 9^2$. So, let's plug in what you know, adjusting the – and + signs as needed to get the right answer. A good first guess here would be that because –81 appears in the original expression, one of its factors would have a + sign and the other a – sign.

$y^2–81 = (y+9)(y–9)$

The final step is to test your answer by expanding it back (multiplying the two factors) to see whether they really do produce the original expression.

$(y+9)(y–9) = y*y – 9y + 9y + (9)(–9) = y^2–81$

So, the final answer is:

$y^2–81 = (y+9)(y–9)$

Example 3: Factor the expression $x^2+3x–4$.

Solution: This expression is a bit trickier because it contains three terms. But the same approach you took to solve example 2 will work here.

$x^2+3x–4 = (x \quad)(x \quad)$

So far, so good. Now, you need to figure out what two factors of –4 equal 3 when you add or subtract them. Make a guess and try it out. If it doesn't work, try another combination until you succeed.

$–4*1 = –4$ but $–4 + 1 = –3$ and $–4 – 1 = –5$. No good.

$–1*4 = –4$ and $–1 + 4 = 3$. Success.

$x^2+3x–4 = (x –1)(x +4)$

Now the double check,

$(x –1)(x +4) = x*x + 4x –x –4 = x^2 +3x –4$

So, the final answer is:

$x^2+3x–4 = (x –1)(x +4)$

Inequalities

Whereas equations are mathematical expressions of quantities that are equal to each other, *inequalities* are expressions of unequal quantities. Take a look at Table 5.1 for a review of the inequality symbols and their definitions. You will see these symbols again on the ASVAB and you will be asked to perform operations to solve for inequalities. Solving algebraic inequalities is similar to solving algebraic equations with one *big* exception. Anytime you need to multiply or divide both sides of the inequality, you *must* reverse the direction of the inequality sign. When adding or subtracting, the inequality symbol remains unchanged.

Table 5.1 Inequality Symbols	
Inequality Symbol	**Definition**
$\neq$	Does not equal
$>$	Greater than
$<$	Less than
$\geq$	Greater than or equal to
$\leq$	Less than or equal to

Here is an example to illustrate this point:

Solve for x if $-2x - 7 > 17$.

First, isolate the variable by adding 7 to each side of the greater than symbol and then dividing each side by -2, switching the direction of the inequality to a less than sign. Here's how it looks:

$-2x - 7 > 17$

$-2x > 24$

$x < -12$

To double check your answer, try plugging a value for x that is less than -12 into the original expression and see whether it is valid.

Let's pick $x = -13$.

$-2x - 7 > 17$

$-2(-13) - 7 > 17$

$26 - 7 > 17$

$19 > 17$

True.

Geometry

Using geometry, the entire world opens up to measurement and mathematical analysis. Among other things, geometry deals with the mathematics of shapes, lines, and angles. Using these important tools you can calculate perimeter, circumference, area, and volume. Let's take a look at the key concepts of geometry that appear on the ASVAB.

Lines

A *line* is a continuous set of points that goes on infinitely in both directions in a straight path. *Parallel lines* are lines that never intersect (or cross at any point), as seen in Figure 5.1. *Perpendicular lines* are lines that intersect each other at a right angle (90 degrees), as seen in Figure 5.2. A line can be described by an algebraic equation and plotted on a graph, by assigning coordinate values (x,y) to its points.

Figure 5.1   Parallel lines.

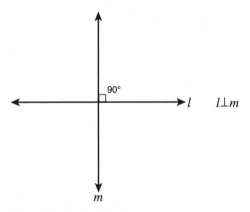

Figure 5.2   Perpendicular lines.

Slope of a Line

You might see a slope question on the ASVAB. If you do, here is how to solve it. The slope of a line is equal to the change in the rise (delta y) divided by the change in the run (delta x). Look at Figure 5.3 to help you visualize this concept. Essentially, slope is a measure of the steepness with which a line rises or falls when compared to a horizontal line. Written as a formula,

Slope $= (y_2 - y_1)/(x_2 - x_1)$

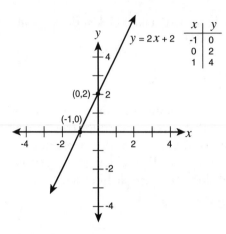

Figure 5.3 Slope of a line.

To calculate the slope of the line y = 2x + 2, you simply pick any two point (x,y) combinations that satisfy the equation (that is, that lie on the line) and plug them into the equation for slope. In this case, if we choose (–1,0) and (0,2), solving for slope would go like this:

slope = $(y_2-y_1)/(x_2-x_1)$

slope = (2--0)/(0--1)

slope = (2)/(1)

slope = 2

Angles

When two lines intersect, they form an angle. Angles can be measured in degrees. Table 5.2 shows you some types of angles.

Table 5.2 Types of Angles	
Type of Angle	**Example**
Straight line	180°
Circle	360°
Right angle (90 degrees)	90°
Acute angle	a < 90°

(continued)

Table 5.2 Types of Angles *(continued)*	
Type of Angle	**Example**
Obtuse angle	$a > 90°$
Complementary angles (two acute angles whose sum equals 90 degrees)	$a + b = 90°$
Supplementary angles (two angles whose sum equals 180 degrees)	$a + b = 180°$

In the special case where a line intersects two parallel lines (this is called *transecting*), the angles formed are related to each other as shown in Figure 5.4, where angles A and B are supplementary. Take a good look, because you are likely to see this again later.

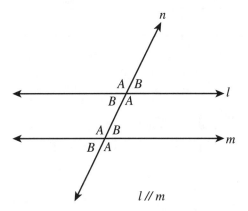

Figure 5.4 Angles formed by transecting parallel lines.

Triangles

Triangles are geometric shapes formed by the intersection of three line segments. Triangles, therefore, have three sides and three angles. The sum of the angles of a triangle is always equal to 180 degrees. Table 5.3 describes different types of triangles you need to be aware of for the ASVAB.

Table 5.3	Types of Triangles		
Type of Triangle	Equilateral	Isosceles	Right
Example	$a = b = c$ $<ac = <cb = <ba$	$a = c \neq b$ $<ab = <cb$	$a^2 + b^2 = c^2$ $<ab = 90°$ $<ac + <cb = 90°$
Sides	All three sides have equal length	Two sides have equal length	According to the Pythagorean Theorem, $a^2+b^2=c^2$
Angles	All three angles have equal measurement (60 degrees)	The two angles across from the two equal sides have equal measurement	The angle across from the hypotenuse (side c) is a right angle (90 degrees and the other two angles are complementary

Two other significant quantities to describe triangles can be calculated. The perimeter of a triangle is found by summing the lengths of the three sides. Area, the measure of the surface within a particular region (such as a triangle), can also be calculated. Here is the formula for the area of a triangle:

Area = 1/2(base)(height) = 1/2(b)(h)

Figure 5.5 shows a triangle that has both the base and height labeled.

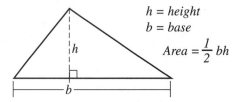

$h = height$
$b = base$
$Area = \frac{1}{2} bh$

Figure 5.5 A triangle with base and height labeled.

Quadrilaterals

Four-sided geometric shapes are called *quadrilaterals*. Quadrilaterals come in several different forms, but in addition to their four sides, they all have four angles whose sum is equal to 360 degrees. Table 5.4 shows the quadrilaterals.

Table 5.4	Types of Quadrilaterals			
Type	**Square**	**Rectangle**	**Parallelogram**	**Trapezoid**
Example	$P = 4s$ $A = s^2$	$P = 2(l + w)$ $A = l\,w$	$A = bh$	$A = \frac{1}{2}(b_1 + b_2)h$
Sides	Opposite sides parallel. All four sides same length.	Opposite sides parallel. Opposite sides same length.	Opposite sides parallel. Opposite sides same length.	One pair of opposite sides parallel, other pair not.
Angles	All four angles are right angles	All four angles are right angles.	Opposite angles are equal.	Sum of four angles equals 360 degrees.
Perimeter	Sum of lengths of four sides.	Sum of lengths of four sides.	Sum of lengths of four sides.	Sum of lengths of four sides.
Area	$A = s^2$	$A = lw$	$A = bh$	$A = 1/2(b_1+b_2)h$

Circles

Circles are formed by a curved line with each of its points located an equal distance from a given point (the center of the circle). That distance is called the *radius* of the circle. The straight-line segment that passes through the center of the circle and also contacts two points on the circle is called the *diameter*. The diameter is equal to two times the length of the radius. Figure 5.6 shows a circle with diameter and radius labeled.

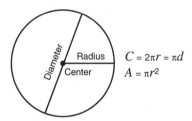

$C = 2\pi r = \pi d$

$A = \pi r^2$

Figure 5.6 The circle.

The term *circumference*, not perimeter, is used to define the distance all the way around a circle. The following is the formula for circumference:

Circumference (C) = $(\pi)d = (\pi)2r$

where π is a constant that can be approximated as 22/7 or 3.14.

The area of a circle is obtained by using the formula

Area (A) = (π)r2

Volume

The concept of *volume* requires you to think in three dimensions. So far, all the geometric shapes you have considered existed within a plane (that is, a flat surface extending continuously in all directions). Real-life objects, however, are solids that take up space and are three-dimensional. Volume allows you to calculate just how much space is contained in these objects.

Table 5.5 demonstrates some common examples of volumetric calculations that might appear on the ASVAB.

Table 5.5 Volume of Common Solids		
Object	**Drawing**	**Formula for Volume**
Rectangular solid		$V = lwh$
Cube		$V = s^3$
Cylinder		$V = (π)r^2h$

Exam Prep Questions

1. Find the slope of the line running through the points (–3,–2) and (–1,4).
   - ❑ A. –3/2
   - ❑ B. –1
   - ❑ C. 2/3
   - ❑ D. 3

2. What is the volume of a 4-inch high rectangular box with sides measuring 5 inches and 6 inches?
   - ❑ A. 30 in²
   - ❑ B. 44 in³
   - ❑ C. 120 in²
   - ❑ D. 120 in³

3. If lines l and m are parallel, what is the value of z (see Figure 5.7)?

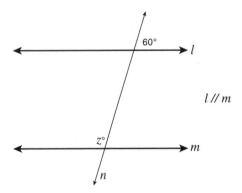

Figure 5.7 Figure for question 3.

   - ❑ A. 30
   - ❑ B. 60
   - ❑ C. 120
   - ❑ D. 180

4. If x = –2 and y = 10, what is the value of the expression, $3x^2 + xy^2 - 5y$?
   - ❑ A. –238
   - ❑ B. –48
   - ❑ C. 138
   - ❑ D. 150

5. If the $11,274 Rob spent on his fiancée's engagement ring cost him three months' salary, how much does Rob make each month?

  ❏ A. $1,879
  ❏ B. $3,758
  ❏ C. $7,516
  ❏ D. $33,822

6. Solve the inequality: $-3y > 5y + 32$.

  ❏ A. $y < 4$
  ❏ B. $y > -4$
  ❏ C. $y < -4$
  ❏ D. $y > 16$

7. $(x + 3)(x - 1) =$

  ❏ A. x^2+2x-3
  ❏ B. x^2-2x+3
  ❏ C. x^2+2x+3
  ❏ D. x^2-2x-3

8. $8! =$

  ❏ A. 5,040
  ❏ B. 20,160
  ❏ C. 32,464
  ❏ D. 40,320

9. What is the cube root of 27?

  ❏ A. 3
  ❏ B. 3.14
  ❏ C. 3 *(square root of 2)
  ❏ D. 9

10. $x^9 / x^6 =$

  ❏ A. x^{-3}
  ❏ B. x^3
  ❏ C. $3x^6$
  ❏ D. x^{15}

Exam Prep Answers

1. **The correct answer is D.** The slope of a line is equal to the change in the rise (delta y) divided by the change in the run (delta x). Applied to this problem where you are given the coordinates (–3,–2) and (–1,4), you find that

    Slope = $(y_2–y_1)/(x_2–x_1)$ = [4–(–2)]/[–1–(–3)]

    = 6/4

    = 3/2

2. **The correct answer is D.** Remember that the formula for the volume of a rectangular solid is V = lwh. Plugging in the lengths you are given, you get V = (6in)(5in)(4in) = 120in³. The trick here is to remember that volume is expressed in cubic inches, not square inches like area.

3. **The correct answer is C.** Because line n intersects line l at a 60-degree angle and line m is parallel with line l, line n must intersect line m at a 60-degree angle as well. As you can see in Figure 5.8, once that is established z can be found by subtracting 60 degrees from 180 degrees (as they are supplementary angles).

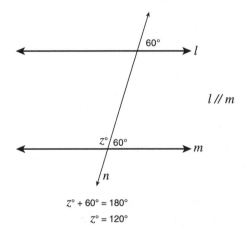

Figure 5.8 Figure for answer 3.

4. **The correct answer is A.** All you need to do here is plug the values of x and y into the algebraic expression and perform the operations it calls for to reach the answer, as seen here.

    $3x^2+xy^2–5y$ = 3(–2)² + (–2)(10)² – 5(10)

    = 3(4) + (–2)(100) – 50

    = 12 + (–200) – 50

    = –238

5. **The correct answer is B.** Write a simple equation to relate the two quantities you are given (cost of ring and number of months' salary it represents) to the quantity you want to know: Rob's monthly salary. Assigning the variable m for monthly salary, you have

$$3m = \$11,274$$
$$m = \$11,274 / 3$$
$$m = \$3,758$$

6. **The correct answer is C.** Remember the rule that the inequality sign must be reversed when dividing (or multiplying) by a negative number, and you'll have no problem with this one.

$$-3y > 5y + 32$$
$$-3y - 5y > 32$$
$$-8y > 32$$
$$y < -4$$

7. **The correct answer is A.** Multiply the two expressions, like this:

$$(x + 3)(x - 1) = (x)(x) - (x)(1) + (3)(x) - (3)(1)$$
$$= x^2 - x + 3x - 3$$
$$= x^2 + 2x - 3$$

8. **The correct answer is D.** No difficult math here, but no shortcuts, either. You must remember that 8! = 8*7*6*5*4*3*2*1, and then you must do the multiplication carefully enough not to fall for one of the wrong answers.

9. **The correct answer is A.** The cube root of a number (x) is the number (y) which, when multiplied by itself three times (y*y*y) equals x. In this case 3*3*3=27, so 3 is the cube root of 27.

10. **The correct answer is B.** When dividing exponents that have the same base variable, simply subtract the exponents to find the answer.

6

Electronics Information

Terms you'll need to understand:

- ✓ Schematics
- ✓ Switch
- ✓ Electrical circuit
- ✓ Resistor
- ✓ Free electrons
- ✓ Transistor
- ✓ Direct current
- ✓ Capacitor
- ✓ Alternating current
- ✓ Insulator
- ✓ Frequency
- ✓ Magnets
- ✓ Voltage

- ✓ Electromagnets
- ✓ Electromotive force
- ✓ Inductor
- ✓ Power
- ✓ Step-up transformer
- ✓ Resistance
- ✓ Step-down transformer
- ✓ Impedance
- ✓ Class C fire extinguisher
- ✓ Conductor
- ✓ Magnetic Flux
- ✓ Rectifier
- ✓ Inverter

Techniques you'll need to master:

- ✓ Recognizing the definitions of basic AC and DC terms
- ✓ Knowing Ohm's Law and how to apply it
- ✓ Understanding how electricity flows through a circuit
- ✓ Discerning the difference between series, parallel, and series-parallel connections
- ✓ Knowing Fleming's Right Hand Rule and Left Hand Rule
- ✓ Understanding basic electrical safety

The Electronics Information (EI) module of the ASVAB contains 20 questions, which you will need to answer in 9 minutes. To achieve your 70%, you must answer 14 of the questions correctly; to achieve 80%, you must answer 16 questions correctly. Although the EI module is really one of overt knowledge, if you take your time and read the questions carefully, you should do well, but don't take too much time on any one question. Above all, pay attention to the Exam Alerts and make sure that you understand the information that the Cram Sheet outlines.

Schematics

During the course of this discussion on the fundamentals of electricity, we will use *schematics* to illustrate the principles discussed. Schematics are line drawings of electrical and electronic circuits and components.

An electric *circuit* is a path through which electricity flows. This path contains one or more components or devices and has a load, or something that is drawing the electricity—an end-user, if you will. Electricity can flow through a circuit when the path is complete (closed) and is connected to an energy source. An open circuit is one that has an incomplete path, and electricity cannot flow all the way through it to a load.

An entire circuit has one or more schematic drawings, and each component within that circuit has a drawing representation. In each of the following sections we discuss the most common electronic and electrical components and their respective schematic symbols. With each section, you will have an opportunity to become more familiar with schematic details, as well as the principles behind the drawings.

Principles of Electricity

In science class, you learned that atoms comprise all matter, including air, and that an atom consists of three distinct particles:

➤ Positively charged particles, or protons

➤ Negatively charged particles, or electrons

➤ Neutrally charged particles, or neutrons

Protons and neutrons make up the nucleus of an atom, whereas *electrons* maintain a circular orbit around the nucleus. Sound familiar? Figure 6.1 illustrates the basic structure of an atom. This illustration, which is of a copper atom, is a little different from one you might have seen in your science book, because it shows more than one layer—or shell—of electron orbits. The outermost shell of electrons is the most loosely bound to the nucleus. For that reason, atoms can more easily exchange electrons from the outer shell.

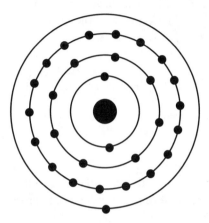

Figure 6.1 Atomic structure.

When we talk about electricity, the primary concern is electrons, for in essence, electricity is the movement of *free electrons* through a given medium. A free electron is one that is not in a tightly bound orbit around a nucleus. When a conductive material receives an external electrical charge, the electrons gain enough energy to leave the outermost shell of the atom and become free electrons.

The most basic principle of electricity is that of *Ohm's Law*, which entails three primary measurements: current, voltage (or electromotive force), and resistance. The following sections discuss each of these constituents, and then provide a discussion on how to use Ohm's Law to find these properties.

Current

Within an electrical conductor, such as electrical wire, there are billions of free electrons at rest, and until an outside force imposes an electrical force on them, they will remain at rest. However, once you activate an electrical source to the electrons, they will begin to move.

You can think of electron movement, or electrical flow, like that of a river. By looking at a landscape, you can determine which way a river will flow; namely, from a higher point to a lower point, according to the laws of gravity. When you think of electricity, you can also determine which way the electrons will flow, although the laws of magnetism, rather than the laws of gravity, govern the flow of electrons.

Just as gravity dictates that water will flow downhill, the inherent charge of the electrons will cause them to move in a predefined direction, which is away from the voltage source toward the load. The electron's electrical charge acts like a magnetic field in which negative charges repel each other, creating the movement within the electrical field. That movement is called *current*. You measure the strength, or rate of movement of the current in amperes (A), and represent this force by the symbol I (for intensity).

Current is the rate of the flow of electrons, measured in amperes (A)—or amps— and is determined by this formula in DC circuits: I = E/R, where E is electromotive force and R is resistance.

In AC circuits, current is determined by this formula: I = V/Z, where V is the voltage and Z is the impedance.

Different loads, or draws on the electrical system, require differing amounts of current, and for devices with an induction motor, the startup draw is more than the normal operating draw. You can read more about induction later in this chapter in the section titled, "Inductors, Inductance, and Inductive Reactance." The electric company sets up most households for 100 Amp (also stated 100 A) service, which is sufficient for most applications.

The following sections discuss the two forms of electrical current, which are *direct current* and *alternating current*.

Direct Current

Direct current (DC) is the flow of electrons in only one, consistent direction, usually maintained by a constant voltage source, such as a battery. Direct current is most like our river analogy, as water flows in only one direction, according to the force exerted upon it, and so does direct current, as Figure 6.2 illustrates.

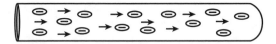

Figure 6.2   Direct current electron flow.

Because transmission lines have a constant resistance, a lower current will decrease the power loss in it. However, by its nature, direct current cannot easily travel great distances without experiencing considerable power loss. This is because direct current has only one current value and one voltage value, and its input voltage cannot be increased without also increasing the current proportionally. In addition, transmitting a direct current with suffi-cient voltage to carry the transmission for the desired distance is not financially feasible in most cases. However, today's technology is introducing new ways to carry the extremely high DC voltage (higher than that for high-voltage AC transmissions) by using rectifiers and inverters to change DC to AC and vice versa.

A battery is the most common source of DC power. In a battery, whether it is a small, AAA battery that you put in your television's remote control or a large, industrial battery, the principle is the same: The battery develops a lack of electrons at the positive terminal and develops a surplus at the negative terminal. The number of surplus electrons indicates the voltage level of the battery. Because electrons are negatively charged and repel each other, and because electrons in a DC circuit travel in only one direction, when a load is applied to the circuit, the surplus electrons leave the crowded, hostile environment of the negative terminal and travel toward the more magnetically friendly, positive terminal to create electricity. This manner of creating voltage is induced voltage, or electromotive force (emf). Figure 6.3 illustrates the constant current flow and voltage in a DC circuit.

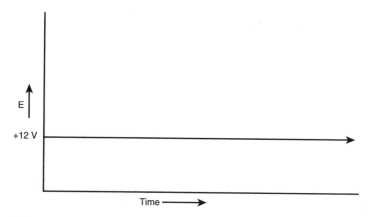

Figure 6.3   Waveform for direct current.

Alternating Current

Most electric devices that we use every day, with the exception of battery-operated cordless tools, use *alternating current* (AC). In alternating current, the flow of electrons periodically and regularly reverses its direction. This reversal of direction is caused by a changing—or alternating—voltage in a circuit. This causes the current to flow first clockwise, then counterclockwise. Figure 6.4 shows the electron flow in an AC circuit.

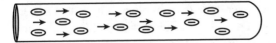

Positive Alternation

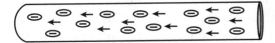

Negative Alternation

Figure 6.4 Alternating current electron flow.

The device that produces the voltage causing an alternating current is the AC voltage source. An alternator, also called an AC generator, is another machine that produces AC voltage.

Alternating current is more widely used because it can carry a high voltage over long distances. During any power transmission, power losses occur because the conductive material (in an electrical wire, the copper wire through which the electricity travels) heats up. Applying a very high voltage in a transmission line makes it possible to reduce the power loss in the line. A low current at a high voltage or a proportionally high current at low voltage transmit the same amount of overall power.

An AC current exhibits a sine wave signature, as Figure 6.5 shows. Each AC cycle consists of two flow alternations per cycle; a positive alternation, or the amount of time that the power output is above the axis, and a negative alternation, or the amount of time that the power output is below the axis. The negative alternation represents the flow reversal in the AC current flow. The AC output repeats these cycles as long as the conductor is receiving power. Both voltage and current in an AC circuit exhibit a sine wave.

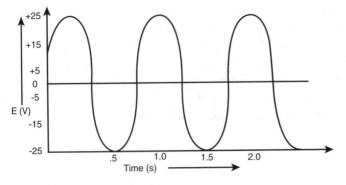

Figure 6.5 A waveform for alternating current.

You use the cycle rate, or *frequency*, to assess the rate at which AC current is flowing. The frequency—measured in *hertz (Hz)*—indicates the number of cycles that the AC flow completes in one second. The electricity that you receive through the outlets in your home operates at about 60 cycles. In this case, the duration of one cycle is 1/60 s, meaning that the AC current performs about 60 complete cycles per second, which is stated as 60 Hz.

Electromotive Force and Voltage

Remember the analogy used previously of current being like a river? Let's take that illustration one step further, and because you normally experience electricity through the medium of electrical wiring, let's liken it to water flowing through a pipe. Just as a pump must force water from the ground into a pipe, so a source must "pump" electrical charge into the wire. With water, the more powerful the pump, the greater water flow you will have. In like manner, the greater *voltage* you have the greater will be the rate that electrons pass through the wire.

 Remember that voltage is the pressure that makes the stream of electrons flow, and current is the rate of flow of the electrons.

The letter E indicates voltage, for *electromotive force* in DC circuits, and V indicates voltage in AC circuits, and in both cases is measured in volts (v).

 Voltage is the energy or pressure that makes the stream of electrons flow, is measured in volts, and is represented by this formula in DC circuits: E = IR, where E is electromotive force. In AC circuits, voltage is derived by this formula: V = IZ, where V is the voltage and Z is the impedance.

Resistance and Impedance

All materials, regardless of how electrically conductive they are, have some resistive properties, or properties that oppose the flow of electrons. In any electrical circuit, the inherent resistance of the conductive material will slow down the electron flow. The more resistive the conductor is, the slower the flow will be. The resistance of the conductors depends on the type of material and the size of the conductors.

It is important to know that *line drop* is indicative of a decrease in voltage due to line impedance. A lower current and higher voltage across the transmission line will help compensate for line drop.

Materials with high resistance have low conductivity and materials with low resistance have high conductivity. This is because high-resistance materials have more free electrons than an insulator, but not as many as a conductor. As the resistance increases, the material acts more like an insulator; as the resistance decreases, the material acts more like a conductor. All materials, even those such as copper and silver that are good conductors, have at least some resistance factor. For more information, see the "Insulators" and "Conductors and Conductivity" sections in this chapter.

In DC circuits, R represents resistance and in AC circuits, Z represents impedance. Although Ohm's Law uses R and Z in the same capacity, impedance differs slightly from resistance in that impedance is a calculation of both resistance and inductive reactance. You measure resistance in ohms, represented by omega symbol (Ω). The formula for finding resistance in a DC circuit is R=E/I, and Z=V/I in AC circuits.

Resistance is the opposition to electron flow within the conductive material, is measured in ohms, and is represented by this formula in DC circuits: R = E/I, where E is electromotive force. In AC circuits, we find impedance, which includes resistance, by this formula: Z = V/I, where V is the voltage and Z is the impedance.

Ohm's Law

Ohm's Law is the most fundamental law of electricity. A set relationship exists between voltage, resistance, and current in an electrical circuit, which Ohm's Law expresses as follows:

➤ *Current* equals voltage divided by resistance, and stated by these formulas: I=E/R (DC) or I=V/Z (AC).

➤ *Resistance* equals voltage divided by current, and stated by these formulas: R=E/I (DC) or Z=V/I (AC).

➤ *Voltage* equals resistance multiplied by current, and stated with these formulas: E=IR (DC) or V=IZ (AC).

In the preceding formulas, I is the intensity (current), E is the electromotive force, and R is resistance. However, Ohm's Law varies somewhat between AC and DC circuits, as Figure 6.6 and Figure 6.7 illustrate, with Ohm's Law triangles for AC and DC circuits.

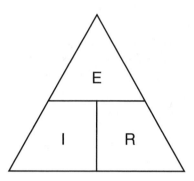

Figure 6.6 Ohm's Law triangles for DC circuits.

To find the correct formula using the triangles, simply cover the value that you want to find, and what you see remaining is the formula for that value. For example, if you want to know the formula for finding current, cover the I; what you see remaining is E/R. Therefore, the formula you are looking for is this: I=E/R, which we know to be true.

On the Electronic Information module, you must know Ohm's Law and be able to apply it. Ohm's Law states that current equals voltage divided by resistance (I=E/R); Resistance equals voltage divided by current (R=E/I); and Voltage equals current multiplied by resistance (E=IR). Be sure that you understand this section thoroughly.

You can use Ohm's Law triangle for DC circuits for AC only if the load is purely resistive. However, in most AC circuits, the load, input, or output is a combination of resistance, capacitance and inductance. The general representation for impedance is Z. In addition, current flow in an AC circuit is not in phase with the voltage and will either lead or lag the voltage. Therefore, Figure 6.7 shows the impedance triangle for AC circuits. The triangle is the same as Ohm's Law at DC, except that impedance replaces resistance and voltage replaces electromotive force.

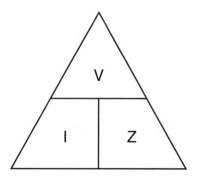

Figure 6.7 Ohm's Law triangle for AC circuits.

Using Ohm's Law to Find Resistance

If you know both the current through a circuit and the voltage applied to the circuit, you can find the resistance of the circuit by using the Ohm's Law formula for resistance, which is R= E/I for DC circuits or Z=V/I for AC circuits. In Figure 6.8, what is the resistance of the circuit?

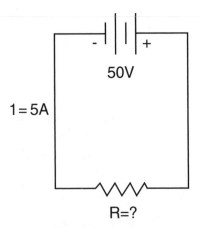

Figure 6.8 Finding resistance in a simple circuit.

Because the current is 5A and the voltage is 50V, the resistance is equal to the voltage divided by the current, so 50/5=10 ohms.

Using Ohm's Law to Find Current

If you know the voltage applied to a circuit and the resistance of the circuit, you can use the Ohm's Law formula for current, which is I = E/R for DC circuits and I = V/Z for AC circuits. in Figure 6.9, what is the current through the circuit?

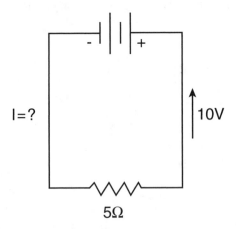

Figure 6.9 Finding current in a simple circuit.

Because the voltage is 10V and the resistance is 5 ohms, the current is equal to the voltage divided by the resistance (or impedance), so 10/5 = 2A.

Using Ohm's Law to Find Voltage

If you know the current flowing through a circuit and the resistance of the circuit, you can determine the voltage applied to the circuit by applying Ohm's Law formula for voltage, which is $E = IR$ for DC circuits and $V = IZ$ in AC circuits. In Figure 6.10, what is the voltage being applied to the circuit?

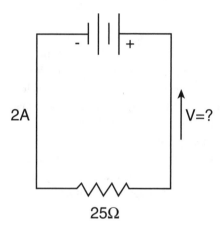

Figure 6.10   Finding voltage for a simple circuit.

Because the current is 2A and the resistance is 25 ohms, the voltage is equal to the current multiplied by the resistance/impedance, so $2 \times 25 = 50V$.

Power

Another common measurement, in addition to those that Ohm's Law addresses, is that of overall *power*. Knowing the power of an electrical circuit, piece of equipment, or entire electrical system is crucial in knowing how much electricity you need to deliver. Power represents the rate of work, or the overall amount of electricity that a device needs to operate, and is measured in watts (w).

To find power, you must know that 1 watt equals 1 ampere multiplied by 1 volt, or $P = E \times I$. So, if you have a piece of equipment that is rated for 2 amps at 110 volts, the overall power consumption is 220W, because $2 \times 110 = 220$.

Electrical Components and Properties

Now that we have discussed the basic principles that govern an electrical circuit, let's discuss the components that affect the way that an electrical circuit works.

Batteries

Batteries are essentially electrical generation devices, adhering to the voltage-generation principle discussed in the "Direct Current" section in this chapter. The three most common types of batteries are *dry cell*, which is the kind you buy to put in your Walkman or children's toys; *wet cell*, which is for cars and boats; and *storage batteries*, also called deep-cycle batteries and are used in remote, backup, emergency, and industrial electrical systems. Figure 6.11 illustrates the schematic symbols for a single-cell and a multi-cell battery. The symbol consists of a long bar and a shorter bar. Although schematics might not always indicate the positive and negative terminals, the long bar always represents the positive terminal and the shorter bar the negative terminal.

Single-cell battery   Multi-cell battery

Figure 6.11   Schematic symbols for single- and multi-cell batteries.

When you want more energy than a single battery or power source can provide, you have several options that will provide more voltage, more current, or modest improvements on both. Although this discussion pertains only to batteries, it is applicable to any form of multiple power sources.

Series Connection

When you connect batteries in series, you can achieve an overall voltage that is equal to the sum of the individual voltages of the cells, but you will get only as much current as any one cell in the battery chain can supply. For example, if you connect six, 12-volt batteries with an individual amperage of 15 amps, in series, you will achieve 72 volts, but will maintain a total current of only 15 amps.

Connecting batteries in series equals the sum of the voltages and maintains single-cell current.

To connect power sources in series, you connect the positive terminal of the power distribution panel to the positive terminal of the first battery. Then, you connect the negative terminal of the first battery to the positive terminal of the second battery, the negative terminal of the second battery to the positive terminal of the third battery, and so on, until you connect the negative terminal of the last battery to the negative terminal of distribution panel. Figure 6.12 illustrates a set of six batteries connected in series.

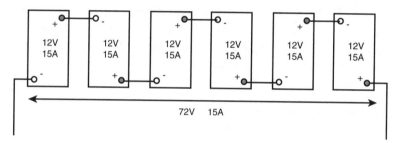

Figure 6.12 Batteries connected in series.

Parallel Connection

When you connect batteries in parallel, you can achieve a total output current that is equal to the sum of the individual amperages of the cells, but you will get only as much voltage as any one cell in the battery chain can supply. For example, if you take the same six, 12-volt, 15 amp batteries discussed previously, and connect them in parallel, you will achieve 90 amps, but will maintain a total voltage of only 12 volts.

Connecting batteries in parallel equals the sum of the amps and maintains single-cell voltage.

To connect power sources in parallel, you connect the positive terminal of the power distribution panel to the positive terminal of the first battery. Then, you connect the positive terminals of each battery in the chain together. Next, you connect the negative terminal of the first battery to the negative terminal of the distribution panel and connect the negative terminals of all the batteries in the chain together. Figure 6.13 illustrates a set of six batteries connected in parallel.

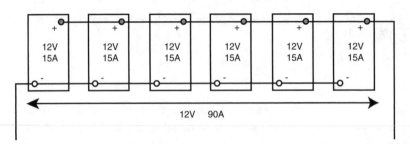

Figure 6.13 Batteries connected in parallel.

Series-Parallel Connection

In some circumstances, you might find that you need to increase both voltage and current. In those cases, you should connect your batteries, or power sources, in a series-parallel configuration. Let's take the same 12-volt, 15 amp batteries that you were using earlier as an example. If you have a system that requires 36 volts at 30 amps, you can connect them in series-parallel, as Figure 6.14 illustrates.

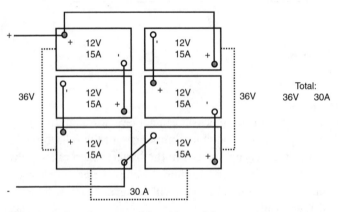

Figure 6.14 Batteries connected in series-parallel.

By connecting three of the batteries in series, you increase the total voltage of those batteries to 36 volts, and then do the same with the other three batteries for another 36 volts. Then, connect the two sets of three batteries in parallel to increase the current to 30 amps.

Wiring

Electric circuits and equipment connect to a power source via electrical wires, or cable. Different electrical applications require different sizes of wire and the amount of current that will be traveling through the cable is the determining factor in choosing wire size. The higher current that a circuit needs, the larger the diameter of the wire must be. Current flow through a wire increases the temperature of the wire. If too small of a wire is used, it will heat up and cause a reduction in voltage and possibly a fire. If the wire is large and the current is small, the heat coefficient is small. The thicker a wire is, the more current it can carry without overheating.

Gauge numbers define wire sizes and get bigger as the wire diameter gets smaller. The amount of current that a given size of copper wire can carry safely, or its amperage capacity, is its ampacity. There are several types of cable:

➤ Plastic-sheathed, indoor-type non-metallic (NM) for indoor household wiring and other dry locations.

➤ Armored cable NM for indoor and other dry locations; armor keeps cable from chafing during and after installation.

➤ NMC (non-metallic corrosion-resistant) for moist, damp, and corrosive locations, including the hollow in concrete block, and for both below and above ground.

Cable Insulation Colors

Most 110 wiring that you will see is either 12- or 14-gauge Romex cable. This cable has three wires inside a sheath and each wire is designated for a specific purpose. Table 6.1 correlates each wire color to its intended function.

Table 6.1 Cable Insulation Colors	
Wire Type	**Insulation Color**
Hot	Black
Neutral	White
Ground	Bare or Green

Splicing Cable

If you need to *splice*, or permanently join wires together, you have three choices: solder the joints, use screw-on wire nut connectors, or use wire crimps.

Soldering takes a bit more time, effort, and tools, but connects the wires electrically as well as mechanically. A properly made solder joint is as strong as the original wire and it offers no additional resistance to the flow of current.

A screw-on connector makes a solderless connection that can be permanent in most applications. To use wire nuts, you put the two ends of clean wire together and push them into the connector. Because the wire nuts are threaded inside, you can then screw the connector down tightly, like a bottle cap, onto the wire.

Finally, you can join wires with wire crimps. Wire crimps are short, copper cylinders into which you insert the ends of the stripped, clean cable wire. You then use wire crimps to squeeze down the crimp firmly around the wire.

For both soldering and crimping, you can protect the finished splice with heat-shrink electrical tubing, depending on the application. Doing so protects not only the join, but also protects people from accidental electrical shock.

Wiring Safety

Most wiring, and all electrical connections, are not intended to be exposed to damp conditions. Even ambient water moisture can provide an arc path for an electric current as it seeks ground. Be sure that you have the proper type of cable installed for moist environments and be sure that it is properly grounded and that no connections are exposed.

The most important thing to remember when you are dealing with electrical wire is that you should never handle electrical wires without first interrupting the electricity in that particular circuit.

If you are experiencing electrical problems, such as smoke, arcing, blowing fuses, or tripping circuit breakers, you should interrupt the electrical supply to that circuit until you can locate the problem. You might have a damaged electrical cable or faulty equipment, or you might be overloading the circuit.

Resistors

A *resistor* is a component that offers more resistance to the flow of current than an ordinary conducting wire, and works by limiting the amount of current flowing in a circuit. Resistors can limit the current or adjust the voltage in a circuit. By choosing the proper value of resistor, you can precisely control the value of the current flowing through a circuit.

You will normally find two types of fixed resistors in electrical work, which are carbon composite and wire wound. A fixed resistor always has the same degree of resistance, but some wire-wound resistors have an adjustable sliding tap that lets you choose a certain value of resistance. In addition, some wire-wound resistors have fixed taps that provide fixed values of resistance between their taps. Potentiometers and rheostats are two types of variable resistors. Figure 6.15 illustrates the schematic symbols for resistors.

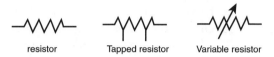

| resistor | Tapped resistor | Variable resistor |

Figure 6.15 Schematic symbols for resistors.

When current flows through a resistance it produces heat, and for that reason, appliances such as heaters and dryers often use wire-wound resistors. However, in many other applications, heat is not a desired effect, and a resistor that gets too hot could destroy itself or cause fire or damage to the equipment.

Transistors

A *transistor* is an electronic component that performs certain electrical functions, such as regulating current or voltage, and acts as a switch or gate for electronic signals. A transistor consists of three layers of semiconducting material, such as germanium or silicon, each capable of carrying a current. A semiconductor is a material that has more current-carrying capabilities than an insulator, but less than a conductor. Figure 6.16 shows the schematic symbol for a transistor.

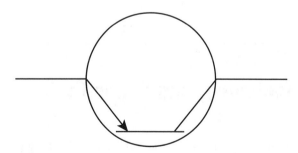

Figure 6.16 Schematic symbols for transistors.

Conductors and Conductivity

An *electrical conductor* is a substance through which electrical current can flow with little resistance, or simply stated, a material in which free electrons can be easily moved from one atom to another by an outside, energizing force. In general, metals are very good electrical conductors, but resistance in any element increases with increasing temperature in conductors.

Because silver and copper can both conduct almost all the applied electricity, you will commonly find these materials as conductors. However, some composite materials also have good conductance properties. Table 6.2 describes the relative conductivity of some of the most common conductive materials.

Table 6.2 Relative Conductivity of Common Elements	
Element	**Relative Conductivity**
Silver	106
Copper	89.5
Gold	65
Aluminum	59
Tungsten	28.9
Zinc	28.2
Brass	28
Iron	17.7
Platinum	15
Tin	13
Nickel	12–16
Lead	7
Titanium	5
Steel	3–15

Capacitors, Capacitance, and Capacitive Reactance

A *capacitor* is a device in an electrical circuit that stores an electric charge. The simplest capacitor consists of two parallel plates, one positive and one negative, of conducting material with non-conducting material (a dielectric) between them. In some capacitors, the dielectric is actually air. You will encounter two types of capacitors: *fixed* and *variable*. Figure 6.17 shows the schematic symbol for a capacitor.

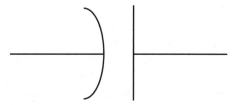

Figure 6.17 Schematic symbol for a capacitor.

As electrons leave the negative terminal of the power source, they move onto the capacitor's negative plate. Because the dielectric between the plates will not allow the electrons to travel freely from one plate to the other, the electrons begin accumulating on the negative capacitor plate until the stored voltage in the capacitor equals the line voltage from the power source. At that point, the voltage is sufficient to force the electrons from the negative plate, through the dielectric, onto the positive plate of the capacitor, and back into the circuit. This process is called *charging the capacitor.*

In your everyday life, you have experience with this phenomenon: Every time you turn on your television, I'm sure that you have noticed a slight delay between the time you press the power button and the time that you see a picture on the screen. That's because your television has a capacitor in its circuit that it must charge.

Capacitors are rated by their capability to store a charge and by the maximum voltage with which they can be used, and measure that capacitance using the farad (F). The capacitance of a capacitor depends on several criteria, which are

➤ The surface area of its plates

➤ The distance between the plates, or rather, the thickness of the dielectric

➤ The type of dielectric

A capacitor that has large plates close together will have a higher capacitance than a capacitor with the same dielectric, but with smaller plates or plates that are farther apart.

After a capacitor becomes fully charged, it acts as an open circuit in DC applications; that is, after the capacitor receives a charge from a DC voltage source, current stops flowing in the branch of the circuit that contains the capacitor. In an AC circuit, capacitors also offer opposition, called capacitive reactance, but do not act as an open circuit when an AC voltage is applied.

Switches

A *switch* is a simple device for opening and closing an electric circuit. When you turn on a light switch, for example, the switch (and the circuit) is closed. This means that the switch completes a conducting path, and the current flows from the voltage source to the lamp, then back to the source. Figure 6.18 shows the schematic symbols for switches. These are the most common types of switches:

➤ **Single-pole, single-throw (SPST)**—Has only two positions, open or closed, and can open or close only one wire in a circuit, such as a light switch for a single lamp.

➤ **Double-pole, single-throw (DPST)**—Has two separate sets of contacts and can open or close two circuits at a time. It also has only two positions, open and closed, such as a light switch for more than one light circuit.

➤ **Single-pole, double-throw (SPDT)**—Has two positions, closed and closed. In essence, it is a toggle switch that enables you to switch between two different circuits. Throwing the switch to one side closes one circuit and opens an adjacent circuit; throwing it to the other side does the reverse. Some SPDT switches have a middle position that leaves both circuits open.

➤ **Double pole, double-throw (DPDT)**—Can make and break contact between two wires at a time. It has six terminals and can have either two or three positions. If there is a center off position, both circuits are open.

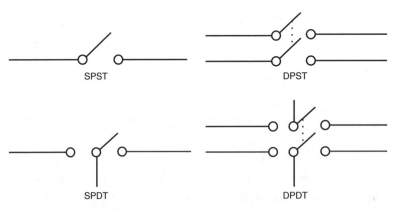

Figure 6.18   Schematic symbol for switches.

Insulators

In an *insulator*, the electrons are more tightly bound to the atom's nucleus and therefore have no free electrons. When you apply a voltage source to an insulating material, you will notice no resulting electric current. Because of the lack of free electrons, the material's electrons have very little electron movement. Materials such as asbestos, glass, rubber, and plastic are good insulators, which is why they often cover wires carrying electrical voltages.

Magnets and Electromagnets

There are two main types of magnets: *natural magnets* and *electromagnets*. Natural magnets are materials that attract pieces of iron, and can be either temporary or permanent magnets.

Electromagnets are artificial magnets made by passing electricity through a coil of wire wound around an iron core, or by inserting a magnetic material into the magnetic circuit of a solenoid. Electromagnetism is the magnetic effect produced when electric current flows through a conductor. Our discussion will focus on electromagnets, which are an integral part of an electrical circuit.

If a piece of magnetic material is anywhere near a magnet, the magnet will affect it. How the material is affected depends on its placement in regard to the magnet. The area around a magnet within which it can produce a magnetic effect, is the magnet's field. You can indicate the shape and strength of a magnet's field by using lines, called *magnetic lines of force*. Notice that the lines of force are closed loops. Every line of force leaves the north pole of a magnet, makes a complete path through the surrounding space or material, and returns to the south pole. The lines run from the north pole to the south pole outside the magnet. They run from south to north inside the magnet. Figure 6.19 shows the magnetic fields of a bar magnet.

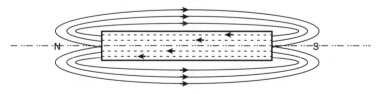

Figure 6.19   Magnetic fields.

Here are several terms that you need to know describing magnets and magnetic materials:

➤ *Permeability* is the ease with which a substance passes magnetic lines.

➤ *Reluctance* is the opposite of permeability, and is the opposition that a substance offers to magnetic lines.

➤ *Retentivity*, or residual magnetism, measures the degree to which a substance remains magnetized after the magnetizing force is removed.

➤ *Magnetic flux* is the quantity of magnetism, expressed by the total number of magnetic lines of force, which passes along the magnetic circuit. Flux density is a measure of the magnet's strength, measured along the number of lines of force in a unit of area, usually one square centimeter.

If you place a small compass near a wire through which a current is flowing, the compass needle will move to indicate the presence of a magnetic field around the wire. The field is circular and its direction depends on the direction of the current.

If a conductor moves through a magnetic field, the field will induce a voltage in it to create magnetic induction. For electromagnetic induction to take place there must be a magnetic field, conductor voltage, and relative movement of the field and the conductor.

Using the Left Hand Rule

Just as a permanent magnet has a north and south pole, so does an electromagnet. Both the direction of the current and the way that the coil is wound affect the coil's polarity. To determine which end of a coil is the electromagnet's north pole, and by extension, direction of current flow, use the illustration in Figure 6.20 and the Left Hand Rule (LHR), which is as follows:

1. The current leaves the negative terminal of the battery and enters the left end of the coil. Place your left hand at the left end of the coil.

2. The wire in this coil goes over the core at the point where current enters the coil. Curl the fingers of your left hand (theoretically) around the coil in the same way the wire winds around the coil.

3. The thumb of your left hand now points in the same direction as the north pole. Because your thumb is pointing to the right, the right end of the coil is the north Pole.

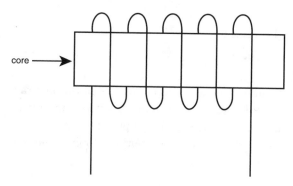

core →

Figure 6.20   Using the Left Hand Rule.

Using the Right Hand Rule

By using the Right Hand Rule (RHR), you can determine the direction of the magnetic field in the area around a current-carrying conductor. The RHR states that if you (theoretically) grasp the current-carrying wire with your right hand in such a way that your thumb points in the direction in which the conventional current is flowing, your fingers will point in the direction of the lines of force, or the magnetic field, encircling the wire.

Use the Left Hand Rule (LHR) to determine magnetic poles, and use the Right Hand Rule (RHR) to determine the direction of the magnetic field.

Inductors, Inductance, and Inductive Reactance

An *inductor* is a component that stores energy in the form of a magnetic field. In its simplest form, an inductor is simply a wire loop or coil, usually wound around a magnetic core. *Inductance* is the property of a circuit or component that opposes the inherent change in current of an ac circuit. The moving magnetic field produced by a change in current causes an induced voltage to oppose the original change. Inductance is directly proportional to the number of turns in the coil and depends upon the radius of the coil and the type of material in the core. Figure 6.21 illustrates the schematic symbol for an inductor.

Figure 6.21 Schematic symbol of an inductor.

If you connect an inductor to an AC voltage source, the current through the inductor will change continuously because the inductor offers continuous opposition to the current flowing through it. This opposition is *inductive reactance* and it depends on the rate at which the current is changing and the inductance (ability to oppose) of the inductor.

Transformers

A *transformer* changes, or transforms, an alternating voltage at a given rate to a higher or lower voltage. If you take a simple transformer apart, you will find two separate coils wound around an iron core, because it is essentially an inductor. Figure 6.22 shows the schematic symbol for a transformer.

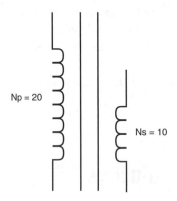

Figure 6.22 Schematic symbol for a transformer.

The alternating voltage from a voltage source (an alternator or a distribution power line) connects to one coil, called the primary winding. The other coil is the secondary winding and does not connect to the primary winding or any voltage source, but connects instead to the load.

To transform an AC input, or affect electromagnetic induction, apply a voltage source to the primary winding. This induces a secondary voltage in the secondary winding, and then the secondary voltage flows through to the load. The voltage that we apply to the primary winding is the primary voltage, and the induced voltage is the secondary voltage.

Voltage transformation depends on the ratio of the number of turns in the primary winding to number of turns in the secondary winding. The formula for determining the transformation ratio is Np/Ns or Np:Ns, where Np is number of turns on the primary and Ns is the number of turns on the secondary so that if Np=200 turns, and Ns=10 turns, then you have a turn ratio of 20:1.

 You need to know how to determine the turns ratio between primary and secondary turns of a transformer. The applicable formula is Np/Ns or Np:Ns.

You should know about two types of transformers: *step-up transformers* and *step-down transformers*. Power companies use both of these types on a large scale. They generate a high alternating voltage, use a step-up transformer to step it up to a still higher voltage, then transmit it through power lines over long distances to the point of usage. At this point, step-down transformers change the high-voltage to a lower value, then the transformed electric power is applied wherever it is needed, at a lower, safer, and more convenient voltage. Transformers may also have an equal number of turns. The purpose of this is to condition the input voltage.

Step-up Transformers

If a transformer has more turns in the secondary winding than in the primary winding, the secondary voltage is higher than the primary voltage and it is a step-up transformer. For example, an alternator generates a voltage of 2300 V but the transmission lines carry the electric power at 230,000 V. A step-up transformer must connect between the alternator and the transmission line and must have 100 times more turns than the primary.

Step-down Transformers

If a transformer has more turns in the primary winding than in the secondary winding, the primary voltage is higher than the secondary voltage. This means that the voltage has been decreased, or "stepped down." For example, the voltage available from the distribution line is 4600 V and the motors used in a plant have a rating of 230 V. A step-down transformer needs to connect between the distribution line and the motor to step down the voltage from 4600 V to 230 V. Because the secondary voltage must be 20 times lower than the primary voltage, the secondary winding of the transformer must have 20 times fewer turns than the primary winding, and the turns ratio will be 20:1.

Rectifiers and Inverters

Two more components that you need to know are *rectifiers* and *inverters*. A rectifier takes an AC input and converts it to DC, such as in a battery charger. An inverter takes a DC input and converts it to AC, such as the inverters that you use when you are traveling to plug your laptop into your car's electrical system.

Electrical Safety

The ASVAB covers a couple of questions on general electrical safety. In the sections that follow, we discuss topics that you need to know for the test.

Discharging a Capacitor

It is important to note that once you have charged a capacitor, it will remain charged even after you have removed the input voltage. How long it remains charged depends on its capacitance. Some capacitors may remain charged for 24 hours or more—some larger capacitors for even years.

 Never touch a capacitor, no matter how small it looks, with your hands, even if you are wearing a grounding strap.

Before you ever work on any electrical or electronic circuit, you must always be sure to discharge the capacitor. To discharge a capacitor safely, you should use a high-wattage resistor comparable to the capacitance of the capacitor, or a capacitor discharge tool.

However, the ASVAB might ask you about discharging a capacitor and gives as the "correct" answer "placing a screwdriver across both the negative and positive terminal of the capacitor." While you need to know the right answer, the practice itself is not sound.

Electrical Fires

An electrical fire is just that: electrical in nature. Electrical fires can result from old, damaged, or overloaded conductor wire. You cannot extinguish an electrical fire with a regular fire extinguisher or with water. To extinguish an electrical fire, use a "C" class fire extinguisher, which is also called a CO_2 or nonconductive extinguisher. If the fire is large, call the fire department immediately. Do not resume using the circuit until you determine the cause of the fire and correct the problem.

Exam Prep Questions

1. What are drawings of electrical circuits called?
   - ❏ A. Sketches
   - ❏ B. Schematics
   - ❏ C. Currents
   - ❏ D. Transistors

2. Which particles are responsible for the generation of an electrical flow?
   - ❏ A. Electrons
   - ❏ B. Protons
   - ❏ C. Neutrons
   - ❏ D. Atoms

3. What principle do you apply to determine voltage across a line?
   - ❏ A. Newton's Law
   - ❏ B. Kepler's Law
   - ❏ C. Fleming's Law
   - ❏ D. Ohm's Law

4. What is current?
   - ❏ A. The amount of power consumption.
   - ❏ B. The rate of the flow of electrons through a circuit.
   - ❏ C. The ohms of an electrical transmission.
   - ❏ D. The magnetic flow of a circuit.

5. Find the current of the circuit in the following figure.

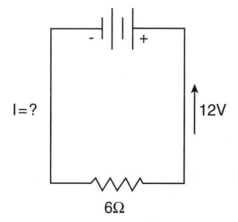

I=?   12V   6Ω

   ❏ A. 2 ohms
   ❏ B. 6 volts
   ❏ C. 6 amps
   ❏ D. 2 amps

6. What is the most common source of DC voltage?
   ❏ A. A battery
   ❏ B. A DC generator
   ❏ C. An Alternator
   ❏ D. A sine wave

7. Which of the following represents the waveform for an AC output?
   ❏ A.
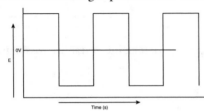

   ❏ B.
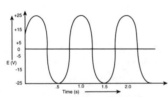

   ❏ C.

   ❏ D.
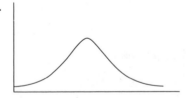

8. What is the most common frequency of AC power that you will see in the United States?
   ❏ A. 1/50s or 50 hertz
   ❏ B. 1/110s or 110 hertz
   ❏ C. 1/60s or 60 hertz
   ❏ D. 450 MHz

9. In a circuit with a current of 2 amps and a resistance of 25 ohms, what is the voltage across the circuit?

❏ A. 50 volts
❏ B. 110 volts
❏ C. 50 farads
❏ D. 110 hertz

10. Calculate the power consumption of an appliance with a rating of 70 volts and 5 amps.

❏ A. 120 watts
❏ B. 350 watts
❏ C. 14 ohms
❏ D. 1:14

11. How are the batteries connected in the following figure?

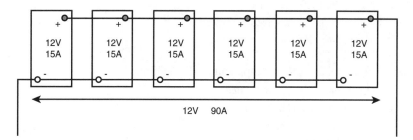

❏ A. In series
❏ B. In sequence
❏ C. In series-parallel
❏ D. In parallel

12. What is the cable insulation color for the "hot" wire in a three-wire Romex cable?

❏ A. Bare
❏ B. Green
❏ C. Black
❏ D. White

13. What is the electronic component in the following figure?

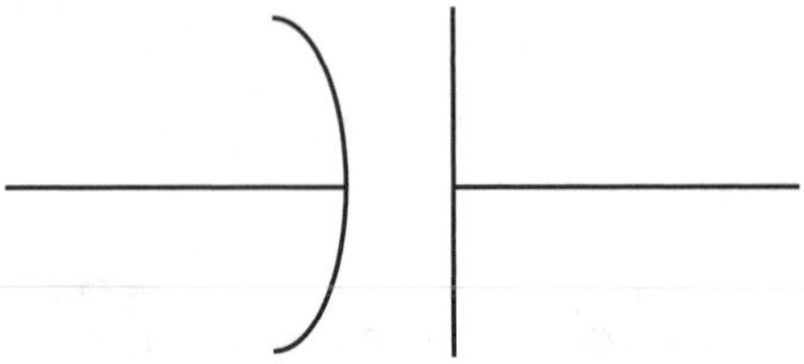

- ❏ A. A capacitor
- ❏ B. A transistor
- ❏ C. A battery
- ❏ D. A conductor

14. What is the property of a conductor?
- ❏ A. Breaks the circuit path
- ❏ B. Allows some electrons to move
- ❏ C. Does not have many free electrons
- ❏ D. Allows free electrons to move readily

15. Fleming's Left Hand Rule helps you to determine what?
- ❏ A. Direction of the magnetic field
- ❏ B. Magnetic poles of a conductor
- ❏ C. Strength of the magnet
- ❏ D. The voltage of a circuit

16. How does inductance affect an AC circuit?
- ❏ A. It opposes current and magnetic field change
- ❏ B. It increases the voltage
- ❏ C. It increases the current
- ❏ D. It has no effect

17. Transformers can perform which of the following?
- ❏ A. Change an input voltage to one of a higher rating
- ❏ B. Change an input voltage to one of a lower rating
- ❏ C. Maintain the same voltage rating, but filter the input
- ❏ D. All of the above

18. What is the turn ratio on the following figure?

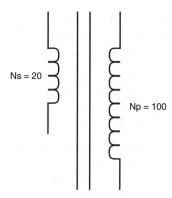

Ns = 20

Np = 100

  ☐ A. 1:5
  ☐ B. 1:40
  ☐ C. 5:1
  ☐ D. 1:1

19. Assuming that your wiring is correctly rated: One of your circuit breakers keeps tripping every time you start your air compressor for more than two minutes. What might be the cause and what is the solution?

  ☐ A. The air compressor draws too much current. Because it works most of the time, just place the breaker back into the On position and keep using it.

  ☐ B. The circuit breaker is faulty; replace it.

  ☐ C. You might have an electrical fault in the wiring or the compressor. Leave that circuit off until you track down the fault and correct it.

  ☐ D. The air compressor draws too much current; get a smaller one.

20. What is the best way to put out an electrical fire?

  ☐ A. Smother it with a blanket
  ☐ B. Use your kitchen fire extinguisher
  ☐ C. Use class "C" extinguisher
  ☐ D. Throw water on it

Exam Prep Answers

1. **Answer B is correct.** Schematics are line drawings of electrical circuits and their components. A sketch is a hand-drawn rendering; current is a measurement in a circuit; a transistor is an electronic component. Therefore, answers A, C, and D are incorrect.

2. **Answer A is correct.** Free electrons are the particles responsible for producing an electrical current. Protons and neutrons comprise the nucleus of an atom. Therefore, answers B, C, and D are incorrect.

3. **Answer D is correct.** You use Ohm's Law to determine voltage across a line. Newton defined the law of gravity; Kepler was an early astronomer; and Fleming defined the rules of magnetism. Therefore, answers A, B, and C are incorrect.

4. **Answer B is correct.** Current is the rate of the flow of electrons and is measured in amps. Power consumption is voltage multiplied by current; Ohms measure resistance in a circuit; and magnetic flow indicates the north and south poles in a circuit. Therefore, answers A, C, and D are incorrect.

5. **The correct answer is D.** Because I (current) = E (voltage)/R (resistance), then $12/6 = 2$ amps. 6 amps is an incorrect rate. Neither volts nor ohms are a measure of current. Therefore, answers A, B, and C are incorrect.

6. **Answer A is correct.** The most common source of DC power is batteries. Although a DC generator creates a DC voltage, it is not as common as a battery, so answer B is incorrect. An alternator puts out AC, so answer C is incorrect. A sine wave is a representation of an AC output, so answer D is also incorrect.

7. **Answer B is correct.** Alternating current generates a sinewave. Answer A is a square wave; C is a DC output from a battery; and D is a Bell curve. Therefore, answers A, C, and D are incorrect.

8. **Answer C is correct.** Although other countries use different frequencies, the United States uses 1/60s or 60 Hz power. Answers A and B are incorrect frequencies and answer C is a common speed for home computer processors.

9. **Answer A is correct.** Because the formula for finding voltage is V = I×Z (or E = I×R), and $2 \times 25 = 50$. 110 volts is not the correct result from this formula, so answer B is incorrect. Neither farads nor hertz are a measurement of voltage. Therefore, answers C and D are also incorrect.

10. **Answer B is correct.** Because the formula for solving power consumption is P = E×I (or P = V×I), and $70 \times 5 = 350$. Answer A indicates

the wrong power consumption; answer C is the result of the formula for resistance (R = E/I); and answer D is a turns ratio.

11. **Answer D is correct.** The batteries are connected in parallel. Answers A, B, and C do not describe the correct connection pattern and are, therefore, incorrect.

12. **Answer C is correct.** In the United States, black is always the "hot" wire. Bare and green wires are ground, and white is neutral, therefore, answers A, B, and D are incorrect.

13. **Answer A is correct.** The diagram shows the schematic symbol for a capcitor. Answers B, C, and D are other components and incorrect.

14. **Answer D is correct.** A conductor's properties allow electrons to move freely, thus enabling the transmission of a current. A switch breaks the circuit, as does a capacitor in a DC circuit; a semiconductor allows the movement of some electrons, and an insulator does not have many free electrons. Therefore, answers A, B, and C are incorrect.

15. **Answer B is correct.** The Left Hand Rule helps you determine the magnetic poles of a conductor, and by extension, the direction of current flow. The Right Hand Rule shows you direction of the magnetic field, so answer A is incorrect. Answers C and D have nothing to do with the Left Hand Rule, so are also incorrect.

16. **Answer A is correct.** Inductance in an AC circuit opposes both the current change and the magnetic field change that stems from the current change. Transformers increase voltage, and transistors can increase both the voltage and current; inductance does have an effect on AC circuits. Therefore, answers B, C, and D are incorrect.

17. **Answer D is correct.** Transformers allow you to step-up, step-down, and filter input voltage.

18. **Answer A is correct.** The turns ratio is 1:5, according to the formula Np/Ns or Np:Ns so that Np=20 and Ns=100, therefore 20/100 = 1/5 or 1:5.

19. **Answer C is correct.** You most likely have an electrical fault somewhere in the path: Find it and fix it to prevent a possible fire or fatal electrical shock. Because the compressor works at first, this indicates that once the current through the line generates heat in the wire, the electrical path creates a short. Resetting the breaker does not fix the problem, therefore answer A is incorrect. The fact that the breaker does not immediately trip indicates electrical feedback or overload in the circuit. It is an indicator of a problem, and replacing the breaker won't fix it. Therefore, answer B is incorrect. Getting a compressor with a smaller draw doesn't solve the problem, it masks it. The reason a smaller compressor might work without tripping the breaker is that a

smaller compressor presents a smaller load on the circuit, and therefore won't generate as much heat as fast as the larger compressor. Therefore, answer D is incorrect and you still have an electrical problem; fix it.

20. **Answer C is correct.** Use a class "C" extinguisher on the fire; it is CO_2-based, not water-based, and is nonconductive. Answer B is incorrect because most kitchen extinguishers are for grease and oil fires, so don't use them. Answer A is incorrect because placing a blanket on the fire also means placing yourself in close proximity to a live electrical charge. Water is highly conductive, and throwing water on an electrical fire will get you killed. Therefore, answer D is incorrect.

Mechanical Comprehension

Terms you'll need to understand:

✓ Power
✓ Work
✓ Horsepower
✓ Efficiency
✓ Mechanical advantage
✓ Torque
✓ Simple and compound machines
✓ Fluid dynamics
✓ Structures
✓ Loads

Techniques you'll need to master:

✓ Knowing how each of the simple machines work
✓ Using the formula to determine mechanical advantage for each type of simple machine
✓ Understanding various structure types and how they support loads
✓ Discerning how fluids respond to differing conditions

The Mechanical Comprehension (MK) module of the ASVAB tests your understanding of mechanical principles, structural support, and material properties. The questions in this section of the test gauge your knowledge of simple machines, compound machines, mechanical motion, and fluid dynamics. Although it may all sound a little complicated, you will have learned most of it in high school.

The MK contains 25 questions (the CAT-ASVAB has 16 questions), which you will need to answer in 19 minutes. To achieve your 70%, you need to answer 18 questions correctly; to achieve 80%, you need to answer 20 questions correctly. Like the Electronics Information module, much of the MK module is sheer knowledge. Although you can guess some of the questions correctly without knowing the principle, most of the questions are ones for which you need to know the applicable formulas and principles to get the right answer. The good news is that you have a little more time per question than you did in the EI module; however, you still need to move as quickly through the questions as you can. Again, pay attention to the Cram Sheet items.

All forms of motion fall into the branch of science and physics called mechanics. Because the basis of all mechanics is that of machines and motion, we need to begin our discussion with an overview of principles that govern them both.

Mechanical Principles

When you use a machine, even your fingers, you can see two forces at work: the applied force, called effort (E), and the resisting force, called resistance (R).

As an exercise, lay your pencil on your desk, and then pick it up using your forefinger and thumb. Watch your hand and arm carefully as you slowly reach down, squeeze the pencil, and pick it up. You have just witnessed several physical and mechanical principles at work: gravity, Newton's first law of motion, conservation of energy, and lever action with a mechanical advantage. In this case, the pencil was the resistance force, and your fingers and arm were the effort force.

In many cases, machines help you to use more force than simple strength will allow; this is called a mechanical advantage. In essence, if you have a mechanical advantage (more on that later in this chapter) a machine multiplies the input effort to help you overcome the load resistance.

Work and Mechanical Energy

Work is such a commonly used word, that in its frequent usage we tend to forget what it means. Energy is the potential for work, and falls into two categories: potential (inactive energy) and kinetic (active energy). Mechanical energy is matter in motion or with the potential of motion. This matter can be large, as of that in a machine, or as minute as the atomic level.

Work, by definition, is the movement of an object by a force. We use foot-pounds (ft lb) to measure mechanical work, and this formula to calculate work:

Work(W) = force(f) × distance(d) or W = fd

Let's put this formula into practical application: If you lift a 20 lb. rock 3 feet from the ground, what is the amount of work that you have done? Because W = 20 lb × 3 ft; W = 60 ft lb

Let's take that one step further: You know that work input is the effort that you put into a machine, calculated by effort force x distance; work output is the work that the machine does, calculated by resistance force x distance. The Law of Work states that the work put into a machine is equal to the work received from the machine under ideal conditions, or in equation form:

(effort force)(effort distance) = (resistance force)(resistance distance)

Therefore, you should understand that both sides of the equal sign should come out the same, or that work input will equal work output. Let's use Figure 7.1 to estimate how much effort force (input) you need to lift the box.

In Figure 7.1, the work input needed to lift the 240-pound box one foot off the floor is 60 pounds times 4 feet, or 240 ft lb of work, so that fd = fd is reflected by 240(1) = 60(4), or 240 = 240. Under ideal conditions the amount of work is 240 ft lbs of work.

If you have an equation that requires you to calculate how much effort that you need to apply, you must solve for the unknown variable, which is effort force represented by x. So if you have a box that weighs 400 lbs. that you must lift 2 feet, and you have an input distance of 5 feet, your formula will look like this: 400(2) = 5x; 800 = 5x; and 160 = x. So, you require 160 pounds of input force to move the box.

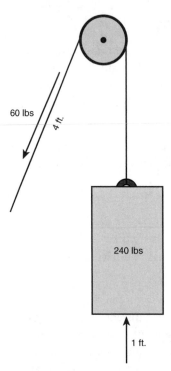

60 lbs

4 ft.

240 lbs

1 ft.

Figure 7.1   Calculating work.

NOTE

You must understand how to calculate work for simple machines. You use this formula to calculate work: work output = work input.

Power (P) is the rate of doing work, and time (t) is an important element in calculating the rate of work. Power is directly related to work such that more work in the same amount of time means greater power. As an example, by using a backhoe to dig a hole, you can do much more work in the same amount of time than you could if you were using a shovel: That means that the backhoe has more power. You calculate power with this formula:

$P = W/t$

Time is inversely related to power so that the more time it takes a machine to do a certain amount of work, the less power is involved, and vice versa.

Horsepower (hp) is a common way of measuring power. A one-horsepower engine does 550 ft lbs of work in 1 second. Hence, if an engine has 3 hp, then it has the power to do the work of 1650 ft lb per second ($3 \times 550 = 1650$). Further, horsepower calculated per minute equals 33,000 ft lb per minute (550 lbs. $\times$ 60 sec.).

Mechanical Advantage

Mechanical advantage (MA) is the force-multiplying ability that machines provide, and it indicates the ratio of the resistance force to the applied (or effort) force.

You need to understand how to solve for mechanical advantage. On the exam you may be called to solve for either the ideal MA or the actual MA. The formulas are: IMA = input distance/output distance; AMA = force output/force input. See what information the question provides and solve accordingly: if it provides distances, then solve for IMA; if it provides force amounts, then solve for AMA.

The MA tells you the number of times that a machine multiplies your input effort, which means that a machine with an MA of 4 multiplies the input effort 4 times. Thus, the ratio of input effort to output effort is 1:4 and the machine operator has to apply only 1/4 as much force as he would if he did not use the machine. The formula that you can use to estimate mechanical advantage is

MA = R/E

For example, if a man is using 70 lbs. of effort to lift a 280 lb. box, to find the MA, you substitute the values for R and E, like this: MA = R/E; MA = 280/70; MA = 4. In this case, the machine multiplied the input effort by 4 times, for a work ratio of 1:4. Clearly, it is easier for the man to apply an effort of 70 pounds to the machine than for him to apply an effort of 280 pounds to the box.

However, because of the decreased input effort, the input distance must increase to accomplish the same amount of work, because according to the Law of Conservation of Energy, energy cannot be spontaneously created. In other words, the man must back up and exert his 70 pounds of effort over a longer distance than if he just picked up the 280-pound box. But, by applying 70 pounds of effort over 4 times the distance (according to our 1:4 ratio), he can easily lift the box with only 70 pounds of input effort. A shorter work distance will require the man to exert more input effort.

There are two forms of mechanical advantage, which might be on the exam:

➤ Ideal mechanical advantage (IMA)—Calculates mechanical advantage in an ideal, no-friction environment; the formula for IMA is

MA = input distance/output distance

➤ Actual mechanical advantage (AMA)—Takes into consideration the effects of friction on a work process; the formula for AMA is

MA = force input/force output

It sounds complicated, but it's not. Just remember that on the exam, the question will give you all the information that you need to easily solve the problem.

Friction

Under normal conditions, some of the effort force goes to overcome friction within the machine. This affects your mechanical advantage and means a decrease in overall efficiency of the machine. Friction prevents any machine from producing as much work as is applied to it, the result of which is that work input is always greater than work output. The effect of friction in a pulley system is called drag, and you can estimate drag by finding the difference between the work input and the work output.

Some of your test questions will ask you to calculate, as stated previously, the actual mechanical advantage and other questions, as the next section discusses, will ask you to calculate efficiency. These types of questions take into consideration the effects of external resistance, like friction.

Calculating Efficiency

If 75% of the input to a machine is available as output, and 25% is used in overcoming friction within the machine, then the machine has an efficiency of 75%. Because of friction, work input will always be greater than work output, meaning that no machine is 100% efficient.

Some simple machines are very efficient because they have few or no moving parts to produce friction. The efficiency of a well-designed lever may come close to 100%, and some inclined planes can have an efficiency of more than 90%. On the other hand, the efficiency of a block and tackle may vary between 40% and 60%, and the wedge is the most inefficient of the simple machines.

You can reduce friction by polishing surfaces that come into contact, using wheels or bearings between moving surfaces to allow them to roll past each other rather than slide, and lubricating the machine's moving parts.

You can calculate a machine's efficiency by comparing its work output to its work input and multiplying by 100 (the ideal efficiency rate).

The efficiency of a machine is equal to the ratio of its output (resistance multiplied by the distance it is moved) to its input (effort multiplied by the distance through which it is exerted), and is equal to the ratio of the AMA to the IMA. In short, it is the ratio of useful work output to expended energy input. The formula looks like this:

Efficiency = work output/work input × 100%

You have already learned the formula for calculating work, which is W = fd. So, look at the efficiency formula for machines like this:

Efficiency = (force output) (output distance)/(force input) (input distance) × 100%

Therefore, if you have a work output of 125 ft lbs and a work input 250 ft lbs, your efficiency will be 125/250, multiplied by 100%, which is an efficiency rating of 50%.

On the test, you will also need to address electrical efficiency, which is a little different from mechanical efficiency, but operates on the same premise. To calculate electrical efficiency, use this formula:

Efficiency = power output/power input × 100%

For example, if you have a 10 hp engine with a full output, but the engine itself operates at only 85% efficiency, what is the power input? You can use a diagram similar to the Ohm's Law triangle, as Figure 7.2 shows, to reorient the problem.

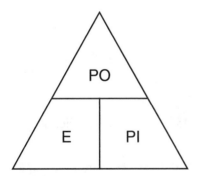

Figure 7.2 Efficiency triangle.

You are looking for the power input, so cover that value on the triangle to see what your equation will be. In this case, you are solving for the power input, so you will place that to the left of the equal sign. Now, convert the efficiency rating to a decimal (.85), plug in the known values, and solve so that your problem looks like this:

PI =PO/E or PI = 10/.85; PI = 11.76

So, your power input is 11.76 hp to make a machine with an efficiency of 85% run at its full 10 hp rating.

Principle of Moments and Torque

The principle of moments dictates that you can maintain equilibrium if the moments (forces) tending to clockwise rotation are equal to the forces tending to counterclockwise rotation. These moments of force are commonly referred to as torque. When equilibrium exists, there is an equality of torque (moments), which is expressed by this equation:

(weight of A)(distance of A) = (weight of B)(distance of B)

Figure 7.3 illustrates a platform balance. The clockwise torque is the product of the weight (resistance) of A (25 lbs.) and its distance (6 inches) from the fulcrum. The counterclockwise torque is the weight of B (30 lbs.) multiplied by its distance (5 inches) from the fulcrum.

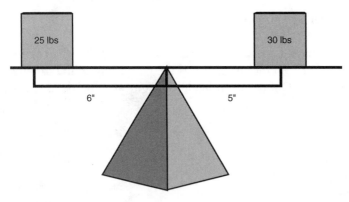

Figure 7.3 Platform balance.

According to the formula (30)(5) = (25)(6); 150 = 150. Because the torques are equal and opposite, the lever balances.

In another type of problem, you might be asked to calculate how much input effort you need to apply to counteract an opposing torque. Figure 7.4 provides an example of such.

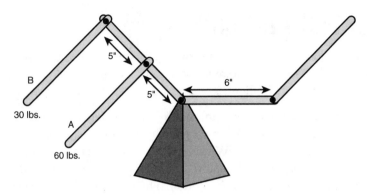

Figure 7.4 Bell crank lever.

Let's take this one step at a time by eliminating B (and its distance) from the equation. That leaves you with only torque A (60 lbs. resistance) and its distance, which is 5 inches. Find out how much input effort you need to counteract the counterclockwise torque by using this formula, substituting effort for weight and x for the unknown input effort:

(resistance A)(distance A) = (input effort)(distance of effort), or

(60)(5) = 6x; 300 = 6x; 50 = x.

That means that you need to exert 50 lbs. of input effort on the crank to counteract the torque of A. Now, let's add B to the equation. The counterclockwise torque is the sum of A and B, which is 90 pounds, and the distance is the sum of the distances of A and B from the fulcrum, which is 10 inches. Use the preceding formula to find the amount of clockwise torque needed to equalize the lever. You should have come up with 150 lbs. as the needed counteracting torque.

When you have more than one force acting on a machine, remember that the total torque is equal to the sum of the forces.

In most problems like this one, the question will specify three of the four quantities in the equation and the fourth will be unknown, meaning that you need to find the unknown value to make the two torques equal.

Mechanical Motion

Mechanics is the branch of physics that deals with motion, and the same laws that govern the motion of a solar system also govern the motion of an airplane in flight and a baseball in flight.

All motion is relative to a reference point, and we use the term position to refer to the location of an object. When we give the position of an object, it is in relation to its reference point. When an object that is located in one position changes positions, then it has moved. When an object has a continuous change of position, the object is in motion. The moving object may be moving differently in relation to its reference, or not at all in relation.

For example, a book lying on a desk is seemingly motionless. In reference to the desk and the objects around it, it is motionless. However, it actually possesses at least four kinds of motion because it shares in the following:

➤ The earth's rotation about its axis

➤ The earth's revolution about the sun

➤ The motion of the solar system

➤ The motion of the galaxy through space

Therefore, technically, the book is in motion and motion itself is relative to the conditions of the situation. The next step is to govern what the rules of motion apply.

Forces of Motion

In the 17th century, Sir Isaac Newton first introduced the three fundamental laws relating particle motion to applied forces. A particle is an object in mechanics that has mass but no size. A particle can be a point mass, even though it might represent something as large as a planet or as small as a pinprick. In particular, a particle cannot rotate, nor can it be subjected to any moments (torque) because it has no lever arms.

Mechanical engineers today still use the laws proposed by Sir Isaac Newton, which apply to all objects and particles, and are as follows:

➤ First Law of Motion—"An object at rest tends to remain at rest unless acted upon by an external force; an object in motion tends to remain in motion at the same speed and in the same direction unless acted upon by an external force."

The tendency of matter to resist changes in motion is inertia, which is directly related to the mass of an object.

➤ Second Law of Motion—"The acceleration of an object acted upon by a force is directly related to the strength of the force and inversely related to the object's mass; the acceleration occurs in the direction of the force."

The acceleration of an object is directly related to the strength of the force applied to it and inversely related to the mass of the object. We can restate this law like this:

Acceleration = Force/Mass, or Force = mass × acceleration (F = ma)

➤ Third Law of Motion—"For every action, there is an equal and opposite reaction."

This means that all forces operate in pairs. Understanding this is fundamental to understanding concepts like equilibrium and resistance. We have already touched lightly on this in our discussion of moments and torque.

A *force* (F) is any effort that can push, pull, or rotate another object. This turning ability depends not only on the strength of the force, but also on the distance (d) away from the object, which is stated as M = Fd.

In this statement, d is the perpendicular distance between the impact point and the line of action of the force. The units of a moment-M (torque) are the product of force and distance and are often expressed as foot pounds (ft lb).

If you apply a force to an object at rest, then the object will tend to translate, rotate, or both. For example, if you apply force to the midpoint of a free, uniform bar, and that force slides the bar so that every point moves an equal distance at the same time, then the bar translates. If you apply the same force to some other point that causes the bar to turn, then the bar translates and rotates.

In mechanics, there are several physical properties that come into play as we seek to solve various mechanical and physical mysteries and how forces affect objects. The scalar, vector, and tensor are fundamental to understanding mechanics and physical properties of materials and objects.

Vectors and Vector Quantities

A diagram may represent a vector quantity with an arrow, called a vector. The length of the arrow, which is drawn to a convenient scale, represents the magnitude (force or speed), and the head of the arrow represents the direction the object is moving. Examples of vector quantities are as follows:

➤ Velocity

➤ Force

➤ Momentum

➤ Spin

➤ Displacement

You can use vectors to solve different types of problems that relate to motion. For lack of a better term, we can call vector quantities two-dimensional, where at least two forces are at work in the movement. For example, if an illustration shows a jet and its corresponding vector, then the length of the vector represents the speed of the jet and the arrow indicates the direction.

Resultants

A resultant is a vector that shows the combined effect of two or more vectors. Therefore, if an object displays both positive and negative motion, the resultant will be the total of those vectors. The process of finding the resultant by adding the initial vectors and calculating the magnitude and direction of the resultant is called vector addition. Vectors are most useful when two vector quantities interact at an angle. However, you can use vector addition to find the resultant even when the vectors do not act at right angles to each other.

Scalar Quantities

Whereas velocity is an example of a vector quantity, physical quantities such as speed that have magnitude (amount or force) but no direction, are scalar quantities. Examples of scalar quantities are

➤ Speed

➤ Work

➤ Length

➤ Area

➤ Mass

➤ Energy

➤ Electric charge

To use geometrical terminology again, scalar quantities are one-dimensional, where only one force is at work against the object. For example, if a force is applied to an object, then the only consideration is the effect of that effort.

If the object is unaffected, then no work has been done.

Tensors

A tensor is a vector quantity described only by referring to more than three components or vectors—three dimensional, if you will. Tensors are important in the theory of elasticity, where they describe stress and strain on an object or material. In mechanics, a tensor refers to the stress-strain relationship for materials whose measurable values are not consistent along different axes. In these materials, stress in one direction creates strains in other directions. Technically, both vectors and scalars are also tensors: a scalar is a zero-order tensor, a vector is a first-order tensor, and a matrix (what we are calling a tensor) is a third-order tensor.

Motion and Mechanical Laws

To measure motion scientifically, you must be able to describe it. Several terms are helpful in describing motion, and we discuss those terms in the following sections.

Speed

Because motion involves changing locations, you can determine how far an object has moved if you know the distance it has traveled, or the length of the path along which it traveled. *Speed* is the distance traveled in a given amount of time, in other words, it is the rate of motion. The more distance an object covers in a certain amount of time, the greater its speed. You calculate speed by dividing the distance traveled by the time elapsed, or:

Speed = distance/time or s = d/t

There are two instances of speed that you can calculate, which are

➤ Average speed is the overall distance that an object travels divided by the rate of travel, or an average of the speed, even though the object will travel at the average speed only occasionally.

➤ Instantaneous speed is the speed of a moving object at any given instant in the path. We measure this speed with a speedometer.

Velocity

Normally, we use the term *velocity* as a synonym for speed. However, speed refers only to the distance that an object covers in a given amount of time, whereas velocity takes into account the direction in which the object is moving. Thus, when we speak of the velocity of a moving object, we are referring to both its speed (how fast it is going) and its direction (where it's headed).

Acceleration

Experience tells us that objects do not move randomly on their own; rather, that an outside force must provide the push or pull necessary to move it. When an object is moving with a constant velocity, neither its speed nor its direction changes. However, objects do not always travel at constant velocity, and they often speed up, slow down, or change direction. We call a change in velocity *acceleration*.

Although the word acceleration is commonly used to mean an increase in velocity, physicists use the term to refer to any change in velocity, whether it is an increase or decrease in speed or a change in direction, and negative acceleration = deceleration.

According to Newton's First Law of Motion, an object must be acted upon by an outside force to create a change in acceleration. Understanding that, you can measure acceleration with the formula a = Vf–Vi/t, or

Acceleration = final velocity–initial velocity/time

Momentum

Momentum is a vector quantity that represents the product of the mass and velocity of an object (momentum = mass x velocity). When an external force acts upon an object in motion, it creates changes in the object's momentum. An object may have both linear momentum, because of its linear motion, and angular momentum because of its rotation. The angular momentum is a product of the instantaneous linear momentum and the distance.

Equilibrium

Equilibrium is a state of balance or the balance of forces acting on an object. When an object is in equilibrium, there is no tendency to change. When no force is moving an object in a line, the object is in translational equilibrium, and when no force is making an object turn, the object is in rotational equilibrium. An object at rest that is also in a state of equilibrium is in static equilibrium. A state of equilibrium does not mean that no forces act on the object, but that those forces are in a state of balance. This is an important concept in determining moments of force and torque.

Simple and Compound Machines

Now that we have discussed the influences on machines and the principles that govern them, let's move our discussion to the different types of machines.

A *machine* is any mechanism that makes work easier by helping to push or pull against a resistant force. Machines can multiply the force that you apply, allowing for less input effort. Alternatively, machines change the direction of the input effort or multiply the speed or distance of the resistance movement.

 You must know the different simple machine types and be able to calculate the mechanical advantage of each.

There are two types of machines: *Simple* and *compound*. We discuss the simple machines in the sections that follow, and compound machines are those that consist of two or more simple machines. An example of a simple machine is a pulley. An example of a compound machine that uses a pulley is a lawnmower.

All complex machines have, as their basis, two or more simple machines that have existed for thousands of years. We discuss the six types of simple machines in the following sections. The simple machines are these: the lever, the wheel and axle, the pulley, the inclined plane, the wedge, and the screw.

Levers

You might not be aware, but you use levers every day: opening your car door, chopping vegetables, and even waving hello to your neighbor. The lever is one of the most versatile of all simple machines because it multiplies force or speed without necessarily changing the direction of effort. Simply put, a *lever* is a rigid bar or beam resting upon a fulcrum (pivot point). You can calculate mechanical advantage of a lever in any of several ways:

➤ By dividing the length of the effort arm by the length of the resistance arm (MA = effort arm/resistance arm)

➤ By dividing the distance the effort moves by the distance the resistance moves (MA = effort distance/resistance distance)

➤ By dividing the resistance force by the effort force (MA = resistance force/effort force)

Let's take the following example: A 50 lb. force applied at the end of a 4.5 ft. crowbar barely moves a 400 lb. rock located under the opposite end of the bar. Where must the fulcrum be located? First, apply the principle of moments (torque), wherein the counterclockwise movement is equal to the clockwise movement or, (rock weight)(distance to fulcrum) = (applied force)(distance from fulcrum)

If x is the distance of the rock from the fulcrum, then you can solve it like this:

(400 lbs.)(x ft.) = (50 lbs.)(4.5–x)ft
400x = 225–50x
400x + 50x = 225
450x = 225
x = 0.5 ft. or 6 inches

Now, you can apply the formula for mechanical advantage, as follows:

MA = effort distance/resistance distance, or MA = 48/6; MA=8

You might have a variety of lever-mechanical advantage questions on the test, and no two of them may be the same. So, become familiar with the different ways to solve MA for levers.

We classify levers according to where the input and output forces are exerted in relation to the fulcrum. We discuss the three types of levers in the sections below.

First Class Levers

First class levers have the input (effort) and output (load or resistance) forces on either side of a fulcrum. In this type, you apply the effort force to one end and the resistance arm moves the resistance force, reversing the direction of the effort force. Figure 7.5 illustrates a first class lever. Examples of first class levers include a see saw, a crowbar, a pole used as a lever, and the oars of a rowboat. Scissors are an example of a compound first class lever.

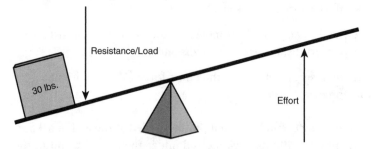

Figure 7.5 First class lever.

The part of the lever that lies between the effort force and the fulcrum is the effort arm; the part between the fulcrum and the load is the load arm, or resistance arm. To calculate mechanical advantage of a first class lever, use the formula that you have learned already, which is:

(resistance A)(distance A) = (resistance B)(resistance B)

If both arms are the same length, the lever does not multiply the input force in any way, and you need to apply an effort equal to the load to move it. That is, 30 pounds of load requires 30 pounds of effort to move it. Because both sides of the equation are equal, then there is no mechanical advantage.

However, if the effort arm is longer than the load arm, then the lever will multiply the effort force, requiring you to exert less effort to move the load than the resistance weighs, thus creating a mechanical advantage. If the effort arm is shorter, then the lever will multiply the effort speed, but will not multiply input effort. By adjusting how far the fulcrum is from the load, you can control the mechanical advantage. The closer it is to the load, the more force you need to apply.

A special application of the first class lever is a torsion spring. You have probably seen them before; a spring with opposing arms or hooks on each end. In this case, the fulcrum, like other first class levers, is in the middle, the resistance is at one end, and the effort arm is the other end. The torsion spring operates by coiling and uncoiling so that it transmits a twist effort instead of a pull or push.

Second Class Levers

A second class lever places the fulcrum at one end of the lever, and you apply the effort force at the other end with the resistance between the effort and the fulcrum. These levers multiply the effort force but cause the load to move in the same direction as the force is applied; that is, it does not change the effort direction. Figure 7.6 shows a second class lever.

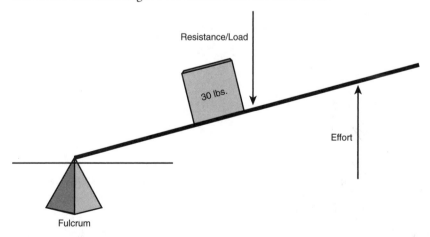

Figure 7.6 Second class lever.

Have you ever tried to move a heavy rock or log with a lever? Then you have used a second class lever. The fulcrum of the lever is the point where it touches the ground, and the load (the rock or log) is between the fulcrum and the point where you are exerting the upward effort.

As with a first class lever, the distance of the load from the fulcrum determines the mechanical advantage. If you want to move a very large load with a small applied force, you must put the load very close to the fulcrum. You use the same formula to estimate mechanical advantage for second class levers as you did for first class levers.

A wheelbarrow is a good example of a second class lever: When you lift the handles of the wheelbarrow (input effort), the load (resistance), located between the effort and the fulcrum, moves up. A nutcracker and a jar opener are also examples of second class levers. Because the fulcrum is at one end, the applied force is at the other, and the load is in between.

Third Class Levers

Third class levers place the fulcrum at one end of the lever, the load at the other end, and you apply the effort between the fulcrum and the load. Third class levers always multiply distance and speed without changing the direction of the effort. That means that the lever will always push the object farther, or faster, than the effort force. Examples of a third class lever include a baseball bat, yard rake, and broom. Figure 7.7 illustrates a third class lever.

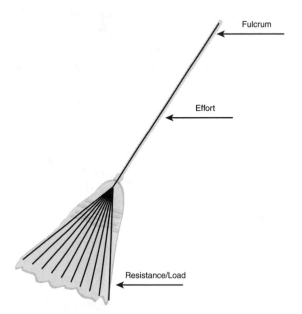

Figure 7.7 Third class lever.

Because the effort is greater than the resistance, this type of lever gives you a mechanical advantage of less than 1, a fractional mechanical advantage. Therefore, the effort must always be greater than the resistance. To find the mechanical advantage, use this formula:

MA = effort arm/resistance arm

So, if you place a 50 pound load, 4 feet from the fulcrum and you are exerting effort 2 feet from the fulcrum, MA = 2/4, or 1/2. That means that you have to exert 100 pounds of effort, or twice as much effort as resistance to move the load.

Wheel and Axle

Essentially, the wheel and axle is a lever that rotates around a center point, which acts as the fulcrum, and has arms of unequal length. The arms are the radius of the wheel and of the axle. The larger, outside wheel rotates around the smaller, inside wheel, which serves as the axle. When the wheel turns, the axle also turns, and the axle multiplies the effort applied to the wheel. Figure 7.8 illustrates a wheel and axle.

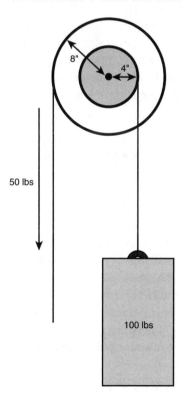

Figure 7.8 Wheel and axle.

Although the effects of friction impair the overall efficiency of a wheel and axle (as compared to a lever), you still don't need to apply as much force to move a load as you do with a lever, but you apply the effort over a greater distance from the fulcrum as compared to the distance of the load. In addition, a wheel and axle can move a load much farther than a lever can.

You can apply the effort or resistance on either the outer wheel or the inner wheel (axle). Depending on where you apply effort and resistance, the wheel and axle can multiply force or multiply speed. We can calculate mechanical advantage by using this equation:

MA = input radius/output radius

The wheel and axle combines the effects of the pulley and the lever by redirecting the force applied through a rope or cable and increasing or reducing the magnitude of the force. The mechanical advantage of a wheel is equal to the ratio of the radius of the wheel to the radius of the axle. You can use the inverse of this ratio to determine the effort needed to balance the load as well as the distance.

MA = load/effort

Suppose the axle radius is 4 inches and the wheel radius is 8 inches. You can determine the ratio between effort and load in the manner described above. A 50-pound force applied to the wheel will balance a 100 pound weight suspended from the axle. The mechanical advantage of this machine is 2. The weight of the object is twice as large as the force required to balance it.

Examples of the wheel and axle that multiply force are a doorknob, a screwdriver, a winch, a windlass, and the pedals and front sprocket of a bicycle. Examples that multiply distance and speed are the rear wheel and sprocket of a bicycle, the blade of a lawnmower, and an airplane propeller.

Pulleys

A *pulley* consists of a belt, rope, cable, or chain wrapped around a single, grooved wheel. Depending on how it is arranged, a pulley may or may not multiply the effort. A pulley can also reverse the effort force applied to the rope; a single pulley mounted on a yardarm allows you to pick up a box by pulling down on a rope. If you have a pulley system, the smaller pulleys will turn at a greater speed than the larger pulleys. There are three pulley configurations that you might see: a fixed pulley, a movable pulley, and a block and tackle, described in the following sections.

Fixed Pulley

A *fixed pulley* does not move with the resistance and does not multiply effort, but it does change the direction of the effort, as Figure 7.9 shows. It has a mechanical advantage of 1 and work output will always equal work input. That means that because the forces of effort and resistance are equal, the distances over which effort is exerted and the resistance is moved are equal.

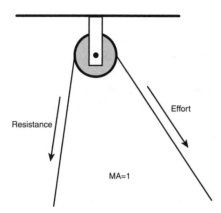

Figure 7.9   Fixed pulley.

Movable Pulley

A *movable pulley* attaches to the resistance and moves with it. This type of pulley multiplies effort, but does not change direction of the effort, as Figure 7.10 shows.

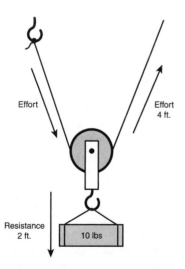

Figure 7.10   Movable pulley.

A movable pulley enables you to apply an effort (discounting friction) of only half of the resistance force, but you must apply the effort from twice the distance as you want to move the resistance. For example, although you would exert a force of only 5 pounds to raise a 10 pound box 2 feet with a moveable pulley, you would have to pull 4 feet of rope through the pulley. Calculate the mechanical advantage by dividing the effort distance by the resistance distance, or MA = effort distance/load distance.

Block and Tackle

A *block and tackle*, also called a pulley system, is a combination of one or more fixed pulleys and one or more movable pulleys. In a block and tackle, the movable pulleys multiply the effort force while the fixed pulleys change the direction of the effort force. Figure 7.11 shows a block and tackle system.

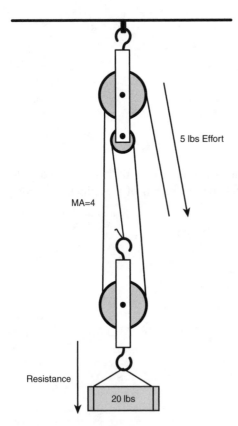

Figure 7.11 Block and tackle.

A block and tackle system provides considerable mechanical advantage, because it increases the effort by the number of times the force changes direction. You can increase the number of pulley wheels indefinitely to get a higher and higher mechanical advantage. By counting the number of ropes that support the resistance in a block and tackle, you can easily determine the mechanical advantage.

For example, a block and tackle with four segments of rope supporting the resistance multiples the effort force by 4, thus the mechanical advantage is 4. That means, if 4 segments support a resistance of 20 pounds, you must apply an effort of only 5 pounds to the rope to raise the resistance, or

Effort = R/MA; Effort = 20/4; Effort = 5 pounds

However, that means you must also pull the rope 4 feet for every foot you move the load.

> When calculating effort (sometimes phrased tension), remember to count the segments of the pulley system and use that number to divide into the load weight to determine the amount of effort that you need to apply. If the question entails a bosun's chair, keep in mind that the chair itself has two segments of rope.

Inclined Planes

An inclined plane, or ramp, consists of a sloping platform that allows us to use a smaller effort to raise a load by providing for a gradual climb, as Figure 7.12 shows. To raise a load vertically, you must apply a force equal to the weight of the load.

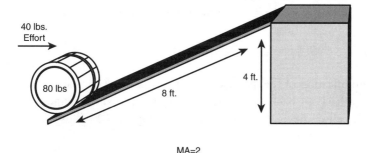

MA=2

Figure 7.12   Inclined plane.

Although using an inclined plane is slower than a vertical lift, you can apply an effort smaller than the weight of the load to raise an object, and the longer the ramp is, the less effort that you must exert. Although lifting a load straight up requires more force over a shorter distance, in the end, you do the same amount of work in either approach.

To calculate the IMA of an inclined plane, you divide the length of the incline (effort distance) by the vertical rise (resistance distance), called a run-to-rise ratio. The mechanical advantage increases as the slope of the incline decreases, but then the load will have to be moved a greater distance. To find the ideal mechanical advantage of an inclined plane, use this equation:

MA = effort distance/resistance distance

The actual mechanical advantage of an inclined plane is equal to the ratio of the load lifted to the force applied, or

MA = resistance force/effort force

However, for calculation, we assume the inclined plane to be frictionless, and if you discount friction, then the work done using an inclined plane is exactly the same as the work done in lifting the load directly.

For example, if you lift an 80-pound barrel onto a platform 4 feet high, it would require an effort of 80 pounds. But if you roll the barrel up an inclined plane 8 feet long, it requires an effort of only 40 pounds. Although the total work of 320 ft lb is the same either way, the mechanical advantage is 1:2, or 2. Remember that the longer the inclined plane, the greater the mechanical advantage, so rolling that same barrel up a ramp that is 16 feet long requires only 20 pounds of effort for a mechanical advantage of 1:4, or 4.

Mountain switchbacks are inclined planes that reduce the effort of a car engine, but increase the distance the car must travel to get up the mountain. Other examples of inclined planes are gangplanks and stairs.

Wedges

A *wedge* is a modification of the inclined plane principle, and consists of two inclined planes, back to back. A wedge multiplies force and changes the direction of the effort from the top to the sides. Figure 7.13 illustrates a wedge.

The mechanical advantage of a wedge depends on the angle of the thin end. The smaller the angle, the less the force required to move the wedge a given distance through, say, a log. At the same time, the amount of splitting is decreased with smaller angles. To find the mechanical advantage of a wedge, use this equation:

MA = length/thickness

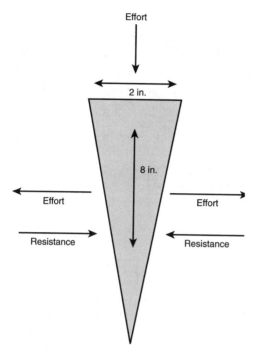

Figure 7.13   A wedge.

For example, if you are using a wedge that is 8 inches long and 2 inches wide, then MA = 8/2 or 4. Long, slender wedges require less effort to overcome resistance than short, thick ones. You use a wedge to split or separate objects (splitting a log), for lifting heavy objects short distances, or for holding objects in place (shims under your wood floor, in your stair risers, or around your window frames).

The end of a nail is also a wedge, and as you force the nail into a block of wood, its sloping surfaces make the job a more gradual one and you need not hammer as hard to get the nail in. Knives, axes, stakes, needles, pins, chisels, and ice picks are among the most common wedges.

Screws

A *screw* consists of an inclined plane wrapped in a spiral around a solid cylinder. Each revolution of the plane around the cylinder is a turn, which may run either clockwise or counterclockwise. The ridges formed by the inclined plane are the threads and the vertical distance from any given point on one thread to a corresponding point on the succeeding thread is the pitch.

Using a Micrometer

A *micrometer* measures drill bits, screws, and other small items. Micrometers come in several different sizes: 1/2 inch, 1 inch, 1 1/2 inches, and 2 inches. The size of the micrometer is usually indicated on the frame. Figure 7.14 shows an outside micrometer. There are several types of micrometers, which we discuss more fully in the Automotive Information chapter.

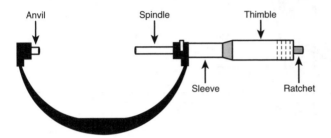

Figure 7.14   A micrometer.

You place the item to be measured between the anvil and spindle. The thimble is rotated until the parts make contact. Then you read the measurement using the graduated markings found on the sleeve and the thimble. The micrometer is marked like this:

➤ The sleeve is divided into ten equal segments, and each segment equals one-tenth of an inch.

➤ Each tenth of an inch segment is further divided into four equal segments of twenty-five thousandths of an inch.

➤ Each twenty-five thousandth of an inch segment is divided into twenty-five equal segments on the thimble.

➤ Each segment on the thimble is equal to one-thousandth of an inch.

So, if your micrometer measures from 0 to 1 inch, your first reading will be 0. Next, look at the sleeve. The last number that you can see is 1, so that is equal to one-tenth of an inch (.1) and you have 0.1 so far. After that, look at the twenty-five thousandth segments. You can see three lines, which equals seventy-five thousandths of an inch (.075). The thimble reading is 11. That equals eleven thousandths of an inch (.011). Now add everything together and the reading is one hundred eighty six thousandths (0.186). Although it seems simple, you may not get the hang of reading a micrometer the first time.

Turnbuckles

A *turnbuckle* is a unique form of screw that provides leverage on both ends, which Figure 7.15 shows. Normally, turnbuckles attach between two segments of rope, cable, or wire to remove slack from the line between two resistances or a fixed point and a resistance load. The way it works is that it has two "screws," one on either end; one end has right-hand threads and turns clockwise to tighten, whereas the other end has left-hand threads and turns counterclockwise to tighten. To calculate mechanical advantage, remember that you need to take both "machines" into account.

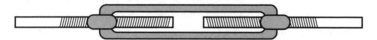

Figure 7.15 Turnbuckle.

Jackscrews

A screw can provide a tremendous mechanical advantage because it allows you to exert an effort force over a very long distance to move the resistance a very short distance. To lift a heavy object, you must use a machine with a large mechanical advantage, such as a jack screw, which Figure 7.16 illustrates.

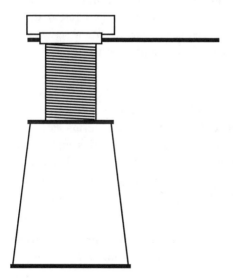

Figure 7.16 Jack screw.

Jackscrews combine the advantages of both the screw and the lever in that a lever turns a screw to lift the load. A *jackscrew* consists of two threaded surfaces; the inner surface of a hollow cylinder (the base of the jack) is threaded, and the outer surface of the internal screw is also threaded with the same pitch as the internal screw. As you rotate the lever on the top of the internal screw, the external screw and the internal screw work against each other to lift the load. Although a jackscrew can lift very heavy loads, you must turn the lever that turns the jackscrew many times to raise the load a very short distance.

However, because there is much friction in the screw operation, the input effort is always greater than the output and the efficiency is small. On the other hand, the effort necessary to turn the handle is considerably small as compared to the enormous weight of the load. In the case of a jackscrew, however, the inherent friction is actually an advantage as it keeps the load from slipping while there is not active effort being applied. The formula for calculating the work input and output is the same as for an inclined plane, which is

(work done in vertical lift) = (work done in pushing handle)

Because work is equal to force x distance, you can restate the equation like so:

(house weight)(pitch of screw) =

(force exerted on handle)(circumference of screw shaft or lever)

To find the mechanical advantage of a jack screw, you calculate the effort distance and compare it to the resistance distance. Because the input effort travels in a circle, the effort distance is the circumference of the circle that the lever makes, and the resistance distance is equal to the pitch of the screw. Use this formula to calculate the mechanical advantage of a screw:

$MA = 2\pi r/\text{pitch}$

The mechanical advantage of other types of screws is the ratio of the circumference of the effort to the distance the screw advances during each revolution. Remember that the length of the lever arm is the radius, and that to find circumference, you use the formula $2\pi r$, and that pi is roughly equal to 3.14. It is important to remember to be sure all your quantities are consistent. If you are using inches to specify your pitch, then you should also use inches to specify circumference.

If you are using a screwdriver with a handle diameter of 3 cm, the radius of the effort is going to be 1.5 cm, so the distance of the effort will be 2 π(1.5) cm per turn of the screw.

In the case of a jackscrew, if a house weighs 4,000 pounds, the pitch of the jackscrew is .250 inches and the length of its handle is 12 inches, find the amount of effort required to move the lever by substituting in the values in the formula for work, which are as follows:

Resistance x pitch = effort force × circumference, or

$\quad$ (4000)(0.250) = F x (2p)(12.0)

$\qquad$ 1000 lbs = 24π(F)

$\qquad\quad$ F = 1000/24(3.14) or 13.3 lbs.

So, you need a force of 13.3 lbs. to turn the handle on the jack to begin to lift the 2-ton house. To find the mechanical advantage, divide 4,000 pounds by 13.3 pounds, for an MA of 302.

Screws can hold together pieces of wood or metal. A jar lid, a piano stool, and a vise are also examples of a screw. In addition, screws can lift heavy objects, or move objects by a precise amount. Screws are used to make delicate adjustments of tools and machines.

Gears and Other Simple Machines

Gears are a form of wheel and axle that have teeth around the edge instead of a groove for a rope. Like a wheel and axle, a gear is a form of lever, wherein the arm of the lever is the radius of the gear and the center of the gear (or the shaft) is the fulcrum. Gears can change the effort direction or increase or reduce a force or the distance over which that effort is applied.

Gears can be a toothed or pegged wheel or a toothed cylinder or cone that meshes with another gear to transmit motion and force. In any pair of gears the larger gear rotates slower than the smaller one does, but rotates with greater force. By meshing gears of two different diameters, you can obtain a variation in both speed and torque between the two shafts. Each gear in a series reverses the direction of rotation of the previous gear.

When you use two or more gears in a single machine effort, then you have created a gear train, as Figure 7.17 shows. Gear trains reduce or increase the speed or torque output of a rotating system, or change the direction of the output of a system. In addition, they provide greater mechanical advantage.

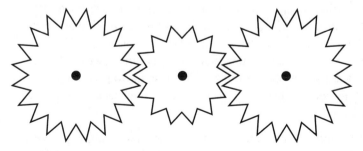

Figure 7.17 Gear train.

The first gear in the train is the driver, and the final gear in the train is the driven gear. Any gears between these two are called *idlers*. Every successive gear in the train reverses the direction of the previous gear, meaning that if the driver gear is turning clockwise, then the next gear in the chain will turn counterclockwise, and the third gear will again turn clockwise and so on. An idler gear does not alter the gear ratio between the driver and driven gear, but serves to conduct effort in the same direction and speed as the driver. However, if the idler gear speeds up or slows down the gear speed, then it is a gear differential (it differs the gear speeds). In addition to these, there are several gear types with which you should be familiar, as the following paragraphs discuss.

▶ **Bevel gears**—This gear type transfers power between two intersecting, nearly perpendicular shafts that have teeth cut on a conical surface instead of a cylinder. The teeth of the gears mesh together at less than a 90° angle. The reduced angle provides change in direction, speed, and force of the effort. Bevel gears transmit rotary motion between shafts that are not parallel and that would intersect at an angle if extended.

▶ **Spur gears**—These gears are what you normally think of when you think of a gear; a disk with teeth cut in the outer edge that mesh together with other gear edges. If the two gears are of different sizes, then the larger gear is a wheel and the smaller a pinion. Spur gears transmit motion between parallel shafts.

Spur gears change both the speed and force of a rotating axle, but how much they are changed depends on the gear ratio. That is, the ratio of the number of teeth on one gear as compared to the number of teeth on the other gear. If you have two gears, and the larger one has 30 teeth, and the smaller has 6, then you have a gear ratio of 30:6, or 5:1. This means that the smaller gear rotates five times for every one time that the larger gear rotates. If the force is moving from the smaller gear to the larger, then your ratio is the reverse, or 1:6.

▶ **Worm gears**—This gear type consists of a single tooth in the form of a screw thread (the worm), with which a helical gear (the wormwheel) meshes. The wormwheel transmits torque and rotary motion at a right angle to the worm screw to change the rotary motion by 90°. Worm gears transmit motion between perpendicular, nonintersecting shafts. They also decrease the speed of turning from screw to gear and increase its force. The worm screw always drives the wormwheel and never the other way round.

▶ **Rack and Pinion Gears**—This gear type consists of a single spur gear (the pinion), which meshes with a sliding toothed rack to convert rotary motion into linear motion.

➤ **Helical gears**—These gears are similar to spur gears, but their teeth are twisted instead of straight. Helical gears can transmit motion between shafts that do not intersect and are at any angle with respect to each other.

You use gear trains to increase mechanical advantage. In fact, wherever you have a speed reduction, you multiply the effect of the effort. The gear ratio provides the basis for understanding the mechanical advantage. In a simple gear train, the total gear ratio is the product of the gear ratios between the pairs of meshed gears. If N represents the number of teeth for each gear, then you can find the total gear ratio like this:

$Vr = Na/Nb \times Nb/Nc = Na/Nc$

We use the gear ratio to find the mechanical advantage of a gear, according to the formula $MA = Na/Nb$. So, if your driver gear has 45 teeth, your idler gear has 7, and your driven gear also has 45 teeth, then your gear ratio will be:

$Vr = Na/Nb \times Nb/Nc; Vr = 45/7 \times 7/45; Vr = 1/1$

This means that your gear ratio is 1:1 and your mechanical advantage is 1. In this case, you have maintained effort, speed, and direction. However, if your driver has 45 teeth, your idler/differential has 7 teeth, and your driven gear has 30 teeth, then your equation will look like this:

$Vr = 45/7 \times 7/30; Vr = 45/30$ or a 1.5:1 ratio, so that $MA = 1.5$

If your gear train has only two gears, then your gear ratio will be a ratio of one gear to the other. For example, if gear one has 12 teeth and the other has 8 teeth, and you need to find out how many revolutions that gear two makes as compared to gear one, then divide gear one by gear two: $12/8 = 1.5$. So, if gear one makes 10 revolutions, how many does gear two make? $10 \times 1.5 = 15$; meaning that gear 2 will make 15 revolutions to 10 revolutions of gear one.

Structural Support

In this section, we discuss forces, moments (torque), and static equilibrium and how they affect different structure types. As in the discussion on simple machines, when we talk about loads, we are talking about force or resistance against a structure. A force represents the action of one body on another and may either push or pull that structure. There are several types of forces that we must consider, which are

➤ Forces that act along the same line of action are collinear. For example, clothes hanging on a segment of clothesline is a collinear force, and all the clothes on that segment exert force on the line.

➤ If the lines of action pass through a common point, then the force system is concurrent. For example, the corner post in a wire fence has force pulling on it from at least two directions.

➤ A system of forces that act in a common plane are coplanar. For example, the snow load on a roof lies on the entire plane of that roof segment.

Especially for collinear forces, the principle of transmissibility is important. It states that the external effect of a force on a body is the same for any point of application along the line of action. For example, imagine a long rope attached to a tree limb. If you pull anywhere on that rope and exert a force of 50 lbs., the rope would apply the same force to the tree. This is an important principle if you have a nondistributive structure, such as a single beam, where the load is concentrated according to placement.

Structure Types

The ability of a structure to carry a load is dependant on both structural design and material properties. You can identify structures, or components of structures, with these basic terms:

➤ Cables

➤ Beams

➤ Membranes

➤ Plates

➤ Trusses

These terms describe the building blocks of structures and are characterized by the way they respond to external loads.

Cables

A *cable* is a very efficient structure with high load-carrying capacity, considering the structure of the material used to make it. Cables support loads through pulling (tensile) forces only. Cables support both horizontal and vertical external forces by the axial force. Axial force means a force that is applied in the direction of the formation of fibers or strands in the material.

Beams

A *beam* bears loads that are applied transversely (across the structure or formation of fibers or strands in the material). Because transverse loads bend the beam, it must offer some internal resistance to bending, and that is where material properties come into play.

A beam does not necessarily have to be horizontal, because a vertical member can be a beam as long as the loads are applied transversely and it can be a load-bearing column if the load is applied in the axial direction. The job that a beam does determines the type of beam that it is. For example, a simple beam is one that has both ends supported. A beam that has one end anchored into a wall or is otherwise fixed on one end and free on the other is a cantilever beam.

Membranes

A *membrane* is a thin-walled substance that is often used to carry transverse loads. A membrane is similar to a cable in two dimensions. The membrane has internal tension only and offers no internal resistance to bending. The membrane forces are determined by its static equilibrium.

Plates

Similar to the beam, a *plate* supports transverse loads through the action of internal moments and forces that resist bending. The internal stresses are like lateral layers of stresses that result from such things as internal bending, twisting, and shear.

Trusses

A *truss* is an assembly of straight members that are pin connected at their ends, causing only the ends to experience load stress. Because trusses essentially operate in planes, they experience no internal bending, but do experience axial tension and compression. A truss is an efficient use of materials commonly used in structural design.

Bridges

There are six basic bridge forms, which are the beam, the truss, the arch, the cantilever, the cable-stay, and the suspension.

➤ **Beam bridges**—Beam bridges are made of long timber, metal, or concrete beams anchored at each end. Load weight is concentrated.

➤ **Truss bridges**—In a truss bridge, the beams form a lattice that evenly distributes the load so that each section of the lattice shares a portion of the load applied to any part of the structure. For this reason, truss bridges can support heavy loads such as trains.

➤ **Arch bridges**—Arch bridges—steel, concrete, or masonry—have a bowed shape that transmits the vertical force of the load to create a horizontal outward force at its ends.

➤ **Cantilever bridges**—Cantilever bridges have self-supporting arms anchored at the ends that project toward one another. The arms, which transfer the load weight, can connect in the center of the span or support a third member.

➤ **Cable-stayed bridges**—Cable-stayed bridges use cables that attach directly to one or more supporting towers to support loads.

➤ **Suspension bridges**—Suspension bridges, used for the longest bridge spans, suspend the roadway from vertical cables that attach to horizontal main cables. The main cables hang from two towers and the ends are anchored in bedrock or concrete.

Bridge types can be used alone or in combination with one another.

Load Types

The force or weight on a structure is its *load*. Structures are frequently subjected to combinations of different types of loads, which consist of concentrated, distributed, static, and dynamic external loads. All these forces may act together or alone on the structure.

The duration of a load is also a contributing factor; a structure may be able to hold a large load (larger than its rated weight) for a short while, but because of the stress on the structure, it will soon experience a failure. Random forces that have no pattern and that do not repeat themselves, such as lateral force during an earthquake, also have an effect on load bearing structures.

In addition to the load types discussed in the following sections, loads can be of a particular type and have their own, specific load effects, which are

➤ **Dead load**—Dead loads are the weight of the building materials alone.

➤ **Live load**—Live loads are the additional weight due to occupancy or use, such as weights of people and traffic.

➤ **Snow load**—Snow load is the weight of accumulated snow on a roof.

➤ **Wind load**—Wind load, or wind shear, is the force of wind pressure against the structure surfaces.

Sometimes the dead weight of a structure does not significantly impact its load-carrying ability. For instance, the dead weight of bridge material is minimal as compared with the applied load. However, the materials for structures such as earth dams and fill for highways weigh a lot more than their external loads. The design of a dam, a retaining wall, or even a foundation would be negatively impacted if the dead weight of the material were disregarded.

Concentrated Load

A concentrated load acts on a relatively small area of a structure, which we can describe as a point. If you place a 300-lb. load in the center of a small bridge, the weight is distributed over a given area, depending on the size of the base of the load. Even if the weight of the load is not evenly distributed along all edges of the load, the total contact area is still small as compared to the total bridge surface. The total 300 lbs. force represents a static concentrated load of 300 lbs. acting at the midpoint of the bridge. If you move that load from the center towards either of the ends, the weight is still distributed, but stresses the weighted end slightly more. The heavier the load, the more stress it will put on the weighted area. In addition, the structure of the bridge itself determines how much the load weight will affect the structure. If you place the same load on a beam structure, the stress will be significantly more than on a truss system. Figure 7.18 shows a concentrated load.

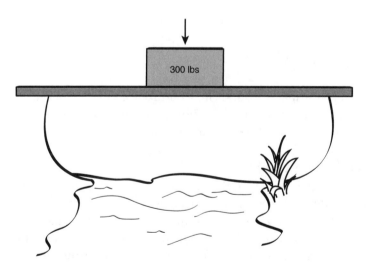

Figure 7.18   Concentrated load.

Static Uniformly Distributed Load

Distributed loads extend their weight across an entire structural area or along a line. The static uniformly distributed load describes a load wherein a structure has a uniformly distributed, permanent load. If the structure load does not vary with time and if the structure is stationary, then the load is static. In this case, the load creates no specific stress point.

For example, a large pipeline that crosses a gulch, and is supported by a truss, adds the weight of the fluid flowing in the pipe to the dead weight of the pipe itself and represents a uniformly distributed load carried by the truss. Other examples include a snow load on a roof, the lift on aircraft wings, and the vertical bearing forces on foundations. Figure 7.19 illustrates a static uniformly distributed load.

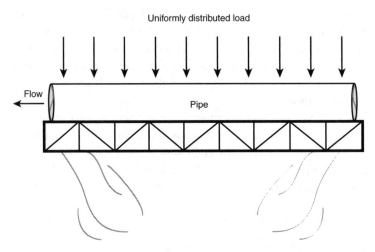

Figure 7.19   Static uniformly distributed load.

A typical uniformly distributed load, such as a blanket of snow, is applied to the central beam, which is assumed to be uniform. Therefore, the distributed force is given in terms of pounds per linear foot along the beam (lb/ft).

Dynamic and Impact Loads

If the applied loads vary with time or the structure experiences a high degree of movement, then the load becomes dynamic. However, if the inertial forces are small compared to other applied forces, then you can consider the load to be static. An example of a periodic dynamic force is that of a motor with an unbalanced rotating shaft mounted on a frame. As the shaft rotates, the magnitude and direction of the force will vary.

Another type of dynamic load is an *impact load*. An air blast or shock wave is a sudden force with a large amplitude and relatively short duration time, as are car crashes and rocket thrusts.

Nonuniformly Distributed Loads

In a uniformly distributed load, the weight or force of the load is distributed evenly across the entire surface of the structure. However, there are cases where the weight or force of the load is not distributed evenly. You can consider an evenly distributed load as a rectangular force and a nonuniformly distributed load as a triangular force against the structure, as Figure 7.20 shows. For example, the horizontal force of water against a dam increases linearly (horizontally) with depth. The soil pressure against a vertical retaining wall is also a linearly distributed force.

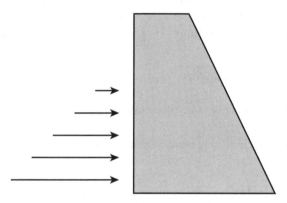

Figure 7.20   Nonuniformly distributed load.

Mechanical and Structural Properties

Mechanical properties describe the response of materials subjected to applied forces and displacements. The properties defined in this section apply to metals, ceramics, organics, and polymers—all of which are primary building materials.

Stress

The strength of a material is typically specified in terms of stress, which is the internal force per unit area within the material. You use this formula to determine stress:

Stress = Force/Area

When you apply a load at a right angle to a structure, that load can cause the members to bend, and result in tension in the fibers on the outside of the bend. The stress distributes uniformly through the cross-section where the force is being applied. The stress is tensile if the member is being "stretched" and compressive if the member is being "squashed." You measure units of stress in pounds per square inch (psi), pounds per square foot (psf) or Newtons per square meter (N/m2). Forces that tend to twist, bend, shear, compress, or elongate a material can induce stress into a material.

Strain

Some materials tend to deform (strain) when you place them under a load. This strain can compress the material or stretch it. To describe material elongation or compression, use this formula in regard to the length of material:

   Strain = change in original length/original length

You must measure the change in length in the same units as the original length so that you can develop a ratio for the two. A positive value indicates elongation, and a negative value indicates compression.

Modulus of Elasticity

The modulus of elasticity (E) tells you how much a material or structure will deflect under a bending load. One important reason for knowing the elasticity of a material is so that you can understand concepts such as vibrational and resonant movement within a material, in addition to how much stress it can take.

All materials do not deform in the same way under the same load, and some stretch more than others under equal tension. Up to a certain point (the elastic limit), most materials act like an elastic spring. The material develops an internal strain that is proportional to the internal stress in the material. For elastic materials under a one-dimensional stress, the relationship between stress and strain can be expressed as

   Stress = Elasticity (strain)

Because all materials do not stress the same, you use three types of elasticity moduli to define elasticity under stress:

➤ **Stretch modulus**—The stretch modulus is the longitudinal stretch (from end to end). You remember the toy, "Stretch Armstrong"? Yeah. It's like that.

➤ **Shear modulus**—The shear modulus does not change the size of the material, only the shape. The stretch is horizontal, like when you apply a force to the top of a stack of magazines. Because the magazine covers are generally "slick", it causes the individual magazines to shift horizontally in relation to the ones under and over them.

➤ **Bulk modulus**—The bulk modulus is a change in volume because of pressure or compression, like when you forget and place the frozen turkey on top of the grocery bag that contains the bread—its the "squash" factor.

Properties of Materials

Since the beginning of the 1800s, the selection of materials from which we build structures has changed dynamically. Prior to that time, most materials were used in a derivative of their raw state. However, since the beginning of the 19th century, scientists have broadened the scope of structural materials to include synthetics and polymers, not to mention ceramics, steel and other alloys. Because of these innovations, engineers can improve the structural integrity of many raw materials, like these:

➤ Textiles, ceramics, and metals are added to plastics to improve flexibility, structure, thermal, or electrical properties

➤ Steel added to concrete improves its flexibility and helps it to resist fracturing

Each type of material, whether it is a pure, semi-pure, or a composite, has its own molecular and conductive properties, which respond to burning, corrosion, degradation, freezing, and chemical reactions.

Thermal properties, such as heat capacity, conductivity, expansion, and contraction, of a material are important to understanding how different materials will respond under different environmental conditions.

Metals

The term *metal* refers to any material, such as steel, that has high-strength characteristics, conducts heat and electricity, and is machinable, hard, and lustrous. Metals are very common and comprise more than 80 elements on the periodic table.

Metals lose electrons in chemical reactions, whereas nonmetals gain electrons. Because of this electron exchange, metal has good molecular integrity, meaning that it is strong. An alloy is a mixture of two or more metals and may also include other additives or impurities. Although many metals may change form in response to temperature changes, metal, particularly steel, is a primary material for weight-bearing structures because of its tolerance for thermal change.

Metal alloys have a high tensile strength, but when they reach their elasticity limit, they begin to deform. If the load continues beyond the elasticity limit, then the material will separate at the fracture point.

Ceramics

Ceramics include several types of materials, such as rock, mineral ores, clay, cement, glass, brick, insulation, abrasives and porcelain. Ceramic withstands extreme thermal, chemical, and pressure environments.

The molecular structure of ceramic material consists of mixtures of metallic and nonmetallic elements. The metal atoms easily lose electrons to the strong attraction of the nonmetal nuclei. Because of these bondings, ceramics have a high melting point, low corrosive action, and overall chemical stability.

Because of their low reactivity and relative strength, ceramics such as rocks, sand, and cement are used in highway construction, buildings, pipelines, cutting tools, and dams. In addition, many metal structures have a ceramic coating, called stresscoat. Stresscoat, because it is ceramic, cracks at lesser strain levels than metals do. This allows engineers to see problem areas before they become points of failure.

Organics

Substances that are based on carbon are called *organics*. Organics exist in the form of solids, liquids, or gases. Wood, petroleum, natural gas, natural rubber, coal, collagen in connective tissue, and proteins are examples of organic materials that occur in nature. Drugs, adhesives, detergents, plastics, nylon, insecticides, rubber, and some foods are typical synthetic organics that have been developed through chemistry.

Organics are responsive to most environmental conditions, such as temperature, humidity, and degradation/decomposition. As far as structural components go, you will see some organics and some synthetic organics, wood being the primary organic, and synthetic rubber as the primary synthetic organic.

Synthetics and Polymers

Synthetic materials are made by chemically connecting long chains of carbon molecules together. Although organic molecules are resistant to sharing electrons, forcing them to do so creates a strong, stable material, called *polymer*. Some polymers, such as nylon, have a high degree of elasticity. Other materials, like some plastics, can be very elastic under a load force, but do not return to their former position after the force is removed. PVC, on the other hand, is very rigid and stable over a long period of time.

The behavior of polymers subjected to mechanical force depends on two variables: time and temperature. Temperature negatively affects polymers. The deformation, tensile strength, and modulus of elasticity of polymers depend on the rate at which the force is applied. Furthermore, deformation continues at a slow rate if the load is maintained.

Fluid Dynamics

Although water, which is a liquid, and air, which is a gas, may seem to have little in common, they share one important characteristic; each is a fluid. While they both flow as fluids, they differ in other characteristics. Liquids have a definite volume but no definite shape, and a liquid will change shape to that of its container, but will not expand to fill it completely. On the other hand, gases have no definite volume or shape, but a gas will change both shape and volume to completely fill a container.

A *fluid* includes any substance that has no rigidity, lending explanation to why both liquids and gases are fluids. Here are some characteristics of fluids that you should know:

➤ *Diffusion* is when molecules of one fluid mix through the molecules of another fluid, motivated only by random molecular action.

➤ *Cohesion* occurs when molecules of the same type stick together.

➤ *Adhesion* occurs when molecules of different types stick together.

When you put water into a container, the molecules are attracted to each other because of cohesion. However, the water molecules at the surface do not have any molecules above them, so they are attracted to the molecules beneath and beside them. The stronger the cohesion within the liquid, the greater the tendency of the molecules at the surface to pull together to create surface tension. That is why when you throw a stone into a pool of water, it creates first a splash, then a wave. The splash and wave are a combination of energy transference from a disrupting factor on the surface of the water and rapid water displacement.

Specific Gravity

Although we can compare the densities of two objects by comparing the mass per cubic centimeter, it is more convenient to compare the density of an object to that of water, which gives us the specific gravity of that object. In other words, the specific gravity is the ratio of the weight or mass of any volume of a substance to the weight or mass of an equal volume of water.

Specific gravity = Density of object/density of water

Why measure specific gravity? By measuring specific gravity, you can determine the fat content of milk or the purity of gasoline. You can even determine the amount of charge in your car's battery by measuring the specific gravity of the fluid in the battery.

A hydrometer measures the specific gravity of a liquid. One type of hydrometer is a long, narrow float with a graduated scale on the side and a weight at the bottom (see Figure 7.21). The denser the liquid, the higher the scale sticks up out of the liquid as the hydrometer floats.

Figure 7.21 Hydrometer.

Pressure

Pressure is the force per unit area, understanding that the force is perpendicular to the area. If you have ever swum to the bottom of a lake or a deep pool, you may have felt like your chest and eardrums were being squeezed. In actuality, the weight of the water above you was pressing down on you and from all sides. By understanding this, you also understand that fluids at rest exert force. That force, exerted per unit of area, is what we call pressure. We can express this relationship between force and area as an equation, like this:

Pressure(P) = Force(F)/Area(A)

When you inflate an automobile tire to a pressure of 30 pounds per square inch, you do not put 30 pounds of air into the tire, but the total force pushing outward against the walls of the tire with a pressure of 30 psi is about 12 tons over the entire tire surface.

Compression Pressure

An external force applied to a fluid by its container can raise the fluid's pressure. For example, the air inside a tire, a balloon, or an air tank is kept at a higher than normal pressure by its container. The walls of an inflated balloon, for example, try to contract and pull the air within into the smallest volume possible. If you remember blowing up a balloon, you realize that the balloon would expel the air already in the balloon. In other words, the balloon was trying to contract the air into the smallest volume possible until it was equal to the natural volume of the balloon. The force that you exert upon the air as you blow it up is transmitted equally to all surfaces inside the balloon.

Likewise, when you add air to a tire, the pressure you add at the valve stem is spread equally throughout the whole tire. Pressure caused by the "squeezing" of a fluid by its container acts equally in all direction and is transmitted equally to all surfaces.

Depth and Pressure

Another cause of increased pressure in a fluid is gravitational pressure. The fluid's weight causes it to exert more pressure at greater depths. Remember the greater pressure at the bottom of the swimming pool? That pressure is caused by the pull of gravity, as is the pressure of the air around us. The increase in pressure at the bottom of an 8-foot deep swimming pool is about 3.5 psi because of the water weight overhead. At the bottom of the deepest part of the ocean, the pressure is over 8 tons per square inch. Although it varies with depth, the gravitational pressure exerted by a fluid at a given depth is applied equally in every direction.

As an exercise, let's put into practice some of this theory. Calculate the pressure, in pounds per square inch, of the water at the bottom of a tank that is 10 feet square and 20 feet deep.

First, remember your formula for determining pressure, which is pressure equals force divided by area, or P = F/A. Now, what are the values for force and area?

Force = weight × volume; the weight of fresh water is 62.4 lb per ft³, and volume is calculated by length times width times depth, so that F = 62.4 lb/ft³ × (10 × 10 × 20ft); F = 62.4 (2000); and F = 124800 ft².

Now, back to our original formula of P = F/A. You now have P = 124800/A, where A is the area (length times width) of the tank, so that P = 124800/100 ft². Because you normally see pressure stated as pounds per square inch, multiply 100 ft² by 144, or the area of a square foot stated in square inches, so that P = 124800/14400, and P = 8.66 lbs. pressure per cubic inch.

Gravitational pressure is determined not only by depth but also by the density of the fluid. Denser fluids exert more pressure at a given depth because they are heavier and more forcefully attracted by gravity. Sea water, which is slightly denser than fresh water, exerts about 3% more pressure than fresh water at all depths. Mercury, the densest liquid, exerts more pressure at a depth of 3 feet than water does at 30 feet. Gravitational pressure depends upon depth and the density of the liquid, while pressure caused by an external force spreads equally through the fluid regardless of density or location within the container.

Pressure and Pascal's Law

When a fluid at rest is pressed upon, either from an external force or from the force of its own weight, it moves around and adjusts itself until the force, or pressure, at any point is exactly the same in all directions. Blaise Pascal first asserted this principle with this statement: "The pressure applied to any surface of a confined fluid is transmitted equally in every direction throughout the fluid."

Gases and Pressure

You measure pressure as the amount of force pressing upon each unit of area. For every pound-per-square-inch (psi) of pressure, one pound of force presses upon each square inch of an object's surface. At sea level, normal atmospheric pressure is about 14.7 psi, and Force = Pressure × area. This quantity changes with altitude, depth, and overall pressure changes.

When you lower the pressure on a gas, the volume of the gas increases. According to Boyle's Law: "If the temperature of a gas remains constant, its volume and pressure are inversely related." We can express that principle with this equation:

$P1/P2 = V2/V1$

For example, when 100 in³ of a gas under a pressure of 20 psi is compressed to a volume of 5 in³, what will be the new pressure if the temperature remains unchanged?

First, look at how the volume changes. By dividing 100 in³ by 5 in³, we see that the volume decreased by a factor of 20 (100 in³ ÷ 5 in³ = 2). According to Boyle's Law, if the volume decreases by a factor of 20, then the pressure must also increase by a factor of 20. Therefore, you can find the new pressure by multiplying the current pressure 20 psi by 20 to get 400 psi.

In addition to Boyle's assertions, Charles's Law states that: "If the pressure of a gas is constant, its volume and temperature are directly related. If either temperature or volume changes, the other must also change in the same direction and to the same extent." You can restate this with this equation:

$$V1/T1 = V2/T2$$

To take that law one step further, if you heat a gas under constant pressure, its volume will increase. But, if you heat the gas in a container of constant volume so that the gas cannot expand, then its pressure must increase instead. If the volume of a gas is constant, its pressure and temperature are directly related: $P1/T1 = P2/T2$.

Archimedes and Fluid Displacement

Have you ever noticed how objects seem to "lose weight" when you immerse them in water? Buoyancy is the tendency for an object to float when it is placed in a fluid and, believe it or not, all objects have buoyancy. Because of their own pressure, fluids exert a buoyant force on the objects within them. This force is due to the difference in fluid pressures at different depths and is exactly equal to the weight of the fluid displaced. Archimedes first discovered this principle and asserted that, "The weight lost by an object immersed in a fluid is equal to the weight of the fluid displaced." Archimedes' Principle applies to objects immersed in any fluid, not just in liquids.

Therefore, an object will float if it is lighter than an equal volume of water, and an object will sink if it is heavier than an equal volume of water. A 75-pound piece of wood, if submerged, might displace 100 pounds of water. The buoyant force would then be greater than the weight of the wood, causing the wood to rise out of the water until it displaces only 75 pounds of water and the forces are balanced.

Have you ever wondered how a ship made of steel, which is much heavier than water, can float? A steel ship is not a solid piece of metal, but is more like a hollow steel box filled with air, and is therefore much less dense than an equal volume of water. A ship in water sinks to a level where the buoyant force pushing upward, due to the weight of the water displaced, just equals the total gravitational force downward, which is due to the weight of the ship and its cargo. At that point of equal balance between the two opposite forces, the ship floats. Once the cargo is unloaded, the ship will rise as its weight decreases. When it is loaded again, it will sink until the weight of the water it displaces is again equal to its own weight.

Another example is a submarine, which can float on top of the water or maneuver under it by changing its buoyancy. A submarine on the surface floats according to Archimedes' principle by displacing volume of water equal to its own weight. However, to submerge, the submarine opens doors that allow water to flood into ballast tanks, which are compartments in the submarine. The tanks are flooded until the submarine becomes heavier and sinks to the point where it weighs exactly as much as the volume of water it displaces. At the point where the submarine is completely under water but not sinking further, it has neutral buoyancy. The submarine can then use its engines, motors, rudders, and hydroplanes to maneuver to any desired depth, according to its ability to withstand the pressure of the water around it. To resurface, the submarine must reduce its weight by releasing compressed air into the ballast tanks to force the water out of the tanks and make the submarine lighter.

To summarize the points of Archimedes' Principle:

➤ An object that is immersed in a fluid displaces a certain amount of the fluid.

➤ An object immersed in a fluid has an upward buoyant force exerted upon it by the fluid; the buoyant force is equal to the weight of the displaced fluid.

➤ For objects that float, the buoyant force equals the weight of the object; a floating object will sink to the level in the fluid where the weight of the displaced fluid equals the weight of the object.

➤ For objects that sink, the buoyant force due to the weight of the fluid displaced is less than the weight of the object, and the volume of fluid displaced equals the volume of the object.

Bernoulli and Fluid Movement

Just as balloons and ships float in the atmosphere and in water, respectively, according to Archimedes' Principle (they are lighter than the air or water that they displace), airplanes and other objects in flight do so according to the Bernoulli Principle. Bernoulli asserted that: "Sideward pressure exerted by a moving fluid decreases as the fluid's velocity increases."

As a plane moves through the air, the air traveling over the curved upper surface of the wing (a design called an airfoil) must travel further up and over the wing than the air traveling under flat part of the wing.

That means that the air traveling above the wing must speed up temporarily and, by the Bernoulli Principle, exert less pressure on the wing than does the air beneath the wing. This difference in pressure over the whole surface of the wing pushes the wing up, toward the lower pressure. This upward force is called lift. There are several factors that affect lift, which are

> ➤ **Speed**—The faster the wing moves through the air, the greater lift it produces as it creates distortion between the pressure field.

> ➤ **Tilt**—A pilot can also increase lift by tilting the wing(s). Perhaps you have noticed that airplanes taking off and landing have their noses higher in relation to the back of the plane than they do in normal flight. This increases the plane's lift at slower speeds.

> ➤ **Shape**—Changing the shape of the wing can also increase wing lift. This is especially important at low speeds, as lift must overcome the force (weight) of gravity if a plane is to fly.

> ➤ **Thrust**—This is the force that drives a plane forward through the air, allowing the wings to create lift.

Gravity and drag resistance are the two forces exhibited by air that tend to slow the movement of a plane. Drag is caused by friction with the airplane's surface, the inertia of the air that is resisting being moved out of the way, and the pressure difference ahead of and behind the airplane caused by its motion.

To reduce drag, the airplane surfaces are smooth and shaped so that they efficiently push air aside and allow the air pressure fields to come smoothly back together behind them. Streamlining is the science of shaping objects so they allow the easy flow of fluids around them. Streamlining is important in the design of airplanes, cars, ships, submarines, and fast trains to allow them to move easily through the fluids that surround them.

Remember Newton's Third Law of Motion, "For every action, there is an equal an opposite reaction"? It is this principle at work that causes resistance and backpressure to build up behind a moving object. Oddly enough, smooth surfaces do not necessarily have less drag than non-smooth surfaces. For instance, the dimples on a golf ball allow the ball to displace less air as it moves, thus creating less resistance, or field of lower pressure, behind the moving ball. In addition, a spinning baseball creates a lower field of pressure on one side of the ball than on the other—the same principle that gives airplanes lift.

Exam Prep Questions

Read each question, and then choose the answer that fits most closely to the question.

1. A 500-lb. barrel is rolled up a 15 ft. plank to a platform whose vertical height above the ground is 3 ft. Disregarding friction, what effort is required to move the barrel?
   - ❏ A. 15 lbs.
   - ❏ B. 2500 lbs.
   - ❏ C. 500 lbs.
   - ❏ D. 100 lbs.

2. What force must you exert (vertically) on the handles of a wheelbarrow 4 ft. from the axle of the wheel in order to lift a weight of 200 lbs. that is concentrated at a point 1.5 ft. from the axle?
   - ❏ A. 100 lbs.
   - ❏ B. 75 lbs.
   - ❏ C. 200 lbs.
   - ❏ D. 4 lbs.

3. What force must you exert on the handle of a jackscrew 16 inches in radius if the pitch is 0.375 inches and the weight of the load is 6,000 pounds?
   - ❏ A. 22.4 lbs.
   - ❏ B. 6,000 lbs.
   - ❏ C. 3,000 lbs.
   - ❏ D. 32 lbs.

4. What is the mechanical advantage of a wheel and axle, where the wheel has a radius of 10 in. and the axle has a radius of 5 in.?
   - ❏ A. MA = 1
   - ❏ B. MA = 10
   - ❏ C. MA = 5
   - ❏ D. MA = 2

5. A mass of air has a pressure of 15 psi and a volume of 75 ft³. If it is compressed to a new volume of 5 ft3, what will be the new pressure?
   - ❏ A. 75 psi
   - ❏ B. 15 psi
   - ❏ C. 225 psi
   - ❏ D. 5 psi

6. What is the pressure, in psi, of a tank of water that measures 12 feet square by 12 feet deep?

❑ A. 5.2 psi
❑ B. 62.4 psi
❑ C. 12 psi
❑ D. 144 psi

7. In Figure 7.22, which end of the bridge is supporting the most of the 800 lb. weight if the bridge is a beam structure?

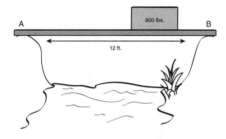

Figure 7.22

❑ A. End A
❑ B. End B
❑ C. Ends A and B are supporting half of the load.
❑ D. Not enough information to answer the question.

8. In Figure 7.22, which end of the bridge is supporting the most weight if the bridge is a truss structure?

❑ A. End A is supporting 200 lbs. and end B is supporting 600 lbs.
❑ B. End B is supporting 800 lbs.
❑ C. Neither end is supporting the weight.
❑ D. Both ends are supporting 400 lbs.

9. How much effort will it take to lift the load in this situation?

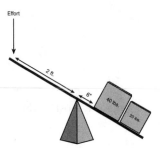

Figure 7.23

- ❏ A. 180 lbs.
- ❏ B. 60 lbs.
- ❏ C. 15 lbs.
- ❏ D. 240 lbs.

10. What is the effort required to move the 200 lb. load 1 foot off the ground?

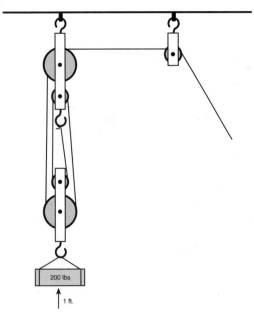

Figure 7.24

- ❏ A. 4 lbs.
- ❏ B. 50 lbs.
- ❏ C. 200 lbs.
- ❏ D. 100 lbs.

Exam Prep Answers

1. **The correct answer is D.** According to the formula wd = wd, then 15x = 500(3); 15x = 1500; x = 100. Answer A represents the MA; answer B indicates that you have reversed the effort distance and resistance distance; because an inclined plane does provide a mechanical advantage, then you do not have to exert an equivalent amount of effort to move the barrel. Therefore, answers A, B, and C are incorrect.

2. **The correct answer is B.** According to our formula wherein wd = wd, then 4x = 300; x = 75. Answer A assumes a mechanical advantage of only 2, which is incorrect. Answer C assumes no mechanical advantage, which is also incorrect. Because 4 represents the mechanical advantage, answer D is incorrect.

3. **The correct answer is A.** According to our formula: resistance × pitch = effort force × 2pr (or circumference); 6,000(.375) = F(2p)(16); 2,250 = 100.48F; 22.4 = F. 6,000 is the resistance force; 3,000 assumes a mechanical advantage of only 2; 32 represents the diameter of the handle. Therefore, answers B, C, and D are incorrect.

4. **The correct answer is D.** MA = radius of wheel/radius of axle; MA = 10/5; MA = 2. Answers A, B, and C are incorrect values.

5. **The correct answer is C.** According to Boyle's Law, pressure and volume are inversely proportional, so that P1/P2 = V2/V1. First, you find the increase value by dividing 75 by 5 to get an increase value of 15. Now multiply the original pressure by the same value of 15 to get the new pressure of 225 psi. Answers A, B, and D are all original values of the equation and are therefore incorrect.

6. **The correct answer is A.** The formula for measuring water pressure (for water at rest) is P = F/A, where F = weight(depth). The weight of water per cubic foot is 62.4 lbs., so F = 62.4 ft³(12 ft.); F = 748.8 ft². Now, apply the original formula P = 748.8 ft²÷144 ft²/in²; P = 5.2 psi. Answer B is incorrect because 62.4 is the weight of water; answer C is incorrect because that is the depth of the water; answer D is incorrect, because 144 is the area of the tank.

7. **The correct answer is B.** Because a beam does not distribute weight evenly, then the end closest to the load is supporting the load. Because the load is at the other end of the platform, end A is not supporting the load. Because the beam is not a truss structure, ends A and B are not sharing the load. In addition, the question provides enough information to answer the question. Therefore, answers A, C, and D are incorrect.

8. **The correct answer is D.** A truss structure distributes the load nearly evenly throughout the structure. Neither end is bearing more weight than the other, therefore, answers A, B, and C are incorrect.

9. **The correct answer is C.** The formula to use is wd = wd, so that 24x = 60(6); 24x = 360; x = 15. 180 pounds indicates that you did not change the 2 ft. to 24 inches, therefore, answer A is incorrect. Always be sure your values are the same. Because the distance on each side of the fulcrum is not the same, then the effort to lift the boxes is not the same as the weight of the boxes. Therefore, answer B is incorrect. 240 lbs. indicates that you exchanged distance values on each side of the equation. Therefore, answer D is also incorrect.

10. **The correct answer is B.** The mechanical advantage is 4, because there are 4 ropes supporting the load. Because Effort = R/Ma, so that E = 200/4; E = 50 lbs. Four pounds is the mechanical advantage, so A is incorrect. Because we have a mechanical advantage of 4, a force equal to the resistance is not required, therefore, C is incorrect. 100 lbs. would indicate an MA of only 2, therefore D is also incorrect.

Shop Information

Terms you'll need to know:

- ✓ Rule
- ✓ Caliper
- ✓ Micrometer
- ✓ Kerf
- ✓ Oxyacetylene torch
- ✓ Brace
- ✓ Auger bit
- ✓ Forstner bit
- ✓ Torque
- ✓ Ratchet
- ✓ Filler rod
- ✓ Soldering
- ✓ Flux
- ✓ Tinning
- ✓ Brazing
- ✓ Turning
- ✓ Milling
- ✓ Grinding
- ✓ Blueprints
- ✓ Layout

Techniques you'll need to master:

- ✓ Identifying a tool by its appearance
- ✓ Identifying the correct use for a given tool
- ✓ Identifying a tool's parts
- ✓ Selecting the proper tool for a given job
- ✓ Understanding basic shop processes

Do you like working with tools? Have you spent a summer working in construction or carpentry? Did you spend a lot of time hanging out in your mom or dad's home workshop? If you answer "yes" to one or more of these questions, then you will probably find this section of the ASVAB easy and even fun. If, however, you've never picked up a wrench or swung a hammer, you are at a disadvantage and this chapter will help you get up to speed.

The purpose of the Shop Information test is to identify people who possess significant know-how in working with shop tools, materials, and processes. The military doesn't need a whole army of carpenters and machinists, but it does need some. If your experience, interests, and career goals don't include shop work, this section is not going to be as important to you. Your score on this test has no impact on your eligibility to enlist in any branch of the military.

Of course, you want to do your very best on every section of the ASVAB. This chapter contains an overview of the material you're most likely to see on the test. We'll start out by looking at a wide variety of tools and then review shop processes and planning techniques. To obtain more detailed information on any area, your best bet is to visit a hardware store or a friend's home workshop where you can see and pick up a tool and ask questions about it. This type of information is most easily picked up and absorbed through hands-on practice. Of course, you can also follow up with a keyword search using your favorite Internet search engine to reinforce your knowledge.

Depending on the version of the ASVAB you take, you may find Shop Information as a separate section of the test (as on the CAT-ASVAB) or combined with the Auto Information test. You can expect to answer 25 questions in 11 minutes.

Tools

Tools are used to make work easier. To make our review of tools, their parts, and their applications easier, we will group them according to use: measuring, cutting, drilling, shaping, and fastening.

Measuring Tools

You've probably heard the old saying, "measure twice, cut once." Measuring is one of the most important shop functions because it is the only way to ensure your project turns out according to plan. Measuring compares an object whose dimension you don't know with an object whose dimension you do know. The known dimension is called a *standard*. Measuring tools provide the standard needed for accurate and precise measurement. You might encounter a wide variety of measuring tools (pictured in Figure 8.1 and numbered to correspond with the list below), depending on your needs:

1. **Tape measure**—A commonly used, general purpose measuring tool, the tape measure is compact and allows you to measure both small and large distances easily.

2. **Rule (scale)**—Used to achieve a higher degree of accuracy in measuring small dimensions. Steel rules (scales) are especially useful in finish work.

3. **Caliper**—Used extensively in metalworking applications, calipers can measure irregular shapes and thick stock. The Vernier caliper combines a steel rule with caliper legs (and sometimes a depth gauge) and can be used to measure thickness and inner and outer diameters (and depth).

4. **Micrometer**—Providing the highest degree of precision in measuring the thickness or the outer diameter of an object, micrometers are accurate to within one thousandth (or even one ten thousandth) of an inch.

5. **Carpenter's square (Try square)**—Used to mark lines at a right angle prior to cutting, or to check corners and joints to verify that they are square (that is, intersecting at a 90 degree angle).

6. **Plumb bob**—The plumb bob is a weight which is pointed at the bottom and hung by a string so that it does not touch the ground. Because gravity pulls the weight down in a perfectly straight path, the plumb bob is used to indicate a perfectly vertical line.

7. **Level**—Used to ensure that surfaces are level or plumb, levels are essential tools during the installation process (for example, setting fence posts, framing, etc.).

Cutting and Shaping Tools

Once you have measured out the required dimensions, you will often need to modify your materials in some way to bring them to the correct size and shape. Cutting and shaping tools remove or separate material by one of a variety of methods: ripping, cutting, slicing, abrading (scraping or rubbing), or burning. We will begin by looking at saws and then review shears or snips, cutting torches, planes, chisels, routers, and files.

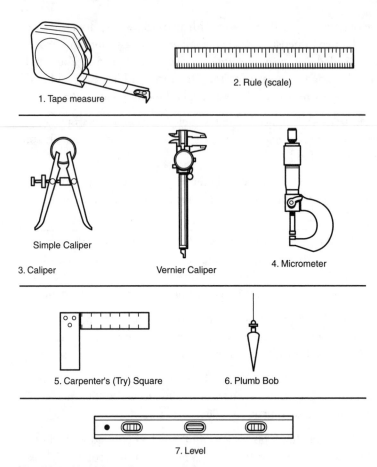

Figure 8.1 Measuring tools.

Saws

Saws are used to cut materials by digging into them with sharp teeth. A saw's teeth are shaped so that the cutting action takes place when you draw the teeth across the wood. When you begin to cut with a saw you should draw the saw backward slowly, guiding the side of the blade with your thumb to create a groove, called a kerf, in the wood. Once you have established the kerf it will help prevent the saw from slipping sideways and allow you to begin the power strokes in which most of the cutting is done.

You need to know the major types of saws for cutting wood (crosscut saw, ripsaw, backsaw, and coping saw) as well as metal (hacksaw). Before we look at each of these saws, you need to understand the basic parts of a saw. Figure 8.2 shows the familiar crosscut hand saw with its parts labeled.

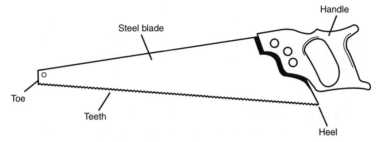

Figure 8.2 The parts of a saw.

Saw blades are described by the number of points (that is, teeth) per inch. So an 8-point saw has 8 teeth per inch and a 12-point saw has 12 teeth per inch. The higher the point value of a saw, the finer the cut will be.

See Figure 8.3 for pictures of the different types of saws. Refer to the list after Figure 8.3 for a description of the different types of saws seen in the figure.

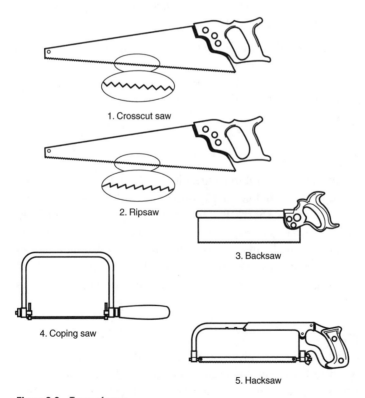

Figure 8.3 Types of saws.

Types of saws include

1. **Crosscut saw**—Used for sawing across the wood grain, the crosscut saw has teeth that act like knife points during the cutting process. Crosscut saws may also be used for ripping (cutting with the wood grain).

2. **Ripsaw**—Used exclusively for maximum efficiency at ripping (that is, cutting with or along the grain), the ripsaw's teeth act like a row of chisels. The result is a rougher cut, unsuitable for crosscutting.

3. **Backsaw**—Used for precise, finish cuts, the backsaw is shorter than the crosscut saw and has smaller teeth with more points per inch. Backsaws are often used with a miter box, which guides the blade and allows a high degree of accuracy on straight or angled cuts. Backsaws also have a rigid, steel "backbone" along the top edge of the blade to prevent the blade from bending from side to side during the cut.

4. **Coping saw**—Used for creating a curved cut, the coping saw is distinctive for its U-shaped frame and narrow blade with a high point count of small teeth for finish cutting.

5. **Hacksaw**—Used to make straight line cuts in metal, the hacksaw can be fitted with a variety of blades depending on the application (as a general rule, the harder the metal being cut, the more teeth or points per inch are required). The teeth of the hacksaw blade are made from hardened steel.

Shears (Snips)

Shears or snips (the terms are interchangeable) are useful for cutting thin, soft metal. They operate with a cutting action like regular scissors and are best when used for relatively short cuts. To make a smooth, continuous cut, open the jaws of the snips all the way and place the sheet of metal all the way back against the jaws. Using hand pressure only, squeeze the handles together to cut until the cut advances to a little over half the distance to the tip of the snips. Then, advance the shears and repeat the process. Figure 8.4 shows a pair of metal snips.

Cutting Torch

Another way to cut metal is by burning through it with a cutting torch. The oxyacetylene torch utilizes a special cutting attachment that forms a flame fed by a mixture of oxygen and acetylene gases (see Figure 8.5). A cutting torch is useful for cutting holes and curved or straight lines in metal that is too hard and/or thick for shears or saws.

Metal Shears (Snips)

Figure 8.4 Metal shears (snips).

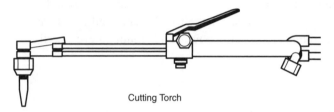

Cutting Torch

Figure 8.5 Oxyacetylene cutting torch.

Shaping Tools

To round out your review of cutting and shaping tools, you need to know a bit about planes, chisels, files, and routers. Figure 8.6 gives an illustration of each type of shaping tool with descriptions of each tool in the list that follows.

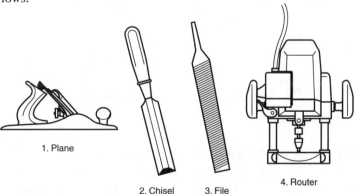

1. Plane

2. Chisel   3. File

4. Router

Figure 8.6 Shaping tools.

1. **Plane**—Used to slice off a thin layer of wood from the edge of a board, the plane is an essential finishing tool. When you pass a plane over an edge you produce a clean, flat, smooth surface.

2. **Chisel**—Used for shaping wood, performing inside cuts (that a plane or saw cannot reach), smoothing surfaces, or removing material so that two parts will fit together. The chisel is a simple, handheld tool with a single cutting edge and a flat head that can be pushed by hand or struck with a mallet when making cuts. The cold chisel is a special type of chisel used for metal cutting applications.

3. **File**—Used to shape and smooth wood or metal (depending on the type of file selected), files are essentially metal bars with toothlike grooves cut into them. Files are also useful for sharpening other tools.

4. **Router**—Used to shape and form edge contours, cut grooves and dadoes (a wide slot that is cut across the wood grain), and trim laminate material. Routers are versatile power tools found in every well-equipped wood shop.

Drilling Tools

Drilling is the process of cutting a hole into a material. In this section we will review the tools and inserts (or bits) used for drilling. Figure 8.7 illustrates three types of drilling tools with descriptions of these tools in the list that follows the figure.

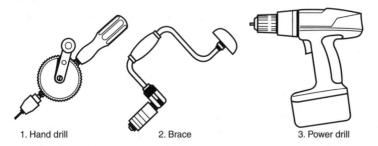

1. Hand drill   2. Brace   3. Power drill

Figure 8.7 Drilling tools.

1. **Hand drill**—Used for drilling small holes, the hand drill can be used to make pilot holes for nails or screws or for countersinking. This simple drill has a handle, a chuck into which the drill bit is secured, and a crank that you turn by hand to turn the drill bit.

2. **Brace**—Used for driving bits, the brace is a kind of hand drill that is excellent for boring wide holes because its design provides powerful leverage for the drilling process. (Boring is a term used to describe cutting a hole that is larger than 1/4 inch into a material.)

3. **Power drill**—Used to increase efficiency across a wide spectrum of drilling applications, the power drill may be adjusted to provide the required torque and speed for any job. Powered by an electric motor, the power drill is a real timesaver on repetitive work.

Drill Bits

After you have selected your drilling tool, you need to choose the appropriate drill bit for your job. The bit is the working surface of the drill that comes in contact with the material. Some common types of drill bits you need to know about are twist, auger, spade, Forstner, reamer, tap, and die. Figure 8.8 shows you each of these drill bits with a description of each bit following the figure.

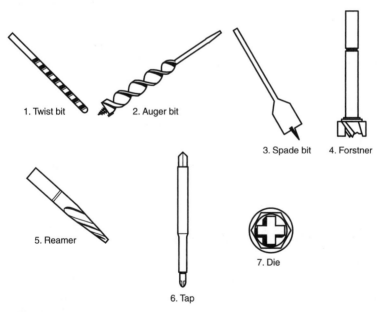

Figure 8.8 Drill bits.

 Can you pick an auger bit out of a line-up? The ASVAB will ask you questions requiring you to identify a tool from its picture, so pay attention to the illustration figures in this chapter. If you are more of a "hands-on" learner, take a few minutes to stop by your local hardware store. There you can see and pick up tools to reinforce your learning.

1. **Twist bit**—Used for drilling wood or metal, the twist bit is the bit of choice for most standard drilling applications. Twist bits come in a wide variety of sizes (diameters), typically from as small as 1/64 inch to as large as 1/2 inch. The hole formed by a twist bit has a tapered bottom, corresponding to the shape of the bit's tip.

2. **Auger bit**—Used for boring and deep drilling. Typically used with a brace in woodworking applications, an auger bit has a self-feeding screw on its tip, which makes it easy to control when drilling deep holes.

3. **Spade bit**—Used in woodworking for drilling or boring larger diameter (up to 1 1/4 inches) or deep holes, spade bits operate much like a rotating chisel, scraping away the wood in its path. Its long center point will leave a hole in the center of the work piece.

4. **Forstner bit**—Used only with power drills, this bit's circular contour has thin, sawtooth-style blades surrounding a center spur that breaks out the chips formed while drilling. Forstner bits are especially useful for boring large holes that are much cleaner than those made by spade bits.

5. **Reamer**—Used to enlarge or taper predrilled holes, the reamer bit's cutting edges are on its outside, not on the tip. For this reason, you would not use a reamer to make a hole deeper, only wider (and smoother).

6. **Tap**—Used in metalworking to cut threads (for receiving threaded fasteners) on the inside of holes.

7. **Die**—Used in metalworking to cut threads on the outside of pipes or metal rods.

Fastening Tools and Fasteners

Fastening tools and fasteners are used to attach objects to each other. You have to know how to distinguish between the major types of fasteners by appearance and use. Screws, nuts and bolts, nails, and rivets are all fasteners that pass through the material and apply pressure to bind objects together. Clamps and vises, necessary tools for holding work pieces together while work is being done, also apply pressure to do their job, but are removed when the work is completed and do not pass into or through the material being worked.

Screwdrivers and Screws

Screws provide strong holding power and have the advantage of being removable for easy disassembly. Screws are inserted using a screwdriver which is twisted around and around to provide the necessary torque (that is, rotating force). Screwdrivers come with different types of heads or tips that correspond to the various types of screws. Figure 8.9 shows several common types of screws and Figure 8.10 gives an example of two screwdrivers: *Slotted* and *Phillips*. Phillips head screws have the added advantage over slotted head screws of allowing a snugger fit with their driver, which minimizes slippage and makes it possible to generate greater torque.

1. Slotted   2. Phillips

Figure 8.9 Types of screws.

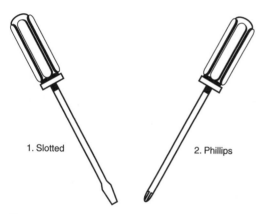

1. Slotted   2. Phillips

Figure 8.10 Slotted and Phillips screwdrivers.

Wrenches, Nuts, and Bolts

Nuts and bolts are threaded fasteners that fit together (interlock) when the bolt is inserted into the nut and rotated. Wrenches are tools that provide the necessary torque to securely fasten together nuts and bolts. Figure 8.11 shows six of the most common types of wrenches, which are described following the figure.

1. **Open-ended wrench**—Built so that its jaw (the crescent-shaped open end) fits exactly over the nut, and as a result you need a different open-ended wrench for each size nut you must turn.

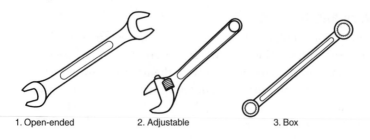

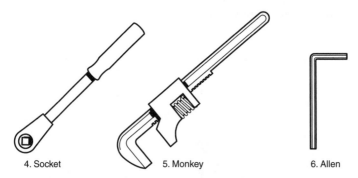

Figure 8.11 Types of wrenches.

2. **Adjustable wrench**—Unlike the open-ended wrenches described previously, the adjustable wrench enables you to move the jaw to exactly fit nuts of various sizes.

3. **Box wrench**—Completely surrounding the nut with its "box", or notched circular opening, box wrenches are sturdy and less likely to slip off the nut while being turned. Box wrenches are not adjustable, so you need a different one for each size of nut you must turn.

4. **Socket wrench**—Using a common driver to turn one of a set of closed wrenches, called sockets, the socket wrench is an excellent tool for rapid tightening (assembly) and loosening (disassembly) tasks. Ratcheting action (the wrench only provides a power stroke in one direction) allows the socket to stay over the nut throughout either process.

5. **Monkey wrench**—An adjustable wrench with its jaws at 90 degrees to its handle, the monkey wrench is used most often for bending or twisting pipes (as in wrought-iron work and some plumbing applications). The monkey wrench has been replaced by the adjustable wrench in most tool boxes.

6. **Allen wrench**—Allen, or hex key wrenches, are used to turn screws with hexagonal (six-sided) socket heads. Hex keys usually come in sets of varying sized wrenches and are often L-shaped. You can also buy a set of straight hex key wrenches that are held together in a knife-style holder.

Hammer and Nails

Another common means of fastening wood together is the nail. Nails are driven into the wood with blows from a hammer and get their holding power from the wood fibers pressing up against their sides. Common types of hammers are shown in Figure 8.12 and Figure 8.13 illustrates the various parts of a standard claw hammer.

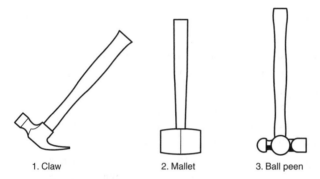

1. Claw   2. Mallet   3. Ball peen

Figure 8.12 Types of hammers.

1. **Claw hammer**—Used for driving and pulling (with the claw end) nails. This type of hammer is also referred to as a carpenter's hammer.

2. **Mallet**—Used for tapping objects such as chisels, dowel pins, plugs, and metal, where the aim is to avoid deforming the surface being struck. Mallets have heads made of softer materials such as rawhide, wood, plastic, or rubber.

3. **Ball peen hammer**—Used for metal work in shaping metal, tapping parts into place, and riveting. Woodworkers also find this hammer useful for tapping pieces into place.

Rivet Gun and Rivets

Rivets are used to permanently join (or fasten) metal. A rivet is a short metal rod with a head that is used for tapping the rivet into a previously drilled hole in the metal sections being joined. The end of the rivet is then flattened out by hammering (for example, with a ball peen hammer) to prevent it from slipping back out of the hole.

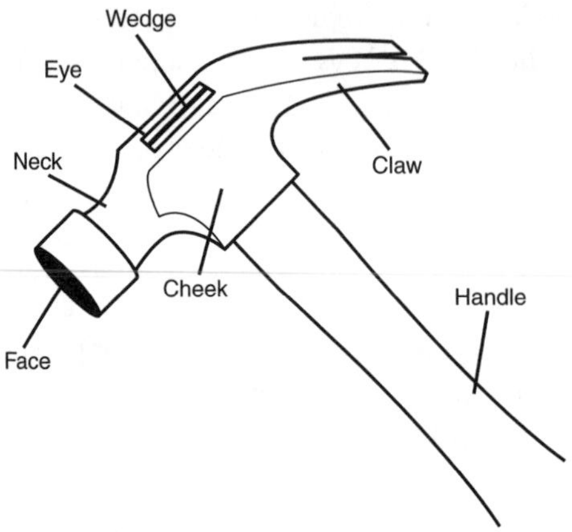

Figure 8.13 shows the parts of a hammer with the following labels: Wedge, Eye, Neck, Claw, Cheek, Handle, Face.

Figure 8.13 Parts of a hammer.

Pop-rivet tools (or rivet guns) are specialized tools used to speed up the riveting process. As you can see in Figure 8.14, the pop-rivet tool looks somewhat like a stapler. You begin by feeding a rivet into the nosepiece of the tool. Squeezing the handles of the tool causes it to grip the rivet. You then place the rivet gun over the predrilled hole and alternately open and close the tool's handles to draw the rivet's mandrel (long, narrow stem) up into the tool. When it becomes difficult to work the handles, you have applied enough pressure for the rivet to hold. Squeeze the tool's handles harder one more time to break off the excess part of the mandrel, and your rivet is set.

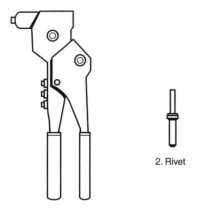

2. Rivet

Figure 8.14 Rivet gun and rivet.

Clamps and Vises

Whenever you work with a material, be it to cut, shape, drill, machine, or fasten (either with fasteners or glue) you need to ensure your work piece is held firmly in place. Clamps and vises are excellent at doing just that. Whereas vises are usually permanently attached to a work bench, clamps are removable and portable. Figure 8.15 shows an example of a clamp and a vise. Choosing the appropriate holding device for your project will allow you to work safely and precisely.

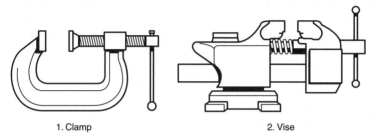

1. Clamp   2. Vise

Figure 8.15   Clamp and vise.

Pliers

Pliers are gripping tools where the user provides all the gripping force by squeezing the handles together. Pliers are useful in a wide range of gripping, pulling, twisting, and holding applications. Figure 8.16 illustrates a few of the hundreds of types of specialized pliers and the following list will give you some more specific detail about each of the pliers.

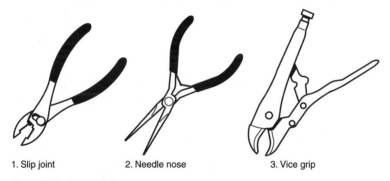

1. Slip joint   2. Needle nose   3. Vice grip

Figure 8.16   Types of pliers.

1. **Slip Joint Pliers**—Used for gripping small objects. They have curved jaws with small grooves (or teeth) that help secure the object being held. Slip Joint pliers get their name from the hinged joint between their jaws, which can be moved (or slipped) to close tightly or open wide, depending on your need.

2. **Needle Nose Pliers**—These are especially useful for gripping very small or delicate objects and for reaching inside a confined space to grip something. They are often used for electrical applications and may come with a built-in wire cutter near their hinge.

3. **Vise Grip Pliers**—Necessary for any application requiring you to hold or grip with a great deal of constant pressure. In this way, they can be used similarly to a clamp. They can also be locked onto an object such as a rusted or frozen nut or bolt and then turned with both hands like a wrench.

Shop Processes

Now that you have familiarized yourself with the most important shop tools, let's take a look at several shop processes that you will need to know for the ASVAB. Do you know the difference between welding and soldering? What does it mean to "machine" something? If you can answer these questions without batting an eye, then you are in good shape. If, like many people, you aren't so sure how to answer those questions, read on.

 These next few paragraphs on shop processes contain information that will be good for at least two or three correct answers on some of the more difficult questions on the Shop Information test. If you are not already familiar with the shop processes described here, please pay extra attention to this section of the review.

Welding

Welding is a process in which two pieces of metal are permanently bonded (or fused) together by heating the two pieces where they join and filling the joint with molten metal. The result, when everything cools down and the metal recrystallizes, is a joint that is as strong as or stronger than the original metal. The heat may either be supplied by the flame from a gas torch, such as an oxyacetylene torch, or from an arc-welding rig that creates heat by the formation of an intense, high-voltage, electrical arc between the welding tool and the metal object being welded. In either form of welding, the joining material is called a welding rod (or filler rod) and may be purchased in varying diameters and alloys depending on the welding task to be performed. Welding is a high-temperature process; the oxyacetylene torch produces a flame that can reach 6,000 degrees and the arc-welder cranks the heat up to over 7,000 degrees. Welding is a process that requires training and plenty of safety precautions.

Soldering

Soldering is another method of permanently bonding together metals, but in this case by using a filler rod (solder) that is an alloy (or mixture of metals). Solder is typically made of a mixture of lead and tin.

The soldering process begins with cleaning the metal pieces that are to be joined. This step is essential for a successfully soldered joint. Next, you apply a chemical material called *flux*, which prevents oxides from forming on the surface of the original metal. Flux also has properties that help break down the surface tension of the solder, allowing it to flow freely into the joint and bond with the original metal.

Solder is applied using a soldering iron as the heat source. There are a number of different types of soldering irons, but no matter which one you use you must first clean and prepare the tip by tinning it. Tinning is the process of heating the tip of the soldering iron (called the bit), coating it with flux, and then applying a thin layer of solder. The bit is then wiped with a clean cloth to remove excess solder before you begin your work.

Brazing

Brazing is a technique of joining dissimilar metals by fusing them with a filler rod made of an alloy such as brass (a mixture of copper and zinc.) Brazing (like soldering) produces a joint that is not as strong as a weld.

Machining

Machining is a term for shaping materials with specially designed machine tools. Although the ASVAB will not delve too deeply into technical information about specific machine tools, it is important that you know a little bit about a few of the most common machining processes, such as turning, milling, and grinding.

➤ **Turning**—Turning reduces the diameter of an object by rotating it around a horizontal axis and then moving a cutting tool against the part. Turning is accomplished with a lathe, a machine tool that is useful for both woodworking and metalworking turning applications.

➤ **Milling**—Milling machines metal with a revolving, multitoothed cutting tool into which the work piece is fed. Milling machines are among the most versatile machine tools and can be used to machine flat surfaces, drill (or bore), and cut slots or even irregular shapes.

➤ **Grinding**—Grinding is a machining process for metal that is analogous to sanding for wood. Some common grinding applications are buffing, polishing, sanding, removing thickness, or leveling off a work piece to achieve flatness. Rather than cutting the metal workpiece, grinding machines remove material by rapidly moving an abrasive material (such as ceramic, aluminum oxide, or composite wheel, block or disk) or a wire brush against it. Grinders vary greatly in size depending on the application, from huge machining centers to smaller bench grinders to handheld disk grinders.

Shop Project Planning

Before moving on to the practice questions, let's take a brief look at the shop project planning process. Complex projects need to be carefully planned and the required steps and specifications should be documented. Blueprints are detailed technical drawings with all key dimensions indicated. They may even call out requirements for specific materials. Before beginning work on any project, you should study the blueprints carefully. The next steps you should take include preparing a complete listing of materials required, preparing templates or patterns for use in fabricating or checking parts, and laying out your project by marking out the blueprint dimensions on the materials you will need to cut or shape.

Exam Prep Questions

1. Which of the following would be a good use for a milling machine?
   - ❑ A. Finish cutting wood
   - ❑ B. Reducing the diameter of pipe stock
   - ❑ C. Cutting slots into metal
   - ❑ D. Joining dissimilar metals

2. What is the term used to describe drilling a large diameter (greater than 1/4″) hole?
   - ❑ A. Turning
   - ❑ B. Planing
   - ❑ C. Reaming
   - ❑ D. Boring

3. Identify the micrometer.

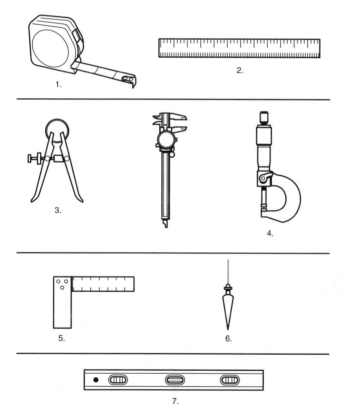

- ❑ A. #2
- ❑ B. #4
- ❑ C. #7
- ❑ D. #3

4. Which tool should you choose for evenly shaving the end of a wood board?

❑ A. Plane

❑ B. File

❑ C. Power sander

❑ D. Sand paper

5. In the figure that follows, identify the part of the hammer indicated by the arrow.

❑ A. Claw

❑ B. Face

❑ C. Neck

❑ D. Cheek

6. Which of the following uses the auger bit?

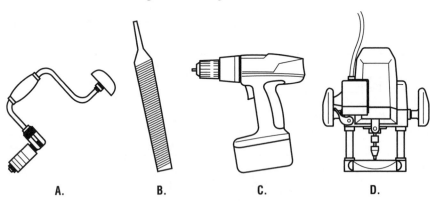

A.   B.   C.   D.

7. The process of cleaning and preparing the tip of a soldering iron for use is called _____.
   - ❑ A. Dipping
   - ❑ B. Hardening
   - ❑ C. Tinning
   - ❑ D. Brazing

8. To make a curved cut in a piece of wood you should select a
   _____.
   - ❑ A. Back saw
   - ❑ B. Coping saw
   - ❑ C. Ripsaw
   - ❑ D. None of the above

9. Which type of drill bit would make the best choice for boring a clean hole in a door for installing a door knob?
   - ❑ A. Auger bit
   - ❑ B. Twist bit
   - ❑ C. Forstner bit
   - ❑ D. Spade bit

10. What is kerf?
   - ❑ A. The long stem of a rivet
   - ❑ B. The cut made by a saw blade's teeth
   - ❑ C. A chemical used to prevent metal oxidation
   - ❑ D. Sawdust

Exam Prep Answers

1. **Answer C is correct.** Milling machines are well suited for cutting slots into metal. Answer A is incorrect because milling machines are metalworking tools and would be unsuitable for finish cutting wood. Answer B is incorrect because a lathe would be the machine tool of choice for reducing the diameter of pipe stock. Answer D is incorrect because dissimilar metals are joined by brazing.

2. **Answer D is correct.** Answer A is incorrect because turning is the process of reducing the diameter of a workpiece. Answer B is incorrect because planing is shaving a thin layer off a board to smooth, reduce thickness, and flatten it. Answer C is incorrect because reaming means expanding the diameter, smoothing, and sometimes tapering a predrilled hole.

3. **Answer B is correct.** The other answer choices are incorrect because Answer A is a rule (or scale), Answer C is a level, and Answer D is a Vernier caliper.

4. **Answer A is correct.** The other answer choices are incorrect because they all remove material by abrasion (rubbing away material) rather than shaving. A plane, once the blade is set and locked in place, will shave off an even amount of wood across the entire length of the board edge.

5. **Answer D is correct.** For a review of all parts of a hammer, you can refer to Figure 8.13 in the chapter.

6. **Answer A is correct.** Answer B is incorrect because it shows a file (which is not a type of drill bit). Answer C is incorrect because it uses a spade bit. Answer D is incorrect because it uses a Forstner bit.

7. **Answer C is correct.** Answers A, B, and D do not apply to soldering.

8. **Answer B is correct.** The coping saw's u-shaped frame and flexible, narrow blade make it ideal for making curved cuts. Answer A is incorrect because the back saw has a rigid "backbone" that prevents its blade from flexing or curving during the cut. Answer C in incorrect because the rip saw is larger and has teeth designed specifically for cutting with the wood grain. Any curved cut requires some cross-grain cutting.

9. **Answer C is correct.** Answer A is incorrect because the auger bit is better suited for deep drilling. Answer B is incorrect because twist bits come in smaller diameters for drilling. Answer D is incorrect because in this case, the question is asking for the best choice for a cleanly bored hole and Forstner bits produce cleaner holes than spade bits.

10. **Answer B is correct.** The path cut into wood by the teeth of a saw's blade is called kerf. Answer A is incorrect because the long stem of a rivet is called a mandrel. Answer C is incorrect because flux is the name of the chemical compound used to prevent metal oxidation in the soldering process. Answer D is incorrect because sawdust is the byproduct of a saw cut, but not the cut itself.

Automotive Information

Terms you'll need to understand:

✓ Engine
✓ Electrical system
✓ Fuel System
✓ Drive Train
✓ Chassis
✓ Valve train
✓ Hydraulics
✓ Piston
✓ Transaxle

✓ Compression stroke
✓ Intake stroke
✓ Power stroke
✓ Exhaust stroke
✓ Crankshaft
✓ Cylinders
✓ Emissions
✓ Transmission
✓ Suspension

Techniques you'll need to master:

✓ Describe the function of each of the four basic components of the automobile.
✓ Describe the function of each of the five engine systems.
✓ Identify the most common automotive tools.
✓ Explain the purpose of each of the automotive systems.

✓ Understand the function of the transmission and transaxle.
✓ Understand the most common exhaust pollutants and how to reduce them.
✓ Describe the process of combustion.

The Automotive Information (AI) module of the ASVAB tests your understanding of automotive maintenance, troubleshooting, and repair. The questions gauge your knowledge of automotive components and systems, tools, terminology, and common practices. Most high school automotive curriculums cover the information that this module tests.

If you are taking the conventional paper ASVAB, the AI combines the Automotive and Shop modules into one module that contains 25 questions, which you will need to answer in 11 minutes. If you are taking the CAT-ASVAB, Automotive and Shop are separate modules. In this case, the Automotive module has 11 questions, which you must answer in 6 minutes. To achieve your 70% on the paper ASVAB, you need to answer 18 questions correctly, and to achieve 80%, you need to answer 20 questions correctly. Those scores are 8 and 9 correct questions, respectively, for the CAT-ASVAB. Again, you just have to know the information that the AI module covers. One advantage of the automotive module is that the names of auto components usually indicate what they do, so that makes it a little easier. However, the troubleshooting and engine operation might give you some problems if you haven't studied. You have less than a minute per question in this module, so don't let it bog you down too much. If you need extra help in this area, try to get a textbook from your high school auto class or consult the information listed in Appendix B, "Need to Know More?".

A Look Under the Hood

Just like a computer, a car is a set of components and systems. Each of these systems interacts to create energy to power and move the automobile. The ignition and electrical systems provide primary power to create energy and activate the other automotive systems. The engine systems create the force to move the vehicle.

To get a feel for where automotive components are located, be sure your car is off and the parking brake is on, then open your hood and have a look. By using the illustrations in this book, you should be able to recognize most components. Next, lie down on the ground and have a look under your car. This is the area where you see most of the components that provide motion to your car.

A Word on Safety

Before we discuss the tools, practices, and components of the automobile, we feel that it is important to touch on a few vital safety practices and considerations.

➤ Always wear safety glasses whenever you are working on a car, especially when you are doing metal work.

➤ Always wear a back brace when you are lifting heavy equipment or components. Don't try to lift more than your known capacity.

➤ Always use the proper tool for any particular job. Improper tool usage can result in injury or even fatality.

➤ Don't wear loose clothing or jewelry when you are working on an automobile; work coveralls are the best clothing.

➤ If you are working with heavy components or equipment, wear safety shoes.

➤ Never work under a vehicle alone. If a heavy component such as an engine or transmission falls, or the car comes off the jack, it might result in serious injury or fatality.

➤ When you jack an automobile up, be sure that you don't use just a car jack, but that you also use a jack stand and wheel chocks.

Tools of the Trade

As with any profession, auto mechanics have their own set of tools. You might be familiar with some of them, whereas others may be new to you, depending on whether you have automotive experience.

 Be sure you know the most common hand and power tools that automotive work entails.

The tools that we discuss in this section are the ones that most commonly comprise an automotive tool kit. We discuss the tools that you will see in a mechanic's shop in subsequent sections, but a tool kit normally includes the following categories of tools:

➤ Hand tools

➤ Power tools (electrical, compressed air, and hydraulic)

➤ Cleaning tools

➤ Metalworking tools

➤ Measuring tools

➤ Fasteners

Hand Tools

Hand tools are those tools that do not require any force, electrical or hydraulic, other than normal physical strength. Of course, like all tools we learned about in Chapter 7, hand tools multiply the power you exert upon them. The sections that follow discuss the most common hand tools.

Wrenches

Because most automotive parts fasten together with bolts and nuts, you use wrenches to tighten or loosen those bolts and nuts. Figure 9.1 shows the most common wrench types. Subsequent to the variety of sizes in which bolts and nuts are available, wrenches are also available in different sizes to accommodate that variance. You determine the size of a wrench by the size of the nut or bolt on which it fits. You can find both metric (usually measured in millimeters) and English system (measured in inches and fractions of an inch) wrenches.

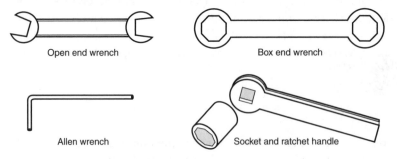

Open end wrench   Box end wrench

Allen wrench   Socket and ratchet handle

Figure 9.1 Wrenches.

Manufacturers normally stamp wrench sizes on the side of the tool. A size of 10 mm means that the opening of the wrench measures 10 millimeters across the flat part of the jaw and that it fits on a bolt head or nut that is 10 millimeters in diameter. Here are the most common wrench types:

➤ Open-end wrenches have an end opening that fits around the bolt or nut. The opening normally sits at a 15-degree angle to the handle to facilitate working in tight spaces. The ends of most open-end wrenches are different sizes.

➤ Box-end wrenches have ends that fit over the top of a bolt or nut. Although the design does not allow for work in very tight spaces, it allows you to apply more force with less slipping.

➤ Combination wrenches have one box end and one open end that are usually the same size.

➤ Socket wrenches, like box wrenches, fit over the bolt or nut, but the design is different than that of a box wrench. A socket is a metal cylinder that has a square drive hole on one end to attach to a ratchet handle, while the other end has a cutout that fits over the bolt or nut. Sockets are available in a variety of sizes, shapes, and depths to accommodate different tasks. Extensions fit between the handle and the socket to allow you to access hard-to-reach components.

➤ A torque wrench is a special type of socket wrench that has a handle that measures the resistance to turning of a bolt or nut. One type of torque wrench uses a beam and pointer to show the torque on a scale and you turn the wrench until the dial indicates the desired torque. Another type has an adjustable drive head that you can set to click when it reaches a certain torque.

➤ Adjustable wrenches adjust to fit bolts and nuts of different sizes and are available in lengths from about 4 inches to about 20 inches. The longer the wrench is, the larger the opening will adjust. Adjustable wrenches look similar to open-end wrenches but have a thumbwheel just below the opening to adjust the jaw size.

➤ Allen wrenches are L-shaped, hexagonal rods that fit in correspondingly shaped hollows in the tops of Allen screws.

Screwdrivers

Many automotive components fasten with screws, for which you need a screwdriver to turn. The Phillips and common screwdriver are two screwdriver types.

➤ Common screwdrivers drive screws that have a straight slot in the top. When you use a common screwdriver, choose a screwdriver with a blade that fits snugly into the slot so that you don't damage the screw head.

➤ Phillips screwdrivers drive screws that have an x-shaped indentation on the head. The blades number from 0 (the smallest) to 6 (the largest).

➤ Nut drivers are part screwdriver and part wrench. A nut driver has a handle and shank like a screwdriver, but in place of a blade it has a driver that accommodates small sockets.

Pliers

Pliers have opposing jaws that grip objects or cut wire, as Figure 9.2 shows. Pliers are available in a number of sizes and are grouped by their overall length. The most common types of pliers are

➤ Combination pliers have a slip joint that enables you to set the jaw openings at either of two settings; one to hold small objects and the other to hold larger objects. You can use these pliers to pull out pins, bend wire, and remove cotter keys.

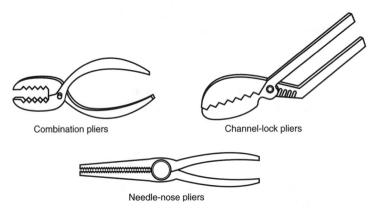

Combination pliers   Channel-lock pliers

Needle-nose pliers

Figure 9.2 Pliers.

➤ Channel-lock pliers grip large objects and have channels that allow you to set the jaw width.

➤ Diagonal cutting pliers have hardened cutting edges that can cut electrical wire and cotter keys.

➤ Needle-nose pliers have long, thin jaws that allow you to grip things in small spaces, and some needle-nose pliers have curved or bent jaws for gripping around obstacles.

➤ Snap-ring pliers remove and replace lock rings on automotive components, especially transmission assemblies, which frequently use lock rings.

➤ Vise-grip pliers lock on to small components to hold them securely during grinding or buffing.

➤ Hose-clamp pliers allow you to remove and install spring-tension hose clamps on radiator and heater hoses. A groove in the jaws grips the hose clamp so that you can squeeze the ends together to remove the hose.

Hammers

Many repair jobs require a hammer, but in automotive work, different hammers accomplish different tasks and are not always interchangeable. Ball peen hammers are the ones most commonly used in automotive repair. They have rounded heads and are used to drive punches and chisels. Never use the ball peen hammer directly on automotive parts because its hardened head can dent or damage the part. For repair jobs that require a softer head, use a soft face hammer, the most common of which are made of brass, rubber, plastic, and rubber-covered steel. Claw hammers are not good for automotive work because the metal part may cause the hammer face to shear.

Punches

Some automotive components fasten with pins, which you remove with a punch and hammer. A punch is a slender, cylindrical tool with a pointed end. A starting punch breaks the pin loose, then a pin punch smaller than the hole drives the pin out. An aligning punch has a long, tapered point that aligns corresponding holes in two separate parts.

Power Tools

Although you can do the same job with a hand tool as you can with a power tool, power tools and equipment make jobs easier and faster, especially if you have a lot of repetitive work. A power tool operates by electricity, air (pneumatic), or hydraulic power. In this section, we discuss the power tools and equipment used most often for general repair jobs.

Electric Power Tools

Most specialized automotive equipment such as oscilloscopes and wheel balancers operate on electrical power. Here are the most common electrical power tools:

➤ Electric wrenches attach to heavy duty sockets via a socket drive on the wrench. Pressing the trigger spins the drive and socket to tighten or loosen bolts and nuts. Electric wrenches are especially useful for parts that have a lot of bolts and nuts, such as engines and transmissions.

➤ Electric drills drive a chuck that holds a drill bit. This tool drills holes, drives engine cylinder hones, deglazers, and brake hones.

➤ Grinders consist of an electric motor that drives a grinding wheel or wire wheel. Grinding wheels remove metal to sharpen tools, such as drills and chisels, and to make metal parts, whereas wire wheels clean components.

Compressed Air Power Tools

Most automotive shops use an air compressor that draws in air, compresses it, and stores it in a tank. Air lines from the tank distribute the compressed air throughout the shop for tasks such as inflating tires, blowing off parts during cleaning, and powering pneumatic tools.

➤ Air impact wrenches consist of a wrench assembly that connects to removable sockets. Many air wrenches have an impact feature that drives the socket and vibrates it in and out. The force of the impact helps to loosen difficult-to-remove bolts and nuts.

➤ Air-operated jacks raise the front or rear of an automobile.

➤ Lifts raise the entire automobile so that a mechanic can work underneath. Some are electrical, but most use compressed air. The lift mechanism is below the shop floor to allow the vehicle to roll onto the lift. A single post lift can adjust for any size vehicle by moving the four wheel pads under the automobile frame. However, the center post makes it difficult to work on the middle of the vehicle. To overcome this, the mechanic can use another type of lift that has two posts to lift the vehicle from the ends or the sides.

Hydraulic Power Tools

Other power tools use hydraulic pressure to operate. In these types of tools, a piston pumps hydraulic fluid, places the fluid under pressure, and uses that pressure to exert greatly multiplied mechanical force. The most common hydraulic tools are

➤ Hydraulic floor jacks operate via a handle on the jack that pumps hydraulic fluid to lift the jack pad and raise an automobile. A control knob on the handle releases the fluid to lower the vehicle. To prevent damaging your bumpers, and causing possible injury to yourself, never jack your car up via the bumper. Always use jack stands with floor jacks.

➤ Mobile floor cranes lift very heavy loads, such as when placing engines in or out of a vehicle. Wheels allow the mechanic to roll the crane into place. A lift chain or cable attaches to the engine and the mechanic uses the control knob to raise the engine out of the vehicle. He may then roll the crane and engine to any location in the shop.

➤ A hydraulic press is a table to which a hydraulic cylinder is mounted. Pumping the cylinder handle lowers a pressing ram with several tons of force. This force can press bearings on and off shafts, in and out of housings, or it can straighten bent components.

Cleaning Equipment

Cleaning is an important step in almost all repair jobs because the mechanic must clean the part before he can find problems and measure for wear. Common cleaning equipment includes:

➤ Steam cleaners generate steam to force soap solution over the part to remove grease and sludge. Portable or stationary cleaners generate steam by burning natural gas or kerosene and are normally for outside use.

➤ Solvent cleaners are for small components and parts. The solvent thins grease, oil, and sludge and washes it away. The cleaner circulates the solvent through a filter to remove impurities for reuse.

➤ Cold tank cleaners contain a soaking solution that removes carbon and paint from nonferrous metal parts, such as carburetors or aluminum engine parts. You must use a face shield and rubber gloves when using a cold tank.

➤ Hot tank cleaners normally use natural gas to heat the cleaning solution for cleaning large ferrous metal parts such as engine blocks and cylinder heads. Most hot tank solutions are strong enough to dissolve nonferrous metals like aluminum.

➤ Glass bead blasters use compressed air and very small glass beads to further clean carbon and paint from parts that have been soaked in a hot or cold tank. Blast tanks can also use sand to clean parts, but the disadvantage of the sand is that it is small enough to become lodged in the crevices of the parts and inhibit movement and increase wear.

Metalworking Tools

You will usually find many metalworking tools in an automotive shop. Mechanics use tools such as files, hacksaws, chisels, drills, reamers, taps, and dies to cut and shape metal. The following list highlights each of the most common metalworking tools.

➤ Files are hardened steel tools that have rows of cutting teeth that smooth or shape metal by manual grinding. The cutting edges on a single-cut file run in only one direction, whereas double cut files have two cross-hatched cutting edges. Figure 9.3 illustrates these files. The cutting edges can be close together or far apart. The more distant cutting edges remove more metal with a single pass, whereas files with close cutting edges remove less metal and are better for smoothing or polishing.

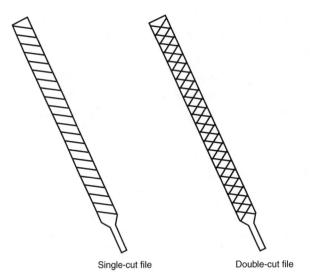

Single-cut file   Double-cut file

Figure 9.3   Files.

➤ Hacksaws are small-bladed tools that cut exhaust pipes and other metal parts. Hacksaws can have a rigid or an adjustable frame, which accommodates blades of different lengths. Hacksaw blades have varying numbers of teeth, stated in teeth per inch (TPI). Blades with fewer and larger teeth allow a hacksaw to remove more metal in a single pass. Soft, wide materials need a 14 TPI blade, while harder materials need an 18 TPI blade. For cutting pipe, tubing, conduit, or metal of an unusual shape, use a blade that keeps two or more teeth in contact with the wall, such as a 24 or 32 TPI blade. Figure 9.4 shows you a picture of a typical hacksaw.

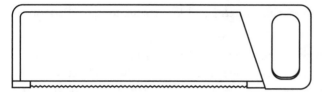

Figure 9.4 Hacksaws.

➤ Chisels consist of a hardened steel bar that has one end ground to a cutting edge and you hit with a hammer to cut or shape metal.

➤ Twist drills (drill bits) mount into an electric drill to create holes. Sharpen bits with a grinding wheel and check the point with a drill point gauge. Before you drill metal, use a center punch to mark the center of the hole. A center punch has a sharp point that makes a dent in the metal when you hit it with a hammer to give the drill a starting place and prevent it from wandering.

➤ Reamers have cutting edges that remove very small amounts of metal from a drilled hole to create a very precise fit. Reamers can be either machine-driven or hand-driven. Both fixed-size and adjustable reamers are available.

➤ Taps make or repair internal threads. Use a tap drill chart to find the correct hole size for a tap and then look on the shank of the tap to find the diameter and thread pattern.

➤ Dies create external threads, and a die stock holds and turns the die during threading. The size and thread pattern are stamped on each die.

➤ Screw extractors remove bolts or studs that have broken off below the surface of an automotive part.

Measuring Systems and Tools

Precision fit and interchangeability are important in automotive repair. For this reason, mechanics have specifications, tolerances, and clearances that they must follow if a vehicle is to work properly. To follow these specifications, a mechanic must be able to measure precisely. In the following sections, we discuss the measuring systems and tools that a mechanic uses in everyday automotive repair.

Measuring Systems

In addition to the tools that he has at his disposal, the mechanic must also understand the two measuring systems and know how to convert between the two.

The English system is the most common measuring system used in the United States. This system states specifications in inches or fractions of an inch, the most common of which are: 1 inch, 1/2, 1/4, 1/8, 1/16, 1/32, and 1/64 of an inch. However, work that requires measurements less than 1/64 of an inch, use decimals of an inch (1.0) to indicate size; one inch is divided by 10 (0.1), each tenth is also divided by 10 (0.01), and so on, to four places after the decimal (ten-thousandths place).

The metric system, also called Systeme International (SI), is the measuring system that most of the rest of the world outside the United States uses. The basic unit is the meter, which is divided by and multiplied by factors of 10. In the metric system, larger and smaller units are relative to the meter, as indicated by a prefix. For example, 1,000 meters is a kilometer (km), kilo meaning thousand. Likewise, one-thousandth of a meter is 1 millimeter (mm). If you need to refresh on the metric system, go to this website: www.bms.abdn.ac.uk/undergraduate/guidetosiunits.htm.

You must know how to convert between the English and metric system. Table 9.1 provides conversion factors.

Table 9.1	English to Metric Conversion Chart			
To Find	**Equals**	**Multiply**	**By**	**Conversion Factor**
Millimeters	=	Inches	×	25.4
Centimeters	=	Inches	×	2.54
Centimeters	=	Feet	×	32.81
Meters	=	Feet	×	0.3281
Kilometers	=	Feet	×	0.0003281
Kilometers	=	Miles	×	1.609
Inches	=	Millimeters	×	0.03937
Inches	=	Centimeters	×	0.3937
Feet	=	Centimeters	×	30.48

Table 9.1 English to Metric Conversion Chart *(continued)*				
To Find	**Equals**	**Multiply**	**By**	**Conversion Factor**
Feet	=	Meters	×	0.3048
Feet	=	Kilometers	×	3048.0
Yards	=	Meters	×	1.094
Miles	=	Kilometers	×	0.6214

Measuring Tools

An automotive mechanic uses a number of measuring tools or instruments to ensure accuracy. Here are the most common measuring tools:

➤ Rulers are flat wood, metal, or plastic instruments that are graduated into a number of spaces. Most rulers have both English and metric measurements with the smallest gradation normally as 1/64 of an inch and millimeters.

➤ Micrometers read the diameter of cylindrical objects like bolts, shaft, or holes. (We have already touched on what a micrometer looks like and how to use it in Chapter 7). Micrometers can measure inside or outside diameters, depending on the design. Outside micrometers measure the external surfaces of cylinders, screws, drill bits, and such. An inside micrometer measures the diameter of holes. You read the scale on an inside micrometer exactly like that of an outside micrometer.

➤ Small hole gauges measure the inside of holes that are too small for an inside micrometer (see Figure 9.5). To use a small hole gauge, place the tool into the hole and adjust the diameter of the gauge sphere by moving an internal wedge up or down until the gauge fits the internal dimension. Then, remove the gauge and use an outside micrometer to measure the diameter of the expanded sphere.

➤ Telescoping gauges also measure holes and consist of a spring-loaded piston that telescopes within a cylinder (see Figure 9.6). To use a telescoping gauge, place it into the hole so that the piston can expand to the hole size. When you get the proper feel, turn the handle to lock the piston in position, then remove the gauge and use an outside micrometer to measure across the two contacts.

➤ Feeler gauges measure the space between two surfaces, like between contact points or a spark plug gap. A feeler gauge is a flat blade or round wire of a precise thickness, which is stamped on the gauge. To use a feeler gauge, place it in the space that you want to measure. If the gauge and the space are the same size, the gauge will feel tight as you move it in and out.

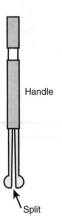

Handle

Split

Figure 9.5 Small hole gauge.

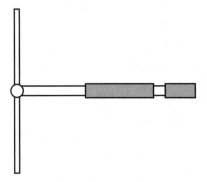

Figure 9.6 Telescoping gauge.

➤ Dial indicators measure movement or play and contour of an automotive part. It uses a plunger or lever that connects a pointer to a built-in gear. The pointer on the face of the gauge shows the measurement.

➤ Calipers look much like a ruler with one stationary bar and one moveable bar. Calipers are used to gauge the thickness of a material or object, or measuring inside or outside diameters of holes or rods. A vernier caliper is a more precise tool than a normal caliper, gauging thicknesses to the hundredths of an inch.

Fasteners

Manufacturers use fasteners, which include bolts, nuts, and screws, to hold together automotive parts. Every repair job involves fasteners, so you must understand proper fastener selection and use.

For the test, be sure that you can recognize the most common fasteners and understand their applications.

Threaded Fasteners

Threaded fasteners use the wedging action of a thread (screw, as defined in Chapter 7) to clamp two parts together. The most common types of threaded fasteners are screws, bolts, studs, and nuts, as highlighted in the following list:

➤ Screws are fasteners that fit a threaded hole. You drive the screw into the hole to clamp two parts together. The most common type is the cap screw, which has a hexagonal head and is sometimes called a hex head screw. You can drive a cap screw with a box, open-end, combination, or socket wrench.

Machine screws often hold together small automotive parts. Machine screws can have either a slotted or a Phillips head and you drive them with a screwdriver. You will see Allen head screws, which you drive with an Allen wrench, used more often in aircraft assemblies than in automotive components.

Sheet metal screws have a wide pitch that does not require a threaded hole, but instead uses the body of the sheet metal to form an internal thread. One type of sheet metal screw is hard enough to be self-tapping and creates its own internal threads in soft metal.

➤ Bolts screw into threads on a nut instead of a threaded hole. Some bolts look like hex head screws, but machine bolts have a square head and are used where strong fasteners or close tolerances are not vital. You normally use two wrenches to tighten or loosen bolts—one to drive the bolt and one to hold the nut. However, the head on a carriage bolt has a square base that locks into the part to keep the bolt from turning as you tighten the nut.

➤ Studs have threads on both ends. One end of the stud fits into a threaded hole in one part, then another part fits over the other end of the stud and the two parts are clamped together with a nut. You will normally see studs in areas where positioning is important. Although a stud can have threads down its entire length, it usually has threads only on the ends.

➤ Nuts are fasteners that have internal threads that accommodate the threads on bolts or studs. You can use a box-end, open-end, or socket wrench to drive a nut. Other types of nuts include wing, stop, and thumb nuts. You tighten wing and thumb nuts by hand, and use stop nuts for permanent fastening.

Hex lock nuts are common in applications where parts undergo a lot of vibration. Its cone-shaped end creates a positive lock against the bolt or stud.

You can also use a castellated nut and a cotter pin to keep a nut from working loose. After you tighten the castellated nut, you insert a cotter pin through slots in both the nut and the bolt and bend the ends of the cotter pin around the nut.

Measuring Pitch for Threaded Fasteners

Although threaded fasteners have any of several types of threads, you cannot use one thread type with another thread type. Nuts and bolts are available in both English and metric system threads.

English system fasteners have either coarse (NC) or fine (NF) thread types. Coarse threads have fewer threads per inch than fine threads. You use coarse threads in aluminum parts because they provide greater holding strength in soft materials. Use fine threads in harder materials, such as cast iron and steel, to provide greater staying action and torque.

Metric system threads indicate pitch size on the fastener with designations like M12 × 1.75. M shows that the fastener has metric threads; the first number is the outside diameter (in millimeters) of a bolt, screw, or stud or the inside diameter of a nut; the second number is the pitch. The larger the pitch number, the greater the spacing between the threads.

Because some vehicles have both metric and English threaded fasteners and all vehicles use both fine and coarse threads, it is sometimes difficult to tell one thread from another. A pitch gauge has blades with teeth and by matching the teeth on a blade with threads on a fastener, you can determine thread size. Each blade has its thread size stamped on the side. Pitch gauges are available for both metric and English threads.

In addition to size, pitch, and type, you must also know fastener grades. Bolts and screws have differing tensile strength according to their application. You should always use replacement fasteners that are of the same grade as the originals. You will find grade markings on the head of a bolt, which are as follows:

➤ Grade 1 bolts have no markings and are not very strong.

➤ Grade 5 bolts have three marks and are much stronger than Grade 1 bolts.

➤ Grade 8 bolts are the strongest bolts for automotive use and have six marks on the head.

Metric fasteners also use numbers to indicate strength, and the higher the number is, the stronger the fastener is. Typical metric bolt strength numbers are 9.8 and 10.9.

Nuts are not always marked for quality, but when they are marked, English nuts use dots to represent grade markings and metric nuts use numbers to represent strength, and the marks carry the same significance as the marks on a bolt.

Nonthreaded Fasteners

In addition to threaded fasteners, manufacturers also use nonthreaded fasteners, such as dowel pins, retaining rings, cotter keys, splines, washers, and rivets, for some applications.

➤ Washers are flat, circular fasteners used with bolts, screws, studs, and nuts. Flat washers normally fit between a nut and an automotive part or under the head of a screw or bolt. The washer distributes the clamping force over a wider area and protects machined surfaces as you tighten the bolt head or nut. Flat washers are flat and continuous (they make an entire circle). Lock washers are also flat, but the surface is not continuous. This "broken surface" digs into the fastener and the component to prevent the fastener from vibrating or working loose. Shake-proof washers are star shaped and have teeth that allow them to grip the component and the fastener. Figure 9.7 shows you these washers in diagram form.

Flat washer   Lock washer   Shake-proof washer

Figure 9.7 Washers.

➤ Dowel pins fit into predrilled holes to position two adjoining parts. Dowel pins require special pliers or a punch and hammer for removal. Dowel pins may be straight or tapered, solid or split.

➤ Retaining rings (snap rings) are either internal or external and often hold transmission assemblies together. An external ring fits in a machined groove on the outside of a shaft, relying on spring tension from the ring to hold it in the groove. An internal ring fits in a machined groove inside a hole. You use retaining ring pliers to install the retaining rings.

➤ Keys are small, hardened pieces of metal that lock a gear or pulley on to a shaft. Half of the key fits into a key seat on the shaft and the other half fits into a keyway on the pulley or gear.

➤ Splines have external teeth that lock gears on a shaft. The teeth on the spline match up with internal teeth cut on the gear. The external and internal splines mate together, allowing the shaft to turn the gear. Splines are common in transmission assemblies.

➤ Rivets are soft metal pins with a head at one end. Rivets hold together two pieces of metal through holes drilled in both components. The rivet goes through both of the holes and then you form the small end of the rivet into a head with a rivet set or a ball peen hammer. Rivets are common in body work.

Engine Classifications

Now that we have covered the preliminaries, let's discuss the construction and purpose of the different automotive systems, starting with the engine.

There are many different ways to classify the variety of engines that are in operation today, for both legacy and current automotive designs. The following are ways to commonly classify engines:

➤ Combustion type

➤ Number of strokes/cycles

➤ Number of cylinders

➤ Arrangement of cylinders

➤ Arrangement of valves

➤ Combustion chamber shape

➤ Ignition method

➤ Cooling system

➤ Carburetion methods

We will examine each of these classifications throughout the rest of this chapter.

Combustion Types

The combustion, or ignition, of the air-fuel mixture can take place either inside or outside the engine.

Internal Combustion

Most automobiles today have an internal combustion engine. In an internal combustion engine, fuel is burned inside the same container where power is developed, that is, inside the engine. A few drops of gasoline injected into the combustion chamber are allowed to vaporize briefly and are then ignited.

External Combustion

The steam engine is an example of an external combustion engine. The burning of an air-fuel mixture heats water in a container, and the resulting steam is piped into the engine and used to develop power. In a steam engine, the fuel can be burned almost anywhere as long as it turns water into steam that can be fed to the engine.

Cylinder Number and Arrangement

You can also classify engines according to the number of cylinders they have or by the arrangement of the cylinders. Throughout history, automotive manufacturers have produced engines with one, two, three, four, five, six, eight, twelve, and sixteen cylinders. Cylinder arrangement can be in-line, V-shape, or opposing each other.

In-Line

An in-line cylinder arrangement configures the cylinders in a row. They can be completely vertical or slanted to lower the engine's height. Although the in-line arrangement works well with four cylinders, it becomes cumbersome with six cylinders and even more so with eight. The more cylinders that an in-line engine has, the more difficult it is to evenly distribute the air-fuel mixture. In addition, more cylinders also mean longer engine length, resulting in a larger hood area and less passenger space.

V-Arrangement

The V-arrangement places two rows of cylinders in a V-shaped block. Pistons from both rows connect to one crankshaft in the bottom of the V. Any even number of cylinders is possible in the V design. Motorcycles commonly use a V-2, whereas automobiles are often V-6s or V-8s, and some V-12s and V-16s have also been made. The V design provides a shorter, more rigid engine and better air-fuel mixture distribution.

Opposed Cylinder Arrangement

Opposed (flat) cylinder designs are common when the engine must fit in a small compartment at the rear of the car. In this design, two rows of cylinders are opposite each other on a flat plane and the two rows of pistons connect to a single crankshaft located between them.

Valve Arrangement

You can also classify engines according to valve arrangement, of which there are two primary designs: the L-head and the I-head. A third design, the overhead, is an extension of the I-head.

L-Head

The L-head valve arrangement is a legacy design that places the entire valve-operating mechanism in the cylinder block, allowing the cylinder heads to be very flat. The intake and exhaust valves are located beside the piston. The camshaft operates a set of valve lifters that push directly on the valves to open them. Because the valves have to open up high for good breathing, the combustion chamber area above the piston has to be large. However, for high compression the combustion chamber should be as small as possible. The result is that the flathead design does not permit both good breathing and high compression.

I-Head

The I-head arrangement is an overhead design that places the valves over the piston in the cylinder head but leaves the camshaft and lifters in the block. The overhead design has more parts, but has a more efficient engine and higher compression ratios. In this arrangement, the air-fuel mixture feeds into the engine and burned gases are exhausted through the cylinder head, so the engine gets better compression and can breathe better.

Overhead Camshaft

The overhead camshaft (OHC) design eliminates pushrods and rocker arm assemblies by placing the camshaft on top of the cylinder head directly above the valves. The camshaft operates a set of lifters that directly contact the valves. It eliminates the weight of the pushrods and provides better breathing because the valves can be placed into the cylinder at a more flexible angle. Some engines use two separate camshafts above the pistons in a double overhead camshaft (DOHC) design.

Cycling

Cycling is the number of strokes that a piston needs to make to generate power. Most vehicles on the road today use four-stroke cycling. However, jet-skis, snowmobiles, and other small engines, such as those used in motorcycles and chain saws, develop power in two strokes. In the following sections, we discuss two- and four-stroke engines.

Two-Cycle

The two-cycle engine does in two strokes what it takes the four-cycle engine four strokes to do. Two-stroke engines fire once every revolution (four-stroke engines fire once every other revolution) to provide more power for the amount of work expended. The advantage of the two-stroke engine is that it does not have valves and is therefore smaller and lighter.

In a two-cycle engine, fuel intake and compression occur on the upward (compression) stroke, and combustion and exhaust occur on the downward (combustion) stroke.

The upward stroke of the piston creates a vacuum in the crankcase that pulls the air-fuel mixture in from the carburetor through an inlet port. At the same time, the piston seals off the exhaust port and compresses the fuel charge in the combustion chamber. Near the top of the upward stroke, the spark fires the fuel charge.

On the downward stroke, the piston seals off the inlet port and begins to develop pressure in the crankcase. As the piston continues downward, the exhaust port opens and releases the burned gases. Near the bottom of the downward stroke, the inlet port starts to open to receive a fresh charge of fuel. To prevent the new fuel from escaping through the exhaust port, the top of the piston in most small engines is shaped so that the air-fuel mixture swirls as it enters the combustion chamber. This clears the combustion chamber of almost all burned gases and keeps the fresh air-fuel mixture from escaping.

Four-Stroke Cycle Engine

Most automotive piston engines develop power in a series of four-strokes. A stroke occurs when a single piston moves from the top of the cylinder, called top dead center (TDC), to the bottom of the cylinder, called bottom dead center (BDC). When the piston moves from BDC back to TDC, another stroke has occurred. A series of four strokes is a complete cycle. The four-stroke-cycle engine develops power in this sequence of piston strokes: intake, compression, power, and exhaust.

➤ **Intake Stroke**—At the beginning of the intake stroke, the piston is at TDC. There are two holes in the top of the cylinder; the intake port to let in air and fuel, and the exhaust port for exhaust gases to leave after combustion. The intake stroke begins with both ports closed. As the piston moves down during the intake stroke, the intake port opens and the vacuum inside the cylinder draws air and fuel into the cylinder. When the piston is at BDC, the crankshaft has turned 180 degrees, the combustion chamber is filled with the air-fuel mixture, and the intake port closes.

➤ **Compression Stroke**—During the compression stroke, the piston travels from BDC back to TDC, compressing the air-fuel mixture in the combustion chamber. During compression, the fuel particles are pressurized, thus increasing heat within the fuel molecules. At the end of the compression stroke, the crankshaft has turned another 180 degrees to complete one revolution. During the compression stroke, the intake and exhaust ports remain closed.

➤ **Power Stroke**—As the piston reaches TDC again, the air-fuel mixture ignites and burns very rapidly. The rapid expansion of gases inside the cylinder forces the piston downward to BDC to accomplish the power stroke. At this time, the crankshaft has turned another 180 degrees, completing one and one-half revolutions. During the power stroke, the intake and exhaust ports remain closed.

➤ **Exhaust Stroke**—As the piston travels back up to TDC for the exhaust stroke, the exhaust port opens to release exhaust gases from the cylinder. When the piston reaches the top of this stroke, the exhaust port closes. The crankshaft has turned another 180 degrees to complete two entire revolutions.

 Be sure that you understand the strokes of both two-cycle and four-cycle engines. Two-cycle engines have an intake-compression stroke and a combustion-exhaust stroke. Four-cycle engines have separate intake, compression, combustion, and exhaust strokes.

Power Overlap

Automotive engines usually have four, six, or eight cylinders. In a four-cylinder engine, because of the crankshaft design, no two cylinders are performing the same stroke at the same time, and one piston is always providing a power stroke to turn the crankshaft. However, the more cylinders that an engine has, the smoother the engine runs. Additional cylinders mean additional power strokes to the crankshaft, and more than four cylinders provides an overlap of power strokes.

Combustion Chamber Shape

We also can classify engines by the shape of their combustion chamber. Overhead valve engines can have a hemispherical, wedge-shaped combustion chamber, or a precombustion chamber, which we discuss in the following sections.

Hemispherical

A hemispherical, or "hemi," combustion chamber places the valves on a slant at either side of the chamber and the spark plug at the center of the chamber. The design of the "hemi" engine provides efficient air-fuel mixture burn-off at high speeds.

Wedge

The wedge combustion chamber provides smooth burning of the air-fuel mixture because the piston squeezes the air-fuel mixture into the chamber in a swirling manner that gives good distribution for complete and smooth burning.

Precombustion Chamber

The precombustion chamber is common in diesel engines and some gasoline engines. This design connects a second, smaller chamber to the main combustion chamber. On a diesel engine power stroke, fuel is injected into the precombustion chamber, whereas gasoline engines use a second intake valve. Combustion starts in the prechamber and spreads into the main chamber by its own energy.

Engine Types

In the automotive world, you will see two main types of engines: the rotary engine, currently exclusive to Mazda, and the piston engine, both diesel and gasoline powered. The engine is the automobile's source of power and is a compound machine consisting of hundreds of moving parts that are supported by many subsystems. The engine converts heat energy from a fuel to a usable form of power. To create this power, the engine mixes a fuel, such as gasoline or diesel, with air and ignites it to produce the heat. The type of vehicle that an engine powers, whether automobile, boat, truck, aircraft, or motorcycle, determines the power and size of that engine.

Rotary Engine

The rotary engine is a type of internal combustion engine that you will currently see only in Mazda vehicles. The rotary engine performs the same job as a four-stroke cycle piston engine, but with a rotary, rather than reciprocating, motion. The rotary engine doesn't use pistons, but uses a rotor attached to an eccentric cam on an output shaft. Figure 9.8 shows the basic construction of the rotor assembly of a rotary engine.

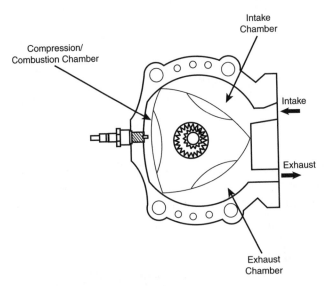

Figure 9.8   Rotary engine.

The rotor is inside an oval firing chamber and has seals on each of its three points so that it can rotate in the chamber and create distinct chambers within the rotary path. Both ends of the firing chamber are closed and sealed. The chamber contains two side ports; one port connects to the fuel system and allows air and fuel to enter the engine and the other connects to the exhaust system. The spark plug screws directly into the chamber.

As one face of the rotor sweeps past the intake port, a partial vacuum occurs in this part of the firing chamber. As the rotor continues to turn, the seal crosses the intake port, sealing off the chamber. The rotor continues to turn, compressing the air-fuel mixture and the spark occurs at a maximum compression. Rapidly expanding gases push against the rotor face and force the rotor to continue to turn in a clockwise direction. Power applied to the face of the rotor transmits over the eccentric shaft to the output shaft. As the apex of the rotor passes the exhaust port, the exhaust gases escape from the chamber.

Although they have a different design, rotary engines require the same support systems—fuel, ignition, lubrication, and cooling—that piston engines require.

Piston Engines

A piston engine, also called a four-stroke-cycle engine or a reciprocating engine, is the heart of most automobiles and the engine type that you will see most commonly. In a piston engine, the pistons and connecting rods move up and down in a reciprocating motion. The piston engine uses a number of systems and subsystems to propel an automobile. The next section discusses the construction and operation of the most important piston engine parts and how they work together to develop power.

Basic Piston Engine Components

Because the engine is the heart of the automobile, let's begin the discussion on piston engines by describing its most significant parts. This section discusses each major automotive system and its subsystems and how they all work together to provide power and motion to an automobile. Refer to Figure 9.9, which illustrates piston engine components, during the discussion on piston engines.

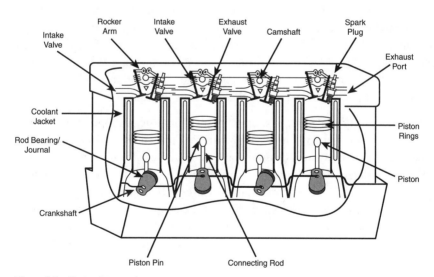

Figure 9.9 Basic piston engine components.

Be sure that you understand all the major components of an automotive engine and types of engine design.

Pistons and Piston Rings

The piston transmits the force created by the combusting fuel through the connecting rods to the crankshaft. In the four-stroke cycle engine, there is always one piston delivering power, one exhausting gases, one drawing in air-fuel, and one compressing the air-fuel mixture.

Ring grooves hold the piston rings in place on the piston. The heat dam is above the top ring groove and prevents heat from extending down into the lower part of the piston (see Figure 9.9). A pin hole is bored through the piston to hold the piston pin, and the distance between the top of the piston head and the center of the pin hole is the compression distance or compression chamber.

Pistons can be forged or cast from aluminum alloys. Cast pistons are very light and can generate higher engine speeds. Forged pistons provide a stronger, denser piston and have better heat distribution throughout the piston, but cast pistons are less expensive.

Cast iron or steel piston rings create a moveable seal between the combustion chamber and the crankcase to prevent compression pressures from leaking around the piston into the crankcase. At the same time, they keep oil in the crankcase from leaking into the combustion chamber. Piston rings also conduct heat from the head of the piston into the cylinder wall so that the cylinder and piston can expand and contract at the same rate.

The piston ring seals are flexible to adjust for differing operating speeds. They are exposed to vacuums, high internal pressures, and extreme heat. Because of this, they must change shape rapidly to conform to shape changes in the cylinder wall. Compression rings in the grooves near the piston head protect the seal from compression pressures. Oil control rings below the compression rings wipe excessive oil from the cylinder wall and route it back into the crankcase to minimize oil consumption.

Crankcase

The crankcase houses and supports the crankshaft and is either split or one-piece. Split crankcases are cast in two pieces and bolted together. During repair, the mechanic takes the two halves apart to remove the crankshaft. However, the one-piece crankcase is more common and during service, the mechanic removes and replaces the entire crankcase. The advantage of a one-piece crankcase is better rigidity and less expense to manufacture than a split crankcase.

Both kinds of crankcases can be either cast iron or cast aluminum. Although aluminum is lighter than cast iron and allows for better head dissipation, cast iron is stronger and provides a more solid housing for the crankshaft. Small, air-cooled engines usually have aluminum crankcases while larger engines have cast iron crankcases.

Cylinder Block

Most automotive engines today combine the cylinders and crankcase in one large metal casting called a cylinder block. All other engine components either fit inside, or fasten to the outside, of the block. Cylinder blocks are either cast aluminum or cast iron. The number and arrangement of cylinders determine the shape of the cylinder block. The two lower block designs are the V design and the Y design. The designs are similar in overall construction, but the Y design flares at the bottom to give better attachment area.

Cylinders

The cylinder is a tube in the cylinder block. The cylinder is closed at the bottom and the piston slides up and down inside of the cylinder. The space between the top of the cylinder and the top of the piston is the combustion chamber where the engine compresses and ignites the air-fuel mixture. The cylinders are usually cast iron and made to very tight tolerances. However, some cylinders are made of aluminum, and although this makes the engine lighter and provides good heat dissipation, aluminum tends to wear rapidly.

Cylinder Heads

The cylinder head is a large aluminum or iron casting bolted to the top of the engine block. A head gasket between the cylinder head and the block forms a gas- and liquid-tight seal. An in-line engine has one cylinder head, and a V-engine has two cylinder heads, one for each bank of cylinders.

The casting of the cylinder head forms the combustion chamber above each piston. Each combustion chamber has a threaded hole for a spark plug and intake and exhaust ports. The intake port connects to the intake manifold, which directs air and fuel into the cylinder head/combustion chamber. On the exhaust stroke, the exhaust port routes burned gases out of the engine. An exhaust manifold attaches to the cylinder head to collect burned gases and send them through the exhaust pipe into the muffler.

Connecting Rods and Crankshaft

To use the power developed by burning gasoline, the piston must connect to other parts. The connecting rods and crankshaft are the components that utilize and transmit this power (see Figure 9.9).

As the combusting air-fuel mixture expands and forces down the piston, the connecting rod that attaches to both the piston pin and the crankshaft causes the crankshaft to turn. This action changes reciprocating motion to rotating motion. The crankshaft's ends are mounted in lubricated bearings so they can turn. To produce a continuous rotary motion, the piston must return to its starting point at TDC. After the piston pushes down the crankshaft, a counterbalancing weight, the crankshaft throw, has enough momentum to return the piston to TDC for the next charge of air and fuel.

Connecting rods are either cast or forged, but most engines today use cast connecting rods. The connecting rod usually has an I-beam cross-section to combine high strength with low weight. The end of the connecting rod through which the piston pin fits is called the small end. If a free-floating pin is used, this end will have a piston pin bushing. The other end of the connecting rod is the big end and has a removable cap that allows it to be bolted around the crankshaft throw. Balancing pads at the ends ensure that the rod weight meets final balancing tolerances. Some connecting rods have an oil spurt hole that distributes oil to other engine parts, and a few engines have a drilled oil passage the length of the rod to provide pressurized oil to the piston pin bushing.

Each connecting rod mounts to a journal on each crankshaft throw. A sprocket or gear attaches to the front end of the crankshaft to drive the valve train, and a drive flange connects a flywheel at the rear to pass on power to the drive train.

The crank converts the piston's reciprocating motion into rotary motion. It also turns the belts for accessories such as the oil, fuel, and water pumps, the valve train, alternator, distributor, and fan. The crankshaft in a four-cylinder, in-line engine has four throws that attach to the connecting rods and are directly in line with the cylinders. The throws are normally spaced 180 degrees apart to allow a different stroke of the four-stroke cycle to occur in one of the cylinders at any given time.

The crankshaft in a six-cylinder, in-line engine has six crank throws that are spaced 120 degrees apart and placed directly in line with the cylinders. V-8 engines have four crank throws and each throw has two connecting rods—one rod for each cylinder. Although the throws of a V-8 crankshaft can be spaced 180 degrees apart like a four-cylinder, in-line engine, most V-8's space the throws 90 degrees apart.

Bushings and Bearings

Friction occurs wherever moving parts meet and cause heat and wear. Lubricants reduce friction, but another way is to make the contacting parts from materials other than the part material. For instance, copper, tin, and lead are good materials for parts that rub against steel or cast iron. For this reason, bushings and bearings at major points in an engine are made of material different from that of the parts they support. Here are the important automotive bearing types:

➤ A bushing is a full round sleeve that is pressed into place in a component hole and machined on the inside to fit a shaft. Insert bearings usually have two halves that fit over a shaft and a cap as part of the housing assembly.

➤ Roller bearings support the front and rear crankshaft main bearing positions in some engines.

➤ Connecting rod bearings are two-piece insert bearings that fit onto the large end of the connecting rods at the journals. The small end of the connecting rod has piston pin bushings.

➤ Main bearings are two-piece insert bearings that hold the main bearing journals. The main bearings support the crankshaft so that it can rotate. Most bearings are slightly larger than the cap or housing in which they fit so that they can snap into place. Other bearings have a locking lip that fits into a slot in the housing, while still others use dowel pins to hold the bearing in place.

All bearings must have oil clearance, which means that when oil is pumped into the oil clearance area of a bearing, the combination of the oil pressure and the rotation of the shaft creates a skin of oil between the shaft and bearing. That way, the shaft doesn't rest on the bearing but on the oil film, and there is no metal-to metal contact.

Seals and Gaskets

Seals and gaskets are important in automotive connections because they minimize friction and prevent lubrication from leaking at the automotive joints and connections.

Gaskets are flat compression seals used between two automotive parts that are bolted together to form a pressure-tight seal. Without a gasket, the tight compression of the two parts would cause irregularities on the part surfaces to leak. Gaskets are soft material that compresses and fills up these irregularities when the two parts are tightened. Gaskets are made of copper for low combustion pressure, steel and graphite (or other non-asbestos material) for higher combustion pressures, and steel and aluminum for very high combustion pressures. Cork, rubber, and paper are used for gaskets in very low-temperature and low-pressure conditions.

One of the most important automotive gaskets is the cylinder head gasket, which seals in the pressures from combustion. The head gasket also seals the lubrication and cooling passages between the block and the cylinder head to prevent cooling and lubricating fluid loss and prevents fluid intermixing.

Seals provide leak protection around rotating or sliding shafts, which a normal gasket cannot do. Of the many different seal types, lip seals and "O" ring seals are the most common.

Lip seals enclose a lubricant inside of a bearing area to keep dirt and other abrasive materials out of the joint. Seals generally have three basic elements:

➤ A casing is a metal housing for the seal assembly that holds the seal in position after installation.

➤ A sealing element is the rubber lip that contacts the shaft and holds the lubricant inside the bearing area.

➤ A spring puts pressure on the sealing element to keep it in contact with the shaft.

O-rings are ring-shaped seals that have an oval cross section. However, some O-rings have cross sections of other shapes. Both static (nonmoving) and dynamic (rotating or sliding motion) situations use O-rings to seal two components. Automotive O-rings are made of synthetic rubber to provide elasticity. When pressure is applied to the joint, the ring shape conforms to the shape of the ring groove and the mating part; when the pressure is removed, the ring goes back to its original shape.

Valve Train

The valve train opens and closes the intake and exhaust ports at the correct time in the cycle. The parts that comprise a valve train are the camshaft, valve lifter, pushrod, rocker arm assembly, and valve assembly (see Figure 9.9).

In the four-stroke cycle, air and fuel enter the cylinder through the intake port, are trapped and burned there, and expelled as exhaust gases through the exhaust port. The valve train is a mechanism above the pistons that regulates the opening and closing of these two ports.

The crankshaft drives the camshaft, which is the heart of the valve train. As the camshaft turns the cam lobes, which are bumps on the camshaft, they push up the valve lifters. Each lifter attaches through a pushrod that runs alongside the cylinder to a rocker arm assembly above the piston. As the valve lifter rises, the rocker arm pushes on the end of the valve and opens it. Further rotation of the camshaft lets the lifter and push rod move down and the valve spring to close the valve. Both valves are closed during the compression and power strokes. As the piston moves up on the exhaust stroke, the exhaust valve opens to release the burned gases.

Camshafts and Camshaft Drives

A small crankshaft gear on the front end of the crankshaft turns the large camshaft gear once every two revolutions of the crankshaft, because valve action is required during only intake and exhaust strokes. The camshaft has a number of cam lobes located along its length. Because there is one cam lobe for each valve, the V-8 camshaft has 16 cam lobes and the V-6 has 12 cam lobes.

The camshaft journals ride in cam bearings in the engine. A large pump on the end of the camshaft drives the fuel pump and a gear on the camshaft drives the distributor and the oil pump.

The camshaft is cast and ground to the proper shape. Each cam is also ground to provide the correct valve action. After grinding, the surface of the cam lobe is hardened to prevent wear.

Valve Lifters

Valve lifters ride on the camshaft and rise as the cam lobe on the camshaft rotates. As the cam lobe rotates, it raises the lifter. The lifter is at its highest point when the nose of the lobe is right under it. As the lobe continues to rotate, the lifter drops along the other flank until it is resting on the lobe heel again. The clearance ramp allows the lifter to travel smoothly down the lobe flank. The shape of the cam nose and flanks determine how long the valves stay open. The number of degrees that the crankshaft rotates while the valve is open determines the lifter time.

Valve lifters are made of high-quality iron and hardened to prevent wear as they slide on the hardened cam lobe. There are two types of valve lifters, solid and hydraulic. Solid lifters are one-piece units that can have a removable seat for a pushrod. Hydraulic lifters provide for changes in valve train length to keep all parts of the valve train in constant contact and cut down on noise.

Push Rods

Overhead valve engines transfer the cam lobe and lifter motion up to the cylinder head by a pushrod. At one end, the pushrod sits in the valve lifter and fits in a rocker arm at the other end. Most pushrods are hollow to lessen weight and allow oil flow. Pressurized oil is sent through the pushrod up to the rocker arm assembly for lubrication.

Rocker Arms

The rocker arm mounts to the cylinder head. When the pushrod lifts one side of the rocker arm, the other side moves correspondingly. The rocker arm converts upward motion to downward motions. If the fulcrum is in the center, a given amount of upward movement will result in exactly the same amount of downward movement for a 1:1 ratio. The fulcrum of many rocker arms is off-center to create a 1:5.1 ratio, meaning that the downward motion to open the valve is 1.5 times greater than the lift of the cam lobe.

Valves, Valve Guides, and Valve Seats

The intake and exhaust valves open and close the intake and exhaust ports. A valve is a shaft with a large round head. The head of the valve has a precision-ground, tapered face that seals against a seat in the cylinder head. When the rocker arm pushes it open, gases move around the valve head into or out of the cylinder. Valves are made from high-quality steels because they get very hot during combustion. The intake valve is larger than the exhaust valve because it controls the slow-moving, low-pressure intake mixture. Exhaust valves are smaller because the exhaust gases are less dense and leave the cylinder under high pressure.

Valve guides support and guide the valve stems in the cylinder. The integral valve guide is part of the cylinder head. Many valve guides can be removed and replaced during an overhaul. Replaceable guides can be made from cast iron or softer materials such as bronze alloys. The clearance between the valve stem and guide must allow the valve to move freely. It must also allow oil to lubricate between the stem and guide. Too much clearance allows oil from the rocker arm to work down the stem and into the combustion chamber. This can create a problem on the intake valve stem because all the while that the intake valve is open, there is a vacuum in the cylinder. On the exhaust valve, there is a vacuum only during valve overlap. Valve guides also disperse heat via coolant passages in the cylinder head near the valve guide area. Heat is moved out of the valve stem, into the valve guide and cylinder head, and into the coolant.

The valve seat is a precision ground area at the entrance of the valve port. It may be a part of the cylinder head or a separate unit installed in the head with a press fit. If the cylinder head is made from aluminum, the seats are cast iron or steel.

Engine Systems

The engine uses several different, interoperating systems to generate energy and motion. The engine system comprises the lubrication, cooling, fuel, ignition, and electrical systems. In the following sections, we discuss each system, its function, and the other systems with which it works.

 Be sure that you know the major automotive systems, their primary components, and understand individual system function and interoperability with other automotive systems.

Lubrication System

The lubrication system circulates oil between moving parts to allow them to move freely and to reduce friction and metal-to-metal contact. The circulating oil also carries heat from the hot engine and cleans dirt and deposits from the engine parts. Oil on the cylinder walls seals the rings to improve engine compression.

All moving engine parts require support, such as guides, shafts, and bearings, and friction increases with the increase of weight or force. When an engine has to compensate for less internal friction, it can develop more power. Most automotive engines use a full-pressure lubricating system wherein pressurized oil is forced to parts such as main, rod, and cam bearings.

Small two-stroke engines used in motorcycles and chain saws use a different lubrication system than a four-stroke engine uses. A special oil-fuel mixture goes into the crankcase. The oil circulates around the components and penetrates into the areas that need lubrication. In some engines, the gasoline and oil are mixed and poured into the fuel tank, while other engines have two separate tanks for fuel and oil.

Our discussion below focuses on the lubrication systems for a four-stroke cycle engine. This discussion includes details on lubricants and components of the oil distribution, filter, and lubrication system as a whole.

Lubricants

Petroleum oil is the most common lubricating fluid. Lubricating oil is made or refined from crude petroleum like gasoline, kerosene, and fuel oil.

Environmental concerns and crude oil shortages led researchers to look for other ways of making a noncarbon-based lubricant, and the result was synthetic oil. Of the four types of synthetic oils available, two belong to the esters class, which are the result of a reaction of alcohol to certain acids, and the other two types are synthesized hydrocarbons that have a molecular structure that is similar to, but more stable than, that of natural petroleum.

Synthetic oils reduce friction better than petroleum oil so that the engine can provide more power and achieve better fuel mileage. Synthetic oils also operate in a wider temperature range than petroleum oil, which means that you don't need to change synthetic oils as often as you do petroleum oil.

The most important property of oil is its viscosity, which is a measure of its fluidity. The Society of Automotive Engineers (SAE) determines the temperature requirements for oil at 0 degrees F (low) and 210 degrees F (high). Thin oil has a low viscosity number, like SAE 20, while thicker oil receives a higher number, like SAE 40 or 50. The oil container states the viscosity number, and your car's owner's manual tells you what grade of oil you should use in your car. Most automobiles need SAE 30 in the summer and SAE 20 in the winter. On the side of the oil container, you might see a designation of 10W-40. The W indicates the oil has met the SAE's low temperature requirements. But if the oil has no W, such as SAE-30, then that oil meets the high temperature ratings.

Bearing grease is a thick, Vaseline-like lubricant specifically for packing bearings. Remember that bearings endure a lot of heat, weight, and motion, so the bearing grease needs to be thick and very stable so that it doesn't break down under the tremendous amount of heat. Like oil, bearing greases are available as petroleum-based and synthetic. Unlike oil the thickness of bearing grease is measured not as viscosity, but as penetration, and the higher the penetration number is, the softer the grease is. Penetration numbers are derived by placing a penetration cone on the surface of a body of bearing grease, then measuring the drop, or penetration, of the cone, in tenths of a millimeter, according to conditions of load, time, and temperature.

Oil Pan

The oil pan stores and collects the oil from the engine. Baffles inside the pan prevent oil from sloshing away from the oil pickup area during hard stops. Some high-performance engines use a shield on the bottom of the crankcase to keep air whipped by the crankshaft from churning up the oil and letting air bubbles enter the oil. The shield also increases the engine's power by reducing the amount of air disturbed by the crankshaft at high speeds.

Oil Pump

The camshaft drives the engine oil pump, which forces oil through the engine. The resistance to this flow results in a pressure buildup that provides more force for the oil distribution. A pickup screen between the oil pan and the oil pump filters large particulate from the oil before passing it through to the oil pump.

If the pressure in the oil lines and system gets too high, the relief valve will compensate. If oil pressure gets too high, a ball or plunger pushes into position to release the pressure and send some oil back into the pan. As soon as pressure returns to normal, the relief valve spring repositions the plunger or ball.

Oil Filter

After the oil goes through the pump and relief valve, it passes through the oil filter, which cleans the oil before it reaches the engine parts. The oil filter threads onto the outside of the cylinder block, so that it can be easily changed.

The filter element and canister assembly are usually one piece, and filter elements can be cotton, wool, or paper, which is the most common.. When the oil passes through the filter, dirt and acids stick to the paper and only the cleaned oil goes through to the engine block. After a lot of use, the oil filter becomes clogged, and if oil is not passing through the element, it isn't getting to engine parts, either.

A bypass valve prevents the oil flow from completely stopping. When the filter element clogs, pressure inside the canister pushes the bypass valve open to let the oil, though unfiltered, go around the filter element and directly into the engine.

Oil Passages

From the filter, the oil enters the oil passages of the block and flows into long channels in the cylinder block. From the main header, the oil goes to oil clearance areas at main bearings. Oil also flows through the crankshaft and to the main journals to the connecting rod journals and sometimes through the connecting rods if they are drilled. From the main bearings, oil also flows to the cam bearings through the cylinder block.

Once oil passes through the lubrication system, it runs down the inside of the engine back to the oil pan. Oil from the connecting rod bearings is thrown off the crankshaft to lubricate the cylinders, pistons, and rings. Excess oil that the oil control ring picks up passes through oil holes in the piston and back to the oil pan.

Monitoring Oil Level and Pressure

If the oil level is too low, the pump cannot provide enough oil to lubricate the engine. An oil dipstick extends into the oil reservoir and is used to check the oil level in your car. Markings on the dipstick show how much oil you have and indicate when you need to add oil. You do not add oil at the dipstick, but at the entrance to the oil reservoir, which has a cap that is normally marked "OIL."

A gauge on the instrument panel indicates the oil pressure. The oil pressure warning light warns you if your oil pressure is low. A sending unit on the engine senses the oil pressure, and if it drops below a safe level, the sending unit activates the oil pressure indicator light.

Cooling System

As mentioned before, you can also classify engines by their cooling systems. Normal engine operation creates tremendous amounts of heat, and the cooling system removes some of this heat to maintain efficient engine operating temperatures. The cooling system removes engine heat in two ways, air cooling and liquid cooling.

Air Cooling

An air cooling system circulates air around hot engine parts to dissipate the heat. The components that get the hottest, such as the cylinders and cylinder heads, have fins to direct the most air into contact with the greatest amount of hot metal.

If the engine is draft-cooled, the vehicle must be moving for air to circulate around the engine components. Motorcycle and aircraft engines are cooled in this fashion, but when the vehicle is idling but not moving, it may overheat for lack of draft.

For forced air circulation, an air pump draws air in and forces it around the engine block. The cylinders and cylinder heads are finned and usually covered with sheet metal shrouding to direct the air. A thermostatic control limits air intake when the engine is cold to prevent overcooling. The advantage of air cooling over liquid cooling is that air-cooled engines weigh less and are smaller.

Liquid Cooling

Liquid cooling systems circulate liquid around hot engine parts to dissipate heat. A liquid-cooled engine is cast with coolant passages in the block and cylinder head. These passages surround each cylinder in the block. When the engine is running, engine heat passes through the cylinder walls and transmits to the liquid coolant circulating through the passages.

When an engine overheats, the coolant begins to boil and stops circulating. In addition, the oil in the engine starts to break down because of the heat, which can damage bearings and other moving parts if it continues.

If an engine becomes overcooled, it is less efficient. During the power stroke, combustion heat pushes down the piston. If too much of this heat is lost to the cooling system, power and efficiency are also lost. If the cylinder area is too cool, the fuel will not combust completely and fuel may run down the cylinder walls and wash off the lubricating oil. If this happens, enough gasoline may enter the oil pan to dilute the oil which diminishes its lubricating ability. The advantage of liquid cooling over air cooling is that liquid cooling can dissipate more heat. In addition, liquid cooling passages reduce engine noise.

Although older automobiles used water as a coolant, all vehicles today use a mixture of ethylene glycol (antifreeze) and water as the coolant. Ethylene glycol prevents the cooling system liquid from freezing because freezing coolant in the radiator and block can damage those components. Depending on the percentage of ethylene glycol used, the system can be protected from freezing in temperatures well below zero. Ethylene glycol also has a much higher boiling temperature (212° F at sea level) than water.

An engine accessory belt drives the coolant pump, which circulates coolant throughout the engine and into a heat exchanger. To remove the acquired heat from the coolant, the hot coolant is pumped out of the engine and into the radiator, which removes heat by dissipation from the coolant and sends it back through the engine.

The radiator mounts in front of the engine and contains a top tank, a bottom tank, and a center core or heat exchanger. Hot coolant passes from the engine through a large hose that connects to the top tank. It then enters the radiator core through a series of small copper or aluminum distribution tubes. The heat passes out of the liquid and into the wall of the tubes and air circulated through the core takes the heat from the fins around the tubes. The cooled liquid flows into the bottom radiator tank and a large hose draws the coolant up and back into the engine.

There are two radiator types: down-flow and cross-flow. Down-flow radiators introduce the hot coolant at the top of the radiator and it flows down through the core to the bottom tank. Cross-flow radiators introduce the hot coolant from the engine through an inlet at the top of one side of the radiator. The coolant then flows across the radiator core to a tank on the other side of the radiator, the bottom of which contains an outlet for the coolant. The advantage of cross-flow radiators is maximum cooling capacity in a limited space.

The pressure relief mechanism in the radiator cap connects to an overflow tube that in turn connects to a recovery tank or coolant recovery system. When the coolant becomes hot and expands, the coolant goes through a tube and into the plastic recovery tank. When the system cools down, the coolant is drawn through the overflow by vacuum and reenters the radiator.

While the vehicle is moving, sufficient air moves through the grill and the radiator core, and as long as the vehicle is moving, there is normally enough air flow to provide sufficient cooling. However, when the engine is running but the automobile is not moving, there isn't sufficient natural air flow through the radiator core. Fans solve this problem.

In many automobiles, the fan mounts to the inside of the front grill and uses the same pulley that drives the coolant pump. When the engine is running, a drive belt turns the pulley to turn the fan, and the fan pulls air through the radiator core. These are the fan types in use today:

➤ Fixed blade

➤ Clutch fan

➤ Flex blade fan

On many front wheel drive cars, the engine is mounted sideways in the engine compartment, which keeps the fan from being mounted on the front of the engine. In this situation, the fan mounts to a fan shroud that attaches to the radiator.

A sheet metal or plastic housing, called a fan shroud, increases the amount of air moved by the fan. The shroud attaches to the radiator and acts like a tunnel to direct the air flow from the fan through the radiator core.

In addition to the coolant passages in the engine, the radiator, coolant pump, fans, and coolant recovery, the liquid cooling system also includes these components:

➤ Radiator hoses allow the coolant to flow from the engine to the radiator and from the radiator back to the engine. Radiator hoses are rubber hoses strengthened with steel wire. Two types of hoses are the curved hose, which is molded in the proper shape to fit on a certain engine, and the straight flexible hose, which is available in different lengths and diameters but will flex to most required shapes.

➤ The radiator pressure cap is on the top tank of the radiator and can be removed to add coolant to the radiator. The radiator cap allows a slight buildup of pressure in the radiator. If the pressure becomes too high, a spring-loaded valve in the cap pushes up to allow pressure to escape.

➤ The vacuum valve is another valve in the cap that prevents vacuum buildup in the radiator as the system cools off. A vacuum in the system triggers the vacuum relief valve to allow air to enter.

➤ The thermostat is a temperature-controlled valve that controls coolant flow into the radiator from the engine.

➤ Drive belts from the crankshaft drive the coolant pump and the fan. Belt tension is adjusted by movable mountings.

➤ The temperature monitoring system senses cooling fluid temperature. If the cooling system stops working, the engine could overheat. The sensor connects to a temperature gauge or warning light on the instrument panel.

➤ The coolant temperature warning light indicates when the coolant temperature is too high. A sending unit on the engine senses the engine coolant temperature, and excessive temperature triggers the warning indicator light on the instrument panel.

➤ The coolant temperature gauge shows the coolant temperature on an instrument panel gauge.

Fuel System

The fuel system is responsible for storing enough fuel for several hundred miles of vehicle operation, delivering the fuel to the engine, and mixing the fuel with air in the proper proportions for efficient combustion. The two fuel systems that you need to know are the gasoline and diesel fuel systems.

Gasoline and Gasoline Combustion

This section explains gasoline fuel, its production, its properties, and its ability to produce power in the combustion chamber. Gasoline is a petroleum-based, hydrocarbon fuel. There are many thousands of hydrocarbons, and every batch of gasoline has a different mix, depending on the crude oil it came from and the refining processes it went through. Gasoline is a mixture of the lightest or most volatile liquid hydrocarbons found in crude petroleum oil.

Normal combustion is the proper burning of air and fuel in the combustion chamber. In this case, the spark starts the combustion, the explosion expands evenly through the air-fuel mixture in the combustion chamber, and the force of the combustion pushes down the piston. However, there are two kinds of combustion that indicate problems with the detonation or burning process, which we discuss here.

➤ Detonation is abnormal combustion where only a portion of the mixture combusts initially, then the remaining portion ignites. When this happens, the secondary explosion applies extreme hammering pressures on the piston and other engine parts, and the extreme heat damages spark plugs and pistons.

➤ Pre-ignition results from deposits from fuel and oil buildup in the combustion chamber. These deposits cause high internal pressure and reduce heat transfer to the coolant. The trapped heat then raises the temperature of the air-fuel mixture to the point that it combusts before ignition. This occurs especially when the engine has a heavy operating load or in hot weather. Pre-ignition also causes the engine to run after you turn off the ignition.

Because some gasoline hydrocarbons are more likely to self-ignite and cause detonation, researchers sought means of reducing these combustion problems by modifying the characteristics of the gasoline.

Leaded fuel is gasoline to which tetraethyl lead has been added to increase the fuel's antiknock ability. The lead slows down the wall of flame in the combustion chamber and reduces detonation. However, much of the highly poisonous lead leaves the combustion chamber with the exhaust gases and goes into the air.

Unleaded fuels have an increased antiknock rating because of a synthesizing process wherein the hydrocarbon molecules of gasoline are converted to synthetic hydrocarbons with a higher octane rating.

The octane rating is the standard for rating fuels and is based on the anti-detonation quality of the iso-octane hydrocarbon. Premium gasoline is a high-octane fuel, whereas regular gasoline has a low-octane rating. Octane ratings are determined by comparing a fuel with a mixture of iso-octane, which has a 100 octane rating, and heptane, which has a 0 octane rating. The fuel octane rating that you see on the gas pump is an average of the theoretical and heavy-load octane numbers.

Besides the octane and lead characteristics, there are several other aspects of gasoline that determine its quality:

➤ Performance numbers rate antiknock qualities higher than 100 octane, and relate fuel quality to overall engine power output.

➤ Volatility is the flammable stability of fuel. Good gasoline contains a mixture of liquids with different boiling points so that some liquids evaporate at low temperature to provide easy starting in cold weather and other, less volatile liquids vaporize as the engine warms up. The more volatile a liquid is, the higher its octane rating is.

➤ Sulfur is found in most crude oil, but is undesirable in gasoline for several reasons. Sulfur combines with combustion products to form corrosive acids, causes wear and deposits in the engine, and reduces octane because sulfur interferes with antiknock additives. Gasoline is refined to reduce the sulfur content as low as possible.

➤ Most gasoline contains chemically unstable hydrocarbon compounds that combine to form heavy hydrocarbons in the fuel system, resulting in sticky valves and carburetor parts. Chemical treatment and careful selection of crude oils have greatly increased gasoline stability.

➤ Water vapor is always found in the air, and is impossible to keep out of gasoline. Cool nights cause condensation on the inner surface of the fuel tank. Because water and gasoline do not intermix, the water, which is heavier, settles to the bottom of the tank. Water infiltration in the carburetor is minimized by fuel filters and sediment bowls, and keeping a full tank reduces condensation in the tank.

➤ De-icers are additives that oil companies use in their gasoline to prevent fuel line freeze up and carburetor icing. Fuel line freeze up results from insufficient servicing of the fuel filter or sediment bowl. Moisture buildup from tank condensation freezes in cold weather and blocks fuel flow to the carburetor. Carburetor icing results from condensation freezing in the carburetor, as a result of low ambient temperatures and the heat from metal parts in the carburetor. De-icer additives are either anti-freeze solvents or surface-active agents that coat ice particles to keep them from sticking to metal surfaces.

Diesel Fuel and Diesel Combustion

Diesel fuel is rated by its heat value instead of combustion properties like gasoline. The heat value describes how much heat energy it can supply when it burns. Diesel has a higher heat value than gasoline and is also less volatile than gasoline is. Diesel has a low viscosity index, and because of that it can go through the injectors easily in warm weather, but thickens too much to flow properly in cold weather. For that reason, diesel is available in several grades during the winter months. Winterized diesel fuel, grade D-1, is less viscous than diesel for normal operating temperatures (grade D-2).

Rating the ignition quality of a diesel fuel is similar to the octane rating given to gasoline. A cetane rating scale from 100 to 0 has been established. A cetane hydrocarbon has good ignition quality and carries a rating of 100. If a fuel has the same ignition quality as a 70% cetane mixture, the fuel receives a cetane rating 70. Like octane ratings, cetane numbers are posted on the fuel pump. Diesel vehicle owner's manuals specify what cetane number fuel to use.

Fuel Tank

The fuel tank stores the fuel and normally mounts to the vehicle's undercarriage. If the vehicle's engine is in the front, the fuel tank is in the rear, and vice versa. Placement of the tank away from the engine distributes weight and lowers the risk of fire.

Baffles in the tanks keep the fuel from sloshing around and shifting weight. By reducing agitation, the baffles also keep condensed moisture from entering fuel lines. Some tanks have drains at their lowest point to remove water.

A screen in the fuel pickup line blocks large particles in the tank from the fuel lines. In vehicles with a float pickup, fuel is taken from just below the surface of the fuel rather than the bottom to reduce water intake. Keeping the fuel level high reduces condensation on the inside of the tank.

Fuel lines route fuel throughout the fuel system. The lines are steel tubing except where movement of the line is necessary, in which case the lines are synthetic rubber.

Fuel Pumps

An outlet on the tank connects to the automobile's fuel line, which runs from the fuel tank into the fuel pump in the engine compartment. The fuel pump draws fuel out of the tank and pumps a steady stream into the carburetor. The two types of fuel pumps are electrical and mechanical.

Electric fuel pumps can mount anywhere in or out of the engine compartment, and usually mount near to or inside the fuel tank. When it mounts on the fuel tank, fuel flows around the armature that extends into the fuel tank. An electric fuel pump has two main parts, which are an electric motor and a vane pump. The electric motor couples to the vane pump, which pulls the fuel out of the tank. Turning the key in the ignition activates the electric motor. An oil pressure switch stops the fuel pump if the engine stops. Because the electric fuel pump delivers much more fuel than the carburetor requires, excess fuel is diverted at the pressure regulator and flows under low pressure back to the fuel tank. The check valve prevents an abrupt drop of pressure in the fuel line when the engine is stopped.

Mechanical fuel pumps mount on the engine block and operate by an eccentric on the engine camshaft that moves the pump rocker arm. The pumping action to the carburetor is entirely mechanical, resulting from motion in the rocker arm on the crankshaft. The fuel pump can furnish more fuel than the wide open carburetor needs, so the pump does not operate when the float valve in the carburetor is closed.

Fuel Filters

Gasoline going to the carburetor must be clean to keep from clogging the carburetor jets and passages. Most fuel systems have at least one filter to remove water and impurities from the gasoline. Although the fuel tank can have a sediment bowl where water and particles of dirt settle, sediment bowls have been largely replaced by in-line filters between the fuel pump and the carburetor. Most in-line filters consist of a disposable plastic canister with a paper filter element. The gasoline enters one end, flows through the element and to the outlet.

Another type of in-line fuel filter mounts at the fuel inlet of the carburetor and has a check valve to prevent fuel back flow to the pump when the engine is off. This type of filter can have a paper or screen element. Fuel enters the inlet nut and flows through the filter element before it enters the carburetor.

Because diesel engines require very clean fuel for proper operation, water, acids, and particulate must be removed from the fuel before it enters the injection system. Most diesel fuel systems include both in-tank and in-line fuel filters as well as a water-fuel separator. A typical diesel fuel filter consists of a paper element contained in a metal canister. The water-fuel separator sits between the fuel tank and the fuel filter. A float valve or sensor activates a lamp in the instrument panel that indicates when the separator should be drained.

Carburetion

The carburetor mixes fuel with air in the proper proportions to burn efficiently inside the cylinder. Carburetors all have similar parts and operate by the same principle. A carburetor on a gasoline engine performs three jobs, which are metering, atomization, and fuel distribution through the air flowing into the engine.

➤ **Atomization and vaporization**—Before gasoline can be used as fuel for an engine, it must be atomized, or broken into fine particles so that it

mixes easily with air to form a mixture that will vaporize and easily combust. Vaporization is when the gasoline is changed from a liquid to a gas,
which occurs only when the liquid absorbs enough heat to boil. A carburetor draws gasoline into the incoming air stream as a spray and atomizes it. The resulting air-fuel mixture is drawn into the intake manifold
where the fuel mist vaporizes. Lessened air pressure in the intake manifold lowers the boiling point of the gasoline, which means that it vaporizes more easily than at normal air pressure.

Be sure that you know the correct air-fuel ratio for normal gasoline engine operation,
which is about 15:1.

> **Metering**—To burn efficiently, the air and fuel that the carburetor
  draws in must be in the correct ratio. The carburetor meters this ratio
  during all engine speeds and loads. An analysis of the amounts of hydrogen and carbon in gasoline and the amount of oxygen in the air reveals
  that it takes about 15 pounds of air to completely burn 1 pound of gasoline, to give a 15:1 air-fuel ratio. More fuel gives a richer mixture, and
  less fuel gives a leaner mixture. Air-fuel ratios are based upon weight,
  not volume because the air and fuel volumes change with pressure or
  temperature, but weight remains unaffected. Most engines will operate
  on air-fuel ratios from 11:1 (very rich) to 17:1 (slightly lean), depending
  on operating conditions.

> **Distribution**—For good burning and smooth engine operation, air and
  fuel must be uniformly mixed and must be delivered in equal amounts
  to each cylinder and evenly distributed within the combustion chamber.

Carburetors

In the carburetor, an airstream enters through a barrel at the top of the carburetor. The fuel is vaporized and mixed into the airstream in the barrel.
After that, the air-fuel mixture passes through to the intake manifold and
cylinders.

The manifold creates the vacuum that causes the airstream. In addition, as
the pistons move down on the intake strokes, that action creates a vacuum in
the combustion chamber. Because the intake valves are open during the
intake stroke, the vacuum extends to the intake manifold. Because the air
above the barrel is at normal air pressure, the pressure difference forces air
down the barrel to fill the vacuum. While the engine is operating, a continuous stream of air flows through the barrel.

. . . .

If the engine consistently had the same load at the same speeds, no compensation would be necessary to create a correct air-fuel ratio or a varying rate of injection. However, because the amount and ratio of the air-fuel mixture must change for different speeds and power outputs, there must be other components in the carburetor, which are listed here:

➤ **Throttle valve**—Controls the volume of air flow.

➤ **Float and fuel supply**—Controls the fuel supply to the carburetor.

➤ **Venturi**—Atomizes the fuel.

➤ **Main jet**—Controls the air-fuel mixture by restricting the flow of fuel to the main discharge nozzle in the carburetor.

➤ **Air bleed**—Introduces air into the fuel nozzle.

There are many different types of carburetors, which you can classify according to the direction air enters the carburetor and the number of barrels that the carburetor has. The carburetor classifications are

➤ Air direction (updraft and downdraft) carburetors mount above the engine to move the air-fuel mixture into the combustion chamber by gravity.

➤ Variable Venturi provide good running at low speeds and increased power when it is needed.

➤ Multiple barrel provides better carburetion breathing.

Fuel Injection

Delivery to the engine of a precise amount of air and fuel gives the greatest power and economy along with the lowest emissions.

Diesel engines use mechanical fuel injection to deliver fuel directly into the compressed air inside the cylinder. This system uses a pump to force pressurized fuel into injectors in each combustion chamber. On the intake stroke, only air is pulled into the cylinder. When the engine is ready for the power stroke, the injectors spray a small quantity of fuel into the compressed air. Diesel fuel injection systems differ from those of gasoline engines. Gasoline engine fuel injectors are in the intake manifold, whereas diesel engine injectors are in a swirl chamber inside the combustion chamber. In addition, diesel engines use mechanical fuel injectors to accurately time the fuel injection and hydraulics to overcome pressure in the combustion chamber, whereas gasoline engines use electronics.

In continuous flow fuel injection, a high-pressure pump forces fuel under pressure to injector nozzles mounted in the intake manifold very near the engine's intake valves. The injectors are not activated mechanically but provide a continuous stream of fuel on demand to accommodate high fuel delivery rates for high speed operation. This system is less efficient than the mechanical type but also less complicated.

Electronic fuel injection (EFI) lowers emissions and improves fuel mileage. This system uses fuel spray nozzles in the intake manifold or cylinder head near each of the engine's intake valves. Pressurized fuel flows to the nozzles by a mechanical or electric fuel pump. The nozzles are electronically controlled to ensure that the fuel injected at any given moment is precisely the amount that the engine needs. Sensors on the engine tell the control unit the actual load condition, engine speed, and operating temperature.

Air Cleaner

The engine pulls in a tremendous amount of air through the carburetor or fuel injection air horn. The air cleaner filters the dust and dirt from the air before it enters the engine. This large, round housing is above the carburetor or fuel injection assembly. Inside the housing is a paper or polyurethane foam filter that air passes through to filter out dirt and dust.

The Drive Train

The power that the engine develops is delivered to the driving wheels of the automobile by the power train (drive train). The transmission is a major part of the power train and its job is to multiply the torque developed by the engine. The transmission and the differential compose the two sets of gears in the drive train. The transmission adjusts the gear ratio while the differential lets the drive wheels turn at different speeds. The transmission changes speed and power between the engine and driving wheels of a vehicle. Front wheel drive cars combine the transmission and the differential in one housing to form a transaxle. Figure 9.10 illustrates a basic drive train configuration.

The two types of transmission are automatic and manual. Manual transmissions usually have one reverse and four forward gear speeds, and often have a fifth overdrive gear that lets the output shaft turn faster than the input shaft for better highway fuel consumption. Automatic transmissions normally use three forward gears and a reverse gear.

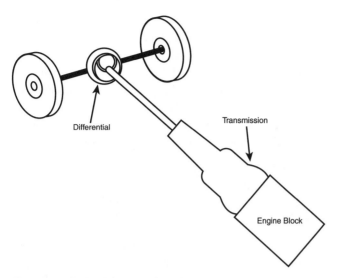

Figure 9.10   Basic drive train configuration.

A manual transmission has a manually operated clutch that the driver uses to shift gears, usually with a stick located on the console and the clutch pedal. An automatic transmission changes gears without the driver shifting. Each shift of the gears is controlled by a shift valve; the gears shift change depending on speed, the road, and load conditions.

Transmission fluid keeps your transmission running well because it lubricates the internal workings of the transmission to keep all the gears and shafts running smoothly. When the gears spin, they fling the fluid around and lubricate all the parts. Oil seals at the front and rear stop the fluid from leaking out of the housing. Always check your transmission fluid when you check your oil or if you notice that your car isn't shifting well. The transmission fluid has its own dipstick, and markings on the stick tell you whether you need to add fluid. Never use any other type of oil in your transmission except transmission fluid.

Manual Transmissions

The manual transmission consists of several gear assemblies, the top row of which is the mainshaft, and the bottom row is the countershaft. A reverse idler assembly is placed off to the side. The clutch disc attaches to a clutch shaft that enters the transmission, and the engine's power enters the transmission when the driver's foot releases the clutch pedal. The manual clutch allows the driver to couple and uncouple the engine from the power train via a clutch pedal. Before the driver can crank the automobile, the engine must be disconnected from the power train.

The manual clutch disconnects the engine from the power train when the driver pushes down the clutch pedal. To move the automobile from a stop, the driver selects low gear, and the shift linkage allows a synchronizer to lock low gear to the mainshaft. As the driver lets up on the clutch pedal, engine power entering the transmission turns the clutch gear and countershaft, which in turn rotates all the gears in mesh with it, but only the low gear is locked to the mainshaft. The power goes through the low gear on the countershaft to the low gear on the larger mainshaft to increase torque.

Rear-wheel drive, front-engine cars place the transmission behind the engine and connect it to a differential or rear axle at the rear with a drive shaft. A front-engine, front-drive vehicle uses a transaxle—a combination of transmission and rear axle in the same housing.

The transmission changes the ratio of the engine speed and the wheels by connecting gears in various combinations. If a gear with 10 teeth is driving a gear with 20 teeth, the drive has a 2:1 ratio, as already discussed in Chapter 7. Automotive engines develop low torque at low rpm, and a transmission provides a way to change the gear ratio between the engine and the rear wheels. Although gear ratios differ for different automobiles, a three-speed engine in low gear carries a gear ratio through the transmission of about 3:1. Second gear has a 2:1 ratio, and when the vehicle is moving fast enough, the automobile no longer requires torque multiplication through the transmission, so the high gear has a 1:1 ratio. An overdrive gear has a gear ratio of higher than 1:1. The advantages of an overdrive are that the engine turns slower for any given speed, resulting in longer engine life, and a slower engine speed uses less fuel. A four-speed offers four possible ratios, starting with a 4:1 ratio, in addition to reverse.

Automatic Transaxle and Transmission

The automatic transmission or transaxle does the same job as the manual clutch and transmission, which is increasing the engine's output torque to move the automobile. However, an automatic transmission is easier to drive than a manual transmission because the driver doesn't have to use a clutch pedal or gearshift lever. The difference is that the engagement and shifting in an automatic transmission or transaxle is done automatically by the torque converter, the planetary gearbox, and the hydraulic control system.

The torque converter is a coupling between the engine and the gearbox that evens out speed changes and multiplies engine torque. The torque converter couples and uncouples the engine from the rest of the drive train, and this is what automatic transmissions use instead of a clutch.

The planetary gearbox is a set of gears that help the converter increase torque. Because the planetary gear arrangement looks like the solar system, the gear at the center is the sun gear, the small planet pinions that are in mesh with the sun gear are held in orbit by a planet carrier. A ring gear surrounds the whole unit and is also in mesh with the planets.

The hydraulic control system regulates the hydraulic pressure through the transmission or transaxle in an automatic transmission. In addition, the hydraulic fluid does the following:

➤ Circulates through the transmission or transaxle components for lubrication.

➤ Dissipates heat from the components and into the radiator heat exchanger.

➤ Transmits engine torque in the torque converter.

➤ Applies the clutches and bands to engage the transmission or transaxle gears.

The hydraulic control system senses driving conditions and shifts the transmission to the correct gear. The hydraulic control system consists of a number of small valves that control the fluid passages leading to the clutches and bans. Which clutch or band is applied depends on which of these valves moves to allow fluid to pass. The three systems that open and close the valves are the manual control linkage, hydraulic pressure from a governor, and hydraulic pressure from a throttle valve or modulator.

Drive Line Arrangements

The drive line is the assembly responsible for getting engine torque to the drive wheels. Front-wheel, rear-wheel, and four-wheel drive vehicles arrange the transmissions/transaxles in different configurations, as discussed here.

Front-Wheel Drive (FWD)

The transmission and differential combine to form the transaxle, which mounts directly to the engine, which normally sits crosswise on front-wheel drive cars. Two drive shafts deliver the power from the transmission/transaxle to the front wheels.

The advantage of front-wheel drive is that combining the transmission and differential into one housing makes the car lighter, which saves fuel. In addition, because the lengthwise drive shaft and drive shaft tunnel are eliminated, that provides more passenger space.

Rear-Wheel Drive (RWD)

In rear-wheel drive cars, the engine mounts lengthwise with a transmission. The clutch housing and transmission bolt to the rear of the engine. A single, long, drive shaft delivers the torque from the transmission to the differential and rear axle at the rear of the car.

The drive shaft must allow for movement because the transmission is stationary, but the rear axle assembly is spring-mounted and can therefore move up and down. The drive line must be able to make changes in both angle and length to compensate for uneven terrain. The drive shaft must also adjust in length because the distance between the transmission and rear axle changes as the rear axle moves up and down.

Four-Wheel Drive (4WD)

A four-wheel drive arrangement allows all four wheels to transfer engine torque to the road. In four-wheel drive vehicles, the engine mounts lengthwise and uses a transmission and transfer case. The transfer case is a system of gears that mount in a separate housing behind the transmission. Two drive shafts, one from the transfer case to the front axle and one from the transmission to the rear axle transmit transmission torque.

The two transfer case types are a part-time transfer and a full-time transfer case. The part-time transfer case always has one drive axle in a four-wheel drive vehicle automatically in use, and the driver must activate and deactivate the second live drive axle. That way the vehicle can use two-wheel drive during normal driving for fuel economy, but lets the driver engage the four-wheel drive system on rough or slippery roads. The full-time transfer case provides full-time torque to all four wheels. Both transfer case types also provide a gear reduction range lower than the transmission's low gear to increase vehicle power in steep conditions.

All-Wheel Drive (AWD)

All-wheel drive vehicles use both live front and rear drive axles. When the front and rear drive axles receive power from the transfer case, the vehicle can function well on off-road terrain, such as sand, rocks, mud, and snow. An all-wheel drive vehicle has both axles live at all times without manually activating or deactivating axles.

Drive Train Components

The primary drive train components consist of the transmission, transaxle, transfer case drive shaft, differential, universal joints, and slip joints. We discuss each of these components in the following sections.

Drive Shaft

The drive shaft is a steel tube that transmits power from the transmission output shaft to the rear axle. To accommodate different wheelbases and transmission combinations, drive shafts have different lengths, diameters, and types of splined yokes.

Because of the vibration that drive shafts experience, cardboard tubes are sometimes pressed into the steel tubes. Some drive shafts have rubber biscuits molded on the outside of the smaller diameter steel tube. This assembly is then pressed into the drive shaft tubes.

Universal Joint

The universal joint consists of two Y-shaped yokes connected by a cross member called a cross or spider. In a typical drive line, the front and rear universal joints are identical in construction and operation. Universal joints make it possible for one shaft to drive another when they are at an angle.

Slip Joints

The front yoke of the universal joint, the slip joint, has splines that mesh to the external splines of the transmission output shaft. Because the rear axle moves up and down on the suspension when the vehicle is on rough terrain, the distance between the transmission and the rear axle subsequently change. For this reason, the drive shaft is not anchored at the front and the slip joint moves in and out on the transmission shaft to allow this change of distance. The spline of the slip joint fits snugly to the transmission output shaft and is free to move in and out. The slip joint spline is lubricated by the transmission's lubricant to permit the yoke to move easily in all driving conditions.

Differential Assembly

The differential allows two drive wheels to turn at different speeds when the vehicle goes around a corner, because the wheel on the inside of the turn travels through a smaller arc than the wheel on the outside of the corner. If the wheels could not turn at different speeds, they would tend to skip around the corner and make steering very difficult.

On front-wheel drive cars, the differential is in the same housing as the transmission and is called the transaxle. On rear-wheel drive cars, the differential is at the rear of the car in the rear axle assembly.

Electrical Systems

The electrical system serves two main functions, that being to supply the electrical energy to start and operate the engine, and to provide power to operate lights, instruments, and other electrical accessories. Figure 9.11 illustrates the automotive electrical subsystems, which are

➤ Charging system

➤ Starting system

➤ Ignition system

➤ Lighting and accessory system

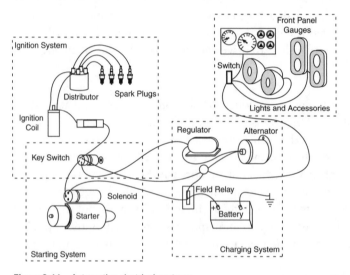

Figure 9.11 Automotive electrical systems.

The discussion in this section focuses on the overall task of these subsystems. We have already provided a detailed discussion on electronics, electricity, and electron theory in Chapter 6, "Electronics Information." If you understand the material in that chapter, then you are prepared to understand automotive electrical systems. Most particularly, you should be sure that you understand these principles and components:

➤ Atomic structure, valence, and free electrons

➤ Electron flow

➤ Common terms and methods of measurement, such as voltage, current, and resistance

➤ Common electronic components, such as conductors, insulators, semi-conductors, and transistors

➤ Electric circuits

➤ Magnetism, electromagnetism, and induction

Charging System

The automobile must always have electrical energy available to operate the engine and power the electrical accessories. The charging system provides this energy by extracting stored energy from the battery and generating electrical power to replace that which was used. The charging system contains three primary components, which are the battery, alternator, and regulator.

Battery

The battery is the stored energy source that provides power to the critical systems and accessories when the engine is not running. It also provides reserve power when the alternator cannot supply all the electrical power that the car needs.

Automobiles use lead-acid storage batteries to store chemical energy and convert it to electrical energy. The battery provides energy for the starter motor and ignition system. When the engine is running, the charging system powers the electrical system and recharges the battery. Most vehicles use 12-volt batteries. Large equipment that needs higher voltages uses two 12-volt batteries connected in series to supply 24 volts.

The battery has a hard plastic case with internal cell partitions, and the end cells have battery terminals that connect to them. The polarity of each terminal is indicated as positive (pos or +) or negative (neg or –) by markings on the battery case near the terminal. From these terminals, the battery connects to the electrical circuit. The top of the battery may have threaded or tapered caps over the cells. You can remove the cap to inspect and refill the water in the cell. The cap has a vent to allow hydrogen and oxygen gases to escape during charging. A maintenance free battery does not have cell vent caps.

Alternator

The alternator must replace electrical energy that an automobile draws from the battery, or the battery will completely discharge and you will have a dead battery on your hands, like when you forget and leave your car lights on.

The alternator consists of a rotor assembly, a stator assembly, and a rectifier mounted in a housing. The housing usually consists of two pieces of die-cast aluminum, which is nonmagnetic, lightweight, and provides good heat dissipation. The front and rear housing contain the bearings that support the rotor. The front bearing is usually pressed into the front housing or onto the rotor shaft.

The alternator works by taking the motion from the rotor to develop electromagnetic induction in the stator coils. Because the alternator has an alternating current (ac) output, the rectifier changes the ac input to direct current (dc) output that the car and battery can use, because both are dc systems.

Regulator

Alternator output voltage increases and decreases with the speed of the rotor. Too much current or voltage output from the alternator can damage the automobile's electrical system and battery. For that reason, electrical output from the alternator passes through a voltage regulator. The regulator keeps the charging output between 13.5 and 14.5 volts. The voltage regulator controls the amount of rotor field current in the alternator.

Starting System

The starting system puts out enough power to crank the engine fast enough to start it. The starting system has five main components, which are

➤ Battery (also part of the charging system)

➤ Starter motor

➤ Starter motor drive

➤ Solenoid

➤ Key switch (also part of the ignition system)

The starting system uses power from the battery to begin the starting process, and the driver controls the starting system via the ignition switch. Because we discuss the key switch (ignition) and the battery elsewhere in this chapter, we will focus our discussion on the components we do not cover elsewhere, which are the starter, starter motor drive, and solenoid.

The Starter Motor

A three-piece housing holds the starter motor: the field frame, the drive end frame, and the commutator end frame. Bearings or bushings in the end frames support the starter armature.

In the starter motor, current passes through the field windings and the armature in series (called a series-wound motor) to provide a great deal of cranking power. To start an engine, the crankshaft must rotate at a fairly high speed. The starter motor converts electrical energy from the battery into mechanical energy to crank the engine.

The starter motor has two major parts, a field winding and an armature. Using another form of electromagnetic induction, the field winding in the starter motor increases the strength of the current and voltage from the battery and stabilizes the output.

The Starter Motor Drive

The starter motor drive meshes the pinion with the engine flywheel to crank the engine and unmeshes them once the engine begins to run. The two types of starter motor drives are the inertia and the overrunning clutch drives. The inertia drive uses inertia to mesh and unmesh the pinion, and the overrunning clutch drive uses a shift lever to work the drive pinion.

The Solenoid

The solenoid is a magnetically operated switch that controls the circuit between the battery and the starter motor. Because the starter motor requires full battery current to operate, large cables must be used for current from the battery. Because voltage drop in the cable makes it unfeasible to key the starter motor from the ignition, the solenoid in the engine compartment acts like a remote switch. When an overrunning clutch drive is used, the solenoid also shifts the pinion into and out of mesh with the flywheel ring gear.

The driver controls the solenoid operation with the ignition switch. Most starting systems also have a neutral or clutch switch to prevent the engine from being started when the transmission is in gear.

Diesel Starting Systems

The diesel engines have problems with cold starts because they use compression ignition. When the engine is first cranked, the air entering the engine is cold, and while the compression stroke increases air temperature, the cold combustion chamber absorbs most of the heat. This means that the air temperature is still too low for ignition.

One solution is the use of a preheating system that uses glow plugs. The glow plug is an electrically heated wire filament that fits into the combustion chamber of each cylinder of the engine. When the driver activates the ignition key, a wait lamp illuminates on the instrument panel while the glow plugs are heating up. When the wait lamp goes off, the combustion chambers are warm enough for starting. After the engine starts, the glow plugs remain on for a short time, then automatically extinguish.

Ignition System

The ignition system provides a series of precisely timed, high-voltage sparks to ignite the compressed air-fuel mixture in the combustion chamber. The main components of the ignition system are

➤ Battery and/or alternator

➤ Ignition key switch

➤ Ignition coil

➤ Distributor

➤ As many spark plugs as there are cylinders

When you activate the ignition switch, that action closes the distributor contact points. Current flows from the power source through the key switch into the primary terminal on the ignition coil. The ignition coil steps up the voltage and sends it out through the secondary terminal into the distributor.

Ignition Switch

The ignition system provides a high voltage spark to each cylinder so the air-fuel mixture ignites at precisely the right time. Twelve volts in the primary circuit are boosted by the coil to 30,000 or more volts at the spark plug. By turning the key in the ignition switch, the driver can control the entire ignition event.

Ignition Coil

The ignition coil steps up the 12 volts available from the battery or alternator to a voltage high enough to arc at the spark plug gap and ignite the air-fuel mixture. The ignition coil's primary winding has about 200 turns of heavy copper wire and the secondary has about 2,100 turns of fine copper wire. (Remember the discussion on step up transformers in Chapter 6?) The ignition coil operates on the same principle. The ignition coil is inside a one-piece steel case filled with tar, epoxy, or oil to displace air. The case has a primary and secondary terminal on the outside for each of the set of windings.

Distributor

The distributor helps the coil develop high voltage, distributes the high voltage to each of the cylinders, and gets the high-voltage to the cylinders at the correct time. The distributor delivers high voltage from the coil through the spark plug wires to each of the engine's spark plugs. When current jumps across the spark plug gap, it creates a spark that ignites the air-fuel mixture.

Spark Plugs

To create a spark in the combustion chamber, the spark plug must have a sufficient gap over which an electrical charge can arc. If the gap were not present, then the electrical charge would simply transmit by conductance and not create an open spark to ignite the air-fuel mixture. If the spark plug and the rest of the ignition system are in good condition, the air-fuel mixture in the cylinder burns smoothly, developing power with very little pollution. Spark plugs must be the right size for the combustion chamber, and different spark plug sizes are required for different engine designs.

Ignition Classifications

You can classify engines by how they ignite the air-fuel mixture in the combustion chamber, of which there are two types: spark ignition and heat ignition.

Spark Ignition

Gasoline engines ignite the air-fuel mixture in the combustion chamber with an electrical spark from the spark plug. The development and control of this electrical spark is the job of the ignition system.

Heat Ignition

Diesel engines use the heat of high compression to ignite the air-fuel mixture. Diesel engines can operate on either the two-stroke or the four-stroke cycle. In the two-stroke engine used in heavy equipment, a supercharger blows air into the cylinder and at the top of the compression stroke a fuel injector sprays fuel into the cylinder, which ignites on contact with the compressed air.

Lighting and Accessory System

The lighting and accessory system consists of many small circuits that operate the lights and accessories on an automobile, such as these:

➤ Headlights

➤ Stop lights

➤ Turn signal indicators

➤ Instrument panel lamps

➤ Gauges

➤ Horns

The system also includes hundreds of feet of wiring that connect these devices to the power source and the many control switches that operate them.

The Chassis Systems

The chassis includes all parts of the automobile except the body and the primary systems that we have already discussed. The chassis systems include the steering, suspension, braking, and emission systems as well as the tires and wheels.

The Steering System

The steering system allows the driver to control the direction of the automobile. The steering system consists of the steering gears, which multiply the driver's effort at the steering wheel, and the steering linkage, which connects the gearbox to the front wheels. The performance of the system is dependent upon proper front wheel alignment for directional control and ease of steering.

The steering wheel attaches to a shaft that runs toward the front of the automobile and enters the steering gearbox. There are two gears in this box; one attaches to the steering shaft and the other attaches to the front wheel linkage. The steering gears change the rotary motion of the steering wheel into straight line motion that will move the steering linkage. It also provides a gear reduction that makes the automobile easier to steer. There are several types of steering available, which we discuss below.

➤ Rack and pinion steering connects the steering wheel and shaft to a small pinion gear. This gear meshes with the teeth on top of a long bar (rack). Turning the steering wheel turns the pinion gear, which moves the rack back and forth. The rack attaches to the steering linkage that turns the wheels. Rack and pinion systems use very little space and are especially suitable for compact vehicles.

➤ Power steering reduces the driver's steering effort. The power steering system requires a pump, usually engine-driven with a belt, connected by hydraulic lines to a cylinder or directly to the steering gearbox.

➤ Variable ratio steering is used in most power steering and some manual units. Variable ratio steering uses a rack-and-pinion gear set that has a different number of teeth in the center than it does on the outside of the gear. This makes the car respond quickly when starting a turn and reduces effort near the wheel's turning limits.

Steering linkage relates to how motion is transferred from the steering gear to the wheels. With rack and pinion steering systems, the rack connects directly to each of the steering knuckles by tie rods. With recirculating ball steering systems, a series of linkages are necessary to transfer the motion from the steering gear to each of the steering knuckles.

All cars today use a collapsible steering column. In a hard front-end collision, the engine and steering linkage are often forced against the steering gearbox, pushing the shaft into the automobile. To prevent serious injury the steering shaft and steering column are made from two pieces that extend like a telescope. During a collision, the column and shaft absorb the energy and the shaft collapses back into the column.

The Suspension System

The automobile's wheels are mounted to the framework through a system of linkages and springs called the suspension system. The suspension system allows the wheels to bounce up and down on rough roads while the rest of the vehicle remains fairly stable. These are the primary components of a suspension system:

➤ Control arms are the linkage that attaches the wheels to the frame.

➤ Steering knuckle and spindle are the suspension system components to which the wheels mount.

➤ Ball joints are the ball shaped bearing used to support suspension system control linkages.

➤ Stabilizer bar reduces body motion.

➤ Coil spring is a large, coil-shaped spring used in suspension system to dissipate chassis movement.

➤ Torsion bar twists at a controlled rate to act as a spring in a suspension system.

➤ Shock absorbers are hydraulic devices that control the up-and-down and rolling motion of an automobile body while also controlling wheel and axle movement.

There are several different suspension designs available, as discussed in the next sections.

Independent Suspensions

In most independent front suspension systems, each front wheel is independent of the other. If the left wheel falls into a hole, the right wheel is unaffected.

Short Long Arm Suspension

This is the most common type of independent suspension. In this system, the front wheels connect to the frame by an upper and a lower control arm which attach to the frame in such a way that they can swivel up and down. The wheels turn on wheel bearings that attach to a steering knuckle and the steering knuckle connects to the control arms through a ball joint. The ball joint allows movement in many directions so that the assembly can swing around as the wheels are turned left and right. It also permits up-and-down motion on rough roads.

McPherson Strut Suspension

This type of suspension uses a single lower control arm that connects to a long, tubular assembly (a strut), which is supported by the coil spring at the upper end and by the lower control arm at the bottom. A ball joint attaches to the lower part of the spindle. Most front wheel drive vehicles use the McPherson strut design.

Rigid Rear Suspension Systems

This is the suspension type that most rear drive automobiles use. It consists of a rigid rear axle that mounts to the frame through a spring system. Each side of the rear axle housing connects to the frame through a spring and shock absorber. The spring absorbs the wheel and axle movement so that the frame, body, and passengers do not bounce.

Independent Rear Suspension

This suspension type is common in front engine, front-wheel drive vehicles. In it, the rear wheels are suspended independently from a rear cross member by arms that go to the back or by a trailing arm independent rear suspension.

Load Leveling Systems

These suspension systems compensate for heavy loads added to the trunk or rear of a vehicle. In weighted conditions, the lowering of the rear affects the operation of both the front and rear suspension, making the vehicle difficult to control. Automatic leveling systems automatically maintain the correct rear height as weight is added to or removed from the vehicle.

The Brake System

The brake system is the most important safety and convenience feature on an automobile. However, it is no small task to stop an automobile that is moving at highway speeds. The heart of the brake system is a master cylinder that connects to the brake pedal. Pushing on the brake pedal causes the master cylinder to force hydraulic fluid through brake lines out to each of the automobile's four wheels. The hydraulic fluid activates the wheel brake assembly on each wheel, which uses friction to stop the wheel from rotating.

Pushing on the brake pedal operates the master cylinder in the engine compartment because of linkage connecting the two. The master cylinder is made up of a container for brake fluid and a piston in a cylinder. A hole in the bottom of the brake fluid container allows brake fluid to fill the area in front of the piston. When the brake pedal is pushed, the piston is pushed forward in the cylinder. As the piston covers the hole, the fluid is trapped and forced out of a line at the back of the cylinder. This fluid is then directed through lines to each of the wheel brake assemblies

The brake lines connected to the master cylinder route the hydraulic pressure to the four wheel brake assemblies. There are two types of wheel brake assemblies in use: drum brakes and disc brakes.

Drum Brakes

Drum brakes are an older brake system, but are still used on most small automobiles and on the rear wheels of many larger vehicles. The brake drum is a large, iron, drum-shaped casting that attaches to each wheel with lug bolts and turns with the wheel. The remaining brake system components are to stop the drum from turning.

The drums are stopped by forcing brake shoes against them. Brake shoes are half circles with high-friction brake lining inside the brake drums. When the brake lining contacts the rotating brake drum, the friction between the lining and the drum stops the drum.

Most drum brake systems are self-energizing, meaning that when the driver presses on the brake pedal and the brake shoes move outward, they contact the drum and tend to rotate with the drum. The primary shoe rotates with the drum and moves away from the anchor pin to apply a rearward force on the adjusting screw. At the same time the secondary shoe rotates around until it contacts the anchor pin.

Disc Brakes

The other type of brake is the disc brake. Disc brakes use the same master cylinder and brake lines as a drum brake system, but differ in the wheel brake assemblies. Instead of a drum, the disc brake system uses a rotor, which is a thick, round piece of cast iron attached to the wheel through the lug bolts. The rotor always turns when the wheel turns. To stop, the disc brake system uses hydraulics to squeeze two brake pads against the rotor. When the brake pads are squeezed against the surface of the rotor, friction stops the rotor from turning.

Emergency and Parking Brakes

All automobiles have an emergency brake system for times when the regular brake system fails or to prevent a parked vehicle from rolling. The system is mechanical in design, so it will continue to work even in the event of a complete hydraulic system failure. Emergency brakes usually operate only on the rear wheels. When the parking brake pedal is pushed down (or when the parking lever is pulled up, depending on your automobile's design), a cable that connects to the rear brake shoes pulls them into contact with the drums and prevents drums and wheels from turning.

Power Brake Systems

Power brakes reduce the driver's braking effort. There are two types of power brakes: One type uses the intake manifold vacuum acting on a diaphragm to assist the driver in applying effort through the master cylinder. The other type uses hydraulic pressure developed by the power steering pump to operate a hydraulic booster that attaches to the master cylinder.

Antiskid Brake Systems

Antiskid (antilock) brake systems prevent the wheels from locking or skidding when the driver is braking heavily. An electrically controlled antiskid system monitors and controls the braking action at each wheel to prevent lockup.

Monitoring devices on each braking wheel sense the wheel rotation speed as compared to overall vehicle speed. If any of the wheels lock up and skid, the logic control unit senses the lockup and reduces pressure on that brake to control the skid. It then re-applies the hydraulic pressure to maintain the best braking action. The system may repeat this cycle about four times a second until the vehicle speed drops or the brake pedal is released.

Tires and Wheels

Tires provide a cushion between the road and the automobile wheels to absorb road shock and they provide frictional contact between the wheels and the road for good traction. This allows the power to go through the tires to the road for rapid acceleration, resists the tendency of the vehicle to skid on turns, and allows quick stops when the brakes are applied.

Tires can either use an inner tube or be tubeless. On tires with an inner tube, the tire, with the tube inside, both mount on the wheel rim. The inner tube is inflated with air via a valve stem that sticks through the tire. The tubeless tire mounts on the rim and air is held between the rim and tire casing when the tire is inflated. The amount of air pressure used in the tire varies with the size of the vehicle and its load.

Tires are made from several different materials. Initially, layers of cord (plies) are formed over a spacing device and rubberized. This form is the casing for the tire and is called the carcass. A steel wire bead, enclosed in an overlap of the carcass fabric, keeps the carcass on the wheel rim. The rubber that forms the tread and sidewall is then vulcanized over the carcass. Although all tires are constructed of the same parts, they are different in the way the layers of cord are arranged.

➤ Bias ply tires form the carcass by layers of cords which run at an angle. The crisscrossing pattern allows the cords to expand and contract. This flexing gives the conventional bias-ply its main advantage, which is a smooth ride. However, as speed increases, the bias-ply begins to roll under, the sidewall begins to contact the ground, and the tread on the opposite side of the tire begins lifting.

➤ Radial ply tires have the cords at right angles. Another structural member, a belt, is added under the tread area of the tire. This combination of radial plies and belts gives a flexible sidewall that is rigid in the tread area, but a harder ride at lower speeds.

➤ Belted bias ply tires have the sidewall softened by adding belts. The result is a better footprint than that of a conventional bias tire.

Wheel Alignment

Wheel alignment is the position of the front and rear wheels in relation to the suspension. Proper alignment makes the automobile easy to turn and keeps it stable at high speeds. Wheel misalignment makes the vehicle difficult to steer and causes rapid tire wear.

Although the suspension system has some alignment factors built in to the design, other factors must be adjusted. Wheel alignment entails accounting for these criteria:

➤ Camber is the inward or outward tilt of the top of a vehicle's tires.

➤ Caster is the backward or forward tilt of the centerline of the ball joints.

➤ Steering axis inclination is based on an angle formed by the centerline of the ball joints and the vertical centerline.

➤ Toe-in is the condition in which the wheels are closer together at the front edge than at the rear edge.

➤ Turning radius is the relative angles of the two front wheels during a turn.

Emission Systems

Emission controls work to eliminate or reduce certain types of pollutants that occur because of the carbon-based fuels that automotive engines use. Exhaust gases contribute about 60% of air pollutants. The automobile is responsible for three major pollutants: hydrocarbons, nitrogen oxides (NOx), and carbon monoxide (CO).

Hydrocarbons

Hydrocarbons (HC) consist of many hundreds of combinations of hydrogen- and carbon-based atoms. All petroleum-based fuels are hydrocarbons. Burning gasoline in automobiles is the major source of hydrocarbon pollutants. Because of unburned fuel in the system, the engine releases hydrocarbons into the air from the carburetor, gas tank, and crankcase vent.

Positive crankcase ventilation (pcv) cleans up crankcase vapors to reduce hydrocarbons. The pcv's closed crankcase ventilation pulls blow-by (unburned fuel and combustion by-products created during the power stroke that leak past the piston rings into the crankcase) vapors out of the crankcase through a tube and into the intake manifold. The vapors enter the cylinders and are burned with the air-fuel mixture.

Nitrogen Oxides

At normal combustion temperatures, nitrogen in the air combines with oxygen to form nitrogen oxides (NOx). Nitrogen oxides are present in the air wherever fuels are burned.

An exhaust gas recirculation (EGR) system controls the emission of nitrogen oxides. NOx can be reduced by adding an inert material, such as those compounds found in exhaust gases, to the air-fuel mixture.

Carbon Monoxide

A third very dangerous pollutant is carbon monoxide (CO). When an engine burns gasoline, it discharges carbon monoxide in the automobile exhaust. Inside an automobile operating in traffic, concentrations of CO may reach levels that are high enough to affect the driver and create a safety hazard.

Reducing Exhaust Emissions

There are currently two ways to reduce exhaust emissions: using an air injection system or a catalytic converter.

An air injection system forces outside air into the exhaust system to reduce HC and CO emissions. The system injects air into the exhaust ports, the catalytic converter, or both places at different times depending on model application and system configuration.

The catalytic exhaust system uses a three-way catalyst to remove hydrocarbons, carbon monoxide, and nitrogen oxides from exhaust gas. A catalyst is a substance that speeds up a chemical reaction, but is not changed itself. The three primary catalysts used in the converter are platinum, palladium, and rhodium. When platinum and palladium combine with heat and unburned fuel, they add oxygen to the reaction (oxidizing). When rhodium is in the presence of heat and nitrogen oxides, it removes the oxygen from the compound to produce nitrogen.

Exam Prep Questions

Read each passage, and then choose the answer that fits most closely to the question.

1. What are wrenches used for?
   - ❏ A. Measuring the diameter of holes.
   - ❏ B. To drive screws.
   - ❏ C. They are used for tightening and loosening nuts and bolts.
   - ❏ D. To measure the diameter of a bolt.

2. If a part is made from aluminum, what type of tank should you use to clean it?
   - ❏ A. Cold tank
   - ❏ B. Hot tank
   - ❏ C. Water tank
   - ❏ D. Oil tank

3. What system takes the power created by the engine and transfers it to the wheels?
   - ❏ A. Drive train
   - ❏ B. Alternator
   - ❏ C. Universal joint
   - ❏ D. Carburetor

4. What happens in the power stroke of a four-stroke cycle engine?
   - ❏ A. Exhaust
   - ❏ B. Intake
   - ❏ C. Compression
   - ❏ D. Combustion

5. What is the purpose of a center punch?
   - ❏ A. To align two adjacent parts.
   - ❏ B. To find the center of a piston.
   - ❏ C. To measure the diameter of a hole.
   - ❏ D. To make a starting divot for a drill.

6. What instrument is used to measure a bolt hole in an engine block?
   - ❏ A. Inside micrometer
   - ❏ B. Small hole gauge
   - ❏ C. Telescoping gauge
   - ❏ D. All of the above

7. What are the two ways of cooling an engine?
   - ❏ A. Water cooling and air cooling
   - ❏ B. Air cooling and liquid cooling
   - ❏ C. Backflushing and air cooling
   - ❏ D. Air conditioning and refrigeration

8. Where is the combustion area in a cylinder?
   - ❑ A. Below the piston
   - ❑ B. In the fuel injectors
   - ❑ C. Above the piston
   - ❑ D. In the intake manifold

9. Between which two parts does a pushrod fit?
   - ❑ A. Between the piston and the valve
   - ❑ B. Between the master cylinder and the brake pads
   - ❑ C. Between the rocker arm and the lifter
   - ❑ D. Between the crankshaft and the camshaft

10. What does viscosity measure?
   - ❑ A. The amount of fuel flow to the fuel injectors.
   - ❑ B. The thickness of oil.
   - ❑ C. The thickness of bearing grease.
   - ❑ D. The burning ability of gasoline.

11. What is the purpose of the radiator?
   - ❑ A. To circulate oil
   - ❑ B. To purify exhaust
   - ❑ C. To store fuel
   - ❑ D. To cool the engine

12. What substances are used in the radiator?
   - ❑ A. Water and oil
   - ❑ B. Water and ethylene glycol
   - ❑ C. 10W-40 oil
   - ❑ D. Grade D-2 diesel

13. What are two forms of faulty combustion?
   - ❑ A. Intake and exhaust
   - ❑ B. Detonation and pre-ignition
   - ❑ C. Carburetion and oxidation
   - ❑ D. Stalling and compression

14. Where do the ignition system, charging system, and starting system get their energy?
   - ❑ A. Distributor
   - ❑ B. Fuel pump
   - ❑ C. Gasoline
   - ❑ D. Battery and alternator

15. What are two ways to reduce harmful exhaust pollutants?
   - ❑ A. EGR and catalytic converter
   - ❑ B. Leaded gasoline and additives
   - ❑ C. Diesel fuel and lower operating temperatures
   - ❑ D. Carburetor and the intake manifold

Exam Prep Answers

1. **Answer C is correct.** Wrenches are used to tighten and loosen nuts and bolts. Calipers and micrometers measure the inside diameter of holes; screwdrivers drive screws; micrometers measure the diameter of a bolt. Therefore, answers A, B, and D are incorrect.

2. **Answer A is correct.** Aluminum parts should be cleaned in a cold tank because a hot tank destroys aluminum and other nonferrous metals. A water tank is not for cleaning auto parts and an oil tank is for storing oil. Therefore, answers B, C, and D are incorrect.

3. **Answer A is correct.** The drive train takes the power generated by the engine and translates it to motion in the wheels. An alternator creates electrical energy; the universal joint, although part of the drive train, is not a system; the carburetor regulates the fuel flow to the engine. Therefore, answers B, C, and D are incorrect.

4. **Answer D is correct.** The third stroke, which is the power stroke creates combustion to complete the downward thrust of the piston. The exhaust releases the gases from the combustion; the intake stroke brings in new air and fuel; and the compression stroke compresses the air and fuel mixture to prepare it for combustion. Therefore answers A, B, and C are incorrect.

5. **The correct answer is D.** The purpose of a center punch is to make a beginning dent for drilling metal to prevent "wander." An aligning punch aligns two adjacent parts; there is no tool that is used to find the center of a piston; and an inside micrometer or caliper is used to measure the diameter of a hole. Therefore, answers A, B, and C are incorrect.

6. **The correct answer is D.** An inside micrometer, a small hole gauge, and a telescoping gauge can be used to measure a bolt hole.

7. **Answer B is correct.** The two methods of cooling an engine are air cooling and liquid cooling. Modern automobiles do not use water in the radiator, so answer A is incorrect. Backflushing has nothing to do with auto cooling and air conditioning and refrigeration are not engine cooling system. Therefore, answers A, C, and D are incorrect.

8. **Answer C is correct.** The combustion area is above the piston in the cylinder. No combustion occurs below the piston; the fuel injectors spray fuel into the combustion area; the intake manifold creates the airstream for fuel injection. Therefore, answers A, B, and D are incorrect.

9. **Answer C is correct.** The pushrod fits between the rockerarm and the lifter, which sits on the camshaft. The rockerarm sits between the piston and the valve; The brake lines are between the master cylinder and the brake pads; Nothing sits between the crankshaft and the camshaft. Therefore, answers A, B, and D are incorrect.

10. **Answer B is correct.** Viscosity is the measure of oil's thickness. Viscosity does not measure the amount of fuel flow to the fuel injectors; penetration measures the thickness of bearing grease; octane levels are a measure of the burning ability of gasoline. Therefore, answers A, C, and D are incorrect.

11. **Answer D is correct.** The purpose of the radiator is to help dissipate heat in the engine created by combustion. The lubrication system circulates oil throughout the automobile; the catalytic converter purifies exhaust; the fuel tank stores fuel. Therefore, answers A, B, and C are incorrect.

12. **Answer B is correct.** The substances used in radiators are water and ethylene glycol (antifreeze). You should never put any of these other substances in your radiator. If you see oil in your radiator, chances are good that you have a blown head gasket. Therefore, answers A, C, and D are incorrect.

13. **Answer B is correct.** The two forms of faulty combustion are detonation and pre-ignition. Intake and exhaust are two of the four strokes of a four-stroke cycle engine; Carburetion is the process of mixing air and fuel while oxidation is rust; stalling is when your car won't stay started and compression is another type of engine stroke. Therefore, answers A, C, and D are incorrect.

14. **Answer D is correct.** The ignition, charging, and starting systems receive their initial energy from the battery and/or alternator. The distributor distributes the spark to the spark plugs; the fuel pump provides fuel to the carburetor from the fuel tank; gasoline is the fuel for the engine. Therefore, answers A, B, and C are incorrect.

15. **Answer A is correct.** Exhaust gas recirculation (EGR) and catalytic converters reduce harmful exhaust pollutants. Leaded gasoline and additives increase harmful pollutants; diesel fuel does not decrease pollutants and lower operating temperatures actually increase exhaust pollutants. The carburetor delivers fuel to the engine and the intake manifold creates the airstream for fuel injection. Therefore, answers B, C, and D are incorrect.

Assembling Objects

Terms you need to understand:

✓ Relationships
✓ Puzzle assembly
✓ Labeled part connections

Concepts you'll need to master:

✓ Determining spatial relationships between puzzle pieces
✓ Joining labeled pieces together around a given axis

The Assembling Objects section of the ASVAB is the newest test, taking the place of the Coding Speed and Numerical Operations sections. You won't be tested on your knowledge of facts or your ability to calculate answers here. Assembling Objects is purely a test of your ability to look at a picture or collection of objects and understand the relationships between the different shapes you see. You will be asked to mentally "assemble" these shapes into a completed whole puzzle and then select the correct answer from among four choices. There are two types of Assembling Objects problems:

➤ Puzzle piece assembly

➤ Labeled part connections

This test is unlike any other on the ASVAB, and it tests a different type of intelligence or ability. Although an understanding of spatial relationships has practical application in military activities such as flying fighter jets and ground combat in an urban environment, your performance on this test will not affect your eligibility to enlist in any branch of the service.

If you are a person who excels at these sorts of puzzles, you might want to just skip ahead to the practice problems for a quick "tune up" of your skills. On the other hand, if you struggle to understand how one answer choice differs from another, or worse yet have no idea what to make of these problems, try the tips and examples that follow before attacking the problem sets.

Puzzle Piece Assembly

You are given several disassembled puzzle pieces (usually three or four) of various shapes and then are asked to choose the correct answer from among four combinations of assembled puzzles. Figure 10.1 is an example.

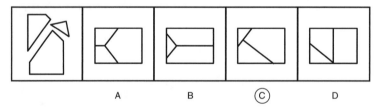

Figure 10.1   Puzzle piece assembly example.

Let's break down Figure 10.1 and look at what you will be expected to do with these types of questions on the ASVAB. Read the following directions, and then follow through the exercise.

Directions: Given the set of pieces in the first box, select the answer choice that correctly assembles those pieces.

At this point, decide which of the choices (A through D) is the correct answer. The following answers and explanations will tell you which is the correct choice and why.

Answers and Explanations

Answer A is incorrect. The fastest way to determine that A is incorrect is to look at the original set of pieces; it contains a triangle. Answer A cannot be correct because it doesn't contain a triangle. Although that difference alone is enough to disqualify answer A, it also contains subtle differences in the shape of the other two pieces.

Answer B is incorrect. You'll notice right away that answer B does have a triangle like the original set and you may also pick up that, also like the original set, it has one four-sided figure and one five-sided figure. On closer inspection, however, you'll observe that the pieces in answer B are longer and have differently angled short sides than those in the original set.

Answer C is the correct answer. By comparing each piece from the original set with its corresponding piece in answer C you'll see that all three pieces match exactly. As a double check, you may look at the original set again and "mentally" assemble its pieces to see whether they fit together in the same way as in this answer choice. Don't let yourself be fooled by answer C being rotated 90 degrees counterclockwise from the pieces as shown in the original set. This is a common distracter technique on the ASVAB.

Answer D is incorrect. This is apparent, almost at first glance, by observing that, unlike the original set of pieces, answer D contains a rectangle. Also, unlike the original set, answer D has no five-sided piece.

Some people have the ability to "think" in shapes and select the correct answer intuitively. Many others need to utilize some form of thought process to succeed on these problems. Here is a workable strategy to demystify the puzzle problems:

1. **Take note of your first impression**—People who have acute sensitivity to spatial relationships can often solve these problems at first glance. Look over the pieces and answer choices quickly and see whether the answer jumps out at you.

2. **Eliminate obvious wrong answers**—Pick a disassembled piece and move through the answer choices looking only for that piece. If that shape doesn't appear in an answer choice, you can eliminate that choice from further consideration. If it does, move on to the next choice.

Repeat this process for each piece until you've eliminated all answer choices except for the correct answer.

3. **Make an informed guess if you must**—Once you've eliminated as many incorrect answer choices as possible, if you still can't positively identify the correct answer, make your best guess from among the remaining selections. Remember that your odds of guessing correctly increase significantly with each wrong answer you can rule out.

That's it. These problems (like riding your bike) are not all that hard once you get the hang of it. And, also like learning to ride a bike, you need to practice your technique until it just seems to come naturally.

Although the puzzle pieces you'll see can come in many shapes, sizes, and combinations, all the problems of this type are basically the same and will succumb to the same systematic approach given previously.

Labeled Part Connections

Have you ever built a model airplane or put together a "some assembly required" project? If you have, then chances are good that you've used a schematic diagram. The ASVAB's labeled part connections problems are similar to this. In these problems you are given two or more pieces to assemble, but this time the pieces are each labeled (a,b,c...). You also are given an "assembly line" onto which the shapes are to be connected. Once again, you are given four possible answer choices from which to select the correct answer. Figure 10.2 shows an example of a labeled part connection.

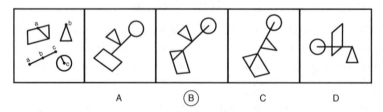

Figure 10.2   Labeled part connection example.

Like you did with Figure 10.1, let's work an exercise here that uses what you see in Figure 10.2. Read the following directions, and then follow through the exercise.

Directions: Given the original set of labeled pieces and the labeled axis line provided in the first box, select the answer choice that correctly connects the pieces in the proper orientation.

Look carefully at these pieces and the "assembly line" (or axis), paying close attention to the location of the labeled points on each. Decide which of the options (A through D) accurately answers this question. The answers and explanations section that follows give you the correct answer and why it is correct.

Answers and Explanations

Answer A is incorrect. Look at the piece labeled "a" in the original set. The axis line segment begins with point "a" at the middle of one side, but then passes through the middle of the quadrilateral to reach its corner. This is not the case in answer A. The other difference is that in the original set the axis line segment ends at point "c" in the center of the circle, but in answer A it stops at the circle's perimeter.

Answer B is the correct answer. By comparing each piece and the axis line segment from the original set with its corresponding piece and orientation in answer B, you'll find that all three pieces match exactly and are arranged in precisely the correct orientation with respect to the axis line.

Answer C is incorrect. Here, pieces "a" and "c" match the original set in shape and orientation to the axis line. Piece "b," however, intersects the axis line along one of its sides instead of at one of its points as required by the original set.

Answer D is incorrect. Here, pieces "b" and "c" match but piece "a" doesn't. Comparing the two quadrilaterals, you will have to look closely to notice that in answer D the axis line never passes through a corner as it does in the original set. This is what you'd call a *distracter*; at first glance it appears correct, but on closer inspection it is just another wrong answer.

The key to completing these connections is to use the labels provided to help you evaluate the possible answer choices. You should begin with the part labeled (a) and check each answer choice to see whether its part (a) is oriented and located correctly in relation to the assembly line. Next, move on to part (b), and so on. On the paper version of the ASVAB you may find it helpful to mark off the labels in your test booklet as you compare them. On the computer version, you can point to the corresponding points on the question and each answer choice. This will help your mind and eye focus on one comparison at a time.

The answer choices will certainly contain a number of distracters. These are answers that may look correct at first glance but are wrong in one detail. Beware, sticking with the systematic approach and verifying each connection one at a time will ensure you distinguish the difference between the right answer and the "almost-right" wrong one.

If you are taking the computer (CAT) ASVAB you will be given the opportunity to work through a sample problem of each type. Don't skip over these examples or rush through them. The time you spend on them does not count against your total time for the test.

Now let's move on to a set of practice questions to help you hone your Assembling Objects skills.

Exam Prep Questions

Of the ten exam prep questions that follow, five are of the puzzle piece assembly variety and five are labeled part connection questions. As you work through these questions, make a special effort to understand why each answer choice is either correct or incorrect. This will help you better learn the thought process that goes into solving these problems and recognize the distracters when they appear on the ASVAB.

Directions: The first five exam prep questions are puzzle piece assembly problems. For each question, you are given the set of pieces in the first box. Your job is to select the answer choice that correctly assembles those pieces.

1.

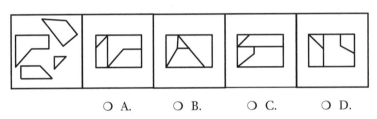

    ○ A.   ○ B.   ○ C.   ○ D.

2.

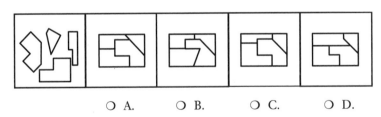

    ○ A.   ○ B.   ○ C.   ○ D.

3.

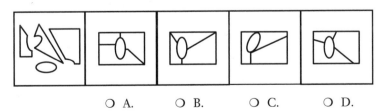

    ○ A.   ○ B.   ○ C.   ○ D.

4.

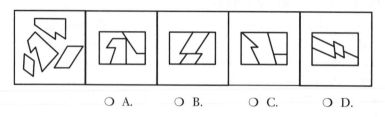

○ A.　　○ B.　　○ C.　　○ D.

5.

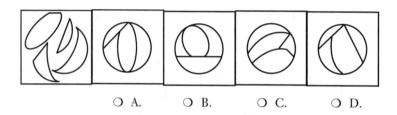

○ A.　　○ B.　　○ C.　　○ D.

Directions: The next five exam prep questions are labeled part connection questions. For each question, you are given a set of labeled pieces and a labeled axis line. Your job is to select the answer choice that correctly connects the pieces in the proper orientation to match the original set.

6.

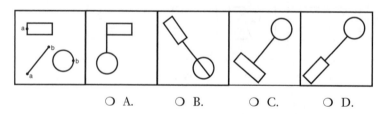

○ A.　　○ B.　　○ C.　　○ D.

7.

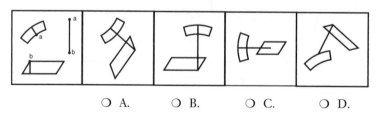

○ A.　　○ B.　　○ C.　　○ D.

8.

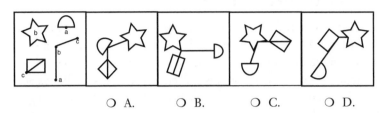

○ A.   ○ B.   ○ C.   ○ D.

9.

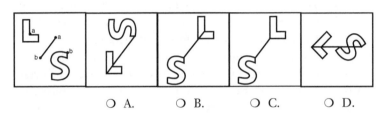

○ A.   ○ B.   ○ C.   ○ D.

10.

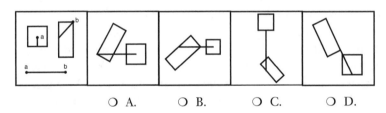

○ A.   ○ B.   ○ C.   ○ D.

Exam Prep Answers

1. **Answer A is correct.** In answer A, all the pieces match the original set and fit together. Answer B is incorrect because it has no five-sided piece and because the bottom and right pieces do not match the original set. Answer C is incorrect because, although its five-sided piece is similarly shaped to the one in the original set, its sides are the wrong lengths. Answer D is incorrect because it has a six-sided shape and its upper-right piece is too small.

2. **Answer C is correct.** In answer C all the pieces match the original set and fit together. Answer A is incorrect because it contains a triangle, unlike the original set, and because its upper-left piece ends with a slanted segment. Answer B is incorrect because it has a five-sided piece and because each of its pieces are different in some way from the original set. Answer D is incorrect because it, too, has a five-sided piece, and because its upper-left piece doesn't match any of the pieces in the original set.

3. **Answer B is correct.** In answer B all the pieces match the original set and fit together. Answer A is incorrect because none of the three pieces surrounding the oval match the original set. Answer C is incorrect because none of the three pieces surrounding the oval match the original set. The most obvious difference is seen in the lower-right piece, which has no curves. Answer D is incorrect despite having three pieces that are fairly close in appearance to the original set. Its right piece is the giveaway, noticeably different in appearance from any piece in the original set.

4. **Answer B is correct.** In answer B all the pieces match the original set and fit together. Answer A is incorrect because it contains no parallelograms (the original set contains two). Answer C is incorrect because it contains one parallelogram, whereas the original set contains two. Answer D is incorrect because its bottom piece has three sawtooth-shaped peaks; the most similar piece in the original set has only two. Also, the parallelogram piece in answer D protrudes too deeply into the top piece.

5. **Answer A is correct.** In answer A all the pieces match the original set and fit together. Answer B is incorrect because its middle piece, with two curved edges, doesn't come to a point at one end. Also, neither of the sidepieces comes to a point on both ends. Answer C is incorrect because the small piece on the right side has no match in the original set. Also, it has no perimeter piece with a straight-line side to it like the piece in the original set. Answer D is incorrect because it contains

two perimeter pieces, each with one straight line, whereas the original set has only one. Also, the centerpiece in answer D doesn't quite match any piece in the original set.

6. **Answer D is correct.** In answer D all the pieces match the original set and are oriented correctly along the axis (or "assembly") line. Answer A is incorrect because its axis line intersects the rectangle at a corner, not in the center of its short side as in the original set. Answer B is incorrect because its axis line bisects the circle. Answer C is incorrect because its axis line intersects the rectangle at the center of its long side, instead of its short side.

7. **Answer A is correct.** In answer A all the pieces match the original set and are oriented correctly along the axis (or "assembly") line. Answer B is incorrect because the axis line doesn't end at the longer of the two concave sides of the curved piece as it does in the original set. This is a difficult distracter, it is easy to confuse with the correct answer. You need to go back to the original piece and look at where the point "a" is located on the piece and the axis. Answer C is incorrect for the same reason, and also because the axis line penetrates the parallelogram and ends in the middle. Answer D is incorrect because its axis line fails to pass through the curved piece and intersects it only on its longer curved "side."

8. **Answer C is correct.** In answer C all the pieces match the original set and are oriented correctly along the axis (or "assembly") line. Answer A is incorrect because its semicircle intersects what would be point "b" instead of "a" and its star shaped piece intersects point "a" instead of "b." Answer B is incorrect because the axis line intersects the rectangle at a right angle instead of at a diagonal. Also, the star piece intersects point "b" at one of its points instead of its interior angles. Answer D is incorrect because the star-shaped piece is shown intersecting either point "a" or "c" (both would be wrong) and because the other two pieces both fail to properly intersect the axis line at the correct orientation.

9. **Answer B is correct.** In answer B all the pieces match the original set and are oriented correctly along the axis (or "assembly") line. Answer A is incorrect because the axis line does not stop at point "a" on the L-shaped piece. Answer C is incorrect for the same reason; in this case, the axis line doesn't penetrate the L-shaped piece, instead stopping at its lower-left corner. Answer D is incorrect because the axis line intersects the S-shaped piece's perimeter at two other places besides point "b." In the original set, the axis line only intersects the S at point "b."

10. **Answer A is correct.** In answer A all the pieces match the original set and are oriented correctly along the axis (or "assembly") line. Answer B is incorrect because, if you consider point "a" to be the center of the square piece, then the rectangle is oriented wrong so that the axis line continues past point "b" to the other side of the rectangle. Answer C is incorrect because its rectangle is oriented wrong (just as in answer B) and because the axis line never reaches point "a," which is located in the original set at the center of the square. Answer D is incorrect because its axis line intersects the square at two points and the rectangle only once.

Practice Exam 1

Word Knowledge

For each question that follows, choose a definition from those in the list that most completely and accurately has the same meaning as the underlined word in the question.

1. What does the underlined word mean?

   Mr. Harris's <u>assent</u> was forthcoming.
   - ❏ A. Rise upward
   - ❏ B. Consent
   - ❏ C. Downwards slope
   - ❏ D. Disallow

2. Sue was <u>wary</u> of the impending trip alone to Chicago.
   - ❏ A. Cautious
   - ❏ B. Tired
   - ❏ C. Anxious
   - ❏ D. Excited

3. Henry's addition to the project was <u>superfluous</u>.
   - ❏ A. Better
   - ❏ B. Fake
   - ❏ C. Unnecessary
   - ❏ D. Excellent

4. The Naval Observatory in Bethesda, Maryland, keeps <u>inerrant</u> time.
   - ❏ A. Incorrect
   - ❏ B. Military time
   - ❏ C. Astronomical
   - ❏ D. Infallible

5. The soldier prepared his <u>quarters</u> for inspection.
   - ❑ A. Dwelling
   - ❑ B. Uniform
   - ❑ C. Rifle
   - ❑ D. Foot locker

6. The Allied Forces exacted <u>retribution</u> on Adolf Hitler's regime.
   - ❑ A. Force
   - ❑ B. Defeat
   - ❑ C. Removal
   - ❑ D. Recompense

7. Golda Meir was <u>dauntless</u> in her pursuit of establishing and governing the nation of Israel.
   - ❑ A. Resolute
   - ❑ B. Fearless
   - ❑ C. Unsure
   - ❑ D. Arrogant

8. Many people are <u>acrophobic</u>.
   - ❑ A. Don't like being photographed
   - ❑ B. Afraid of crowds
   - ❑ C. Afraid of heights
   - ❑ D. Allergic to rabbit fur

9. The <u>monolithic</u> form of the Vietnam Veteran's Memorial inspires awe and solemnity in the onlooker.
   - ❑ A. Large
   - ❑ B. Black
   - ❑ C. Stone
   - ❑ D. Columnar

10. We considered the menu offerings at the new restaurant rather <u>mundane</u>.
    - ❑ A. Unappetizing
    - ❑ B. Unimaginative
    - ❑ C. Exotic
    - ❑ D. Uncooked

11. Joan of Arc's <u>exploits</u> are famous throughout all of France.
    - ❑ A. Discoveries
    - ❑ B. Deeds
    - ❑ C. Extortions
    - ❑ D. Tests

12. The candidate's confidence that he would win the election was somewhat <u>speculative</u>.
    - ❏ A. Assured
    - ❏ B. Mistaken
    - ❏ C. Deceptive
    - ❏ D. Assumed

13. Because of his <u>skullduggery</u>, Tom was becoming well known at the precinct.
    - ❏ A. Trickery
    - ❏ B. Benevolence
    - ❏ C. Crimes
    - ❏ D. Laziness

14. An advance team is usually the <u>precursor</u> to a full-scale invasion.
    - ❏ A. Beginning
    - ❏ B. End
    - ❏ C. Forerunner
    - ❏ D. Replacement

15. The teacher <u>chastened</u> the energetic child.
    - ❏ A. Pursued
    - ❏ B. Disciplined
    - ❏ C. Expelled
    - ❏ D. Calmed

16. The novice chef demonstrated great <u>facility</u> in the kitchen.
    - ❏ A. Ease
    - ❏ B. Difficulty
    - ❏ C. Assistance
    - ❏ D. Confusion

17. Charlotte put the unused wedding dress on <u>consignment</u>.
    - ❏ A. In storage
    - ❏ B. For exhibit
    - ❏ C. For donation
    - ❏ D. For sale by another

18. The man entered into the agreement with a great deal of <u>ostentation</u>.
    - ❏ A. Hostility
    - ❏ B. Pretense
    - ❏ C. Trepidation
    - ❏ D. Authority

19. The old man in the rocking chair was <u>inert</u> all afternoon.
    - ❏ A. Asleep
    - ❏ B. Moving
    - ❏ C. Unmoving
    - ❏ D. Occupied

20. It seemed as though nothing could break through Mrs. Simpson's <u>despondency</u>.
    - ❏ A. Anger
    - ❏ B. Hopelessness
    - ❏ C. Mental focus
    - ❏ D. Joy

Paragraph Comprehension

For the questions in this section, answer each question according to context, word knowledge, connotation, and inference.

21. Quite often, we see a startling lack of virtue and modesty displayed in contemporary writing. Why can't modern-day writers display some degree of decency, especially when the writing has no historical relevance. In these written pieces, the author should take every opportunity to display the most noble of human characteristics, especially that of moral goodness and virtue. I am not suggesting that the character of mankind should be portrayed as divine, or that the expectation for behavior be more than what human nature can attain, for if we cannot attain it, then we will never pursue it. However, contemporary writing should exalt the highest and purest behavior humankind can attain, as shown through daily valor and by overcoming certain trials in one's life and by persevering through others. By documenting such character, we may imitate those things which we can perform, and derive hope through other's modeling. Whenever vice is shown in a writing, it should repulse us, neither should we assign pleasure or courage to pursuing those things which are base in nature, for to unite vice with beneficence, we lose the ability to reconcile virtue and vice, each to their own domain.

    According to the passage, what is the problem with contemporary writing?
    - ❏ A. Society is not virtuous.
    - ❏ B. Contemporary writing exalts vice over virtue.
    - ❏ C. History is not accurate.
    - ❏ D. Society has no good role models.

22. The man rocked sedately in his chair all afternoon, little regarding the heat rising from the ground, the chirp of the cicadas, or the grass creeping up onto the sidewalk.

   According to this statement, what time of year can you assume that this takes place?

   ❏ A. Spring
   ❏ B. Summer
   ❏ C. Winter
   ❏ D. Fall

23. Voice over Internet protocol (VoIP) transmits phone calls in the same way that emails are sent over Internet broadband connections. Although VoIP is not new technology, it has grown recently due to improvements in technology and the spread of broadband Internet connections that make it easy to use the service. The cost savings of VoIP makes it a threat to big telecommunications carriers, and AT&T said that it will no longer seek new residential customers and will concentrate on corporate clients instead, due to rising competition in long-distance services such as VoIP. Global wholesale VoIP minutes during 2001 exceeded 10 billion minutes and will reach 300 billion by 2006. In addition, forecasts indicate that VoIP services will replace about 17 percent of North American phone lines by 2008.

   According to the passage above, what is the main advantage of VoIP?

   ❏ A. It is new technology
   ❏ B. It uses existing broadband lines
   ❏ C. Cost savings
   ❏ D. It can compete against the big telecommunications carriers

24. The little boy pressed his face eagerly against the glass, hoping against hope that the object of his affection was still on display. A moment of breathlessness anticipation as he looked inside. There it was! What joy! The brilliant white lettering contrasted against candy-apple red; The new rubber of all four wheels glinted at him; The handle rested nonchalantly against the edge, beaconing the boy to come inside the store.

   According to this passage, what is the little boy looking at in the window?

   ❏ A. Bicycle
   ❏ B. Wagon
   ❏ C. Train set
   ❏ D. Hobby horse

25. "The youth went slowly toward the fire indicated by his departed friend. As he reeled, he bethought him of the welcome his comrades would give him. He had a conviction that he would soon feel in his sore heart the barbed missiles of ridicule. He had not strength to invent a tale; he would be a soft target." — Stephen Crane, *The Red Badge of Courage*

    In this passage, what is the boy expecting will happen?

    ❑ A. He will be shot at
    ❑ B. He wished to die
    ❑ C. He will faint
    ❑ D. His friends will make fun of him

26. In a wired network, a local area network (LAN) adaptor replaces the network interface card (NIC) to allow wireless devices to communicate through a wireless network. The LAN adaptor has either an internal or an external antenna that replaces the physical connector on an Ethernet network to connect with the network and servers. That the LAN adaptor is wireless is transparent to the network operating system (NOS). Notebook and palmtop computers implement the adapters as PC cards, desktops implement them as add-on cards, and handheld computers implement them as integrated components (IC).

    According to the passage, how does a wireless laptop communicate with a network?

    ❑ A. Through a LAN adaptor
    ❑ B. Through an Ethernet connection
    ❑ C. Through a server
    ❑ D. Through a network interface card

27. Jacob arose from the table and went to the window, quietly meditating on the vista before him. The earlier magnificence of the day had faded gently away, and only a thin stream of yellow light showed where the sun had been.

    What is the setting of the passage?

    ❑ A. Before a storm
    ❑ B. Sunset
    ❑ C. An eclipse
    ❑ D. Sunrise

28. Gabriel repeatedly misinterpreted Greta's actions and attitudes, making it apparent that he has not taken the time to delve into the complexities that comprise the person that is his wife. He attributed her flush and bright eyes on the staircase to happiness instead of the deep, sorrowful emotion that it was. He also determined that her thoughtful state was fatigue, and that her approaching him in the hotel was desire instead of the need for emotional security.

    According to this passage, what can you infer about the state of the relationship between Gabriel and Greta?

    ❏   A. He didn't want her to be happy
    ❏   B. Gabriel is not concerned about Greta
    ❏   C. They do not communicate very well
    ❏   D. They had a warm, close relationship

29. Recently, scientists created the first synthetic prion, which is a rogue protein that is thought to cause mad cow disease and other, similar illnesses, such as scrapie in sheep and Creutzfeldt-Jakob disease (CJD) in humans. These diseases are believed to occur when a normal protein folds into an abnormal shape to create a prion, and sets off a chain reaction of misfolds that eventually leaves clumps of dead brain cells. Unlike viruses or bacteria, prions contain no genetic material, which was thought vital to causing infection, and repeated attempts to prove prion infectiousness have failed. These scientists attest that the man-made prion does not have any brain tissue, but is infectious in nature.

    In this passage, what causes the mentioned brain diseases?

    ❏   A. Dead brain cells
    ❏   B. Bacteria
    ❏   C. Virus
    ❏   D. Abnormal protein

30. Information passed between an online client and an e-commerce server should be protected. The most commonly encrypted information is credit card information and private data. Encryption scrambles the information in a way that only the client and server can de-scramble and effectively makes for a secure connection, but the Web server and client browser must have compatible encryption and decryption capabilities. The protocol creates a unique session key during secure communications that serves as the code to scramble and de-scramble the transaction. The session's encryption strength is measured in bits and the greater the number of bits, the stronger the encryption. Financial institutions and government agencies use very strong encryption.

According to this passage, what component of a secure communication is used to provide encryption?

- ❑ A. The protocol
- ❑ B. The client
- ❑ C. The server
- ❑ D. Credit card information

31. Because of their shared hubris, Lewis and Clark believed that they did not need Sacagawea's interpreting capacity for anything other than to trade for horses. This self-confidence and chauvinism led them to deem her unnecessary to establishing contact with the Indians. For this reason, Lewis did not ask Sacagawea to come with him on his quest to find the Shoshones, partly in response to Clark's previous dismissal of Sacagawea's importance in handling the Indians, and partly because the explorer's self-confidence negated any common sense that they may have exercised.

From this passage, what can you infer that the term "hubris" means?

- ❑ A. Temerity
- ❑ B. Arrogance
- ❑ C. Hesitation
- ❑ D. Carelessness

32. In most large airports, travelers can usually get wireless access, but they must either subscribe to a service or bill their credit cards on a pay-as-you-go basis to do so. However, airports in Lexington, Kentucky, and Blountville, Tennessee, are providing free, wireless Internet service throughout their terminals, allowing computer users to log on to the Internet without paying access fees or subscribing to a service. Airport visitors wanting to use the service can connect to the airport's Internet service using a laptop computer or handheld device with a standard wireless access card.

According to this passage, who can access this wireless service?

- ❑ A. Wireless customers who subscribe to a service
- ❑ B. Remote access customers
- ❑ C. Credit card customers
- ❑ D. Airport customers with a wireless access card installed in their laptops or handheld devices.

33. Throughout society, you can find many people who have accumulated more financial gain than they can ever use in this lifetime. Instead of sating their desire to achieve, this accumulation has created and insatiable hunger for more and more, even to the point where they feel no qualms about cheating the unaware and the powerless out of their meager portions just to moderately appease their voracious appetite for more. In all of nature, you will not find any kind of animal, whether domesticated or wild, who will avail themselves of the opportunity to accumulate immense quantities of food.

    What is the main point of this passage?

    ❏ A. People tend to be greedy
    ❏ B. Animals tend to be greedy
    ❏ C. People are wise to store up what they may need
    ❏ D. People will take only what they need

34. Since the concept of Wi-Fi is relatively new, it will take time for attitudes, technology, and regulations to progress. It may eventually mean that the rules for Wi-Fi become stricter, even to the point of outlawing home and personal networks. Conversely, it may mean that the federal government gives greater leeway in providing for and supporting the existence of those networks. Regardless, over time the social and official laws that define the domain in which community wireless networks exist will become clearer. Perhaps that's a good thing, but we will wait and see.

    According to the passage, what can you infer about the current regulations regarding Wi-Fi?

    ❏ A. Current laws are lenient
    ❏ B. Current laws are strict
    ❏ C. There currently exists no defined regulations
    ❏ D. Corporate America will define the direction of Wi-Fi regulations

35. "There was an air of calm and reserved opulence about the Weightman mansion that spoke not of money squandered, but of wealth prudently applied." — Henry Van Dyke, *The Mansion*

    In this passage, what is the inferred meaning of "opulence"?

    ❏ A. Extravagance
    ❏ B. Peacefulness
    ❏ C. Affluence
    ❏ D. Age

36. Radar, which is much like the echo-location that bats and dolphins use, detects the presence of an object by transmitting short bursts of high-frequency radio waves that bounce off an object to give its distance, speed, and dimensions. The reflected signal gives a radar cross-section (RCS) of an airplane or other target. Stealth technology reduces the RCS by using flat, angular designs and coating the airplane with radar-absorbing materials, such as iron ferrites. Although the radar can still "see" the airplane, the combination of design features distorts the RCS and can make the airplane signature appear as small as a bird.

    According to this passage, what is the primary advantage of stealth technology?

    ❑ A. It decreases airplane wind resistance.
    ❑ B. It lets airplanes see missiles.
    ❑ C. It makes the planes invisible to radar.
    ❑ D. It gives the airplanes a very small radar signature.

37. It is a wonderful thing that here and there in this hard, uncharitable world there should still be left a few rare souls who think no evil. This is the great unworldliness. Love "thinketh no evil," imputes no motive, sees the bright side, puts the best construction on every action. What a delightful state of mind to live in! What a stimulus and a benediction even to meet with it for a day! To be trusted is to be saved. And if we try to influence or elevate others, we shall soon see that success is in proportion to their belief of our belief in them." — Henry Drummond, *Love: The Greatest Thing in the World*

    According to this passage, how does love and belief affect another person?

    ❑ A. It makes them believe in themselves.
    ❑ B. It makes us feel good about ourselves.
    ❑ C. We look good to others.
    ❑ D. We can expect them to feel the same way about us.

38. General Robert E. Lee was one of the most significant military leaders in the history of the United States. Although he was a brilliant strategist and had the heart of a lion, his concern was for the safety and well-being of his "boys." All who served under General Lee were devoted to him, and looked to him as a father, devoted more to their leader than to the cause. For that reason, every casualty struck General Lee as if it were his own kin.

    According to the passage, what kind of man can we assume that General Robert E. Lee was?

    ❑ A. Militarily aggressive at all costs
    ❑ B. Intelligent and compassionate
    ❑ C. Timid and uncertain
    ❑ D. Aloof and cold

39. "He unbuttoned his jacket and shirt and drew forth his lunch. The action consumed no more than a quarter of a minute, yet in that brief moment the numbness laid hold of the exposed fingers. He did not put the mitten on but, instead, struck, the fingers a dozen sharp smashes against his leg." — Jack London, *To Build a Fire*

What is the setting or context of this passage?

   ❑ A. The man was tired and weary

   ❑ B. It was winter and he was cold

   ❑ C. The man had hurt his hand

   ❑ D. His hand had fallen asleep

40. In light of the increasingly limited funds available to industry, most companies find that they have specific job requirements, but cannot justify the additional personnel as full-time hires. Due to this trend, telecommuting is on the leading edge of a distinct change in industry practices. The primary disadvantage of using telecommuting employees is that they are not under daily supervision and are left to their own recognizance to complete assignments on time. That consideration aside, telecommuters allow companies to fulfill contract requirements without paying the overhead costs of a full-time employee. Another benefit is that companies do not have to pay for an employee on the time clock when there is no work to do.

According to this passage, what is the corporate drawback of using telecommuters?

   ❑ A. Companies incur lower overhead costs

   ❑ B. Companies do not have to pay for employee "down time"

   ❑ C. Companies cannot supervise telecommuting employees on a daily basis

   ❑ D. Telecommuting is a leading-edge practice

Electronics Information

For the questions in this section please select the best answer for the question.

41. What atomic particle is responsible for creating electricity?

   ❑ A. Nucleus

   ❑ B. Neutron

   ❑ C. Proton

   ❑ D. Electron

42. What value is the rate of the flow of electrons through a conductive medium?

   ❑ A. Voltage

   ❑ B. Resistance

   ❑ C. Current

   ❑ D. Power

43. If an electrical circuit has a current of 10 A, and a voltage of 50 V, then what is the resistance?
    - ❏ A. 0.05 ohms
    - ❏ B. 5 ohms
    - ❏ C. 250 ohms
    - ❏ D. 5 watts

44. How would you connect a set of six - 10 Amp, 12V batteries to achieve a combined power output of 36V at 20 Amps?
    - ❏ A. Series
    - ❏ B. Parallel
    - ❏ C. Series-parallel
    - ❏ D. Parallel-series

45. What are the options for permanently splicing electrical cable?
    - ❏ A. Soldering, wire nuts, and electrical tape
    - ❏ B. Soldering, electrical tape, and crimping
    - ❏ C. Electrical tape, crimping, and wire nuts
    - ❏ D. Soldering, wire nuts, and crimping

46. What does Figure 11.1 represent?

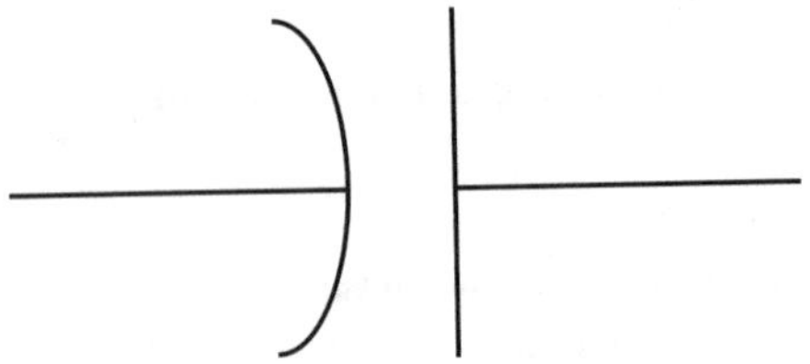

Figure 11.1

- ❏ A. Transistor
- ❏ B. Capacitor
- ❏ C. Resistor
- ❏ D. Switch

47. If the primary input to a transformer is 1,000V and the output is 20,000V, what is the turn ratio and what kind of transformer is it?
    - ❏ A. 20:1; step up
    - ❏ B. 1:20; step up
    - ❏ C. 20:1; step down
    - ❏ D. 1:20; step down

48. Why should you properly discharge a capacitor before working with an electronic circuit?

   ❑ A. Because the retained electrical charge of the capacitor may shock or even kill you.

   ❑ B. Because static electricity from your hand may damage the component.

   ❑ C. To divert static electricity from your body before you work with any other components.

   ❑ D. To ground the equipment.

49. If a circuit has a resistance of 20 ohms and a current of 10 amps, what is the voltage?

   ❑ A. 20w

   ❑ B. 2V

   ❑ C. 0.5V

   ❑ D. 200V

50. What is the overall power output of a generator that has a current of 15 amps at 35V?

   ❑ A. 2.33w

   ❑ B. 525w

   ❑ C. 0.428w

   ❑ D. 233ohms

51. What does Figure 11.2 represent?

Figure 11.2

   ❑ A. Transistor

   ❑ B. Capacitor

   ❑ C. Resistor

   ❑ D. Switch

52. What is the frequency of most household electrical systems?

   ❑ A. 60MHz

   ❑ B. 60Hz

   ❑ C. 110Hz

   ❑ D. 220Hz

53. Which equation should you use to find resistance in a circuit?

   ❑ A. R=E/I

   ❑ B. R=I/E

   ❑ C. R=E × I

   ❑ D. R=I × Z

54. Your outdoor landscaping lights are all connected to the same set of wires. One of them has burned out, but the rest of the lights are still on. How are your lights connected?

❑ A. Serial

❑ B. Parallel

❑ C. Serial-parallel

❑ D. Parallel-serial

55. You have a three-strand, 110 volt, 12-gauge Romex cable, which wire is hot?

❑ A. White

❑ B. Black

❑ C. Bare

❑ D. Green

56. Which of these materials is not a good conductor of electricity?

❑ A. Glass

❑ B. Aluminum

❑ C. Tin

❑ D. Copper

57. What is a dielectric?

❑ A. A magnet created by an electrical charge

❑ B. Materials through which an electrical charge cannot easily travel

❑ C. Materials through which an electrical charge can easily travel

❑ D. The nonconducting material between the plates of a capacitor

58. What is voltage?

❑ A. The amount of power consumption

❑ B. The rate of the flow of electrons through a circuit

❑ C. The magnetic flow of a circuit

❑ D. The energy or pressure that makes the stream of electrons flow through a conductive material

59. Find the current of the circuit in Figure 11.3.

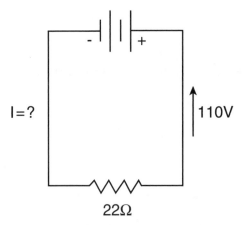

Figure 11.3

    ❑ A. 2 ohms
    ❑ B. 6 volts
    ❑ C. 5 amps
    ❑ D. 2 amps

60. What kind of connection is indicated when all the positive terminals of a set of components are connected together, and all the negative terminals are connected together?
    ❑ A. Serial-parallel
    ❑ B. Parallel
    ❑ C. Parallel-serial
    ❑ D. Serial

Automotive Information

Select the best answer for each question

61. What is the fourth stroke of a four-stroke cycle engine?
    ❑ A. Exhaust stroke
    ❑ B. Intake stroke
    ❑ C. Compression stroke
    ❑ D. Combustion stroke

62. What function does 30W oil perform in a gasoline engine?
    ❑ A. Lubricates the transmission and other drive train components
    ❑ B. Lubricates the engine components and systems
    ❑ C. Lubricates the wheel bearings
    ❑ D. Lubricates the power steering

63. What device would you use to stabilize your car when you jack it up?

   ❏ A. Wheel chocks

   ❏ B. Parking brake

   ❏ C. Jack stand

   ❏ D. All of the above

64. What system translates the energy created by the engine into motive force?

   ❏ A. Differential

   ❏ B. Piston

   ❏ C. Wheel system

   ❏ D. Drive train

65. What does a distributor do?

   ❏ A. Distributes electrical current to the proper spark plug at the proper time.

   ❏ B. Distributes fuel to the proper cylinder at the proper time.

   ❏ C. Distributes oil to the proper cylinder at the proper time.

   ❏ D. Distributes power to the proper wheel at the proper time.

66. What is the function of the piston rings?

   ❏ A. To connect the piston to the piston rod

   ❏ B. To maintain pressure in the combustion chamber above the piston and keep oil from getting into the combustion chamber

   ❏ C. To connect the connecting rod to the crankshaft

   ❏ D. It is the ring at the top of the cylinder that seals the head to the cylinder block.

67. How often does TDC occur during a four-stroke cycle?

   ❏ A. One time

   ❏ B. Two times

   ❏ C. Three times

   ❏ D. Four times

68. What is the purpose of the main bearing?

   ❏ A. To connect the transmission to the differential

   ❏ B. To provide smooth rotation of the wheels

   ❏ C. To support the crankshaft

   ❏ D. To connect the connecting rod to the crankshaft

69. What is the purpose of the valve train?

   ❏ A. Opens and closes each fuel injector port at the correct time

   ❏ B. The stem that lets you put in a tire

   ❏ C. Coordinates timing of the spark plugs

   ❏ D. Opens and closes the intake and exhaust ports at the correct time

70. What is the energy output of an automotive battery?
    - ❏ A. Alternating current
    - ❏ B. Static electricity
    - ❏ C. Direct current
    - ❏ D. Distributed energy

71. What tool has a special socket handle that measures the resistance to turning of a nut or bolt?
    - ❏ A. Torque wrench
    - ❏ B. Socket wrench
    - ❏ C. Box-end wrench
    - ❏ D. Adjustable wrench

72. What is the best tool for removing hose clamps?
    - ❏ A. Channel-lock pliers
    - ❏ B. Hose clamp pliers
    - ❏ C. Snap-ring pliers
    - ❏ D. Vise-grip pliers

73. What equipment can you clean with a hot tank cleaner?
    - ❏ A. Carburetors
    - ❏ B. Aluminum engine parts
    - ❏ C. Engine blocks
    - ❏ D. Brass automotive parts

74. You are cutting an exhaust pipe, what is the proper TPI of hacksaw blade that you should use to cut it so that you have the least chip accumulation?
    - ❏ A. 14 TPI blade
    - ❏ B. 18 TPI blade
    - ❏ C. 32 TPI blade
    - ❏ D. 12 TPI

75. What type of measuring tool would you use to measure a spark plug gap?
    - ❏ A. Micrometer
    - ❏ B. Small hole gauge
    - ❏ C. Caliper
    - ❏ D. Feeler gauge

76. If you have a situation where close tolerances are not necessary, such as attaching the alternator to the engine block, what kind of fastener do you use?
    - ❏ A. Machine bolts
    - ❏ B. Studs
    - ❏ C. Allen head screws
    - ❏ D. Sheet metal screws

77. Which automotive component eliminates pushrods and rocker arms?
    - ❏ A. Connecting rods
    - ❏ B. Overhead camshaft
    - ❏ C. Journals
    - ❏ D. Crankshaft

78. What function does a 2-stroke cycle engine perform on the first stroke?
    - ❏ A. Compression and exhaust.
    - ❏ B. Fuel intake and combustion.
    - ❏ C. Fuel intake and compression.
    - ❏ D. Combustion and exhaust.

79. How many degrees does the crankshaft turn to complete one stroke?
    - ❏ A. 90 degrees
    - ❏ B. 270 degrees
    - ❏ C. 360 degrees
    - ❏ D. 180 degrees

80. What type of engine does not use reciprocating motion?
    - ❏ A. Rotary engine
    - ❏ B. Piston engine
    - ❏ C. Diesel engine
    - ❏ D. Two-stroke cycle engine

Mechanical Comprehension

Using the knowledge that you gained from Chapter 7, "Mechanical Comprehension," choose one answer.

81. A man is using 60 lbs. of effort to lift a 240 lb. crate. What is the mechanical advantage in this situation?
    - ❏ A. MA=14400
    - ❏ B. MA=4
    - ❏ C. MA=0.25
    - ❏ D. MA=1

82. How much work does a 5 hp engine do per minute?
    - ❏ A. 33,000 ft_lb per minute
    - ❏ B. 110 ft_lb per minute
    - ❏ C. 2,750 ft_lb per minute
    - ❏ D. 165,000 ft_lb per minute

83. What force must you exert (vertically) on the handles of a wheelbarrow 4 feet from the axle of the wheel in order to lift a weight of 250 lbs. that is concentrated at a point 2 feet from the axle?

❑ A. 75 lbs.

❑ B. 125 lbs.

❑ C. 250 lbs.

❑ D. 4 lbs.

84. What is the pressure, in psi, of a tank of water that measures 8 feet square by 14 feet deep?

❑ A. 6.07 psi

❑ B. 62.4 psi

❑ C. 14 psi

❑ D. 64 psi

85. What is the mechanical advantage of a wheel and axle, where the wheel has a radius of 8 inches and the axle has a radius of 4 inches?

❑ A. MA=1

❑ B. MA=8

❑ C. MA=4

❑ D. MA=2

86. What is the minimum exerted force needed to lift the load in the Figure 11.4?

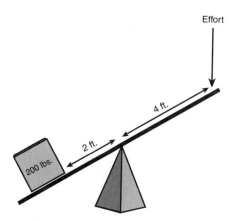

Figure 11.4

❑ A. 100 lbs.

❑ B. 200 lbs.

❑ C. 50 lbs.

❑ D. 150 lbs.

87. What force must you exert on the handle of a jackscrew 12 inches in radius if the pitch is 0.350 inches and the weight of the load is 2,000 pounds?

   ❑ A. 9.28 lbs.
   ❑ B. 2,000 lbs.
   ❑ C. 1,000 lbs.
   ❑ D. 24 lbs.

88. A mass of air has a pressure of 15 psi and a volume of 80 ft². If it is compressed to a new volume of 40 ft², what is the new pressure?

   ❑ A. 80 psi
   ❑ B. 15 psi
   ❑ C. 30 psi
   ❑ D. 40 psi

89. What is the effort required to move a 400 lb. load one foot off the ground?

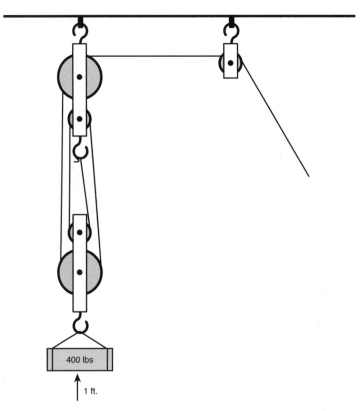

400 lbs

1 ft.

Figure 11.5

   ❑ A. 4 lbs.
   ❑ B. 100 lbs.
   ❑ C. 400 lbs.
   ❑ D. 200 lbs.

90. A 400-lb. barrel is rolled up a 16 ft. plank to a platform whose vertical height above the ground is 4 ft. Disregarding friction, what effort is required to move the barrel?

    ❑ A. 25 lbs.
    ❑ B. 1,600 lbs.
    ❑ C. 400 lbs.
    ❑ D. 100 lbs.

91. What is work?

    ❑ A. The potential for exertion
    ❑ B. The movement of an object by a force
    ❑ C. The rate of motion
    ❑ D. The force-multiplying ability of a machine

92. If you lift a 50 lb. box, 3 ft. from the floor of a loading bay, how much work have you done?

    ❑ A. 25 ft lb
    ❑ B. 50 ft lb
    ❑ C. 100 ft lb
    ❑ D. 150 ft lb

93. If a machine uses 70 lbs. of effort to lift a 140 lb. box, what is the mechanical advantage of the machine?

    ❑ A. 4
    ❑ B. 1
    ❑ C. 2
    ❑ D. 70

94. What is the efficiency of a 6 hp power wench that has a power input of 8 hp?

    ❑ A. 75% efficiency
    ❑ B. 50% efficiency
    ❑ C. 130% efficiency
    ❑ D. 48% efficiency

95. In Figure 11.6, what is the effort needed to balance the bell crank?

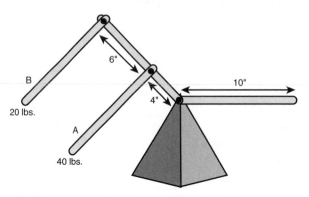

Figure 11.6

    ❑ A. 60 lbs.
    ❑ B. 100 lbs.
    ❑ C. 6 lbs.
    ❑ D. 120 lbs.

96. Velocity and momentum are examples of what type of quantity?
    ❑ A. Scalar quantity
    ❑ B. Vector quantity
    ❑ C. Resultant
    ❑ D. Tensor

97. What type of machine is a pair of vise-grips?
    ❑ A. Simple machine
    ❑ B. Pliers
    ❑ C. Compound machine
    ❑ D. Wrench

98. How much effort will it take to lift the load in this situation?

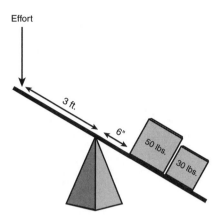

Effort

3 ft.

6"

50 lbs.

30 lbs.

Figure 11.7

❏ A. 180 lbs.
❏ B. 80 lbs.
❏ C. 13 lbs.
❏ D. 480 lbs.

99. A 300-lb. barrel is rolled up a 10 ft. plank to a platform whose vertical height above the ground is 4 ft. Disregarding friction, what effort is required to move the barrel?

❏ A. 2 lbs.
❏ B. 750 lbs.
❏ C. 300 lbs.
❏ D. 120 lbs.

100. What is the power input of a 15 hp engine that is operating at 95% efficiency?

❏ A. 16 hp
❏ B. 15.79 hp
❏ C. 1.58 hp
❏ D. 14 hp

Answers to Practice Test 1

1. B	**21.** B	**41.** D	**61.** A	**81.** B
2. A	**22.** B	**42.** C	**62.** B	**82.** D
3. C	**23.** C	**43.** B	**63.** D	**83.** B
4. D	**24.** B	**44.** C	**64.** D	**84.** A
5. A	**25.** D	**45.** D	**65.** A	**85.** D
6. D	**26.** A	**46.** B	**66.** B	**86.** A
7. B	**27.** B	**47.** B	**67.** B	**87.** A
8. C	**28.** C	**48.** A	**68.** C	**88.** C
9. D	**29.** D	**49.** D	**69.** D	**89.** B
10. B	**30.** A	**50.** B	**70.** C	**90.** D
11. B	**31.** B	**51.** C	**71.** A	**91.** B
12. D	**32.** D	**52.** B	**72.** B	**92.** D
13. A	**33.** A	**53.** A	**73.** C	**93.** C
14. C	**34.** C	**54.** B	**74.** C	**94.** A
15. B	**35.** C	**55.** B	**75.** D	**95.** A
16. A	**36.** D	**56.** A	**76.** A	**96.** B
17. D	**37.** A	**57.** D	**77.** B	**97.** C
18. B	**38.** B	**58.** D	**78.** C	**98.** C
19. C	**39.** B	**59.** C	**79.** D	**99.** D
20. B	**40.** C	**60.** B	**80.** A	**100.** B

Word Knowledge

1. **Answer B is correct.** Assent means agreement or consent. Ascent is a homonym for assent that means a rise upward; Descent is a downward slope; To disallow is to prohibit; therefore, answers A, C, and D are incorrect.

2. **Answer A is correct.** To be wary is to be on one's guard, or cautious. Tired is a synonym for weary; Anxious is to worry; Excited is another word for anticipation; therefore, answers B, C, and D are incorrect.

3. **Answer C is correct.** Superfluous means unnecessary. Better is a synonym for superior; Fake is a synonym for superficial; Excellent is a synonym for superb; therefore, answers A, B, and D are incorrect.

4. **Answer D is correct.** Inerrant means without error or infallible. Incorrect means wrong or inaccurate; Military time is a 24-hour time base, and is not the meaning of inerrant; Astronomical means according to the motion and physical properties of the stars, planets, and other celestial bodies; therefore, answers A, B, and C are incorrect.

5. **Answer A is correct.** Quarters is a military term for a living abode or dwelling. A uniform is clothing that the soldier wears; A rifle is the weapon that the soldier carries; A foot locker is a place where the soldier stores his personal effects; therefore, answers B, C, and D are incorrect.

6. **Answer D is correct.** Retribution is the act of recompensation, whether reward or punishment. While Hitler's regime did experience a show of force, defeat, and eventual removal, those words do not carry the correct meaning; therefore, answers A, B, and C are incorrect.

7. **Answer B is correct.** Dauntless means without fear. Resolute is a synonym for determined; Unsure is a synonym for doubting; Arrogant is a synonym for disdainful; therefore, answers A, C, and D are incorrect.

8. **Answer C is correct.** Acrophobics are afraid of heights. To know this, dissect the word, so that you have acro- and –phobic. For the prefix, think Acropolis, or high city, so you understand that acro means high. Then you have the suffix –phobic, and phobia means fear. So acrophobia is a fear of high places. Being camera shy is more of a disposition than a fear; Agoraphobia is a fear of crowds; A reaction to Angora rabbit fur is a simple allergy. Therefore, answers A, B, and D are incorrect.

9. **Answer D is correct.** A monolith is a smooth, single column. Large is a synonym for massive; Black implies murky; Stone refers to the construction material rather than the construction style; therefore, answers A, B, and C are incorrect.

10. **Answer B is correct.** Mundane means unimaginative. Unappetizing means not appealing to the palate; Exotic means mysterious; and uncooked means raw; therefore, answers A, C, and D are incorrect.

11. **Answer B is correct.** Although exploit has two definitions, the first being a heroic deed, it can also mean to extort. However, according to the context, the term takes on the more favorable connotation of deeds. Discoveries mean explorations, and test means experiments; therefore, answers A, C, and D are incorrect.

12. **Answer D is correct.** Speculative means to assume, usually without sufficient reason. Assured means that he was sure to win the election; although speculation doesn't have a firm basis, it is more of a long shot than a mistake; Deceptive is a synonym for specious, or illusory; therefore, answers A, B, and C are incorrect.

13. **Answer A is correct.** Skullduggery means trickery or underhanded dealing. Benevolence means acts of kindness; crimes are deeds that are punishable by law and are more than just mischief; and laziness is the disinclination to work; therefore, answers B, C, and D are incorrect.

14. **Answer C is correct.** A precursor is a forerunner to, and precedes an incident. It is not the beginning of the incident, neither is it at the end or a replacement; therefore, answers A, B, and D are incorrect.

15. **Answer B is correct.** Chastened means to discipline. Pursued means to give chase; expelled means to ban; Calmed means to bring peace to; therefore, answers A, C, and D are incorrect.

16. **Answer A is correct.** To demonstrate facility is to demonstrate ease or effortlessness. Difficulty means with a great deal of exertion; Assistance means that the novice chef required a lot of help; Confusion means a lack of understanding; therefore, answers B, C, and D are incorrect.

17. **Answer D is correct.** To put something on consignment is to entrust another person to sell it. It does not mean to place in storage, or for exhibit or for donation; therefore, answers A, B, and D are incorrect.

18. **Answer B is correct.** Ostentation means pretense or show. Hostility means under duress or with unfriendliness; Trepidation means with apprehension; Authority means with power or command; therefore, answers A, C, and D are incorrect.

19. **Answer C is correct.** To be inert is to not be moving. If someone is inert, he or she is not asleep, moving, or occupied; therefore, answers A, B, and D are incorrect.

20. **Answer B is correct.** Despondency means a detachment and sense of hopelessness. It does not mean anger, mental focus, or joy. Therefore, answers A, C, and D are incorrect.

Paragraph Comprehension

21. **Answer B is correct.** The passage discusses the way in which contemporary authors exalt vice instead of virtue in their writing. The author does not indicate that he thinks that society is not virtuous, neither does he indicate that history is not accurate or that contemporary society has no virtuous role models; therefore, answers A, C, and D are incorrect.

22. **Answer B is correct.** According to the setting, you can assume that the scene takes place in the summer. Although both spring and fall can have warm days, cicadas usually make their appearance in the summer time, and the setting is all wrong for winter; therefore, answers A, C, and D are incorrect.

23. **Answer C is correct.** The primary advantage, according to the passage is the significant cost savings of VoIP. Although VoIP is a recent technology that uses existing broadband lines and can compete against the big telecommunications carriers, none of these are the main point of the passage; therefore, answers A, B, and D are incorrect.

24. **Answer B is correct.** The little boy is looking at a wagon. You can infer this by the fact that most wagons are red with white or black lettering. In addition, wagons have four wheels and a handle. Bicycles do not have four wheels, a train set does not have a handle; and the description does not fit a hobby horse; therefore, answers A, C, and D are incorrect.

25. **Answer D is correct.** The youth is afraid that his friends will make fun of him. Although the passage uses creative imagery to describe his feelings, he is not afraid that he will be shot at or that he will faint. Neither does he wish to die; therefore, answers A, B, and C are incorrect.

26. **Answer A is correct.** According to the passage, a wireless laptop accesses a network through a LAN adapter. Ethernet connections are for wired networks; a server is part of a network, but does not provide the interface; and wired connections use network interface cards; therefore, answers B, C, and D are incorrect.

27. **Answer B is correct.** The passage describes the sky just after the sun has set. It does not describe the sky before a storm, during an eclipse, or at sunrise; therefore, answers A, C, and D are incorrect.

28. **Answer C is correct.** From the passage, we can clearly understand that Gabriel misinterpreted Greta's demeanor because they didn't communicate well enough for him to be able to interpret correctly. Because he misinterpreted her demeanor as happy, when it was not, he does want her to be happy, so answer A is incorrect. The fact that Gabriel is attentive to Greta's responses indicates that he is concerned for her; therefore, answer B is incorrect. The fact that he lacks the ability to interpret Greta's moods correctly indicates that they do not have a warm, close relationship; therefore, answer D is also incorrect.

29. **Answer D is correct.** The brain diseases are caused when protein cells fold abnormally. Dead brain cells are a result of the infection, and neither bacteria nor viruses cause it. Therefore, answers A, B, and C are incorrect.

30. **Answer A is correct.** The protocol provides the code to scramble and descramble the transactions. Neither the client nor the server provides that code, and credit card information is part of the reason for needing encryption; therefore, answers B, C, and D are incorrect.

31. **Answer B is correct.** Hubris means pride, arrogance, or self-confidence. Temerity means shyness; Hesitation indicates caution or carefulness; and carelessness indicates that not much thought was given to their actions. Therefore, answers A, C, and D are incorrect.

32. **Answer D is correct.** The wireless service in these two airports is free to any customer with a wireless access card in their wireless device. Because there is no charge for the wireless service within the airport, answers A, B, and C are incorrect.

33. **Answer A is correct.** People tend to take not only what they need, but even more, even to the point of depriving others. The author is not saying that animals are greedy, nor is he criticizing those people who store what they need. Above all, he is not pointing out that people are reserved and take only what they need. Therefore, answers B, C, and D are incorrect.

34. **Answer C is correct.** As far as the passage goes, there are currently no defined regulations, a point that is inferred by the wide range of direction that Wi-Fi regulations could go in the future. Because of this inference, you can assume that no official laws currently exist. Whereas Corporate America can determine trends, it cannot determine law; therefore, answers A, B, and D are incorrect.

35. **Answer C is correct.** Opulence means affluence, which can be inferred by the referrals of money and wealth. Opulence does not necessarily entail extravagance and has nothing to do with peacefulness or age; therefore, answers A, B, and D are incorrect.

36. **Answer D is correct.** Stealth design features allow airplanes to have a very small radar signature. Stealth design does not decrease wind resistance, neither does it let airplanes see missiles. Although stealth makes the airplane's signature very small, it does not make the airplane invisible; therefore, answers A, B, and C are incorrect.

37. **Answer A is correct.** The passage infers that when we express belief in, and acceptance of, another person, that we can affect their ability to succeed in life. It does not infer that we will feel good about ourselves, though that may be an added benefit. Nor does it indicate that others will respect us for our attitudes or that our sentiments will be reciprocated. Therefore, answers B, C, and D are incorrect.

38. **Answer B is correct.** General Robert E. Lee was both intelligent and compassionate. These characteristics brought him great favor and devotion from his troops. His concern for his troops indicates that he was not militarily aggressive at all costs. Because he had the heart of a lion, he was not timid and uncertain. People who are aloof and cold do not generally curry the devotion of their followers; therefore, answers A, C, and D are incorrect.

39. **Answer B is correct.** Clues that tell you that it was winter include the mittens and the numbness of exposed fingers. The passage does not indicate that he was tired or that he had hurt his hand. Although an asleep hand may be numb, it won't be that way from exposure; therefore, answers A, C, and D are incorrect.

40. **Answer C is correct.** The biggest disadvantage of using telecommuting employees is that they cannot be supervised and are left to their own recognizance. Lower overhead costs and unpaid down-time are advantages to companies, not disadvantages. That telecommuting is a leading-edge practice is not a disadvantage; therefore answers A, B, and D are incorrect.

Electronics Information

41. **Answer D is correct.** Atomic exchange of free electrons from the valence shell is responsible for creating electricity. The nucleus is the neutron and proton at the center of the electron orbit; The neutron is the neutrally charged particle in the atom; The proton is the positively charged particle in the atom. Therefore, answers A, B, and C are incorrect.

42. **Answer C is correct.** Current is the rate of electron flow through a conductive medium. Voltage is the intensity of the current flow; Resistance is the characteristics of the conductive medium that oppose the electron flow; Power is the overall energy requirements or output of an electric device; therefore, answers A, B, and D are incorrect.

43. **Answer B is correct.** According to Ohm's Law, R=E/I, so R=50/10 or, 5 ohms. Answer A implies R=I/E (R=5/50); Answer C implies R=IE (R=5 x 50); and answer D is a measure of power, not resistance; therefore, Answers A, C, and D are incorrect.

44. **Answer C is correct.** To achieve a total power output of 36 v at 20 amps, you divide the set of six batteries into two groups of three. You then connect each set of three in series, then connect the two sets together in parallel. Series connection alone will not increase the current; Parallel connection alone will not increase voltage; and parallel-series connection is not viable for this type of connection. Therefore, answers A, B, and D are incorrect.

45. **Answer D is correct.** The recommended ways to create a cable splice are soldering, wire nuts (screw-on connector), and crimping. Splicing a cable and then covering it with electrical tape is never a good idea for permanent electrical connections. Therefore, answers A, B, and C are incorrect.

46. **Answer B is correct.** The figure represents a schematic representation of a capacitor. Answers A, C, and D are incorrect. Refer to the Electronics information chapter to see schematic drawings of a transistor, resistor, and switch.

47. **Answer B is correct.** The ratio between the power input and the power output is 1:20, therefore the turns ratio will also be 1:20 and because the transformer has a higher output than input, it is a step-up transformer. Answers A, C, and D indicate wrong ratios and power transformation, and are therefore incorrect.

48. **Answer A is correct.** You should always discharge a capacitor, regardless of its capacitance or size, before you work with an electronic circuit. Doing so will prevent you from being shocked, perhaps fatally. Refer to the Electronics Information chapter in this book to understand how to discharge a capacitor. While static electricity does damage electronic components, that is not the primary concern with capacitors. To divert static electricity from you body, you use a grounding strap, not discharge on an electronic component. Discharging the capacitor does not ground the equipment. Therefore, answers B, C, and D are incorrect.

49. **Answer D is correct.** According to Ohm's Law, E=IR, then E=20(10); E=200v. Answer A is an incorrect value stated in watts, which is a rating for power; Answer B assumes that E=R/I, which is incorrect; Answer C assumes that E=I/R, which is also incorrect.

50. **Answer B is correct.** According to the formula for determining power, P=EI, or P=35(15) for a total power output of 525 watts. Answer A assumes that P=E/I and is incorrect; Answer C assumes that P=I/E and is incorrect; Answer D is a wrong value and incorrect rate and is also incorrect.

51. **Answer C is correct.** The figure represents a schematic representation of a resistor. Answers A, B, and D are incorrect. Refer to Chapter 6, "Electronics Information," for schematic drawings of a transistor, capacitor, and switch.

52. **Answer B is correct.** The electrical service to most modern households is 60 Hz. 60 MHz is an incorrect value; 110 and 220 are the voltages of the household service, but not the frequency; therefore, answers A, C, and D are incorrect.

53. **Answer A is correct.** The Ohm's Law equation for finding resistance in a circuit is R=E/I. I/E not an Ohm's Law formula; E × I is the formula for finding power, and I × Z is the formula for finding voltage in an AC circuit; therefore, answers B, C, and D are incorrect.

54. **Answer B is correct.** Because one of your lights has burned out, but the others are still working, that indicates that the lights are connected in parallel. If the lights were connected in serial, all the lights would have gone out, even though only one was burned out. Lights are not connected in serial-parallel or parallel-serial; therefore, answers A, C, and D are incorrect.

55. **Answer B is correct.** If your household wiring was properly installed, then the hot wire in a three-strand, 110 volt wire is always black. The white wire is neutral and the green, or bare, wire is the ground; therefore, answers A, C, and D are incorrect.

56. **Answer A is correct.** Glass, rubber, and plastic are examples of materials that are poor conductors of electricity. Aluminum, tin, and copper are all good conductors of electricity.

57. **Answer D is correct.** A dielectric is the nonconducting material between the positive and negative plates of a capacitor. A magnet created by an electrical charge is an electromagnet. Materials through which an electrical charge does not easily travel are insulators. Materials through which an electrical charge easily travels are conductors; therefore, answers A, B, and C are incorrect.

58. **Answer D is correct.** Voltage is the energy or pressure that makes the stream of electrons flow through a conductive material. Power consumption is a result of multiplying the voltage times the current; the rate of electron flow is the current; the magnetic flow indicates the negative-to-positive flow of the electrons through a circuit or component; therefore, answers A, B, and C are incorrect.

59. **Answer C is correct.** Because I (current) = E (voltage)/R (resistance), then 110/22=5 amps. Ohms are a measure of resistance and volts are a measure of voltage; 2 amps is an incorrect rate. Therefore, answers A, B, and D are incorrect.

60. **Answer B is correct.** When all the negative terminals of the circuit components are connected together and all the positive terminals of the components are connected together, then the connection is a parallel connection. The connection scenario does not fit that for serial, serial-parallel, or parallel-serial connections. Therefore, answers A, C, and D are incorrect.

Automotive Information

61. **Answer A is correct.** The fourth stroke of a four-stroke cycle is the exhaust stroke. The first stroke is intake; the second stroke is compression, the third stroke is combustion; therefore, answers B, C, and D are incorrect.

62. **Answer B is correct.** 30W oil lubricates the engine components and associated engine systems. Transmission fluid lubricates the transmission and drive train components; bearing grease lubricates wheel bearings; power steering fluid lubricates the power steering system. Therefore, answers A, C, and D are incorrect.

63. **Answer D is correct.** When you use a automotive jack, you should also use a jack stand and wheel chocks, and pull the parking brake to stabilize the vehicle and keep it from rolling, to prevent damage to the vehicle or injury or fatality to yourself or others.

64. **Answer D is correct.** The drive train takes the raw energy developed by the engine and converts it to lateral motion in the wheels. The differential is part of the drive train, but is not a system and does not create motion by itself. The pistons are part of the engine; the wheels are not a system and do not create the motion, they simply act upon the motion that is created. Therefore, answers A, B, and C are incorrect.

65. **Answer A is correct.** The distributor distributes an electrical current from the alternator and/or battery to the proper sparkplug, in sequence, at the proper time. The carburetor and/or fuel injectors provide fuel to the cylinders; The lubrication system distributes oil throughout the engine system; The drive train delivers power to the wheels; therefore, answers B, C, and D are incorrect.

66. **Answer B is correct.** The piston rings create a seal that separates the combustion chamber to maintain combustion pressure while at the same time keeping oil from getting into the combustion chamber. The piston connects to the piston rod via the piston bushing; the journal connects the connecting rod to the crankshaft; the head gasket is at the top of the cylinder to seal the head to the cylinder block; therefore, answer A, C, and D are incorrect.

67. **Answer B is correct.** TDC (Top Dead Center) occurs twice during a four-stroke cycle, once at the beginning of the intake stroke and once at the beginning of the combustion stroke; therefore, answers A, C, and D are incorrect.

68. **Answer C is correct.** Main bearings hold the main bearing journals and support the crankshaft so that it can rotate. The driveshaft connects the transmission to the differential; the wheel bearings provide smooth rotation of the wheels; the journals connect the connecting rods to the crankshaft; therefore, answers A, B, and D are incorrect.

69. **Answer D is correct.** The valve train opens and closes the intake and exhaust ports at the correct time in the cycle. The valve train does not open and close the fuel injectors, neither is it the stem on your tire, nor does it coordinate the timing of the spark plugs; therefore, answers A, B, and C are incorrect.

70. **Answer C is correct.** An automotive battery, regardless of amperage or voltage, has a direct current output. The alternator changes the battery output to alternating current; Batteries do not discharge static electricity; and distributed energy is not a battery output; therefore, answers A, B, and D are incorrect.

71. **Answer A is correct.** A torque wrench has a special socket handle and uses either a beam and pointer or a clicking drive head to measure the resistance to turning of a nut or bolt. Socket wrenches, box-end wrenches, and adjustable wrenches do not measure torque; therefore, answers B, C, and D are incorrect.

72. **Answer B is correct.** Hose clamp pliers enable you to remove and install spring-tension hose clamps on the radiator and heater hoses. Neither channel-lock, snap-ring, nor vise-grip pliers are especially designed for this purpose. Therefore, answers A, C, and D are incorrect.

73. **Answer C is correct.** Hot tanks are for cleaning engine blocks, cylinder heads, and other, large ferrous metal parts. You use a cold tank to clean carburetors, aluminum engine parts, and brass automotive parts; therefore, answers A, B, and D are incorrect.

74. **Answer C is correct.** To cut pipes, tubing, or conduit, you should choose a hacksaw blade with 32 TPI. Hacksaws with 12, 14, or 18 TPI cause too much chip accumulation; therefore, answers A, B, and D are incorrect.

75. **Answer D is correct.** You use a feeler gauge to measure spark plug gaps. Micrometers measure holes and circumferences; small hole gauges measure holes, and calipers measure holes, circumferences, and thicknesses; therefore, answers A, B, and C are incorrect.

76. **Answer A is correct.** You use machine bolts whenever close tolerances are not necessary. Studs are used whenever proper alignment is necessary; Allen head screws are used primarily on aircraft; and sheet metal screws are used for sheet metal and body panels. Therefore, answers B, C, and D are incorrect.

77. **Answer B is correct.** The overhead camshaft eliminates the need for pushrods and rocker arms. The connecting rods, journals, and crankshaft do not replace the function of the pushrods and rocker arms; therefore, answers A, C, and D are incorrect.

78. **Answer C is correct.** A two-stroke cycle engine performs fuel intake and compression on the first stroke and combustion and exhaust on the second stroke; therefore, answers A, B, and D are incorrect.

79. **Answer D is correct.** The crankshaft turns 180 degrees to complete one stroke. 90 degrees is one half of a stroke; 270 degrees is one and one half strokes; and 360 degrees is two full strokes; therefore, answers A, B, and C are incorrect.

80. **Answer A is correct.** Rotary engines do not produce combustion by reciprocating motion. Piston, diesel, and two-stroke cycle engines are all reciprocating engines; therefore, answers B, C, and D are incorrect.

Mechanical Comprehension

81. **Answer B is correct.** According to the formula, MA=Resistance/Effort, or MA=240/60; MA=4. Answer A assumes that MA=RE; Answer C assumes that MA=E/R; Answer D assumes that there is no mechanical advantage. Therefore, answers A, C, and D are incorrect.

82. **Answer D is correct.** A 5 hp engine can do 165,000 ft_lb of work per minute, because 60(5 x 550)=165,000. Answers A and B indicate an incorrect rate, and answer C indicates the amount of work output per second; therefore, answers A, B, and C are incorrect.

83. **Answer B is correct.** According to the formula wd=wd, then 4x=500; x=125. Answer A assumes a mechanical advantage of only 2, which is incorrect. Answer C assumes no mechanical advantage, which is also incorrect. Because 4 represents the mechanical advantage, answer D is incorrect.

84. **Answer A is correct.** The formula for measuring water pressure (for water at rest) is P=F/A, where F=weight × volume, divided by A (area). The weight of water per cubic foot is 62.4 lbs/ft^3., so F=62.4 ft^3 × (8 × 8 × 14 ft.); F=62.4 lbs/ft^3 × 896 ft^3; F=55910.4 lbs. The area of the bottom of the tank is 8 ft by 8 ft, or 64 ft^2. Now, go back to your original formula, P=F/A, so that P=55910.4 lbs/64 ft^2. The result is P-873.6 lbs/ft^2. Since the answer needs to be in psi, we must convert pressure per square foot to pressure per square inch. To convert, divide 873.6 lbs/ft^2 by 144 in^2/ft^2. P=(873.6 lbs/ft^2)/(144 in^2/ft^2); and P=6.07 lbs/in^2, or 6.07 psi.

Answer B is incorrect because 62.4 is the weight of water per cubic foot; answer C is incorrect because that is the depth of the water; answer D is incorrect, because 64 is the area of the tank.

85. **Answer D is correct.** MA=radius of wheel/radius of axle; MA=8/4; MA=2. Answer A indicates no mechanical advantage; Answer B is the size of the wheel; Answer C is the size of the axle.

86. The correct answer is A. According to our formula, work(distance) = work(distance), then 200(2)=4x; x=100. Answer B assumes no mechanical advantage; Answer C is insufficient to lift the weight; Answer D will lift the weight but is not the minimum force needed; therefore, answers B, C, and D are incorrect.

87. **Answer A is correct.** According to our formula: resistance x pitch = effort force x $2\pi r$; 2000(.350)=F(2π)(12); 700=75.39F; 9.28=F. 2000 is the resistance force; 1000 assumes a mechanical advantage of only 2; 24 represents the diameter of the handle. Therefore, answers B, C, and D are incorrect.

88. **Answer C is correct.** According to Boyle's Law, pressure and volume are inversely proportional, so that P1/P2 = V2/V1. First, we find the increase value by dividing 80 by 40 to get an increase value of 2. Now multiply the original pressure by the same value of 2 to get the new pressure of 30 psi. Answers A, B, and D are all original values of the equation and are therefore incorrect.

89. **Answer B is correct.** The mechanical advantage is 4, because there are 4 ropes supporting the load. Since Effort=R/Ma, so that E=400/4; E=100 lbs. Four is the mechanical advantage, so answer A is incorrect. Because we have a mechanical advantage of 4, a force equal to the resistance is not required; therefore, answer C is incorrect. 200 lbs. would indicate an MA of only 2, therefore answer D is also incorrect.

90. **Answer D is correct.** According to our formula wd=wd, then 16x=400(4); 16x=1600; x=100. Answer A represents the MA; Answer B indicates that you have reversed the effort distance and resistance distance; because an inclined plane does provide a mechanical advantage, then you don't have to exert an equivalent amount of effort to move the barrel; therefore, answers A, B, and C are incorrect.

91. **Answer B is correct.** Work is defined as the movement of an object by a force. The potential for exertion is energy; the rate of motion is speed; and the force-multiplying ability of a machine is mechanical advantage; therefore, answers A, C, and D are incorrect.

92. **Answer D is correct.** Using the formula W=fd, we can plug in the values W=50(3); W=150 ft lb of work. The other values are incorrect; therefore, answers A, B, and C are incorrect.

93. **Answer C is correct.** Using the formula MA=R/E, then MA=140/70, or MA=2. 4, 1, and 70 are all invalid values, therefore, answers A, B, and D are incorrect.

94. **Answer A is correct.** Using the formula E=work output/work input, then E=6/8; and E=.75%. 50%, 130%, and 48% are all invalid values; therefore, answers B, C, and D are incorrect.

95. **Answer A is correct.** Using the formula (Work a)(distance a)=(Work b)(distance b), then (20 + 40)(10)= 10x; 600=10x; 60=x. Values of 100 lbs, 6 lbs, and 120 lbs are invalid; therefore, answers B, C, and D are incorrect.

96. **Answer B is correct.** Velocity and momentum are vector quantities. Length and area are examples of scalar quantities; a resultant is the combined effect of two or more vectors; and a tensor is a vector quantity; therefore, answers A, C, and D are incorrect.

97. **Answer C is correct.** A pair of vise grips is a compound machine, which consists of two or more simple machines. While vise grips are pliers, that is not the type of machine that they are. Vice grips are not wrenches; therefore, answers A, B, and D are incorrect.

98. **Answer C is correct.** The formula to use is wd = wd, so that 36x = 80(6); 36x = 480; x = 13.33 lbs. 160 pounds indicates that you did not change the 3 ft. to 36 inches, therefore, answer A is incorrect. Always be sure your values are the same. Because the distance on each side of the fulcrum is not the same, then the effort to lift the boxes is not the same as the weight of the boxes. Therefore, answer B is incorrect. 480 lbs. indicates that you exchanged distance values on each side of the equation; therefore, answer D is also incorrect.

99. **Answer D is correct.** According to the formula wd = wd, then 10x = 300(4); 10x = 1200; x = 120. Answer A represents the MA; answer B indicates that you have reversed the effort distance and resistance distance; Answer C represents no mechanical advantage. Because an inclined plane does provide a mechanical advantage, then you do not have to exert an equivalent amount of effort to move the barrel; therefore, answers A, B, and C are incorrect.

100. **Answer B is correct.** Power input=power output/efficiency, therefore, PI=15/.95, so that PI=15.79 hp. 16 hp, 1.58 hp, and 14 hp are invalid values; therefore, answers A, C, and D are incorrect.

Practice Exam 2

General Science

1. Which of the following steps is *not* part of the scientific method?
   - ❑ A. Making observations of natural phenomena
   - ❑ B. Taking measurements
   - ❑ C. Conducting experiments
   - ❑ D. Formulating a statement of absolute truth

2. When you swing a hammer and strike a nail, the resulting work is done by what kind of energy?
   - ❑ A. Kinetic energy
   - ❑ B. Potential energy
   - ❑ C. Thermal energy
   - ❑ D. Chemical energy

3. A mutually beneficial relationship between two or more species is known as
   - ❑ A. Parasitism
   - ❑ B. Symbiosis
   - ❑ C. A community
   - ❑ D. Predation

4. The thyroid gland is a part of what bodily system?
   - ❑ A. Reproductive system
   - ❑ B. Circulatory system
   - ❑ C. Endocrine system
   - ❑ D. Lymphatic system

5. Dinosaurs lived during which geologic era?
   - ❑ A. Paleozoic
   - ❑ B. Mesozoic
   - ❑ C. Cenozoic
   - ❑ D. Precambrian

6. Which is the largest planet in the solar system?
   - ❏ A. Jupiter
   - ❏ B. Saturn
   - ❏ C. Neptune
   - ❏ D. Uranus

7. The periodic table of elements lists elements in order of their atomic number. What does the atomic number represent?
   - ❏ A. The number of protons in its nucleus
   - ❏ B. The number of neutrons in its nucleus
   - ❏ C. The number of its electrons
   - ❏ D. The mass of its nucleus

8. The chemical equation $H + O_2 \rightarrow H_2O$ represents what kind of chemical reaction?
   - ❏ A. Decomposition reaction
   - ❏ B. Replacement reaction
   - ❏ C. Synthesis reaction
   - ❏ D. Chain reaction

9. Which of the following is a function of the musculoskeletal system?
   - ❏ A. To provide structural support for the body
   - ❏ B. To protect the internal organs
   - ❏ C. To produce blood cells
   - ❏ D. All of the above

10. Which of the following lists is arranged in order from broadest to narrowest classification?
   - ❏ A. Kingdom, phylum, genus, class
   - ❏ B. Species, genus, family, order
   - ❏ C. Kingdom, class, family, species
   - ❏ D. Phylum, genus, species, order

11. Find the correct order, from largest to smallest, of metric system prefixes.
   - ❏ A. Nano-, centi-, kilo-
   - ❏ B. Mega-, kilo-, centi-
   - ❏ C. Kilo-, micro-, mega-
   - ❏ D. Centi-, nano-, kilo-

12. Atoms of the same element, which possess different numbers of neutrons, are called?
   - ❏ A. Solvents
   - ❏ B. Isotopes
   - ❏ C. Inert
   - ❏ D. Non-metals

13. Which of the following statements about the earth's core is false?
- [ ] A. It is responsible for generating Earth's magnetic field
- [ ] B. It has a fluid outer layer and a solid inner core
- [ ] C. It is made up of mainly granite
- [ ] D. It is approximately 1,400 miles across

14. What is the main difference between mitosis and meiosis?
- [ ] A. Mitosis results in two exact copies of the original cell
- [ ] B. Mitosis refers to cell division
- [ ] C. Meiosis occurs in most of the human body's cells
- [ ] D. None of the above

15. What is the difference between velocity and speed?
- [ ] A. Velocity is a scalar unit
- [ ] B. Speed is given in English units, velocity in metric units
- [ ] C. There is no difference
- [ ] D. Velocity contains quantity and direction information

16. A difference between a gas and a liquid is
- [ ] A. Liquids do not have definite shape
- [ ] B. Gases have definite mass
- [ ] C. Liquids have definite mass and volume
- [ ] D. None of the above

17. Which biome is characterized by its coniferous forests?
- [ ] A. Taiga
- [ ] B. Savannah
- [ ] C. Tropical rainforest
- [ ] D. Tundra

18. Which group of organisms within the food chain is responsible for recycling organic material by breaking it down into simple compounds?
- [ ] A. Producers
- [ ] B. Tertiary consumers
- [ ] C. Secondary consumers
- [ ] D. Decomposers

19. Microwave ovens heat food through which form of thermal energy transfer?
- [ ] A. Convection
- [ ] B. Conduction
- [ ] C. Radiation
- [ ] D. All of the above

20. Which of the following parts of the circulatory system are used by blood on its return trip to the heart?
    - ❏ A. Arteries
    - ❏ B. Veins
    - ❏ C. Both of the above
    - ❏ D. Neither of the above

21. Which organelle functions within a cell to extract energy from carbohydrates?
    - ❏ A. Lysosomes
    - ❏ B. Mitochondria
    - ❏ C. Nucleus
    - ❏ D. Endoplasmic reticulum

22. The layers of the earth's atmosphere, in order of increasing altitude, are
    - ❏ A. Mesosphere, troposphere, thermosphere, stratosphere
    - ❏ B. Thermosphere, mesosphere, stratosphere, troposphere
    - ❏ C. Stratosphere, mesosphere, troposphere, thermosphere
    - ❏ D. Troposphere, stratosphere, mesosphere, thermosphere

23. Light hitting a surface and "bouncing" back toward its source, is called
    - ❏ A. Reflection
    - ❏ B. Refraction
    - ❏ C. Radiation
    - ❏ D. Convection

24. Which two planets are closer to the sun than the earth?
    - ❏ A. Mercury and Neptune
    - ❏ B. Saturn and Mars
    - ❏ C. Mars and Venus
    - ❏ D. Mercury and Venus

25. The temperature at which water vapor condenses into droplets is called the
    - ❏ A. Precipitation point
    - ❏ B. Dew point
    - ❏ C. Melting point
    - ❏ D. Triple point

Arithmetic Reasoning

26. A landscaping company charges 5 cents per square foot to apply fertilizer. How much would it cost for them to fertilize a 30 foot by 50 foot lawn?

   - ❑ A. $7.50
   - ❑ B. $15.00
   - ❑ C. $75.00
   - ❑ D. $150.00

27. The triathlon course included a 400 meter swim, a 50.6 kilometer bike ride, and a 5.75 kilometer run. What was the total length of the race course?

   - ❑ A. 56.75 meters
   - ❑ B. 56.75 kilometers
   - ❑ C. 456.35 kilometers
   - ❑ D. 567.5 kilometers

28. How many 15 passenger vans will it take to drive all 52 members of the football team to the stadium?

   - ❑ A. 2
   - ❑ B. 3
   - ❑ C. 4
   - ❑ D. 5

29. If all a roofing company's 12 workers are required to staff 3 roofing crews, how many workers need to be added during the busy season in order to send 6 complete crews out on jobs?

   - ❑ A. 4
   - ❑ B. 12
   - ❑ C. 18
   - ❑ D. 24

30. If Paul's recipe calls for 1 1/4 cups of sugar, but he only has 2/3 cup left in his pantry, how much sugar will he need to borrow to follow the recipe?

   - ❑ A. 7/12 cup
   - ❑ B. 2/3 cup
   - ❑ C. 3/4 cup
   - ❑ D. 1 cup

31. How many 2 1/2 gallon cans worth of gas would you need to pour into an empty 11 gallon tank in order to fill it exactly halfway?

   - ❑ A. 2
   - ❑ B. 2 1/5
   - ❑ C. 3
   - ❑ D. 5 1/2

32. What is the next number in the series {16, 18, 22, 28,⊃}?
    - ❏ A. 26
    - ❏ B. 30
    - ❏ C. 34
    - ❏ D. 36

33. A shoe store is having a sale. The ad promises, "Buy one pair of shoes at full price and get a second pair for 30% off." If Barbara buys two pairs of shoes, each with a regular price of $49.50, how much money will she save?
    - ❏ A. $14.85
    - ❏ B. $34.65
    - ❏ C. $49.50
    - ❏ D. $64.35

34. If a car travels 384 miles in 6 hours, what is its average speed?
    - ❏ A. 46 mph
    - ❏ B. 64 mph
    - ❏ C. 65 mph
    - ❏ D. 68 mph

35. If a customer pays for a $17.39 item with a twenty dollar bill, how much change will he get back?
    - ❏ A. 61 cents
    - ❏ B. $1.61
    - ❏ C. $2.39
    - ❏ D. $2.61

36. If the ratio of Cubs fans to Brewers fans in the crowd is 3:1 and all 42,000 seats are filled, how many Cubs fans are in the ballpark?
    - ❏ A. 14,000
    - ❏ B. 24,500
    - ❏ C. 31,500
    - ❏ D. 40,250

37. What is the quotient of .724/.16?
    - ❏ A. 4.525
    - ❏ B. 4.53
    - ❏ C. 45.25
    - ❏ D. 452.50

38. If the new mayor was elected with 60% of the votes cast and only 50% of the town's 35,000 registered voters cast ballots, how many votes did she receive?
    - ❏ A. 7,500
    - ❏ B. 10,500
    - ❏ C. 17,500
    - ❏ D. 21,000

39. What are the next two numbers in the series {3, 9, 7, 21, 19,⊃}?
    - ❏ A. 21, 7
    - ❏ B. 38, 35
    - ❏ C. 5, 57
    - ❏ D. 57, 55

40. What is the product of 1 1/3 and 4/5?
    - ❏ A. 1/15
    - ❏ B. 3/5
    - ❏ C. 1 1/15
    - ❏ D. 1 2/3

41. If Maija deposits $700 into a savings account with a 4% annual interest rate and doesn't take out any of her money for two years, how much interest will she have earned on her original investment?
    - ❏ A. $28
    - ❏ B. $29.12
    - ❏ C. $57.12
    - ❏ D. $757.12

42. If there were a total of 50 raffle tickets sold and David bought 2 tickets, what is the probability that he will win the raffle?
    - ❏ A. 2%
    - ❏ B. 4%
    - ❏ C. 5%
    - ❏ D. 8%

43. Find the average of 32, 19, and 24.
    - ❏ A. 21.3
    - ❏ B. 23
    - ❏ C. 24.8
    - ❏ D. 25

44. A machine has an error rate of 3 parts per 100. If the machine normally runs 24 hours/day at a rate of 60 parts/hour, but yesterday was shut down for 4 hours for maintenance, how many good (that is, error free) parts did it produce yesterday?
    - ❏ A. 36
    - ❏ B. 97
    - ❏ C. 1164
    - ❏ D. 1200

45. If a rectangle is twice as long as it is wide and its perimeter is 54, then what is its area?
    - ❏ A. 54
    - ❏ B. 81
    - ❏ C. 144
    - ❏ D. 162

Mathematics Knowledge

46. If x=3, what is the value of $3x^2 + 4x - 12$?

   ❑ A. 18
   ❑ B. 27
   ❑ C. 32
   ❑ D. 39

47. Which has the greater volume, a cylinder with a radius of 3 inches and a height of 2 inches or a cube with sides of 4 inches (use the approximation 3.14 for pi)?

   ❑ A. The cube
   ❑ B. The cylinder
   ❑ C. They have the same volume
   ❑ D. Not enough information is given

48. What is the value of $6! - 5!$?

   ❑ A. 1
   ❑ B. 11
   ❑ C. 120
   ❑ D. 600

49. Find the slope of the line running through the points (5,–3) and (–4,6).

   ❑ A. –3
   ❑ B. –1
   ❑ C. 1
   ❑ D. 3

50. $(y - 3)(y^2 + y + 2) = ?$

   ❑ A. $y^3 - 2y^2 - y - 5$
   ❑ B. $y^3 - 4y^2 - y - 6$
   ❑ C. $y^3 - 2y^2 - y - 6$
   ❑ D. $y^3 - 2y^2 - y + 6$

51. For the triangle pictured below, find the value of the angle c?

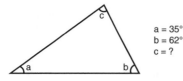

a = 35°
b = 62°
c = ?

   ❑ A. 83
   ❑ B. 180
   ❑ C. 263
   ❑ D. Not enough information given

52. Solve the inequality: x – 3 >= –2
    - ❏ A. –5
    - ❏ B. –1
    - ❏ C. 1
    - ❏ D. 5

53. If z = 5 and y = –7, what is the value of the expression, $-z^3 - z^2y + 3y^2 - zy + 4$?
    - ❏ A. –989
    - ❏ B. 61
    - ❏ C. 236
    - ❏ D. 361

54. It takes Karl twice as long as Amy to read a book. If their book club meets in 12 days and Amy starts to read the new book today, how many days can she take to read the book and still give Karl enough time to finish reading their one copy of the book before the meeting?
    - ❏ A. 4 days
    - ❏ B. 6 days
    - ❏ C. 8 days
    - ❏ D. 10 days

55. Find the cube root of 343.
    - ❏ A. –8
    - ❏ B. –7
    - ❏ C. 6
    - ❏ D. 7

56. If lines i and j are parallel, what is the value of angle m?

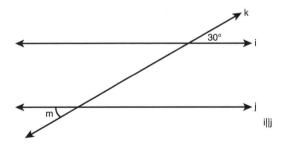

    - ❏ A. 15 degrees
    - ❏ B. 30 degrees
    - ❏ C. 150 degrees
    - ❏ D. 180 degrees

57. What is the area of the unshaded region?

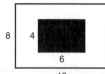

- ❑ A. 24
- ❑ B. 72
- ❑ C. 96
- ❑ D. 120

58. What is the reciprocal of $x^2/3$?

- ❑ A. $3/x^2$
- ❑ B. $x^2 - 3$
- ❑ C. $1 - x^2/3$
- ❑ D. $x^2/9$

59. 1,345.87219 rounded to the nearest thousandth is _____.

- ❑ A. 1,000
- ❑ B. 1,345.870
- ❑ C. 1,345.872
- ❑ D. 1,345.873

60. If, in the right triangle shown in the following figure, side a = 3 and side b = 4, what is the length of side c?

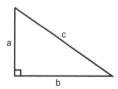

- ❑ A. square root (5)
- ❑ B. 5
- ❑ C. 7
- ❑ D. 12

61. If x is a positive number and y is a negative number, which of the following statements must be true?

- ❑ A. xy is a positive number
- ❑ B. $-xy < 0$
- ❑ C. $-xy^2 > 0$
- ❑ D. xy^2 is a positive number

62. Which of the following answer choices lists numbers in increasing order?

    ❑ A. $-3, 0, 3^0, 3^1$
    ❑ B. $3^1, 3^0, -3, 0$
    ❑ C. $3^0, 0, -3, 3^1$
    ❑ D. $-3, 3^0, 0, 3^1$

63. How many 2×2 squares can fit inside a rectangle with a length of 12 and a width of 10?

    ❑ A. 20
    ❑ B. 30
    ❑ C. 40
    ❑ D. 60

64. If $y = 0$, then $\dfrac{y^2 + 3xy - 3}{2y} = $?

    ❑ A. -3
    ❑ B. $-3/2$
    ❑ C. 0
    ❑ D. Not defined

65. $x^5 / x^2 = ?$

    ❑ A. x
    ❑ B. 3x
    ❑ C. x^3
    ❑ D. x^7

Shop Information

66. Measuring tools are used to determine the dimension of an object by comparing it with a _____.

    ❑ A. Blueprint
    ❑ B. Standard
    ❑ C. Scale model
    ❑ D. None of the above

67. To indicate a perfectly vertical line you should use which of the following?

    ❑ A. Micrometer
    ❑ B. Caliper
    ❑ C. Plumb bob
    ❑ D. Carpenter's square

68. Identify this tool.

- ❏ A. Box wrench
- ❏ B. Socket wrench
- ❏ C. Allen wrench
- ❏ D. Die

69. Which saw blade would produce a finer, cleaner cut?
- ❏ A. 8 point blade
- ❏ B. 10 point blade
- ❏ C. 12 point blade
- ❏ D. All of the above cut the same

70. Name this part of a saw.

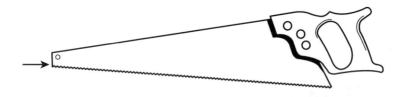

- ❏ A. Kerf
- ❏ B. Nose
- ❏ C. Heel
- ❏ D. Toe

71. Which of the following tools would be most suitable for cutting a metal pipe?
- ❏ A. Rip saw
- ❏ B. Hacksaw
- ❏ C. Coping saw
- ❏ D. Router

72. The purpose of a tap is to _____.
- ❏ A. Drill large diameter holes
- ❏ B. Provide electrical power for a welder
- ❏ C. Cut threads into the outside of a pipe or rod
- ❏ D. Cut threads into the inside of a hole

73. What is a dado?
    - ❑ A. A wide slot cut across the wood grain
    - ❑ B. A tool used for slicing thin layers of wood
    - ❑ C. The groove cut by a saw's blade
    - ❑ D. A circular, small toothed drill bit

74. Which of the following statements does *not* apply to a mallet?
    - ❑ A. Useful for tapping dowel pins into place
    - ❑ B. Has a soft head to absorb shock of impact
    - ❑ C. Can be used in riveting
    - ❑ D. Unable to pull nails

75. The long, narrow stem of a rivet is called a _____.
    - ❑ A. Mandrel
    - ❑ B. Filler rod
    - ❑ C. Neck
    - ❑ D. Post

76. Which drill bit should you select to put a taper on a pre-drilled hole?
    - ❑ A. Forstner bit
    - ❑ B. Spade bit
    - ❑ C. Reamer bit
    - ❑ D. Auger bit

77. What is the strongest method of permanently joining two pieces of like metal?
    - ❑ A. Brazing
    - ❑ B. Welding
    - ❑ C. Soldering
    - ❑ D. Crimping

78. Which tool should you select for gripping a small object inside a tight space?
    - ❑ A. Slip-joint pliers
    - ❑ B. Bench vise
    - ❑ C. C-clamp
    - ❑ D. Needle nose pliers

79. In the soldering process, which of the following is *not* a use for flux?
    - ❑ A. Tinning
    - ❑ B. Creating an electrical arc
    - ❑ C. Preventing oxide formation
    - ❑ D. Breaking down the solder's surface tension

80. The filler rod used in brazing is made from which material?
    - ❑ A. Tin
    - ❑ B. Lead
    - ❑ C. Copper
    - ❑ D. Brass

81. Which machine tool is used for turning?
    - ❑ A. Lathe
    - ❑ B. Bench grinder
    - ❑ C. Milling machine
    - ❑ D. Drill press

82. The shop planning document that contains detailed technical drawings showing dimension information is called a _____.
    - ❑ A. Bill of materials
    - ❑ B. Layout
    - ❑ C. Blueprint
    - ❑ D. Schematic

83. Which measuring tool provides the greatest degree of precision in measuring the thickness or outer dimension of an object?
    - ❑ A. Micrometer
    - ❑ B. Level
    - ❑ C. Carpenter's square
    - ❑ D. Steel rule

84. Identify the backsaw from among the following figures.
    - ❑ A.

    - ❑ B.

    - ❑ C.

    - ❑ D.

85. Which of the following figures shows a chisel?

❑ A.

❑ B.
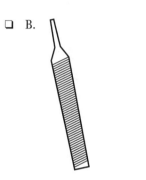

❑ C.

❑ D.
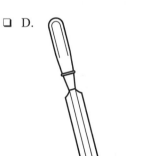

Assembling Objects

For each puzzle piece assembly problem, you are given the set of pieces in the first box. Your job is to select the answer choice that correctly assembles those pieces. For each part connection problem, you are given a set of labeled pieces and a labeled axis line. Your job is to select the answer choice that correctly connects the pieces in the proper orientation to match the original set.

86.

❏ A.   ❏ B.   ❏ C.   ❏ D.

87.

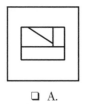      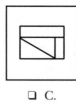   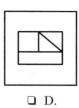

❏ A.   ❏ B.   ❏ C.   ❏ D.

88.

❏ A.   ❏ B.   ❏ C.   ❏ D.

89.

❑ A.   ❑ B.   ❑ C.   ❑ D.

90.

❑ A.   ❑ B.   ❑ C.   ❑ D.

91.

❑ A.   ❑ B.   ❑ C.   ❑ D.

92.

❑ A. ❑ B. ❑ C. ❑ D.

93.

❑ A. ❑ B. ❑ C. ❑ D.

94.

❑ A. ❑ B. ❑ C. ❑ D.

95.

    ❑ A.      ❑ B.   ❑ C.   ❑ D.

96.

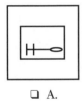   ❑ A.   ❑ B.   ❑ C.   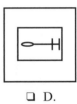   ❑ D.

97.

    ❑ A.   ❑ B.   ❑ C.   ❑ D.

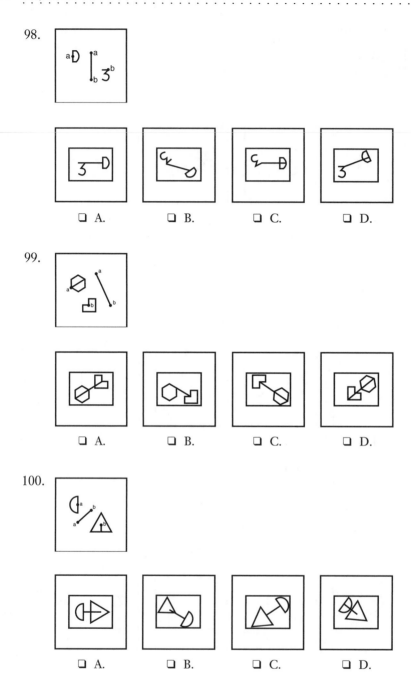

98.

❑ A.   ❑ B.   ❑ C.   ❑ D.

99.

❑ A.   ❑ B.   ❑ C.   ❑ D.

100.

❑ A.   ❑ B.   ❑ C.   ❑ D.

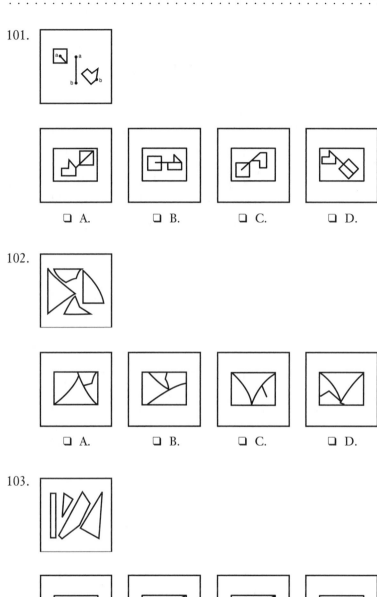

101.

❑ A.   ❑ B.   ❑ C.   ❑ D.

102.

❑ A.   ❑ B.   ❑ C.   ❑ D.

103.

❑ A.   ❑ B.   ❑ C.   ❑ D.

104.

❏ A.   ❏ B.   ❏ C.   ❏ D.

105.

❏ A.   ❏ B.   ❏ C.   ❏ D.

106.

 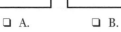 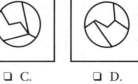

❏ A.   ❏ B.   ❏ C.   ❏ D.

107.

❏ A.　　　　❏ B.　　　　❏ C.　　　　❏ D.

108.

❏ A.　　　　❏ B.　　　　❏ C.　　　　❏ D.

109.

❏ A.　　　　❏ B.　　　　❏ C.　　　　❏ D.

110.

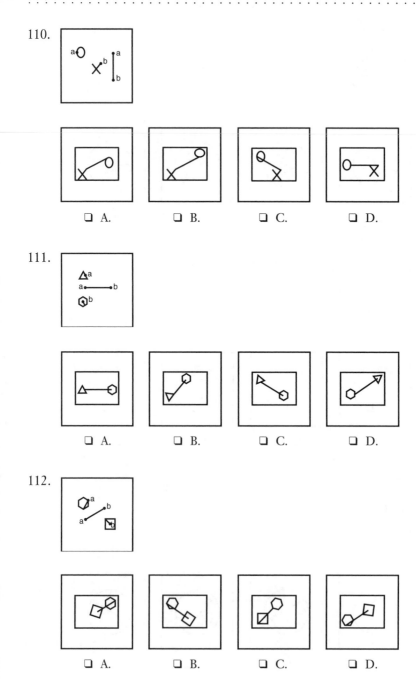

❑ A.　　　　❑ B.　　　　❑ C.　　　　❑ D.

111.

❑ A.　　　　❑ B.　　　　❑ C.　　　　❑ D.

112.

❑ A.　　　　❑ B.　　　　❑ C.　　　　❑ D.

113.

   ❏ A.   ❏ B.   ❏ C.   ❏ D.

114.

   ❏ A.   ❏ B.   ❏ C.   ❏ D.

115.

   ❏ A.   ❏ B.   ❏ C.   ❏ D.

116.

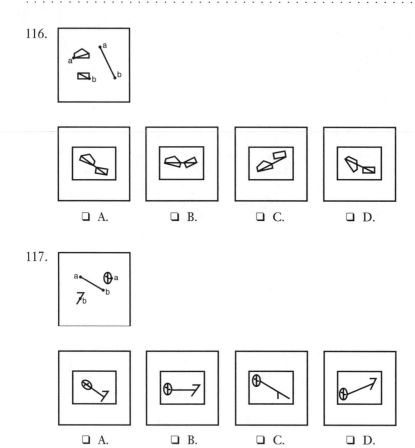

❑ A.   ❑ B.   ❑ C.   ❑ D.

117.

❑ A.   ❑ B.   ❑ C.   ❑ D.

Answers to Practice Exam 2

Answers to General Science

1. D
2. A
3. B
4. C
5. B
6. A
7. A
8. C
9. D
10. C
11. B
12. B
13. C

14. A
15. D
16. C
17. A
18. D
19. C
20. B
21. B
22. D
23. A
24. D
25. B

Answer Explanations for General Science

1. **Answer D is correct.** Answers A, B, and C are incorrect because making observations, taking measurements, and conducting experiments are all part of the Scientific Method. The other step in the method is formulating hypotheses, *not* absolute truths. The Scientific Method does not presume to result in the discovery of absolute truth, merely to develop workable theories and laws based on the best available information and experimentation.

2. **Answer A is correct.** Kinetic energy is the energy of motion. Answer B is incorrect because potential energy is stored energy due to the position of an object. Answer C is incorrect because thermal energy is heat energy. Answer D is incorrect because chemical energy relates to the energy stored in the chemical bonds between atoms.

3. **Answer B is correct.** Answer A is incorrect because parasitism is when one organism (the parasite) benefits from its close interaction with another (the host), which suffers. Answer C is incorrect because a community is defined as the sum of various populations that live within a particular habitat. Answer D is incorrect because predation is the condition of one organism preying on another.

4. **Answer C is correct.** Answer C is correct, and the other answers are incorrect, because the endocrine system is the only bodily system that controls the body through a release of hormones that are produced in the endocrine glands (including the thyroid gland).

5. **Answer B is correct.** Answer A is incorrect because the Paleozoic Era predated dinosaurs. Answer C is incorrect because the Cenozoic Era, in which we are living today, began after the dinosaurs became extinct. Answer D is incorrect because the Precambrian Era, which began with earth's formation, saw the development of only the most primitive life forms.

6. **Answer A is correct.** Answer B is incorrect because Saturn is the second largest planet in the solar system. Answer C is incorrect because Neptune is the fourth largest planet in the solar system. Answer D is incorrect because Uranus is the third largest planet in the solar system.

7. **Answer A is correct.** Answers B, C, and D are all incorrect because the periodic table of elements is arranged in numerical order according to atomic number, which is defined as the number of protons in the nucleus of an atom. The atomic number is like an atom's fingerprint, positively identifying it as being of a certain element.

8. **Answer C is correct.** Answer A is incorrect because a decomposition reaction results in the breakdown of one compound into two or more different substances. Answer B is incorrect because a replacement reaction results in the exchange of elements or compounds. Answer D is incorrect because a chain reaction is the term used to describe a self-sustaining nuclear reaction.

9. **Answer D is correct.** Each of the answer choices A, B, and C describes a function of the musculoskeletal system.

10. **Answer C is correct.** The other answer choices are incorrect because they do not follow the Linnaean classification system from broadest to narrowest. The complete series of classifications from broadest to narrowest is: kingdom, phylum, class, order, family, genus, and species.

11. **Answer B is correct.** Answer A is incorrect because its prefixes are arranged from smallest to largest. Answer C is incorrect because its prefixes are in no order. Answer D is incorrect because its prefixes are in no order.

12. **Answer B is correct.** Answer A is incorrect because solvents are substances into which other substances are dissolved. Answer C is incorrect because the term *inert* refers to elements that do not react readily (or react at all) with other elements. Answer D is incorrect because non-metals encompass a number of different elements.

13. **Answer C is correct.** Answers A, B, and D are incorrect because they all contain true statements about the earth's core. The earth's core is made up of nickel-iron.

14. **Answer A is correct.** Answer B is incorrect because, although mitosis does refer to cell division, so does meiosis. Answer C is incorrect because meiosis only occurs in the human body's sex cells. Answer D is incorrect because for it to be correct none of the other answer choices could be correct.

15. **Answer D is correct.** Answer A is incorrect because velocity is a vector (containing displacement and direction information), not a scalar (containing only displacement information) quantity. Answer B is incorrect because speed can be given in either English or metric units. Answer C is incorrect because there is a difference between velocity and speed.

16. **Answer C is correct.** Answer A is incorrect because neither liquids nor gases have definite shape. Answer B is incorrect because, like gases, liquids do have definite mass. Answer D is incorrect because for it to be correct none of the other answer choices could be correct.

17. **Answer A is correct.** Answer B is incorrect because the savannah is grasslands with few trees and unreliable rainfall. Answer C is incorrect because the tropical rain forest is a region of extremely high humidity, rainfall, and temperature, containing dense, leafy vegetation. Answer D is incorrect because the tundra has permanently frozen soil and its only plant life is comprised of short, rooted plants and shrubs.

18. **Answer D is correct.** Answer A is incorrect because producers use the simple organic compounds for their food source and, in turn, become the food source for primary consumers. Answer B is incorrect because tertiary consumers eat secondary consumers. Answer C is incorrect because secondary consumers eat primary consumers.

19. **Answer C is correct.** Answer A is incorrect because convection is heat transfer through actual displacement of a lower temperature part of a medium by a higher temperature part. Answer B is incorrect because conduction is heat transfer within a medium through the flow of free electrons. Answer D is incorrect because the correct answer is radiation (C).

20. **Answer B is correct.** Answer A is incorrect because arteries are a part of the circulatory system used to circulate blood away from the heart to other parts of the body. Answers C and D are incorrect because the correct answer is veins (B).

21. **Answer B is correct.** Answer A is incorrect because lysosomes recycle materials. Answer C is incorrect because the nucleus controls cell functions and contains the cell's genetic information. Answer D is incorrect because the endoplasmic reticulum's function is to manufacture proteins and lipids.

22. **Answer D is correct.** Answers A, B, and C all fail to list the atmosphere's layers in order from lowest to highest altitude.

23. **Answer A is correct.** Answer B is incorrect because refraction is the bending of light as it passes from one medium into another. Answer C is incorrect because radiation is a form of heat transfer. Answer D is incorrect because convection is also a form of heat transfer.

24. **Answer D is correct.** Answer A is incorrect because, although Mercury is closer to the sun than Earth, Neptune isn't. Answer B is incorrect because both Mars and Saturn are farther away from the sun than Earth. Answer C is incorrect because, although Venus is closer to the sun than Earth, Mars isn't.

25. **Answer B is correct.** Answer A is incorrect because "precipitation point" is not the proper meteorological term for this phenomenon. Answer C is incorrect because melting point describes the point at which a solid transforms into a liquid. Answer D is incorrect because the triple point describes the exact temperature and pressure combination at which a given substance can exist simultaneously and in contact as a solid, liquid, and gas.

Answers to Arithmetic Reasoning

26. C	**36.** C
27. B	**37.** A
28. C	**38.** B
29. D	**39.** D
30. A	**40.** C
31. B	**41.** C
32. D	**42.** B
33. A	**43.** D
34. B	**44.** C
35. D	**45.** D

Answer Explanations for Arithmetic Reasoning

26. **Answer C is correct.** To solve this problem, first find the square footage (that is, area) of the lawn: Area = l * w

$$= 30ft * 50ft$$
$$= 1,500 \ ft^2$$

Then calculate the total cost.

Total cost = (cost/ ft^2)(total ft^2)
$$= (\$0.05)(1,500 \ ft^2)$$
$$= \$75$$

27. **Answer B is correct.** The first step is to convert all distances to the same unit. Then it's just a matter of adding decimals to get the total distance.

    Swim: 400 meters (m) = 0.4 kilometers (km) [Remember: 1 km = 1,000 m]

    Bike:　　　=50.6 km

    Run:　　+ = 5.75 km

    　　　　56.75 km

28. **Answer C is correct.** This is a simple division problem with a small twist. Once you get your answer (a decimal) you must apply common sense. Three vans won't be quite enough; to get everyone to the game you'll have to take a fourth van even though it won't be full. You've got to round up to 4.

    (52 passengers)(1 van / 15 passengers) = 52 / 15 = 3.466 (the .466 extra people go in van 4)

29. **Answer D is correct.** To solve this problem, first figure out how many workers are needed to make up a crew: 12 workers / 3 crews = 4 workers/crew. Next, multiply by the number of crews needed during the busy season to get your answer. Set up a proportion, making x= the number of workers needed to staff 6 crews.

    4 workers = x workers

    1 crew　　6 crews

    (1)(x) = (4)(6)

    　x = 24 workers

30. **Answer A is correct.** This is a subtraction with fractions problem. The first step in subtracting fractions is always to find their common denominator. Begin by converting 1 1/4 from a mixed number into an improper fraction:

    1 1/4 = [(1)(4)+1]/4

    　= (4+1)/4

    　= 5/4

    Then find the common denominator for 5/4 and 2/3:

    5/4 = 5(3)/4(3) = 15/12 and 2/3 = 2(4)/3(4) = 8/12

    Now you are ready to subtract:

    15/12 – 8/12 = 7/12

31. **Answer B is correct.** First of all, figure out how much gas needs to go into the tank to fill it exactly halfway: 11 gallons / 2 = 5 1/2 gallons

Now you have a dividing with fractions problem: (5 1/2 gallons / 2 1/2 gallons)

Begin by converting the mixed numbers into improper fractions:

5 1/2 = [(5)(2) + 1] / 2 = (10+1)/2 = 11/2
2 1/2 = [(2)(2) + 1] / 2 = (4+1)/2 = 5/2

Remember, when you divide fractions, you take the reciprocal of the divisor and then multiply:

(11/2)/(5/2) = (11/2)*(2/5)

    = (11)(2)/(2)(5)

    = 22/10

Finally, convert the improper fraction back into a mixed number and simplify:

22/10 = 2 2/10 = 2 1/5

32. **Answer D is correct.** To find the pattern and determine the operation being performed to obtain the next number, you must look at the relationship of each number with the number that follows in the series. So, you'll notice that:

16 + 2 = 18
18 + 4 = 22
22 + 6 = 28

Following this pattern, your next number will be

28 + 8 = 36

33. **Answer A is correct.** By reading this problem carefully you'll see that it isn't asking for the sale price of the second pair of shoes, or the total amount of money Barbara spent. The only reason you care that she bought two pairs of shoes is that it qualified her to receive the sale price on the second pair. So, all you have to do is calculate the value of her 30% savings on the second pair of shoes:

Regular price of second pair = $49.50

Savings = ($49.50)(30%)

Remember 30% = 30/100 = 0.30

= ($49.50)(0.30)

= $49.50

 x .30

 0000

148500

$14.85

34. **Answer B is correct.** The average speed is given in units of miles/hour. In this case, the car traveled 384 miles in 6 hours. You can write this as: 384 miles / 6 hours. Dividing, you get 64 miles/hour.

35. **Answer D is correct.** This is a straight subtracting with decimals problem. Remember to line up the decimal points before subtracting!

$20.00

− $17.39

$ 2.61

36. **Answer C is correct.** A ratio of 3:1 means that for every 4 fans, 3 are Cubs fans and 1 is a Brewers fan. Knowing that you can set up a proportion to find the number of Cubs fans (x):

3 Cubs fans = x

4 fans   42,000

4x = (3)(42,000)

4x = 126,000

x = 31,500

37. **Answer A is correct.** This is nothing more than a dividing with decimals problem. To solve for the quotient, move the decimal point in the divisor 2 spaces to make a whole number and then move the decimal point in the dividend the same number of spaces. Now you can divide like normal:

$$
0.16\overline{)0.724} = 16\overline{)72.400}
$$

```
          4.525
0.16 )0.724 = 16)72.400
          64
          84
          80
          40
          32
          80
          80
           0
```

38. **Answer B is correct.** To solve this problem, first find out how many people voted:

    50% of 35,000 = (0.50)(5,000) = 17,500

    Then you can calculate how many of those who voted, voted for the new mayor:

    60% of 17,500 = (0.60)(17,500) = 10,500

39. **Answer D is correct.** In this series there are two different operations being performed. Again, look at the relationship between each number and the number that follows it:

    3 * 3 = 9
    9 − 2 = 7
    7 * 3 = 21
    21 − 2 = 19

    See the pattern? The operations alternate between multiplying by 3 and subtracting 2. So, continuing the pattern gives you:

    19 * 3 = 57
    57 − 2 = 55

40. **Answer C is correct.** To multiply fractions, first convert the mixed number to an improper fraction

1 1/3 = [(3)(1) + 1]/3 = (3+1)/3 = 4/3

Then multiply the numerators and denominators of the two fractions:

(4/3)(4/5) = (4)(4)/(3)(5) = 16/15

Finally, convert the product back into a mixed number:

16/15 = 1 1/15

41. **Answer C is correct.** The best way to solve this interest rate problem is to create a simple table to keep track of the growing savings account:

Year	Interest	$ in Account	Calculation
0	$0	$700	$700*4%=(700)(.04)=$28
1	$28	$728	$728*4%=(728)(.04)=$29.12
2	$29.12	$757.12	————————————

The question asks for the total amount of interest Maija will have earned after 2 years. Simply add $28 and $29.12 to find the answer: $57.12

42. **Answer B is correct.** The probability of David winning the raffle is the number of chances he has (2) out of the total opportunities for picking a winning ticket (50). This is because each of the raffle tickets has the same chance of being selected. You can express David's probability of winning as 2/50 = (2)(2)/(50)(2) = 4/100 = 4%

43. **Answer D is correct.** To find the average of three numbers, you must add the three numbers together and divide by the total number of numbers (i.e., 3). In this case, then:

Average = (32 + 19 + 24)/3 = 75/3 = 25

44. **Answer C is correct.** To solve this problem, first find the machine's run time:

    24 hours - 4 hours downtime = 20 hours run time

    Next, find the total number of parts it made during its run time:

    (20 hours)(60 parts/hour) = 1,200 parts

    Finally, establish a proportion to find the number of parts made which had errors (you can call that number "x"):

    3 errors = x

    100 parts 1,200 parts

    $\quad$ 100x = (3)(1,200)

    $\quad$ 100x = 3,600

    $\qquad$ x = 36 parts with errors

    Subtracting the number of parts with errors from the total number of parts made yesterday, gives you your answer: 1,200 – 36 = 1,164 parts without errors

45. **Answer D is correct.** This is a two part problem that requires you to remember the definition of perimeter and area of a rectangle. Given the perimeter and the length of the rectangle in terms of its width, you can solve for both length and width. Once you have the length and width, you simply need to multiply them together to find the area.

    Given: l = 2w

    $\quad$ P = 2w + 2l = 54

    So, P = 2w + 2(2w) = 2w + 4w = 6w = 54

    $\qquad\qquad$ w = 54/6

    $\qquad\qquad$ w = 9

    and $\qquad$ l = 2w = 9*2 = 18

    Thus, A = l*w

    $\qquad$ = 9 * 18

    $\qquad$ = 162

Answers to Mathematics Knowledge

46. B	**56.** B
47. A	**57.** B
48. D	**58.** A
49. B	**59.** C
50. C	**60.** B
51. A	**61.** D
52. C	**62.** A
53. C	**63.** B
54. A	**64.** D
55. D	**65.** C

Answer Explanations for Mathematics Knowledge

46. **Answer B is correct.** To solve this problem, substitute 3 for x in the algebraic expression:

$$3x^2 + 4x - 12 = 3(3)^2 + 4(3) - 12 = 3(9) + 12 - 12 = 27$$

47. **Answer A is correct.** You must recall the formulas for volume of a cylinder and a cube. Then you plug in the information given and compare the results. Answer D is incorrect because there is sufficient information provided. Here are the calculations:

Cylinder: Volume = Pi * radius^2 * height = $(3.14)(3)^2(2) = (3.14)(9)(2) = (28.26)(2) = 56.52\text{in}^3$
Cube: Volume = (side)^3 = 4^3 = 4*4*4 = 64 in^3

48. **Answer D is correct.** The only trick here is to remember the definition of a factorial. Once you've calculated each factorial's value, all you have to do is subtract.

    $6! = 6*5*4*3*2*1 = 720$

    $5! = 5*4*3*2*1 = 120$

    So, $6! - 5! = 720 - 120 = 600$

49. **Answer B is correct.** The slope of a line is equal to the change in the rise (delta y) divided by the change in the run (delta x). You are given the coordinates $(5,-3)$ and $(-4,6)$, so all you have to do is plug them into the equation to find the slope of the line running through both points:

    $$\text{Slope} = (y_2-y_1)/(x_2-x_1) = [6-(-3)]/(-4-5)$$
    $$= (6 + 3)/(-9)$$
    $$= 9 /(-9)$$
    $$= -1$$

50. **Answer C is correct.** Remember the distributive property of multiplication? Here's how it works: First multiply the y by each term in the second grouping, then multiply the -3 by each term in the second grouping. Next, group the similar terms and simplify the expression.

    Solution:

    $$(y - 3)(y^2 + y +2) = [(y)(y^2) + (y)(y) + (2)(y)] + [(-3)(y^2) + (-3)(y) + (-3)(2)]$$
    $$= y^3 + y^2 + 2y + (-3y^2 -3y - 6)$$
    $$= y^3 + y^2 + 2y + (-3y^2 -3y - 6)$$
    $$= y^3 + y^2 -3y^2 + 2y -3y - 6$$
    $$= y^3 -2y^2 - y - 6$$

51. **Answer A is correct.** The key to this problem is to remember that the sum of the three angles in any triangle is equal to 180 degrees. So, because you are given the other two angles, you do have enough information to solve for the third angle.

    Solution:

    angle c $= 180 -$ angle a $-$ angle b
    $$= 180 - 35 - 62$$
    $$= 83 \text{ degrees}$$

52. **Answer C is correct.** Here is how the solution looks:

    x - 3 >= –2

    x >= –2 + 3

    x >= 1

53. **Answer C is correct.** To solve this equation you need to plug in the numerical values for y and z and then perform the operations in the proper order:

$$-z^3 - z^2y + 3y^2 - zy + 4 = -(5^3) - [5^2(-7)] + [3(-7)^2] - [(5)(-7)] +4$$
$$= -125 - [(25)(-7)] + [(3)(49)] - [(5)(-7)] + 4$$
$$= -125 - (-175) + 147 + 35 + 4$$
$$= -125 + 175 + 147 + 35 + 4$$
$$= 236$$

54. **Answer A is correct.** This word problem requires you to read closely, organize the information you are provided into equation form, and then solve.

    Solution:

    Because Karl takes twice as long to read as Amy,

    k = 2a

    Next, write the equation for time left until the meeting (remember both Karl and Amy need to read the book within the next 12 days):

    a + k = 12

    Substituting the first equation into the second allows you to create an algebraic expression in only one variable, which you can easily solve:

    a + 2a = 12

    3a = 12

    a = 4

    Now you have your answer; however, you can easily double check yourself by solving for Karl's time and seeing if it, plus Amy's time you calculated really add up to 12 days.

    If a = 4, then k = 2a = 2*4 = 8, and k + a = 8 + 4 = 12. It checks out!

55. **Answer D is correct.** The cube root of a number (x) is the number (y) which, when multiplied by itself three times (y*y*y) equals x. In this case 7*7*7=343, so 7 is the cube root of 343. Don't be taken in by the distracter answer B: –7*(–7)*(–7) = –343

56. **Answer B is correct.** Because line k intersects line i at a 30 degree angle and line j is parallel with line i, line k must also intersect line j at a 30 degree. As you can see in Figure 14.1, once that is established m can be found in two steps by applying the rule of supplementary angles (angles that are supplementary must add up to 180 degrees, i.e., a straight line.) Therefore, angle m = 30 degrees.

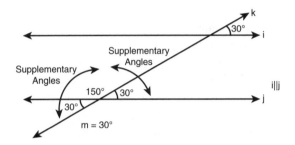

57. **Answer B is correct.** The key to solving this problem is to recognize that the unshaded region is merely the difference of the area of the large, outer rectangle and the small, inner (and shaded) rectangle.

Solution: $A_{unshaded} = A_{large} - A_{shaded}$

$\quad\quad A_{large} = l * w = 12 * 8 = 96$

And $\quad A_{shaded} = l * w = 6 * 4 = 24$

So, $\quad A_{unshaded} = A_{large} - A_{shaded} = 96 - 24 = 72$

58. **Answer A is correct.** Taking the reciprocal of a fraction means flipping it over so that the numerator becomes the denominator and vice versa.

59. **Answer C is correct.** Answer A is incorrect because it represents the original number rounded to the thousands (not thousandths) place. Answer B is incorrect because it represents the original number rounded to the hundredths place. Answer D is incorrect because it represents the original number rounded incorrectly.

60. **Answer B is correct.** Remember the Pythagorean Theorem from the review? Here's where you get to use it. You are given the length of the two legs (a and b) of the right triangle and asked to calculate the hypotenuse (c). You've got all the information you need and now simply have to plug it into the formula: $c^2 = a^2 + b^2$

$c = \sqrt{[a^2 + b^2]}$

$c = \sqrt{[3^2 + 4^2]}$

$c = \sqrt{[9 + 16]}$

$c = \sqrt{[25]}$

$c = 5$

61. **Answer D is correct.** A negative number multiplied by another negative number (even itself, as is the case when a number is squared) produces a positive number. So, after you complete the y^2 operation, you have a positive number multiplied by a positive number, which yields a positive number. Answer A is incorrect because a positive number (x) times a negative number (y) produces a negative number. Answer B is incorrect because a negative number times a negative number produces a positive number (i.e., >0). Answer C is incorrect because a negative number times a positive number produces a negative number (i.e., <0).

62. **Answer A is correct.** This problem is a piece of cake if you are clear on your rules for exponents. Let's review again: a number raised to the power of 0 equals 1, and a number raised to the power of one equals the number. In this case, those rules mean that $3^0 = 1$ and $3^1 = 3$. Once you know that, placing the numbers in the correct order from least to greatest is easy.

63. **Answer B is correct.** To find the total number of squares that will fit inside a larger rectangle, you must find the area of the rectangle (A = l * w = 12 * 10 = 120) and the area of each square (A = s^2 = 2^2 = 4). Now you need to divide the total area by the area of a square to find the answer: 120 / 4 = 30. 30 squares will fit inside the rectangle.

64. **Answer D is correct.** Answers A, B, and C are incorrect because in mathematics the result of any quantity being divided by zero is not defined. There is no numerical answer to this question.

65. **Answer C is correct.** When dividing exponents that have the same base variable ("x" in this problem), just subtract the exponents to find the answer.

So, $x^5 / x^2 = x^3$

Answers to Shop Information

66. B	**76.** C
67. C	**77.** B
68. A	**78.** D
69. C	**79.** B
70. D	**80.** D
71. B	**81.** A
72. D	**82.** C
73. A	**83.** A
74. C	**84.** B
75. A	**85.** D

Answer Explanations for Shop Information

66. **Answer B is correct.** The standard is the premeasured and known dimension that appears on a measuring tool (such as the scribed lines indicating fractions of an inch on a steel rule). Measuring tools are used by placing the tool next to the object being measured and reading off the number of corresponding standard units. Answer A is incorrect because blueprints are planning documents that show the required dimensions for the finished product, they are not related to any particular measuring tool's operation. Answer C is incorrect because scale models are used to demonstrate what the finished product will look like; they are not related to any particular measuring tool's operation. Answer D is incorrect because the correct answer is standard (B).

67. **Answer C is correct.** The plumb bob uses the force of gravity to indicate perfectly vertical lines. Answer A is incorrect because a micrometer is used to measure thickness or outer dimensions. Answer B is incorrect because calipers are used to measure irregular shapes and thick stock. Answer D is incorrect because the carpenter's square is used to check corners to ensure they are square (i.e., at a 90 degree angle). The carpenter's square can only verify a vertical line if the horizontal base against which it rests is perfectly level, which can not be assumed.

68. **Answer A is correct.** Answer B is incorrect; see number 4 in Figure 8.11 in Chapter 8 for a drawing of a socket wrench. Answer C is incorrect; see number 6 in Figure 8.11 for a drawing of an Allen wrench. Answer D is incorrect; see number 7 in Figure 8.8 for a drawing of a die.

69. **Answer C is correct.** Answers A and B are incorrect because 8 and 10 are less than 12 and the higher the number of points per inch in a saw's blade, the finer (or cleaner) it cuts. Answer D is incorrect because the correct answer is 12 point blade (C).

70. **Answer D is correct.** Answer A is incorrect because kerf is the term for the groove cut into wood by a saw's blade. Answers B and C are incorrect because they refer to different parts of a saw (see Figure 8.2 in Chapter 8 to review the parts of a saw).

71. **Answer B is correct.** Answer A is incorrect because a rip saw is used to cut wood along the grain. Answer C is incorrect because a coping saw is used to make curved cuts in wood. Answer D is incorrect because a router is a power tool used to shape and form edge contours, and to cut grooves and dadoes into wood.

72. **Answer D is correct.** Answer A is incorrect because a tap doesn't drill a hole, it makes a cut into a predrilled hole. Answer B is incorrect because a tap is not a piece of electrical or welding equipment. Answer C is incorrect because a die, not a tap, is used to cut threads into the outside of a pipe or rod.

73. **Answer A is correct.** Answer B is incorrect because a plane is the tool used for slicing thin layers of wood. Answer C is incorrect because the term for the groove cut by a saw's blade is kerf. Answer D is incorrect because a Forstner bit is a circular, small-toothed drill bit.

74. **Answer C is correct.** Ball peen hammers, with their special design and steel head and peen, are used for riveting, not mallets. Answers A, B, and D all are applicable to a mallet.

75. **Answer A is correct.** Answer B is incorrect because filler rod is the name of the material used in welding. Answer C is incorrect because the neck is the name of the part of a hammer (see Figure 8.13 in Chapter 8). Answer D is incorrect because, although it seems to be descriptive of a mandrel, it is not the standard terminology.

76. **Answer C is correct.** Answer A is incorrect because a Forstner bit is used for cleanly boring large diameter holes. Answer B is incorrect because a spade bit is used for boring large diameter or deep holes. Answer D is incorrect because an auger bit, with its self-feeding screw tip, is also used to bore or drill deep holes.

77. **Answer B is correct.** Answer A is incorrect because brazing is a process for permanently joining dissimilar metals. Answer C is incorrect because soldering is a lower temperature process for permanently joining metals where the holding strength required is not as great as in brazing or welding. Answer D is incorrect because crimping is a means of joining metal pieces by folding their edges over each other, not fusing them together as in the other methods mentioned here.

78. **Answer D is correct.** Answer A is incorrect because slip-joint pliers, with their crescent-shaped jaws, are better suited for gripping objects where there is unobstructed access. Answer B is incorrect because a bench vise is typically bolted to a workbench. Answer C is incorrect because c-clamps are also too unwieldy to be useful for small objects in tight spaces.

79. **Answer B is correct.** Flux is a chemical compound; it does not create an electrical arc. Answers A, C, and D are all uses of flux in the soldering process.

80. **Answer D is correct.** Answer A is incorrect because tin is used as part of an alloy, along with lead, for soldering (not brazing). Answer B is incorrect because lead is used as part of an alloy, along with tin, for soldering (not brazing). Answer C is incorrect because the filler rod used in brazing is brass (an alloy of copper and zinc); it is not made of either copper or zinc alone.

81. **Answer A is correct.** Answer B is incorrect because the bench grinder is used for removing material from a metal work piece by rapidly moving an abrasive material across its surface. Answer C is incorrect because the milling machine is used to machine flat surfaces, drill, or cut slots and irregular shapes into metal; it's multi-toothed cutting tool revolves, but unlike a lathe, the work piece does not. Answer D is incorrect because the drill press is used for drilling or boring holes in a work piece, not for turning (i.e., reducing the diameter of an object by rotating it around a horizontal axis and then moving a cutting tool against it.)

82. **Answer C is correct.** Answer A is incorrect because the bill of materials is a listing of all materials required to complete a project. Answer B is incorrect because layout is the name of the process of marking out the blueprint dimensions on the materials you will need to cut or shape. Answer D is incorrect because a schematic is more of a preliminary sketch or diagram showing how an object is to be put together.

83. **Answer A is correct.** Answer B is incorrect because a level is a tool used to ensure that surfaces are level or plumb, they don't measure thickness. Answer C is incorrect because a carpenter's square is used to mark lines at a right angle prior to cutting, or to check the squareness of corners or joints. Answer D is incorrect because the steel rule is not capable of the same level of precision as the micrometer.

84. **Answer B is correct.** Answer A is incorrect because it shows a coping saw. Answer C is incorrect because it shows a hacksaw. Answer D is incorrect because it shows a ripsaw.

85. **Answer D is correct.** Answer A is incorrect it shows a spade bit. Answer B is incorrect because it shows a file. Answer C is incorrect because it shows a plane.

Answers to Assembling Objects

86. B	**102.** C
87. C	**103.** A
88. A	**104.** D
89. C	**105.** B
90. D	**106.** A
91. B	**107.** D
92. D	**108.** C
93. B	**109.** C
94. A	**110.** B
95. C	**111.** A
96. D	**112.** D
97. A	**113.** B
98. B	**114.** C
99. C	**115.** A
100. A	**116.** B
101. C	**117.** D

Answer Explanations for Assembling Objects

86. **Answer B is correct.** Answer A is incorrect because only two of the pieces match the original set. Answer C is incorrect because only the square is correct; the other two pieces on the bottom are similar, but not exact matches. Answer D is incorrect because, although the two pieces on the far right are correct, the others are not part of the original set.

87. **Answer C is correct.** Answer A is incorrect because, although the two rectangles are correct, the other pieces do not match. Answer B is incorrect because none of the pieces are correct. Answer D is incorrect because there is no square in the original set and the triangles in Answer D are too small.

88. **Answer A is correct.** Answer B is incorrect because only one of its pieces matches the original set. Answer C is incorrect because, although the bottom two pieces are similar to those in the original set, they are not exact matches. Answer D contains a triangle, yet there is no triangle in the original set, so it is incorrect too.

89. **Answer C is correct.** Answer A is incorrect because its rounded edge piece does not end in sharp points. Answer B is incorrect because none of the pieces match the original set. Answer D is incorrect because the angles of the two smaller pieces on the top are backward.

90. **Answer D is correct.** Answer A is incorrect because, although the triangles are similar in size, the angles are incorrect. Answer B is incorrect because not all the pieces are triangles. Answer C is incorrect because it contains two sets of identical triangles, whereas the original set contains four different triangles.

91. **Answer B is correct.** Answer A has one incorrect piece. Answer C is incorrect because the triangle is smaller and the zigzag piece is missing its pointed end. Answer D is incorrect because only the square piece is correct.

92. **Answer D is correct.** Answer A contains three incorrect pieces. Answer B is incorrect because the smallest piece should have a longer curved side. Answer C is incorrect because the smallest piece's longest side forms the wrong angle.

93. **Answer B is correct.** Answer A is incorrect because the tear-shaped piece is in the wrong place, with the result that it is cut in half. Answer C is incorrect because the tear-shaped piece is in the wrong place and the bottom-right piece is the wrong shape. Answer D is incorrect because the wedge piece is too narrow.

94. **Answer A is correct.** Answer B is incorrect because only two of the pieces match the original set. Answer C is incorrect because only the upper- right piece matches the original set exactly. Answer D is incorrect because its two lower-right pieces do not match the original set.

95. **Answer C is correct.** Answer A is incorrect because the line cuts through both objects. Answer B is incorrect because the line touches the perimeter of the circle, rather than the middle, and cuts through the star. Answer D is incorrect because the line touches the star's point instead of its angle.

96. **Answer D is correct.** Answer A is incorrect because the line touches the wrong side of the H. Answer B is incorrect because the line touches the center of the oval. Answer C is incorrect because the line bisects the oval.

97. **Answer A is correct.** Answer B is incorrect because the end points of the line are shown at the middle of the right triangle's base and the wrong corner of the left triangle's base. Answer C is incorrect because the end point of the line touches the wrong corner of the right triangle's base. Answer D is incorrect because the line cuts through the left triangle horizontally instead of vertically.

98. **Answer B is correct.** Answer A is incorrect because the line shares the entire top line segment of the number 3. Answer C is incorrect because the line touches the wrong point on the 3 and cuts through the D. Answer D is incorrect because the line cuts through the D to reach the correct point on the straight line segment.

99. **Answer C is correct.** Answer A is incorrect because the line cuts through the L shape to reach the correct point. Answer B is incorrect because the line is on the outside of the hexagon, rather than passing through the middle. Answer D is incorrect because, although the line passes through the correct point of the L shape, it begins by passing through the L.

100. **Answer A is correct.** Answer B is incorrect because the line passes through the triangle's angle, rather than its side, to reach the middle. Answer C is incorrect because the line does not stop in the center of the triangle. Answer D is incorrect because the line should not pass through the semicircle.

101. **Answer C is correct.** Answer A is incorrect because the line cuts through the entire square, rather than stopping at its midpoint. Answer B is incorrect because the line cuts through the side of the square instead of a corner, and it cuts through the other shape instead of attaching to its perimeter. Answer D is incorrect because the line bisects the square by passing through its side instead of passing through its corner and stopping in the middle.

102. **Answer C is correct.** Answer A is incorrect because only the triangular piece is correct. Answer B is incorrect because, although the pieces appear similar, when you compare the largest piece in the original set with the corresponding piece in Answer B you'll notice that Answer B's piece does not end in points. Answer D is incorrect because only the triangular piece is correct.

103. **Answer A is correct.** Answer B is incorrect because the middle and bottom pieces are not part of the original set. Answer C is incorrect because the middle piece is not correct. Answer D is incorrect because only the bottom piece is correct.

104. **Answer D is correct.** Answer A is incorrect because the hockey stick–shaped piece does not belong. Answer B is incorrect because the top, left hand piece is not part of the original set. Answer C is incorrect because none of the pieces match the original set.

105. **Answer B is correct.** Answer A is incorrect because only the top piece is correct. Answer C is incorrect because the bottom two pieces are incorrect. Answer D is incorrect because, although the pieces appear similar to the original set, none matches exactly.

106. **Answer A is correct.** Answer B is incorrect because the semicircle is the only matching piece. Answer C is incorrect because the bottom and the right pieces are not in the original set. Answer D is incorrect because the top two pieces are incorrect.

107. **Answer D is correct.** Answer A is incorrect because the middle two pieces are incorrect. Answer B is incorrect because the pieces on the bottom left and middle are not part of the original set. Answer C is incorrect because the far right piece is incorrect.

108. **Answer C is correct.** Answer A is incorrect because the center piece is not part of the original set. Answer B is incorrect because the angles on the two largest pieces are backward. Answer D is incorrect because the triangle is the wrong shape.

109. **Answer C is correct.** Answer A is incorrect because it only uses three pieces. Answer B is incorrect because the two stair step pieces have been

straightened out. Answer D is incorrect because the stair step piece in it is a mirror image of the one in the original set.

110. **Answer B is correct.** Answer A is incorrect because the line touches the narrow end of the oval instead of the long side. Answer C is incorrect because the line cuts through the oval. Answer D is incorrect because, although the line ends at the correct spot on the X, it cuts across the top instead of just connecting with the one point.

111. **Answer A is correct.** Answer B is incorrect because the line rests on the side of the triangle rather than meeting in only one point. Answer C is incorrect because the line cuts through the hexagon through a corner, rather than a side. Answer D is incorrect because the line ends in the center of the triangle and on the side of the hexagon, rather than the other way around.

112. **Answer D is correct.** Answer A is incorrect because the line cuts through the hexagon in the wrong location. Answer B is incorrect because the line goes through the side, not the corner, of the square. Answer C is incorrect because the line cuts through the entire square instead of stopping at the middle.

113. **Answer B is correct.** Answer A is incorrect because the line touches the wrong end of the curved object. Answer C is incorrect because the line cuts through the star incorrectly. Answer D is incorrect because the line connects at a point on the star without cutting through it.

114. **Answer C is correct.** Answer A is incorrect because the line touches the opposite point on the M. Answer B is incorrect because the line touches the S at two points instead of one. Answer D is incorrect because the line touches the S at three points.

115. **Answer A is correct.** Answer B is incorrect because the line cuts into the diamond. Answer C is incorrect because the line touches the wrong point on the diamond; it should touch the point of the wider angle. Answer D is incorrect because the line goes through the corner of the square instead of on the side.

116. **Answer B is correct.** Answer A is incorrect because the line cuts through the house-shaped piece in the opposite angle as in the original set. Answer C is incorrect because the line does not cut through the rectangle. Answer D is incorrect because the line does not cut through the house-shaped piece in the right spot.

117. **Answer D is correct.** Answer A and Answer B are incorrect because the line does not cut through the oval in the original set. Answer C is incorrect because the line intersects the 7 in only one point, not in a line.

CD Contents and Installation Instructions

The CD-ROM features an innovative practice test engine powered by MeasureUp™, giving you yet another effective tool to assess your readiness for the exam.

Multiple Test Modes

MeasureUp practice tests are available in Study, Certification, Custom, Adaptive, Missed Question, and Non-Duplicate question modes.

Study Mode

Tests administered in Study Mode allow you to request the correct answer(s) and explanation to each question during the test. These tests are not timed. You can modify the testing environment during the test by selecting the Options button.

Certification Mode

Tests administered in Certification Mode closely simulate the actual testing environment you will encounter when taking a certification exam. These tests do not allow you to request the answer(s) and/or explanation to each question until after the exam.

Custom Mode

Custom Mode allows you to specify your preferred testing environment. Use this mode to specify the objectives you want to include in your test, the timer length, and other test properties. You can also modify the testing environment during the test by selecting the Options button.

Adaptive Mode

Tests administered in Adaptive Mode closely simulate the actual testing environment you will encounter taking an Adaptive exam. After answering a question, you are not allowed to go back; you are only allowed to move forward during the exam.

Missed Question Mode

Missed Question Mode allows you to take a test containing only the questions you have missed previously.

Non-Duplicate Mode

Non-Duplicate Mode allows you to take a test containing only questions not displayed previously.

Random Questions and Order of Answers

This feature helps you learn the material without memorizing questions and answers. Each time you take a practice test, the questions and answers appear in a different randomized order.

Detailed Explanations of Correct and Incorrect Answers

You receive automatic feedback on all correct and incorrect answers. The detailed answer explanations are a superb learning tool in their own right.

Attention to Exam Objectives

MeasureUp practice tests are designed to appropriately balance the questions over each technical area covered by a specific exam.

Installing the CD

The minimum system requirements for the CD-ROM are

➤ Windows 95, 98, ME, NT4, 2000, or XP

➤ 7MB disk space for testing engine

➤ An average of 1MB disk space for each test

If you need technical support, please contact MeasureUp at 678-356-5050 or email support@measureup.com. Additionally, you can find Frequently Asked Questions (FAQ) at www.measureup.com.

To install the CD-ROM, follow these instructions:

1. Close all applications before beginning this installation.

2. Insert the CD into your CD-ROM drive. If the setup starts automatically, go to step 6. If the setup does not start automatically, continue with step 3.

3. From the Start menu, select Run.

4. Click Browse to locate the MeasureUp CD. In the Browse dialog box, from the Look In drop-down list, select the CD-ROM drive.

5. In the Browse dialog box, double-click on Setup.exe. In the Run dialog box, click OK to begin the installation.

6. On the Welcome screen, click MeasureUp Practice Questions to begin installation.

7. Follow the Certification Prep Wizard by clicking Next.

8. To agree to the Software License Agreement, click Yes.

9. On the Choose Destination Location screen, click Next to install the software to C:\Program Files\Certification Preparation.

If you cannot locate MeasureUp Practice Tests through the Start menu, see the section titled "Creating a Shortcut to the MeasureUp Practice Tests," later in this appendix.

10. On the Setup Type screen, select Typical Setup. Click Next to continue.

11. In the Select Program Folder screen, you can name the program folder where your tests will be located. To select the default, simply click Next and the installation continues.

12. After the installation is complete, verify that Yes, I Want to Restart My Computer Now is selected. If you select No, I Will Restart My Computer Later, you cannot use the program until you restart your computer.

13. Click Finish.

14. After restarting your computer, choose Start, Programs, MeasureUp, MeasureUp Practice Tests.

15. On the MeasureUp Welcome Screen, click Create User Profile.

16. In the User Profile dialog box, complete the mandatory fields and click Create Profile.

17. Select the practice test you want to access and click Start Test.

Creating a Stortcut to the MeasureUp Practice Tests

To create a shortcut to the MeasureUp Practice Tests, follow these steps.

1. Right-click on your Desktop.

2. From the shortcut menu, select New, Shortcut.

3. Browse to C:\Program Files\MeasureUp Practice Tests and select the MeasureUpCertification.exe or Localware.exe file.

4. Click OK.

5. Click Next.

6. Rename the shortcut MeasureUp.

7. Click Finish.

After you complete step 7, use the MearureUp shortcut on your Desktop to access the MeasureUp products you ordered.

Technical Support

If you encounter problems with the MeasureUp test engine on the CD-ROM, please contact MeasureUp at 678-356-5050 or email support@measureup.com. Technical support hours are from 8 a.m. to 5 p.m. EST Monday through Friday. Additionally, you can find Frequently Asked Questions (FAQ) at www.measureup.com.

If you would like to purchase additional MeasureUp products, call 678-356-5050 or 800-649-1MUP (1687) or visit www.measureup.com.

Glossary

acceleration

The change in the velocity of an object over the amount of time required to make that change. (The acceleration of gravity on an object is independent of the object's mass and is a universal constant, $g = 9.8$ meters/second^2.)

acid

Substances that give up a proton (producing an H+ ion) when in an aqueous (water) solution. They turn blue litmus paper red and have low pH numbers.

algebraic expression

A mathematical statement that contains *constants* (definite numbers), *variables* (letter representations of number values), *mathematical operations*, and *grouping symbols* (such as parentheses).

alternating current (ac)

An electrical current that has a regular and recurring change in flow direction.

amplitude

The value of the maximum height of the wavelength above the mean value of the wave.

angle

The shape or space between two lines that intersect.

antonyms

A word that has an opposite meaning to the one given.

Archimedes' principle

An object that is submerged (either completely or in part) in a fluid is buoyed up by a force that is equal to the weight of the fluid it displaces. The ability to predict the force of buoyancy, which operates in opposition to gravity and keeps ships and swimmers afloat, also allows for advances in lighter than air travel.

area

The measure of the amount of a surface within a particular, defined region.

atmosphere

A blanket of gases surrounding the planet. The atmosphere makes life on Earth possible and protects all living things from the sun's harmful ultra-violet rays.

auger bit

Used for boring and deep drilling. Typically used with a brace in woodworking applications, auger bits have a self-feeding screw on their tips which makes the bit easy to control when drilling deep holes.

axle

A shaft that transfers power from the differential to the driving wheels.

base

A substance that accepts a proton (producing an OH- ion) when in aqueous solution. Bases turn red litmus paper blue and have high pH numbers.

battery

An electrical storage device.

Bernoulli's principle

As the velocity of a moving fluid increases, its ability to exert pressure decreases. This principle, when applied to the fluid called air, is at the root of hydrodynamics and aerodynamics and explains how an airplane's wings produce the lift required for flight.

biome

Regions that share similar climate and soil type, resulting in similar populations of plant and animal life.

blueprints

Detailed technical drawings with all key dimensions indicated.

brace

Used for driving bits, the brace is a kind of hand drill that is excellent for boring wide holes because its design provides powerful leverage for the drilling process.

brazing

A technique of joining dissimilar metals by fusing them with a filler rod made of an alloy such as brass (a mixture of copper and zinc). Brazing (like soldering) produces a joint that is not as strong as a weld.

caliper

Used extensively in metalworking applications, calipers can measure irregular shapes and thick stock.

camshaft

A shaft with lobes used to open the engine intake and exhaust valves at the proper time.

capacitor

An electronic component that stores an electric charge.

carburetor

Part of the fuel system that mixes air and fuel in the correct amounts to burn in the engine.

cell

The smallest unit of life. Cells contain distinct parts (organelles), which perform the basic functions of life.

charging system

The system that provides electrical energy for the automobile.

chemical bonds

Forces that cause two or more different kinds of elements to combine to form a compound.

chemical reaction

The interaction that takes place when chemical elements or compounds come together and undergo changes in energy and/or physical properties.

chromosomes

Microscopic objects within a cell's nucleus that contain the cell's hereditary information.

circulatory system

A bodily system that transports oxygen and nutrients throughout the body and removes waste.

circumference

The distance found by measuring or calculating the entire distance around a circle.

clutch

A device used to connect and disconnect the engine from the drive train.

community

The sum of the various populations that live within a particular habitat (common geographic location).

composite numbers

A number that can be expressed as a product of two or more natural numbers other than itself and 1.

comprehension

The process and knowledge gained by understanding a subject.

compression

To apply pressure to a substance without changing the volume.

concentration

The measure of the relative strength of a solution. Solutions with higher concentrations have a larger quantity of solute per unit of solvent.

conduction

A method of heat transfer that occurs within a medium (such as a steel rod or a copper wire) through the flow of "free" electrons.

conductor

A material that allows the flow of electrical current.

connotation

The interpretive meaning of a word or passage.

constant

A definite quantity whose value does not change.

consumers

Consumers are unable to produce their own food so they feed on other organisms. Primary consumers feed on producers; secondary consumers feed on primary consumers, and so on.

context

The setting or environment of a situation.

convection

A method of heat transfer that occurs through actual displacement of a lower temperature part of a medium by a higher temperature part. Because physical mass movement is required, convection can only take place in a fluid.

coolant

Liquid used in liquid cooling system to carry away heat; usually a mixture of ethylene glycol and water.

cooling system

An engine system used to keep the engine's temperature within limits.

core

The center of the earth that is made up of nickel-iron; it has a fluid outer layer and a solid inner core. The core is responsible for generating the earth's magnetic field and is approximately 1,400 miles across, representing about one-third of the earth's mass.

crust

The outermost layer of the earth; the crust varies in thickness from as little as 5 miles under the ocean to 40 miles beneath mountain ranges. It is made up of rock, mainly granite and basalt.

current

The flow of electrons in an electrical circuit.

cylinder head

A large casting bolted to the top of the engine that contains the combustion chamber and valves.

decimal

A numerical expression of a fraction with a base of 10.

denotation

The literal meaning of a word or passage.

diesel engine

An engine that uses the heat of compression to burn the air-fuel mixture in the cylinders.

difference

The result of the arithmetic operation of subtraction.

differential

A system of gears in the rear axle assembly that allows the rear wheels to turn at different speeds when cornering.

digestive system

A bodily system that is comprised of the mouth, esophagus, stomach, small intestine, large intestine, rectum, and anus. The digestive system ingests and breaks down food. The usable nutrient particles are absorbed into the body and the unusable particles are removed and evacuated from the body.

direct current

An electrical current that flows in one direction only, also called continuous current.

DNA *Deoxyribonucleic acid* (DNA)

Molecules which provide a set of instructions that governs the entire cell's function, growth, development, susceptibility to disease, and more.

Doppler effect

A phenomenon of waves generated by a moving source or detected by a moving observer. In the case of sound waves, when a listener hears a noise source approaching, its *pitch* (frequency) appears to increase the closer it gets. The moment the noise source passes its nearest point to the listener and begins moving away, its pitch appears to decrease.

drive shaft

A large steel tube that transfers engine power form the transmission to the rear-axle assembly

eclipse

The obscuring of the moon (lunar eclipse) when the earth's shadow passes over it, or the obscuring of the sun (solar eclipse) when the moon passes directly between the earth and sun.

ecosystem

A community and its environment.

efficiency

The ratio of the useful energy output to the energy input.

elasticity

The ability of a strained body or structure to recover its size and shape after deformation from load weight.

electrical system

The system that provides electrical energy to both start and operate the engine as well as to power all the electrical components

electricity

The exchange of free electrons between atoms.

electromagnetism

A magnetic field induced by an electric current.

electromagnets

A temporary magnet magnetized by an electric current.

electromotive force

The amount of energy output from an electrical source.

electrons

One of three atomic particles that make up atoms of matter; electrons orbit the nucleus and carry a negative charge.

elements

Substances made up of only one kind of atom.

endocrine system

A bodily system that controls the body through a release of *hormones* (produced in the endocrine glands) into the blood stream. Specific hormones target specific organs and only affect them.

energy

The ability to do work. The SI unit of work is the *Joule (J)*.

era

The main grouping of geologic time, based on groupings of significant geological events in the formation and development of planet Earth.

excretory system

A bodily system that filters out waste products from the blood (using the kidneys) and transports them via the ureter to the bladder, where they are stored until removed from the body via the urethra in a process called urination.

exponent

A notation used in higher-level arithmetic and algebra to indicate when a number is multiplied by itself a specified number of times.

factorial

The product of all the natural numbers from one through the number preceding it and is represented by the exclamation mark (!) in mathematical formulas.

figurative

Expressing one thing by using words that describe another.

filler rod

The joining material used in the welding process, also called a welding rod. It comes in varying diameters and alloys depending on the welding task to be performed.

fluid dynamics

The physical properties that fluids, including air and other gases, exhibit.

fluids

Substances that can *flow*. Both liquids and gases are fluids. Fluids exert pressure on their containers due to the constant, random motion of their molecules.

flux

A chemical material that prevents oxides from forming on the surface of the original metal. Flux also has properties that help break down the surface tension of the solder, allowing it to flow freely into the joint and bond with the original metal.

food chain

The interrelationships of the various organisms within a community. Members of a food chain include producers and multiple levels of consumers.

Forstner bit

Used only with power drills, its circular contour has thin, sawtooth-style blades surrounding a center spur that breaks out the chips formed while drilling. Forstner bits are especially useful for boring large holes that are much cleaner than those made by spade bits.

fraction

Another way of expressing proportion, by means of a quotient of whole numbers.

frequency

The number of repetitions of a periodic process in a unit of time, such as the complete alternations per second of an alternating current, or the number of sound waves per second produced by a sounding boyd.

friction

The resistant force that is created by sliding one object on another.

front

The line along where two air masses of differing temperature and humidity come into contact.

fuel injection

A fuel mixing device that injects the fuel directly into the cylinders or intake manifold.

greatest common factor

The largest whole number that may be exactly divided into two given whole numbers.

grinding

A machining process for metal that is analogous to sanding for wood. Rather than cutting the metal workpiece, grinding machines remove material by rapidly moving an abrasive material or a wire brush against it.

homonyms

Words that sound alike, but that are spelled differently and have different meanings.

horsepower

A unit for measuring the power of motors or other machines; the power needed to raise 550 pounds at the rate of 1 foot per second.

igneous rock

Rock that was formed by cooling lava.

ignition

The process that provides an electrical charge to the air-fuel mixture in an engine to begin combustion.

ignition system

The electrical system that provides the high-voltage spark to ignite the air-fuel mixture in the cylinder of an automobile.

impedance

A combination of resistance and reactance in a circuit. Impedance is measured in Ohms.

inductance

The property of a circuit or component that induces a magnetic field or electrical current without actual contact.

inequalities

Mathematical expressions of unequal quantities.

inference

The process of drawing conclusions from stated facts.

insulator

A material that prevents or inhibits electric flow.

interest rate

A percent that expresses the rate of return which is paid on money that is borrowed or lent.

inverter

A device that changes dc input to ac output.

irony

The use of words to express an opposite situation or sentiment.

kerf

The path cut into wood by the teeth of a saw's blade.

layout

The process of marking out the blueprint dimensions on the materials you will need to cut or shape.

least common multiple

The smallest positive whole number into which two whole numbers may be exactly divided.

Linnaean system

The commonly accepted system, dating back to the 18th century, whereby all organisms are classified according to shared characteristics, physical structures, or traits.

literal

Adhering to the primary meaning of a word or expression.

load

A draw on an electrical circuit; the resistance force on a machine.

lubrication

Reducing friction in an engine by providing oil between moving parts.

lymphatic system

A bodily system that supports the circulatory system by returning fluids to the blood and helping to fight infections.

machine

Any device for doing work and that multiplies force, changes the direction of a force, or multiplies the speed of that force.

magnet

An object that attracts iron and produces an external magnetic field by virtue of its natural composition.

magnetism

The study of magnets, their properties, and their effects on other materials. Magnetism also is the term for the force by which magnets attract iron, steel, and other materials with high iron content.

mantle

Located directly beneath the crust, the mantle makes up approximately 85% of the earth's volume. The upper mantle is rigid like the crust. The thicker, lower mantle behaves more like a slowly moving fluid and contains pockets of molten rock. The mantle reaches approximately 1,800 miles below the earth's surface.

mass

A measure of the quantity of matter in an object. An object's mass is constant, regardless of the gravitational force acting on it.

matter
Anything having mass and occupying space; may exist in solid, liquid, or gaseous state.

mechanical advantage
The ratio of the effort input to the work output of a machine.

meiosis
A specialized, two-step process leading to the production of sex cells. One parent cell produces four daughter (or son) cells, each with half the number of chromosomes of the parent cell.

metals
Chemical elements that share certain physical properties, including electrical and thermal (heat) conductivity, hardness, a high melting point, and a shiny appearance.

metamorphic rock
Rock formed by the transformative effects of extreme heat, pressure, or chemical action on existing rock.

metaphor
The use of one word or phrase in place of another with a different literal meaning to suggest likeness.

micrometer
A precision measuring device that can be used to measure the thickness or outer diameter of an object with accuracies to within a thousandth or ten thousandth of an inch.

milling
A process for machining metal with a revolving, multi-toothed cutting tool into which the workpiece is fed.

mitosis
A process in which a cell makes two exact copies of itself by first duplicating its chromosomes and then splitting in two. Each new cell receives a set of chromosomes that perfectly matches that of the parent cell. Mitosis occurs in most of the human body's cells.

multiple
The set of numbers formed by multiplying a number by other numbers.

musculoskeletal system
A bodily system that is made up of bones, which provide strength, protect the internal organs, and produce blood cells. Muscles attach to the skeleton, allowing the body to move and perform vital functions.

nervous system
A bodily system that receives stimuli from the surrounding environment and transmits those stimuli to the brain in the form of electrical impulses. The brain processes this input and controls the body's response.

Newton's laws of motion
A set of basic principles that govern the motion of objects.

non-metals

Chemical elements that combine with metals and sometimes with each other. Their physical and chemical properties are roughly the opposite of metals. Non-metals are poor conductors, are soft, and have lower melting and boiling points than metals.

Ohm's Law

The law that describes the relationship between voltage, current, and resistance.

oil

A petroleum-based or synthetic fluid used for lubrication.

orbit

The path an object follows through space as it travels around another object. The shape of an orbit is determined by the force of gravity acting on the objects and by the laws of motion

order of operations

A set of rules for solving expressions or equations containing multiple operations.

organism

An individual, distinct, living being.

oxyacetylene torch

A cutting tool that cuts metal by burning through it. The oxyacetylene torch utilizes a special cutting attachment that forms a flame fed by a mixture of oxygen and acetylene gases. It is useful for cutting holes or curved or straight lines in metal that is too hard and/or thick for shears or saws.

parallel lines

Lines that never intersect or cross at any point.

Pascal's principle

Any change in pressure applied to a confined, incompressible fluid is transmitted uniformly to every part of the fluid. This principle underlies the incredibly useful mechanical advantage provided by hydraulics.

percent

A way to express the frequency of some occurrence by stating how many times it happens out of each 100 chances of it happening.

perimeter

The distance found by summing the length of each side of a geometric shape.

perpendicular lines

Lines that intersect each other at a right angle (90 degrees).

personification

Assigning human properties to a thing or abstract concept.

pH

A measurement of the relative acidity or alkalinity of a solution, which is determined by its concentration of hydrogen ions. Chemists have created a pH scale that ranges from 0 to 14. Solutions with pH less than 7 are acids and those with pH greater than 7 are alkalines (also called bases).

photosynthesis

The process by which plants create their own food. Chloroplasts within the plants' leaves absorb light (solar energy), which is then used to convert carbon dioxide (CO_2) and water (H_2O) into carbohydrates, which the plant uses for food. A beneficial byproduct of this reaction is the release of oxygen (O_2) and water (H_2O) to the atmosphere.

plot

The story line of a written work.

population

A grouping of a certain species within a habitat.

power

The rate at which work is done. Also, an estimation of the overall energy requirements of a circuit or load. The SI unit of power is the *Watt (W)*.

pre-ignition

Abnormal combustion in which something other than the ignition system explodes the air-fuel mixture.

pressure

The force exerted by a fluid upon a surface, measured as force per unit of area.

prime number

A number whose only factors are itself and 1.

probability

A ratio of the number of times an event occurs to the number of possible occurrences.

producers

Producers are organisms (such as plants) that make their own food. They form the base of the food chain pyramid.

product

The result of the arithmetic operation of multiplication.

proportion

An equality that is established between two fractions. Proportions are used to find an unknown quantity when the other three of the four elements of the proportion are known.

quotient

The result of the arithmetic operation of division.

radiation

A method of heat transfer that occurs through electromagnetic waves and so does not require direct contact between the two mediums. In fact, energy transfer through radiation does not even require a connecting medium.

radiator

A large heat exchanger located in front of the engine.

ratchet

A device that allows rotational motion in one direction only. It is comprised of a toothed wheel, whose teeth slope in one direction, and a pawl, which travels over the teeth in the direction of motion and lodges against the teeth when rotation is attempted in the opposite direction.

ratio

A fixed relationship between two things, expressed as a proportion of the first thing to the second.

rectifier

An electrical device that changes ac current to dc current.

reflection

The "bouncing" back of light rays toward their source when they hit a surface.

refraction

The bending of light when it passes from one medium (such as air) into another (such as the glass of a prism).

reproductive system

The system of organs, male or female, which allow for reproduction.

resistance

The opposition offered to the free flow of electrons; measured in ohms and stated as R.

resistor

An electronic component that limits the flow of current.

respiratory system

A bodily system that enables the body to inhale air, filter out the oxygen needed for life, and exhale the unnecessary (waste) gases (primarily carbon dioxide). The lungs transfer oxygen to the blood stream where it is transported throughout the body via the circulatory system. The respiratory system includes the mouth, nose, throat, and lungs (and other organs).

root

The root of a given number is the whole number that, when multiplied by itself a certain number of times, produces the given number.

rule

A tool that is used to achieve a higher degree of accuracy in measuring small dimensions. Rules (scales) are especially useful in finish work.

schematic

A line drawing representation of an electrical or electronic circuit.

scientific law

Hypotheses that stand up to experimentation.

scientific method

The way in which scientists seek to explain the phenomena they observe. This method includes: making observations, taking measurements, formulating hypotheses, and conducting experiments to test the hypotheses.

sedimentary rock
Rock that was formed by the compacting and cementing together of sediment (small rock, mineral, and even organic particles).

series
A sequence of numbers or terms that are arranged in a particular pattern.

simile
A figure of speech that compares two unlike things.

slope
The property of a line equal to the change in the rise (delta y) divided by the change in the run (delta x).

solar system
The sun and all objects in orbit around it, including the nine planets.

soldering
A method of permanently bonding metals together, by using a filler rod (solder) that is an alloy (or mixture of metals). Solder is typically made up of a mixture of lead and tin.

solute
A substance that is dissolved into a solvent to produce a solution.

solution
A homogeneous (uniform throughout) mixture comprised of a *solute* (a substance that is dissolved) dissolved into a *solvent* (the dissolving substance).

solvent
A substance that dissolves a solute to produce a solution.

specific gravity
A number that compares and object's density to the density of water.

starting system
The electrical system that provides the power for starting the engine of an automobile.

structure
Any constructed platform, whether vertical, horizontal, or elevated plane.

sum
The result of the arithmetic operation of addition.

summary
A synopsis, or brief explanation, of the contents of a story or passage.

switch
An electrical component that closes or opens an electrical path within a circuit.

symbolism
Expressing invisible or intangible things with tangible things.

synonyms
Words that are spelled differently, but that have similar meanings.

synthetic oil
Oil made from a material other than petroleum.

theme

The main idea of a story or passage.

tinning

The process of preparing a soldering iron for use by heating the tip of the soldering iron (called the bit), coating it with flux and then applying a thin layer of solder. The bit is then wiped with a clean cloth to remove excess solder before you begin your work.

torque

A force that produces rotation, as in a torque wrench.

transformer

An electrical device that steps up or steps down an input voltage.

transistor

A semiconductor device used to control current flow.

turning

The process of reducing the diameter of an object by rotating it around a horizontal axis and then moving a cutting tool against the part.

valve

A device for opening and closing a port.

valve train

The assembly of parts that opens and closes the ports of an engine.

variable

A term that may have a number of different values.

velocity

The speed and direction of an object.

viscosity

The thickness or thinness of oil.

voltage

The source of potential energy in an electrical system; measured in volts and abbreviated E.

volume

The measure of the inside space of a three dimensional geometric object.

wavelength

The distance between two consecutive peaks in the wave.

work

The movement of an object by force; the product of the force times the distance the object is moved.

Index

· ·

chemistry, 4
  acids, 9
  atoms, 5
  bases, 10
  carbon, 10
  chemical bonding, 7
  concentration, 8
  elements, 5-6
  equations, 7
  matter, 4
  moles, 8
  organic, 10
  pH, 10
  reactions, 8
  solutions, 8
  solvents, 8
chisels, 239
chloroplasts, 18
circles (geometry), 113-114
circuits, 120
circulatory system, 20
cirrus clouds, 26
clamps, 218
classifications
  organisms, 16
  rocks, 25
claw hammers, 217, 235
clothing styles, 75
clouds, 26
clues
  action/plots, 76
  words, 54-56
cohesion, 193
cold tank cleaners, 237
colors (wiring), 133
combination pliers, 234
combination wrenches, 233
combustion chamber shapes, 251
combustion engines, 247
common denominators, 36
communities, 21
comparison clues (words), 56
comparisons, 81-82
complex machines, 167
composite numbers, 99
compound interest, 41
comprehension (reading), 85
  action, 76-77
  applied level, 82-83
  details, 73
  improving, 84-85
  interpretive level, 79-82

  literal level, 78-79
  main characters, 74
  plots, 76-77
  points of view, 76
  sequences, grouping, 77-78
  settings, 75-76
  subject matter, 74
  summaries, 83-84
  Web sites, 404 (on the CD)
compressed air power tools, 236
compression
  pressure, 195
  strokes, 250
concentrated loads, 187
concentrations (chemicals), 8
conduction, 13
conductors, 136
coniferous forests, 22
connecting rods (piston engines), 256
connections (batteries), 130-132
connotation (words), 61-62
consumers, 24
content (reading)
  applied level, 82-83
  interpretive level, 79-82
  literal level, 78-79
context (words), 53-54
  comparison/contrast clues, 56
  example clues, 55
  experience clues, 54
  paraphrase clues, 55
contrast clues (words), 56
convection, 13
cooling systems (engines), 264-267
coping saws, 210
core (earth), 25
covalent bonds, 7
crankcases (piston engines), 254
crankshaft (piston engines), 256
crosscut saws, 210
crust (earth), 24
cube roots, 101
cumulus clouds, 26
currents, 121-122
  alternating, 123-125
  direct, 122-123
  Ohm's Law, 128
cutting tools, 207
  cutting torches, 210
  saws, 208-210
  shears, 210
cutting torches, 210

Q - R

If you need more answer sheets for practice, visit this book's website at www.examcram.com and download the answer sheets. You then can print as many as you need!

Chapter 1 Answer Sheet

Directions: Read each question carefully and choose the best answer. Fill in the appropriate oval completely with a soft lead pencil.

1. Ⓐ Ⓑ Ⓒ Ⓓ   5. Ⓐ Ⓑ Ⓒ Ⓓ   8. Ⓐ Ⓑ Ⓒ Ⓓ

2. Ⓐ Ⓑ Ⓒ Ⓓ   6. Ⓐ Ⓑ Ⓒ Ⓓ   9. Ⓐ Ⓑ Ⓒ Ⓓ

3. Ⓐ Ⓑ Ⓒ Ⓓ   7. Ⓐ Ⓑ Ⓒ Ⓓ   10. Ⓐ Ⓑ Ⓒ Ⓓ

4. Ⓐ Ⓑ Ⓒ Ⓓ

Chapter 2 Answer Sheet

Directions: Read each question carefully and choose the best answer. Fill in the appropriate oval completely with a soft lead pencil.

1. Ⓐ Ⓑ Ⓒ Ⓓ   5. Ⓐ Ⓑ Ⓒ Ⓓ   8. Ⓐ Ⓑ Ⓒ Ⓓ

2. Ⓐ Ⓑ Ⓒ Ⓓ   6. Ⓐ Ⓑ Ⓒ Ⓓ   9. Ⓐ Ⓑ Ⓒ Ⓓ

3. Ⓐ Ⓑ Ⓒ Ⓓ   7. Ⓐ Ⓑ Ⓒ Ⓓ   10. Ⓐ Ⓑ Ⓒ Ⓓ

4. Ⓐ Ⓑ Ⓒ Ⓓ

Chapter 3 Answer Sheet

Directions: In the following questions, look at the underlined word and pick out the most appropriate synonym or definition from the list. Pay attention to context as you choose your answer. Fill in the appropriate oval with a soft lead pencil.

1. Ⓐ Ⓑ Ⓒ Ⓓ   5. Ⓐ Ⓑ Ⓒ Ⓓ   8. Ⓐ Ⓑ Ⓒ Ⓓ

2. Ⓐ Ⓑ Ⓒ Ⓓ   6. Ⓐ Ⓑ Ⓒ Ⓓ   9. Ⓐ Ⓑ Ⓒ Ⓓ

3. Ⓐ Ⓑ Ⓒ Ⓓ   7. Ⓐ Ⓑ Ⓒ Ⓓ   10. Ⓐ Ⓑ Ⓒ Ⓓ

4. Ⓐ Ⓑ Ⓒ Ⓓ

Chapter 4 Answer Sheet

Directions: Quickly read each paragraph for important details; answer each question based only on information from the passage. Fill in the appropriate oval with a soft lead pencil and move on. If you take the computerized exam version, remember it is timed and you will not be allowed to return to a question to rethink your answer.

1. Ⓐ Ⓑ Ⓒ Ⓓ   5. Ⓐ Ⓑ Ⓒ Ⓓ   8. Ⓐ Ⓑ Ⓒ Ⓓ

2. Ⓐ Ⓑ Ⓒ Ⓓ   6. Ⓐ Ⓑ Ⓒ Ⓓ   9. Ⓐ Ⓑ Ⓒ Ⓓ

3. Ⓐ Ⓑ Ⓒ Ⓓ   7. Ⓐ Ⓑ Ⓒ Ⓓ   10. Ⓐ Ⓑ Ⓒ Ⓓ

4. Ⓐ Ⓑ Ⓒ Ⓓ

Chapter 5 Answer Sheet

Directions: Read each question carefully and choose the correct answer based on information in the chapter. Fill in the appropriate oval with a soft lead pencil.

1. Ⓐ Ⓑ Ⓒ Ⓓ   5. Ⓐ Ⓑ Ⓒ Ⓓ   8. Ⓐ Ⓑ Ⓒ Ⓓ

2. Ⓐ Ⓑ Ⓒ Ⓓ   6. Ⓐ Ⓑ Ⓒ Ⓓ   9. Ⓐ Ⓑ Ⓒ Ⓓ

3. Ⓐ Ⓑ Ⓒ Ⓓ   7. Ⓐ Ⓑ Ⓒ Ⓓ   10. Ⓐ Ⓑ Ⓒ Ⓓ

4. Ⓐ Ⓑ Ⓒ Ⓓ

Chapter 6 Answer Sheet

Directions: Read each question carefully and choose the correct answer based on information in the chapter. Fill in the appropriate oval with a soft lead pencil.

1. Ⓐ Ⓑ Ⓒ Ⓓ   8. Ⓐ Ⓑ Ⓒ Ⓓ   15. Ⓐ Ⓑ Ⓒ Ⓓ

2. Ⓐ Ⓑ Ⓒ Ⓓ   9. Ⓐ Ⓑ Ⓒ Ⓓ   16. Ⓐ Ⓑ Ⓒ Ⓓ

3. Ⓐ Ⓑ Ⓒ Ⓓ   10. Ⓐ Ⓑ Ⓒ Ⓓ   17. Ⓐ Ⓑ Ⓒ Ⓓ

4. Ⓐ Ⓑ Ⓒ Ⓓ   11. Ⓐ Ⓑ Ⓒ Ⓓ   18. Ⓐ Ⓑ Ⓒ Ⓓ

5. Ⓐ Ⓑ Ⓒ Ⓓ   12. Ⓐ Ⓑ Ⓒ Ⓓ   19. Ⓐ Ⓑ Ⓒ Ⓓ

6. Ⓐ Ⓑ Ⓒ Ⓓ   13. Ⓐ Ⓑ Ⓒ Ⓓ   20. Ⓐ Ⓑ Ⓒ Ⓓ

7. Ⓐ Ⓑ Ⓒ Ⓓ   14. Ⓐ Ⓑ Ⓒ Ⓓ

Chapter 7 Answer Sheet

Directions: Read each question carefully and choose the answer that fits most closely with the question. Fill in the appropriate oval with a soft lead pencil.

1. Ⓐ Ⓑ Ⓒ Ⓓ 5. Ⓐ Ⓑ Ⓒ Ⓓ 8. Ⓐ Ⓑ Ⓒ Ⓓ
2. Ⓐ Ⓑ Ⓒ Ⓓ 6. Ⓐ Ⓑ Ⓒ Ⓓ 9. Ⓐ Ⓑ Ⓒ Ⓓ
3. Ⓐ Ⓑ Ⓒ Ⓓ 7. Ⓐ Ⓑ Ⓒ Ⓓ 10. Ⓐ Ⓑ Ⓒ Ⓓ
4. Ⓐ Ⓑ Ⓒ Ⓓ

Chapter 8 Answer Sheet

Directions: Read each question carefully and choose the correct answer based on information in the chapter. Fill in the appropriate oval with a soft lead pencil.

1. Ⓐ Ⓑ Ⓒ Ⓓ 5. Ⓐ Ⓑ Ⓒ Ⓓ 8. Ⓐ Ⓑ Ⓒ Ⓓ
2. Ⓐ Ⓑ Ⓒ Ⓓ 6. Ⓐ Ⓑ Ⓒ Ⓓ 9. Ⓐ Ⓑ Ⓒ Ⓓ
3. Ⓐ Ⓑ Ⓒ Ⓓ 7. Ⓐ Ⓑ Ⓒ Ⓓ 10. Ⓐ Ⓑ Ⓒ Ⓓ
4. Ⓐ Ⓑ Ⓒ Ⓓ

Chapter 9 Answer Sheet

Directions: Read each question carefully and choose the answer that fits most closely with the question. Fill in the appropriate oval with a soft lead pencil.

1. Ⓐ Ⓑ Ⓒ Ⓓ 6. Ⓐ Ⓑ Ⓒ Ⓓ 11. Ⓐ Ⓑ Ⓒ Ⓓ
2. Ⓐ Ⓑ Ⓒ Ⓓ 7. Ⓐ Ⓑ Ⓒ Ⓓ 12. Ⓐ Ⓑ Ⓒ Ⓓ
3. Ⓐ Ⓑ Ⓒ Ⓓ 8. Ⓐ Ⓑ Ⓒ Ⓓ 13. Ⓐ Ⓑ Ⓒ Ⓓ
4. Ⓐ Ⓑ Ⓒ Ⓓ 9. Ⓐ Ⓑ Ⓒ Ⓓ 14. Ⓐ Ⓑ Ⓒ Ⓓ
5. Ⓐ Ⓑ Ⓒ Ⓓ 10. Ⓐ Ⓑ Ⓒ Ⓓ 15. Ⓐ Ⓑ Ⓒ Ⓓ

Chapter 10 Answer Sheet

Directions: Look at each figure carefully. Choose the best answer and fill in the appropriate oval with a soft lead pencil.

1. Ⓐ Ⓑ Ⓒ Ⓓ 5. Ⓐ Ⓑ Ⓒ Ⓓ 8. Ⓐ Ⓑ Ⓒ Ⓓ
2. Ⓐ Ⓑ Ⓒ Ⓓ 6. Ⓐ Ⓑ Ⓒ Ⓓ 9. Ⓐ Ⓑ Ⓒ Ⓓ
3. Ⓐ Ⓑ Ⓒ Ⓓ 7. Ⓐ Ⓑ Ⓒ Ⓓ 10. Ⓐ Ⓑ Ⓒ Ⓓ
4. Ⓐ Ⓑ Ⓒ Ⓓ

Chapter 1 Answer Sheet

Directions: Read each question carefully and choose the best answer. Fill in the appropriate oval completely with a soft lead pencil.

1. (A) (B) (C) (D)   5. (A) (B) (C) (D)   8. (A) (B) (C) (D)

2. (A) (B) (C) (D)   6. (A) (B) (C) (D)   9. (A) (B) (C) (D)

3. (A) (B) (C) (D)   7. (A) (B) (C) (D)   10. (A) (B) (C) (D)

4. (A) (B) (C) (D)

Chapter 2 Answer Sheet

Directions: Read each question carefully and choose the best answer. Fill in the appropriate oval completely with a soft lead pencil.

1. (A) (B) (C) (D)   5. (A) (B) (C) (D)   8. (A) (B) (C) (D)

2. (A) (B) (C) (D)   6. (A) (B) (C) (D)   9. (A) (B) (C) (D)

3. (A) (B) (C) (D)   7. (A) (B) (C) (D)   10. (A) (B) (C) (D)

4. (A) (B) (C) (D)

Chapter 3 Answer Sheet

Directions: In the following questions, look at the <u>underlined word</u> and pick out the most appropriate synonym or definition from the list. Pay attention to context as you choose your answer. Fill in the appropriate oval with a soft lead pencil.

1. (A) (B) (C) (D)   5. (A) (B) (C) (D)   8. (A) (B) (C) (D)

2. (A) (B) (C) (D)   6. (A) (B) (C) (D)   9. (A) (B) (C) (D)

3. (A) (B) (C) (D)   7. (A) (B) (C) (D)   10. (A) (B) (C) (D)

4. (A) (B) (C) (D)

Chapter 4 Answer Sheet

Directions: Quickly read each paragraph for important details; answer each question based only on information from the passage. Fill in the appropriate oval with a soft lead pencil and move on. If you take the computerized exam version, remember it is timed and you will not be allowed to return to a question to rethink your answer.

1. Ⓐ Ⓑ Ⓒ Ⓓ   5. Ⓐ Ⓑ Ⓒ Ⓓ   8. Ⓐ Ⓑ Ⓒ Ⓓ

2. Ⓐ Ⓑ Ⓒ Ⓓ   6. Ⓐ Ⓑ Ⓒ Ⓓ   9. Ⓐ Ⓑ Ⓒ Ⓓ

3. Ⓐ Ⓑ Ⓒ Ⓓ   7. Ⓐ Ⓑ Ⓒ Ⓓ   10. Ⓐ Ⓑ Ⓒ Ⓓ

4. Ⓐ Ⓑ Ⓒ Ⓓ

Chapter 5 Answer Sheet

Directions: Read each question carefully and choose the correct answer based on information in the chapter. Fill in the appropriate oval with a soft lead pencil.

1. Ⓐ Ⓑ Ⓒ Ⓓ   5. Ⓐ Ⓑ Ⓒ Ⓓ   8. Ⓐ Ⓑ Ⓒ Ⓓ

2. Ⓐ Ⓑ Ⓒ Ⓓ   6. Ⓐ Ⓑ Ⓒ Ⓓ   9. Ⓐ Ⓑ Ⓒ Ⓓ

3. Ⓐ Ⓑ Ⓒ Ⓓ   7. Ⓐ Ⓑ Ⓒ Ⓓ   10. Ⓐ Ⓑ Ⓒ Ⓓ

4. Ⓐ Ⓑ Ⓒ Ⓓ

Chapter 6 Answer Sheet

Directions: Read each question carefully and choose the correct answer based on information in the chapter. Fill in the appropriate oval with a soft lead pencil.

1. Ⓐ Ⓑ Ⓒ Ⓓ   8. Ⓐ Ⓑ Ⓒ Ⓓ   15. Ⓐ Ⓑ Ⓒ Ⓓ

2. Ⓐ Ⓑ Ⓒ Ⓓ   9. Ⓐ Ⓑ Ⓒ Ⓓ   16. Ⓐ Ⓑ Ⓒ Ⓓ

3. Ⓐ Ⓑ Ⓒ Ⓓ   10. Ⓐ Ⓑ Ⓒ Ⓓ   17. Ⓐ Ⓑ Ⓒ Ⓓ

4. Ⓐ Ⓑ Ⓒ Ⓓ   11. Ⓐ Ⓑ Ⓒ Ⓓ   18. Ⓐ Ⓑ Ⓒ Ⓓ

5. Ⓐ Ⓑ Ⓒ Ⓓ   12. Ⓐ Ⓑ Ⓒ Ⓓ   19. Ⓐ Ⓑ Ⓒ Ⓓ

6. Ⓐ Ⓑ Ⓒ Ⓓ   13. Ⓐ Ⓑ Ⓒ Ⓓ   20. Ⓐ Ⓑ Ⓒ Ⓓ

7. Ⓐ Ⓑ Ⓒ Ⓓ   14. Ⓐ Ⓑ Ⓒ Ⓓ

Chapter 7 Answer Sheet

Directions: Read each question carefully and choose the answer that fits most closely with the question. Fill in the appropriate oval with a soft lead pencil.

1. Ⓐ Ⓑ Ⓒ Ⓓ   5. Ⓐ Ⓑ Ⓒ Ⓓ   8. Ⓐ Ⓑ Ⓒ Ⓓ
2. Ⓐ Ⓑ Ⓒ Ⓓ   6. Ⓐ Ⓑ Ⓒ Ⓓ   9. Ⓐ Ⓑ Ⓒ Ⓓ
3. Ⓐ Ⓑ Ⓒ Ⓓ   7. Ⓐ Ⓑ Ⓒ Ⓓ   10. Ⓐ Ⓑ Ⓒ Ⓓ
4. Ⓐ Ⓑ Ⓒ Ⓓ

Chapter 8 Answer Sheet

Directions: Read each question carefully and choose the correct answer based on information in the chapter. Fill in the appropriate oval with a soft lead pencil.

1. Ⓐ Ⓑ Ⓒ Ⓓ   5. Ⓐ Ⓑ Ⓒ Ⓓ   8. Ⓐ Ⓑ Ⓒ Ⓓ
2. Ⓐ Ⓑ Ⓒ Ⓓ   6. Ⓐ Ⓑ Ⓒ Ⓓ   9. Ⓐ Ⓑ Ⓒ Ⓓ
3. Ⓐ Ⓑ Ⓒ Ⓓ   7. Ⓐ Ⓑ Ⓒ Ⓓ   10. Ⓐ Ⓑ Ⓒ Ⓓ
4. Ⓐ Ⓑ Ⓒ Ⓓ

Chapter 9 Answer Sheet

Directions: Read each question carefully and choose the answer that fits most closely with the question. Fill in the appropriate oval with a soft lead pencil.

1. Ⓐ Ⓑ Ⓒ Ⓓ   6. Ⓐ Ⓑ Ⓒ Ⓓ   11. Ⓐ Ⓑ Ⓒ Ⓓ
2. Ⓐ Ⓑ Ⓒ Ⓓ   7. Ⓐ Ⓑ Ⓒ Ⓓ   12. Ⓐ Ⓑ Ⓒ Ⓓ
3. Ⓐ Ⓑ Ⓒ Ⓓ   8. Ⓐ Ⓑ Ⓒ Ⓓ   13. Ⓐ Ⓑ Ⓒ Ⓓ
4. Ⓐ Ⓑ Ⓒ Ⓓ   9. Ⓐ Ⓑ Ⓒ Ⓓ   14. Ⓐ Ⓑ Ⓒ Ⓓ
5. Ⓐ Ⓑ Ⓒ Ⓓ   10. Ⓐ Ⓑ Ⓒ Ⓓ   15. Ⓐ Ⓑ Ⓒ Ⓓ

Chapter 10 Answer Sheet

Directions: Look at each figure carefully. Choose the best answer and fill in the appropriate oval with a soft lead pencil.

1. Ⓐ Ⓑ Ⓒ Ⓓ   5. Ⓐ Ⓑ Ⓒ Ⓓ   8. Ⓐ Ⓑ Ⓒ Ⓓ
2. Ⓐ Ⓑ Ⓒ Ⓓ   6. Ⓐ Ⓑ Ⓒ Ⓓ   9. Ⓐ Ⓑ Ⓒ Ⓓ
3. Ⓐ Ⓑ Ⓒ Ⓓ   7. Ⓐ Ⓑ Ⓒ Ⓓ   10. Ⓐ Ⓑ Ⓒ Ⓓ
4. Ⓐ Ⓑ Ⓒ Ⓓ

Answer Sheet for Practice Exam

Directions: Read each question carefully and choose the best answer. Fill in the oval completely with a soft lead pencil.

1. (A) (B) (C) (D)
2. (A) (B) (C) (D)
3. (A) (B) (C) (D)
4. (A) (B) (C) (D)
5. (A) (B) (C) (D)
6. (A) (B) (C) (D)
7. (A) (B) (C) (D)
8. (A) (B) (C) (D)
9. (A) (B) (C) (D)
10. (A) (B) (C) (D)
11. (A) (B) (C) (D)
12. (A) (B) (C) (D)
13. (A) (B) (C) (D)
14. (A) (B) (C) (D)
15. (A) (B) (C) (D)
16. (A) (B) (C) (D)
17. (A) (B) (C) (D)
18. (A) (B) (C) (D)
19. (A) (B) (C) (D)

20. (A) (B) (C) (D)
21. (A) (B) (C) (D)
22. (A) (B) (C) (D)
23. (A) (B) (C) (D)
24. (A) (B) (C) (D)
25. (A) (B) (C) (D)
26. (A) (B) (C) (D)
27. (A) (B) (C) (D)
28. (A) (B) (C) (D)
29. (A) (B) (C) (D)
30. (A) (B) (C) (D)
31. (A) (B) (C) (D)
32. (A) (B) (C) (D)
33. (A) (B) (C) (D)
34. (A) (B) (C) (D)
35. (A) (B) (C) (D)
36. (A) (B) (C) (D)
37. (A) (B) (C) (D)
38. (A) (B) (C) (D)

39. (A) (B) (C) (D)
40. (A) (B) (C) (D)
41. (A) (B) (C) (D)
42. (A) (B) (C) (D)
43. (A) (B) (C) (D)
44. (A) (B) (C) (D)
45. (A) (B) (C) (D)
46. (A) (B) (C) (D)
47. (A) (B) (C) (D)
48. (A) (B) (C) (D)
49. (A) (B) (C) (D)
50. (A) (B) (C) (D)
51. (A) (B) (C) (D)
52. (A) (B) (C) (D)
53. (A) (B) (C) (D)
54. (A) (B) (C) (D)
55. (A) (B) (C) (D)
56. (A) (B) (C) (D)
57. (A) (B) (C) (D)

58. (A) (B) (C) (D)   73. (A) (B) (C) (D)   87. (A) (B) (C) (D)

59. (A) (B) (C) (D)   74. (A) (B) (C) (D)   88. (A) (B) (C) (D)

60. (A) (B) (C) (D)   75. (A) (B) (C) (D)   89. (A) (B) (C) (D)

61. (A) (B) (C) (D)   76. (A) (B) (C) (D)   90. (A) (B) (C) (D)

62. (A) (B) (C) (D)   77. (A) (B) (C) (D)   91. (A) (B) (C) (D)

63. (A) (B) (C) (D)   78. (A) (B) (C) (D)   92. (A) (B) (C) (D)

64. (A) (B) (C) (D)   79. (A) (B) (C) (D)   93. (A) (B) (C) (D)

65. (A) (B) (C) (D)   80. (A) (B) (C) (D)   94. (A) (B) (C) (D)

66. (A) (B) (C) (D)   81. (A) (B) (C) (D)   95. (A) (B) (C) (D)

67. (A) (B) (C) (D)   82. (A) (B) (C) (D)   96. (A) (B) (C) (D)

68. (A) (B) (C) (D)   83. (A) (B) (C) (D)   97. (A) (B) (C) (D)

69. (A) (B) (C) (D)   84. (A) (B) (C) (D)   98. (A) (B) (C) (D)

70. (A) (B) (C) (D)   85. (A) (B) (C) (D)   99. (A) (B) (C) (D)

71. (A) (B) (C) (D)   86. (A) (B) (C) (D)   100. (A) (B) (C) (D)

72. (A) (B) (C) (D)

Answer Sheet for Practice Exam

Directions: Read each question carefully and choose the best answer. Fill in the oval completely with a soft lead pencil.

1. Ⓐ Ⓑ Ⓒ Ⓓ
2. Ⓐ Ⓑ Ⓒ Ⓓ
3. Ⓐ Ⓑ Ⓒ Ⓓ
4. Ⓐ Ⓑ Ⓒ Ⓓ
5. Ⓐ Ⓑ Ⓒ Ⓓ
6. Ⓐ Ⓑ Ⓒ Ⓓ
7. Ⓐ Ⓑ Ⓒ Ⓓ
8. Ⓐ Ⓑ Ⓒ Ⓓ
9. Ⓐ Ⓑ Ⓒ Ⓓ
10. Ⓐ Ⓑ Ⓒ Ⓓ
11. Ⓐ Ⓑ Ⓒ Ⓓ
12. Ⓐ Ⓑ Ⓒ Ⓓ
13. Ⓐ Ⓑ Ⓒ Ⓓ
14. Ⓐ Ⓑ Ⓒ Ⓓ
15. Ⓐ Ⓑ Ⓒ Ⓓ
16. Ⓐ Ⓑ Ⓒ Ⓓ
17. Ⓐ Ⓑ Ⓒ Ⓓ
18. Ⓐ Ⓑ Ⓒ Ⓓ
19. Ⓐ Ⓑ Ⓒ Ⓓ

20. Ⓐ Ⓑ Ⓒ Ⓓ
21. Ⓐ Ⓑ Ⓒ Ⓓ
22. Ⓐ Ⓑ Ⓒ Ⓓ
23. Ⓐ Ⓑ Ⓒ Ⓓ
24. Ⓐ Ⓑ Ⓒ Ⓓ
25. Ⓐ Ⓑ Ⓒ Ⓓ
26. Ⓐ Ⓑ Ⓒ Ⓓ
27. Ⓐ Ⓑ Ⓒ Ⓓ
28. Ⓐ Ⓑ Ⓒ Ⓓ
29. Ⓐ Ⓑ Ⓒ Ⓓ
30. Ⓐ Ⓑ Ⓒ Ⓓ
31. Ⓐ Ⓑ Ⓒ Ⓓ
32. Ⓐ Ⓑ Ⓒ Ⓓ
33. Ⓐ Ⓑ Ⓒ Ⓓ
34. Ⓐ Ⓑ Ⓒ Ⓓ
35. Ⓐ Ⓑ Ⓒ Ⓓ
36. Ⓐ Ⓑ Ⓒ Ⓓ
37. Ⓐ Ⓑ Ⓒ Ⓓ
38. Ⓐ Ⓑ Ⓒ Ⓓ

39. Ⓐ Ⓑ Ⓒ Ⓓ
40. Ⓐ Ⓑ Ⓒ Ⓓ
41. Ⓐ Ⓑ Ⓒ Ⓓ
42. Ⓐ Ⓑ Ⓒ Ⓓ
43. Ⓐ Ⓑ Ⓒ Ⓓ
44. Ⓐ Ⓑ Ⓒ Ⓓ
45. Ⓐ Ⓑ Ⓒ Ⓓ
46. Ⓐ Ⓑ Ⓒ Ⓓ
47. Ⓐ Ⓑ Ⓒ Ⓓ
48. Ⓐ Ⓑ Ⓒ Ⓓ
49. Ⓐ Ⓑ Ⓒ Ⓓ
50. Ⓐ Ⓑ Ⓒ Ⓓ
51. Ⓐ Ⓑ Ⓒ Ⓓ
52. Ⓐ Ⓑ Ⓒ Ⓓ
53. Ⓐ Ⓑ Ⓒ Ⓓ
54. Ⓐ Ⓑ Ⓒ Ⓓ
55. Ⓐ Ⓑ Ⓒ Ⓓ
56. Ⓐ Ⓑ Ⓒ Ⓓ
57. Ⓐ Ⓑ Ⓒ Ⓓ

Answer Sheet

58. Ⓐ Ⓑ Ⓒ Ⓓ   73. Ⓐ Ⓑ Ⓒ Ⓓ   87. Ⓐ Ⓑ Ⓒ Ⓓ

59. Ⓐ Ⓑ Ⓒ Ⓓ   74. Ⓐ Ⓑ Ⓒ Ⓓ   88. Ⓐ Ⓑ Ⓒ Ⓓ

60. Ⓐ Ⓑ Ⓒ Ⓓ   75. Ⓐ Ⓑ Ⓒ Ⓓ   89. Ⓐ Ⓑ Ⓒ Ⓓ

61. Ⓐ Ⓑ Ⓒ Ⓓ   76. Ⓐ Ⓑ Ⓒ Ⓓ   90. Ⓐ Ⓑ Ⓒ Ⓓ

62. Ⓐ Ⓑ Ⓒ Ⓓ   77. Ⓐ Ⓑ Ⓒ Ⓓ   91. Ⓐ Ⓑ Ⓒ Ⓓ

63. Ⓐ Ⓑ Ⓒ Ⓓ   78. Ⓐ Ⓑ Ⓒ Ⓓ   92. Ⓐ Ⓑ Ⓒ Ⓓ

64. Ⓐ Ⓑ Ⓒ Ⓓ   79. Ⓐ Ⓑ Ⓒ Ⓓ   93. Ⓐ Ⓑ Ⓒ Ⓓ

65. Ⓐ Ⓑ Ⓒ Ⓓ   80. Ⓐ Ⓑ Ⓒ Ⓓ   94. Ⓐ Ⓑ Ⓒ Ⓓ

66. Ⓐ Ⓑ Ⓒ Ⓓ   81. Ⓐ Ⓑ Ⓒ Ⓓ   95. Ⓐ Ⓑ Ⓒ Ⓓ

67. Ⓐ Ⓑ Ⓒ Ⓓ   82. Ⓐ Ⓑ Ⓒ Ⓓ   96. Ⓐ Ⓑ Ⓒ Ⓓ

68. Ⓐ Ⓑ Ⓒ Ⓓ   83. Ⓐ Ⓑ Ⓒ Ⓓ   97. Ⓐ Ⓑ Ⓒ Ⓓ

69. Ⓐ Ⓑ Ⓒ Ⓓ   84. Ⓐ Ⓑ Ⓒ Ⓓ   98. Ⓐ Ⓑ Ⓒ Ⓓ

70. Ⓐ Ⓑ Ⓒ Ⓓ   85. Ⓐ Ⓑ Ⓒ Ⓓ   99. Ⓐ Ⓑ Ⓒ Ⓓ

71. Ⓐ Ⓑ Ⓒ Ⓓ   86. Ⓐ Ⓑ Ⓒ Ⓓ   100. Ⓐ Ⓑ Ⓒ Ⓓ

72. Ⓐ Ⓑ Ⓒ Ⓓ

Answer Sheet for Practice Exam

Directions: Read each question carefully and choose the best answer. Fill in the oval completely with a soft lead pencil.

1. Ⓐ Ⓑ Ⓒ Ⓓ
2. Ⓐ Ⓑ Ⓒ Ⓓ
3. Ⓐ Ⓑ Ⓒ Ⓓ
4. Ⓐ Ⓑ Ⓒ Ⓓ
5. Ⓐ Ⓑ Ⓒ Ⓓ
6. Ⓐ Ⓑ Ⓒ Ⓓ
7. Ⓐ Ⓑ Ⓒ Ⓓ
8. Ⓐ Ⓑ Ⓒ Ⓓ
9. Ⓐ Ⓑ Ⓒ Ⓓ
10. Ⓐ Ⓑ Ⓒ Ⓓ
11. Ⓐ Ⓑ Ⓒ Ⓓ
12. Ⓐ Ⓑ Ⓒ Ⓓ
13. Ⓐ Ⓑ Ⓒ Ⓓ
14. Ⓐ Ⓑ Ⓒ Ⓓ
15. Ⓐ Ⓑ Ⓒ Ⓓ
16. Ⓐ Ⓑ Ⓒ Ⓓ
17. Ⓐ Ⓑ Ⓒ Ⓓ
18. Ⓐ Ⓑ Ⓒ Ⓓ
19. Ⓐ Ⓑ Ⓒ Ⓓ

20. Ⓐ Ⓑ Ⓒ Ⓓ
21. Ⓐ Ⓑ Ⓒ Ⓓ
22. Ⓐ Ⓑ Ⓒ Ⓓ
23. Ⓐ Ⓑ Ⓒ Ⓓ
24. Ⓐ Ⓑ Ⓒ Ⓓ
25. Ⓐ Ⓑ Ⓒ Ⓓ
26. Ⓐ Ⓑ Ⓒ Ⓓ
27. Ⓐ Ⓑ Ⓒ Ⓓ
28. Ⓐ Ⓑ Ⓒ Ⓓ
29. Ⓐ Ⓑ Ⓒ Ⓓ
30. Ⓐ Ⓑ Ⓒ Ⓓ
31. Ⓐ Ⓑ Ⓒ Ⓓ
32. Ⓐ Ⓑ Ⓒ Ⓓ
33. Ⓐ Ⓑ Ⓒ Ⓓ
34. Ⓐ Ⓑ Ⓒ Ⓓ
35. Ⓐ Ⓑ Ⓒ Ⓓ
36. Ⓐ Ⓑ Ⓒ Ⓓ
37. Ⓐ Ⓑ Ⓒ Ⓓ
38. Ⓐ Ⓑ Ⓒ Ⓓ

39. Ⓐ Ⓑ Ⓒ Ⓓ
40. Ⓐ Ⓑ Ⓒ Ⓓ
41. Ⓐ Ⓑ Ⓒ Ⓓ
42. Ⓐ Ⓑ Ⓒ Ⓓ
43. Ⓐ Ⓑ Ⓒ Ⓓ
44. Ⓐ Ⓑ Ⓒ Ⓓ
45. Ⓐ Ⓑ Ⓒ Ⓓ
46. Ⓐ Ⓑ Ⓒ Ⓓ
47. Ⓐ Ⓑ Ⓒ Ⓓ
48. Ⓐ Ⓑ Ⓒ Ⓓ
49. Ⓐ Ⓑ Ⓒ Ⓓ
50. Ⓐ Ⓑ Ⓒ Ⓓ
51. Ⓐ Ⓑ Ⓒ Ⓓ
52. Ⓐ Ⓑ Ⓒ Ⓓ
53. Ⓐ Ⓑ Ⓒ Ⓓ
54. Ⓐ Ⓑ Ⓒ Ⓓ
55. Ⓐ Ⓑ Ⓒ Ⓓ
56. Ⓐ Ⓑ Ⓒ Ⓓ
57. Ⓐ Ⓑ Ⓒ Ⓓ

58. (A) (B) (C) (D) 73. (A) (B) (C) (D) 87. (A) (B) (C) (D)

59. (A) (B) (C) (D) 74. (A) (B) (C) (D) 88. (A) (B) (C) (D)

60. (A) (B) (C) (D) 75. (A) (B) (C) (D) 89. (A) (B) (C) (D)

61. (A) (B) (C) (D) 76. (A) (B) (C) (D) 90. (A) (B) (C) (D)

62. (A) (B) (C) (D) 77. (A) (B) (C) (D) 91. (A) (B) (C) (D)

63. (A) (B) (C) (D) 78. (A) (B) (C) (D) 92. (A) (B) (C) (D)

64. (A) (B) (C) (D) 79. (A) (B) (C) (D) 93. (A) (B) (C) (D)

65. (A) (B) (C) (D) 80. (A) (B) (C) (D) 94. (A) (B) (C) (D)

66. (A) (B) (C) (D) 81. (A) (B) (C) (D) 95. (A) (B) (C) (D)

67. (A) (B) (C) (D) 82. (A) (B) (C) (D) 96. (A) (B) (C) (D)

68. (A) (B) (C) (D) 83. (A) (B) (C) (D) 97. (A) (B) (C) (D)

69. (A) (B) (C) (D) 84. (A) (B) (C) (D) 98. (A) (B) (C) (D)

70. (A) (B) (C) (D) 85. (A) (B) (C) (D) 99. (A) (B) (C) (D)

71. (A) (B) (C) (D) 86. (A) (B) (C) (D) 100. (A) (B) (C) (D)

72. (A) (B) (C) (D)

Answer Sheet for Practice Exam

Directions: Read each question carefully and choose the best answer. Fill in the oval completely with a soft lead pencil.

1. Ⓐ Ⓑ Ⓒ Ⓓ
2. Ⓐ Ⓑ Ⓒ Ⓓ
3. Ⓐ Ⓑ Ⓒ Ⓓ
4. Ⓐ Ⓑ Ⓒ Ⓓ
5. Ⓐ Ⓑ Ⓒ Ⓓ
6. Ⓐ Ⓑ Ⓒ Ⓓ
7. Ⓐ Ⓑ Ⓒ Ⓓ
8. Ⓐ Ⓑ Ⓒ Ⓓ
9. Ⓐ Ⓑ Ⓒ Ⓓ
10. Ⓐ Ⓑ Ⓒ Ⓓ
11. Ⓐ Ⓑ Ⓒ Ⓓ
12. Ⓐ Ⓑ Ⓒ Ⓓ
13. Ⓐ Ⓑ Ⓒ Ⓓ
14. Ⓐ Ⓑ Ⓒ Ⓓ
15. Ⓐ Ⓑ Ⓒ Ⓓ
16. Ⓐ Ⓑ Ⓒ Ⓓ
17. Ⓐ Ⓑ Ⓒ Ⓓ
18. Ⓐ Ⓑ Ⓒ Ⓓ
19. Ⓐ Ⓑ Ⓒ Ⓓ

20. Ⓐ Ⓑ Ⓒ Ⓓ
21. Ⓐ Ⓑ Ⓒ Ⓓ
22. Ⓐ Ⓑ Ⓒ Ⓓ
23. Ⓐ Ⓑ Ⓒ Ⓓ
24. Ⓐ Ⓑ Ⓒ Ⓓ
25. Ⓐ Ⓑ Ⓒ Ⓓ
26. Ⓐ Ⓑ Ⓒ Ⓓ
27. Ⓐ Ⓑ Ⓒ Ⓓ
28. Ⓐ Ⓑ Ⓒ Ⓓ
29. Ⓐ Ⓑ Ⓒ Ⓓ
30. Ⓐ Ⓑ Ⓒ Ⓓ
31. Ⓐ Ⓑ Ⓒ Ⓓ
32. Ⓐ Ⓑ Ⓒ Ⓓ
33. Ⓐ Ⓑ Ⓒ Ⓓ
34. Ⓐ Ⓑ Ⓒ Ⓓ
35. Ⓐ Ⓑ Ⓒ Ⓓ
36. Ⓐ Ⓑ Ⓒ Ⓓ
37. Ⓐ Ⓑ Ⓒ Ⓓ
38. Ⓐ Ⓑ Ⓒ Ⓓ

39. Ⓐ Ⓑ Ⓒ Ⓓ
40. Ⓐ Ⓑ Ⓒ Ⓓ
41. Ⓐ Ⓑ Ⓒ Ⓓ
42. Ⓐ Ⓑ Ⓒ Ⓓ
43. Ⓐ Ⓑ Ⓒ Ⓓ
44. Ⓐ Ⓑ Ⓒ Ⓓ
45. Ⓐ Ⓑ Ⓒ Ⓓ
46. Ⓐ Ⓑ Ⓒ Ⓓ
47. Ⓐ Ⓑ Ⓒ Ⓓ
48. Ⓐ Ⓑ Ⓒ Ⓓ
49. Ⓐ Ⓑ Ⓒ Ⓓ
50. Ⓐ Ⓑ Ⓒ Ⓓ
51. Ⓐ Ⓑ Ⓒ Ⓓ
52. Ⓐ Ⓑ Ⓒ Ⓓ
53. Ⓐ Ⓑ Ⓒ Ⓓ
54. Ⓐ Ⓑ Ⓒ Ⓓ
55. Ⓐ Ⓑ Ⓒ Ⓓ
56. Ⓐ Ⓑ Ⓒ Ⓓ
57. Ⓐ Ⓑ Ⓒ Ⓓ

Answer Sheet

58. Ⓐ Ⓑ Ⓒ Ⓓ 73. Ⓐ Ⓑ Ⓒ Ⓓ 87. Ⓐ Ⓑ Ⓒ Ⓓ

59. Ⓐ Ⓑ Ⓒ Ⓓ 74. Ⓐ Ⓑ Ⓒ Ⓓ 88. Ⓐ Ⓑ Ⓒ Ⓓ

60. Ⓐ Ⓑ Ⓒ Ⓓ 75. Ⓐ Ⓑ Ⓒ Ⓓ 89. Ⓐ Ⓑ Ⓒ Ⓓ

61. Ⓐ Ⓑ Ⓒ Ⓓ 76. Ⓐ Ⓑ Ⓒ Ⓓ 90. Ⓐ Ⓑ Ⓒ Ⓓ

62. Ⓐ Ⓑ Ⓒ Ⓓ 77. Ⓐ Ⓑ Ⓒ Ⓓ 91. Ⓐ Ⓑ Ⓒ Ⓓ

63. Ⓐ Ⓑ Ⓒ Ⓓ 78. Ⓐ Ⓑ Ⓒ Ⓓ 92. Ⓐ Ⓑ Ⓒ Ⓓ

64. Ⓐ Ⓑ Ⓒ Ⓓ 79. Ⓐ Ⓑ Ⓒ Ⓓ 93. Ⓐ Ⓑ Ⓒ Ⓓ

65. Ⓐ Ⓑ Ⓒ Ⓓ 80. Ⓐ Ⓑ Ⓒ Ⓓ 94. Ⓐ Ⓑ Ⓒ Ⓓ

66. Ⓐ Ⓑ Ⓒ Ⓓ 81. Ⓐ Ⓑ Ⓒ Ⓓ 95. Ⓐ Ⓑ Ⓒ Ⓓ

67. Ⓐ Ⓑ Ⓒ Ⓓ 82. Ⓐ Ⓑ Ⓒ Ⓓ 96. Ⓐ Ⓑ Ⓒ Ⓓ

68. Ⓐ Ⓑ Ⓒ Ⓓ 83. Ⓐ Ⓑ Ⓒ Ⓓ 97. Ⓐ Ⓑ Ⓒ Ⓓ

69. Ⓐ Ⓑ Ⓒ Ⓓ 84. Ⓐ Ⓑ Ⓒ Ⓓ 98. Ⓐ Ⓑ Ⓒ Ⓓ

70. Ⓐ Ⓑ Ⓒ Ⓓ 85. Ⓐ Ⓑ Ⓒ Ⓓ 99. Ⓐ Ⓑ Ⓒ Ⓓ

71. Ⓐ Ⓑ Ⓒ Ⓓ 86. Ⓐ Ⓑ Ⓒ Ⓓ 100. Ⓐ Ⓑ Ⓒ Ⓓ

72. Ⓐ Ⓑ Ⓒ Ⓓ